Multilingual Education

Volume 24

The book series Multilingual Education publishes top quality monographs and edited volumes containing empirical research on multilingual language acquisition, language contact and the respective roles of languages in contexts where the languages are not cognate and where the scripts are often different, in order to be able to better understand the processes and issues involved and to inform governments and language policy makers. The volumes in this series are aimed primarily at researchers in education, especially multilingual education and other related fields, and those who are involved in the education of (language) teachers. Others who will be interested include key stakeholders and policy makers in the field of language policy and education. The editors welcome proposals and ideas for books that fit the series. For more information on how you can submit a proposal, please contact the publishing editor, Jolanda Voogd. E-mail: jolanda.voogd@springer.com

More information about this series at http://www.springer.com/series/8836

Andy CURTIS • Roland SUSSEX

Editors

Intercultural Communication in Asia: Education, Language and Values

 Springer

Editors
Andy CURTIS
Graduate School of Education
Anaheim University
Anaheim, CA, USA

Roland SUSSEX
School of Languages and Cultures,
and Institute for Teaching and Learning
Innovation
The University of Queensland
St Lucia, QLD, Australia

ISSN 2213-3208   ISSN 2213-3216   (electronic)
Multilingual Education
ISBN 978-3-319-69994-3   ISBN 978-3-319-69995-0   (eBook)
https://doi.org/10.1007/978-3-319-69995-0

Library of Congress Control Number: 2018931919

Printed on acid-free paper

This Springer imprint is published by the registered company Springer International Publishing AG
part of Springer Nature
The registered company address is: Gewerbestrasse 11, 6330 Cham, Switzerland

Acknowledgment

On behalf of the participants in the Third Macao International Forum, we wish to express our warm thanks and appreciation to Professor Lei Heong-Iok, president of Macao Polytechnic Institute; Professor Mao Sihui, who chaired the Forum's Organizing Committee; Professor Joanna Radwańska-Williams; and members of the Organizing Committee. Without their inspiration and contribution, the Forum could not have been realized.

Professor Andy CURTIS, Conference Convener
Emeritus Professor Roland SUSSEX, Conference Secretary

The Macao International Forum

The Macao International Forum is a research initiative of the Macao Polytechnic Institute. The goal of the Forum is to bring together leading international experts in key areas of global inquiry to focus on questions of current intellectual and strategic significance. It is both disciplinary and interdisciplinary. The Macao International Forum is held every two years and is a platform for sharing new ideas among leading international scholars and also for enhancing intercultural communication in the global context.

Each Forum:

- Addresses the current state of knowledge in the designated area of inquiry
- Considers current questions (theory, methodology, analysis), together with their interdisciplinary implications
- Presents research to illuminate the present state of knowledge, current questions, and issues lying ahead
- Recommends and elaborates key questions to inform future directions in the field
- Publishes the results of the forum in book form and appropriate electronic formats

The first Macao International Forum was held at the Macao Polytechnic Institute in December 2010. The proceedings were published as *English as an International Language in Asia: Implications for Language Education* (Berlin and London: Springer-Verlag) by Andy Kirkpatrick and Roland Sussex (eds) (2012).

The second Macao International Forum was held in December 2012. The proceedings were published as *Power Transition and International Order in Asia: Issues and Challenges* (Asian Security Studies) (Abingdon, Oxon.: Routledge) by Peter Shearman (ed.) (2013).

This volume presents the results of the third Macao International Forum, which was held in Macao in December 2014. The papers cover a range of themes in intercultural communication in Asia, with a special emphasis on education, language, and values.

President   Professor Lei Heong-Iok
Macao Polytechnic Institute

Chair, Organizing Committee   Professor Mao Sihui
Macao International Forum
Shantou University
December 2017

Formatting Notes

Naming Conventions

In order to respect the authors' wishes for the order of their given name/family name, we have adopted a convention which is becoming widely used in Asia when names from different cultural backgrounds are written in Roman script. According to this convention, family names are capitalized:

Andy CURTIS
Yihong GAO

This convention applies only to the Table of Contents, to the title page of each chapter, to the Introduction, and to the bio-notes about the contributors at the end of the book. Elsewhere, and especially in the References at the end of each chapter, international conventions make the identity of given and family names transparent.

Index

Following a growing convention in book production, we have not provided this book with an index. Most libraries are now purchasing books in e-format, where it is faster and more natural for readers to conduct their own digital searches.

Andy CURTIS and Roland SUSSEX
Editors

Contents

Introduction.   1
Roland SUSSEX and Andy CURTIS

Part I   Models, Intercultural Competence and Education

Individual, Institutional and International: Three Aspects
of Intercultural Communication   21
Andy CURTIS

Toward a Critical Epistemology for Learning Languages
and Cultures in Twenty-First Century Asia   37
Andrew LIAN and Roland SUSSEX

Intercultural Communication in English Courses in Asia:
What Should We Teach About?   55
Don SNOW

Part II   Values and Communication in Cultural Contexts

Confucian Values as Challenges for Communication in Intercultural
Workplace Contexts: Evidence from the Motivational Concerns
in Vietnamese Politeness Behaviour   75
Thi Hong Nhung PHAM

Part III   English as a Lingua Franca and in Inter/Intra-cultural
          Communication

The Impact of English as a Global Lingua Franca
on Intercultural Communication.   97
Juliane HOUSE

**How Does Intercultural Communication Differ
from Intracultural Communication?** 115
Istvan KECSKES

Part IV   Focal Areas of Intercultural Communication

**Reading the City: The Linguistic and Semiotic Landscape
of Macao's San Ma Lo** (新馬路) 139
Joanna RADWAŃSKA-WILLIAMS

Intercultural Communication About Pain 181
Roland SUSSEX

**Functions of Humor in Intercultural Communication
and Educational Environments** 205
Kimie OSHIMA

Part V   Identity

**Emotional Branding on Social Media: A Cross-Cultural
Discourse Analysis of Global Brands on Twitter and Weibo** 225
Doreen D. WU and Chaoyuan LI

**China's Fluctuating English Education Policy Discourses
and Continuing Ambivalences in Identity Construction** 241
Yihong GAO

Part VI   Conclusion

Conclusion 265
Roland SUSSEX and Andy CURTIS

Contributors 275

Introduction

Roland SUSSEX and Andy CURTIS

Abstract In the modern world intercultural communication is increasing rapidly, as people and their messages become more mobile. Asia is one of the areas where this increase is particularly evident, as its nations and peoples are becoming richer and more mobile than before. Effective communication between languages and cultures, whether between homeland languages or using an international language like English, requires enhanced levels of linguistic competence and intercultural understanding. There has been a corresponding surge of activity in pure and applied research into intercultural communication in Asia. One aspect of this work has involved English, especially American English, as a vehicle of communication. And even where studies of intercultural communication have involved Asian languages, the dominant frameworks from the literature have been Western in terms of theory and methodology, and in the parameters of intercultural communication, such as the "individualism ~ collectivism" dichotomy/continuum which were proposed by scholars like Hofstede (1984).

This book explores the challenges now facing intercultural communication in relation to cultural boundaries, to ideology and values, and for institutions and individuals in an internationalising environment, especially educationally. Its eleven chapters address models, values and communication, English as a lingua franca, three key focal areas (city landscape, pain and humour), and identity.

R. SUSSEX (✉)
School of Languages and Cultures, and Institute for Teaching and Learning Innovation,
The University of Queensland, St Lucia, QLD, Australia
e-mail: sussex@uq.edu.au

A. CURTIS
Graduate School of Education, Anaheim University, Anaheim, CA, USA
e-mail: andycurtiswork@gmail.com

© Springer International Publishing AG, part of Springer Nature 2018
A. CURTIS, R. SUSSEX (eds.), *Intercultural Communication in Asia:*
Education, Language and Values, Multilingual Education 24,
https://doi.org/10.1007/978-3-319-69995-0_1

1 Introduction

This book is about intercultural communication in Asia – people communicating across cultural boundaries, the characteristics and values of the cultures which can affect the success or otherwise of communication, and the broader implications of these issues for education.

Intercultural communication in Asia is increasing rapidly, as indeed it is world-wide. This is partly the result of the increased physical mobility of people, which itself is the consequence of a number of social, political and economic changes. Asia itself is more accessible to tourism, not only from outside Asia, but also between Asian countries. Statistica reports that world-wide in 2015 there were nearly 1.2 billion tourism arrivals worth $7.27 trillion (https://www.statista.com/topics/962/global-tourism/). Geo-political borders are now more open than they were even a decade ago, and the opening up of Myanmar leaves North Korea as the only country in Asia with relatively hermetic borders.

Economically Asia is now much more prosperous. Physical mobility is increasing rapidly: tourism into and out of Asia; education of Asians overseas; the rise of Asian middle classes with a thirst for foreign culture, English language, and travel, as well as education; globalisation and commerce; European tourists in rural China and Vietnam and Laos; Japanese and Chinese and Korean tourists abroad, in Asia and beyond; Asian students in European or English-dominant countries. In short, people are on the move, now more than ever before, and contacts between speakers of different languages and cultures are rising comparably. In this international, intercultural world English is, by a wide margin, not only the lingua franca of Asia (House 2018; Lian & Sussex 2018) but also what we might call the "cultura franca" – a broadly common set of practices and values ranging from ad hoc, almost pidgin, practices negotiated in real time and *in situ* for interpersonal communication, all the way to elaborate codes of values and interaction. If the twenty-first century is the Asian century, then Asia, with 60% of the world's population (http://worldpopulationreview.com/continents/asia-population/), is providing major, and rapidly growing, contexts of intercultural interactions (Chitty 2010).

In this twenty-first century world we have not only physical but also digital mobility, facilitating cultural contact and with it communication. Digital technology has supplemented, and in some cases supplanted, physical contact with virtual. Japan and Korea are among the most digitally connected nations in the world, and China has accelerated dramatically over the last 5 years to become numerically the world leader in digital connexions (for data see the World Bank: http://data.worldbank.org/indicator/IT.NET.USER.P2).

Communicating interculturally requires that people from different languages and cultures interact. And that brings us at once to an issue of terms and definitions. There is some consensus, but only inconsistent observance, in the use of these terms. "Intercultural communication" is more associated with people from different languages and cultures communicating. In contrast, "cross-cultural communication" is more usually understood contrastively, and deals with the factors of the cultures which are relevant to actual or potential communication. However, both "intercultural communication" and "cross-cultural communication" are commonly used for communicating across cultural boundaries (https://en.wikipedia.org/wiki/Intercultural_communication).

For intercultural communication to happen, people from different languages and cultures have to be able to come into contact: they need to come physically face to face, or be culturally in contact through their writings or cultural products. More recently they have been digitally in communication, with contact facilitated by technology, especially the Internet. This requires either that people travel, or that their messages and/or cultural products do.

For many centuries, intercultural communication in Asia – as indeed in Europe, Africa and the Americas – was restricted by limitations on personal mobility and communications. In the world after the various agrarian revolutions most people – other than nomads – did not travel very far from their birthplace during their entire lives. So local languages and cultures, together with folklore, grew and flourished and consolidated. There was less input from people outside this relatively enclosed local context. National boundaries were less well-defined and more porous, so that in principle, people could travel. But in practice it was difficult, often dangerous, inconvenient and expensive to travel, and they tended not to (Snow 2018). And thus intercultural communication was not as widespread as it is today. There were some exceptions. There are the Norman French, the Middle English and the Church-based Latinate cultures in English after the Norman conquest in 1066, and indeed the Latinate Church culture parallel to indigenous cultures through the world of the Catholic Church. Armies travelled, for instance in the Crusades from the eleventh century. So did ships, with exploration and navigation as part of the great European expansion from the fifteenth century, with settlement following in most countries outside Europe. Urbanisation brought rural people to towns and cities as a form of economic migration, creating intercultural contexts through the contacts of languages and dialects.

Intercultural communication was formerly much less of a regular occurrence than it is today. If people do not travel, cultures cannot easily come face to face, except through their messages; and the pace and outreach of messages and people movement was slow, even after the introduction of printing, and in spite of later – pre-digital – advances in transport and communications. Intercultural communication has become endemic and a natural and necessary concomitant of the new world order. And all this is continuing to change with relentless speed and thoroughness.

2   The Domain of Intercultural Communication

As an area of intellectual enquiry with the task of understanding, analysing and addressing all these factors, intercultural communication is of necessity inherently interdisciplinary (https://en.wikipedia.org/wiki/Intercultural_communication). So in intercultural communication we find education; anthropology and ethnography; linguistics and applied linguistics, as well as pragmatics; sociology; psychology and social psychology; communication studies; critical theory; humanities; media studies; information theory; politics and policy, including language planning and policy; and applications to communication in any thematic or scientific area.

In this network of disciplines, language and education are central. Assessed performance in the homeland language and English is now standard in education systems across Asia, and second language competence, especially in English, is a core feature of education, commerce, culture and tourism. The older homeland language pedagogies, founded on centuries of tradition in grammar and normative, native-user models, have been progressively incorporating more communicative approaches and frameworks, prompted especially by English and the Common European Framework of Reference for Languages (www.commoneuropeanframework.org). We see here an additional juxtaposition of values, in terms of shifting educational models. Homeland languages in Asia, like second languages elsewhere, have joined this trend, especially Japanese, Korean, and Chinese, with their dominant position in international commerce and culture, both in courses offered by bodies like the Confucius Institute (Chinese), and in the education systems of other Asian countries. English has an additional role as an international lingua franca, together with the emerging localised norms like Chinglish (Chinese-English) in China, and Japlish (Japanese-English) in Japan, which are now achieving greater acceptability and prominence as English develops growing roles alongside the homeland language. In this broadly based, and hugely expensive, activity, communication has joined normative performance as a key goal, again prompted by curriculum and pedagogy. It is now possible to propose that we are moving, not into a post-communicative framework for language education, but into one enhanced by a major focus on intercultural communication. Some of this movement is focused on language skills and performance, especially intercultural communicative competence (Alptekin 2002; Barker 2015; Byram et al. 2001a, b; Deardorff 2010), including its teaching and assessment (Byram 1997). Intercultural competence is also a feature of language-in-education planning and pedagogy (Byram 2010). The goal is a principled approach to intercultural awareness for the purposes of communication (Snow 2018). And here competence is seen within the wider remit of intercultural communication.

Intercultural communication shows many of the characteristics of an emerging domain of intellectual enquiry. It has international organisations like the International Association for Intercultural Communication Studies (IAICS: http://web.uri.edu/iaics/), with its own journal *Intercultural Communication Studies*. As we shall see in the following section, across its interdisciplinary space, intercultural communication is both catholic, in the older sense of universal and inclusive, as well as eclectic, choosing and activating material and ideas from across a wide spectrum. In theory and methodology it is centripetal, importing what it needs from other disciplines in terms of theory and methodology for the research goals at hand. There is no style of inquiry which is distinctively that of "intercultural communication", other than its thematic focus and interdisciplinarity. Most of its research to date has been descriptive, analytical and comparative, empirical and inductive, and qualitative: there is some evidence of formal observation and quantitative methods from the social sciences. There is some work in the framework of critical theory (Cheong et al. 2012; Halualani 2008; Nakayama and Halualani 2011; Ono 2010; Willink et al. 2014). But on the whole, the core of intercultural communication is a-theoretical. This can be expected to self-correct as researchers progressively define and deepen the areas of enquiry.

The discipline area – it is not yet possible to talk of a "discipline" – of intercultural communication is certainly growing dynamically, and in some cases dramatically. Education in intercultural communication is responding decisively in both curriculum and materials. Courses are being introduced across the educational spectrum, at secondary and especially tertiary levels. Language courses, which before tended to include intercultural communication in a more occasional and unstructured way, are now starting to incorporate it as part of standard curricula. There are over a dozen good introductory textbooks, supported by books of readings, and increasing numbers of monographs and monograph series, like:

Multilingual Matters: Languages for International Communication & Education
Peter Lang: Critical Intercultural Communication Studies
Routledge: Routledge Studies in Language & Intercultural Communication

The annual IAICS conference is specifically devoted to intercultural communication, but many other conferences in the areas listed above include themes and sections focused on intercultural communication. Journals specifically devoted to intercultural communication were mostly established in the first decade of this century, and include:

Intercultural Communication Studies
Journal of Intercultural Communication Research
Journal of International and Intercultural Communication
Language and Intercultural Communication

Among other journals in the communication field which are increasingly devoting space and attention to intercultural communication are:

International Journal of Intercultural Relations
International Journal of Language and Culture
Journal of Multilingual and Multicultural Development
Intercultural Pragmatics

And, of particular interest to this book, there are English language journals with a specifically Asian focus on communication and intercultural communication:

Asian Journal of Communication
Asian Communication Research
Chinese Journal of Communication
Keio Communication Review

(and see So 2010). Most of these journals are part of the stables of international publishers like Elsevier, Multilingual Matters, Routledge, and Taylor & Francis.

In terms of the focal themes of intercultural communication research, Arasaratnam (2015) selected three key journals:

Journal of Intercultural Communication Research
International Journal of Intercultural Relations
Journal of International and Intercultural Communication

and identified eight key themes in their coverage: identity; acculturation and global migration; communication dynamics; intercultural competence; theories, models and scales; perception, stereotypes and discrimination; cross-cultural differences; and intercultural education and study abroad. We have confirmed her results by an independent scan of another journal, *Language and Intercultural Communication*.

One theme which has become increasingly evident is the rapid increase in intercultural communication research relating to China and Chinese, which, on an informal count of the papers published since 2010, now ranks second only to America and American English (with the exception of studies comparing the US and Japan). But the sheer numbers and increasing electronic influence of China are attracting research interest, principally but by no means solely from scholars based in Asia, both Chinese and otherwise. This journal activity is supported by a growing number of introductions to intercultural communication (e.g. Martin and Nakayama 2012, Neuliep 2014), and books of readings (e.g. Samovar et al. 2014). There are also a few, but only a few, books which deal specifically with Asia (Kirkpatrick and Sussex 2012).

3   English and American English

English is not only the dominant language of scholarship in intercultural communication. It is also, by a wide margin, the most prominent second language studied, with English being the anchor, or at least a partner, in languages researched in this domain. And American English has not unexpectedly been the most prominent variety of English in this work. However, for all its dynamism and central location in so many social, technological, political and cultural agendas, the USA is only one exemplar of only one model of cultural identity and practice. The literature is starting to show an emerging trend for intra-Asia comparative studies in intercultural communication. The dominant pairing has been American English with Japanese, corresponding to Japan's position as a trading partner (Ito 1992). But contrastive studies of English with Chinese are accelerating (Zhang et al. 2013). And we are starting to see intra-Asian pairings like Cambodia and Vietnam (Sar and Rodriguez 2014), or Singapore and Taiwan (Zhang 2012). While the preferred focus is still on two-language comparisons, the literature shows some analyses of more than two languages in empirical research, which goes beyond areal "Asian" stereotypes and targets inductively a richer understanding of commonalities and differences (Morris 2014).

Parallel to this development there is also the question of which model of English we are dealing with. There is the "edifice" view of English (Sussex and Kirkpatrick 2012, p. 223), including both dominant L1 models and English as an International Language (EIL). Then there is English as a Lingua Franca (House 2018), seen essentially as a code employed in intercultural contexts (and see Baker 2011). And finally we have what Canagarajah (2007) has called "Lingua Franca English", an emergent, negotiated medium where speakers "activate a mutually recognised set of attitudes, forms, and conventions that ensure successful communication in LFE when they find themselves interacting with each other" (2007, p. 925).

4   Western Bias

The literature on intercultural communication in general, and intercultural communication in Asia in particular, has a strong Western bias. Part of this arises from the well-known international domination of English as the language of scholarship, which in some disciplines exceeds 90% of leading journals. Too few non-Asian scholars outside Asia read Asian languages for scholarship, so that research on intercultural communication in Asia, when written in Asian languages, remains inaccessible except to a small specialised group. In terms of topics and subjects in the behavioural sciences there is a further bias which has skewed the balance away from Asia. This is the "WEIRD" phenomenon, as documented by Henrich et al. (2010), where they analysed people who took part as subjects in research in psychology, cognitive science and economics. "WEIRD" stands for "Western", "educated", "industrialised", "rich" and "democratic". Henrich et al. refer to a study by Arnett (2008) which found that in the top journals in six sub-disciplines of psychology, 96% of the subjects were from WEIRD countries, specifically North America, Europe, Australia and Israel. Fully 99% of the first authors were from Western countries. In their abstract Henrich et al. state that "[…] researchers – often implicitly – assume that either there is little variation across human populations, or that these 'standard subjects' are as representative of the species as any other population". They continue:

> WEIRD subjects are particularly unusual compared with the rest of the species – frequent outliers. The domains reviewed include visual perception, fairness, cooperation, spatial reasoning, categorization and inferential induction, moral reasoning, reasoning styles, self-concepts and related motivations, and the heritability of IQ. The findings suggest that members of WEIRD societies, including young children, are among the least representative populations one could find for generalizing about humans. Many of these findings involve domains that are associated with fundamental aspects of psychology, motivation, and behavior – hence, there are no obvious a priori grounds for claiming that a particular behavioral phenomenon is universal based on sampling from a single subpopulation. Overall, these empirical patterns suggest that we need to be less cavalier in addressing questions of human nature on the basis of data drawn from this particularly thin, and rather unusual, slice of humanity (Henrich et al. 2010, p. 61).

Related aspects of this skewing of subjects and their behaviour were anticipated by Kim's 2002 book *Non-Western perspectives on human communication,* which targets both Western-centrism and particularly US-centrism, in the contexts of topics like individualism, conflict negotiation, and silence.

The pro-Western bias documented in studies like these has not yet been substantially realised, let alone addressed or corrected, in international scholarship. However, there has been some movement to rebalance the Western bias in linguistics, communication studies and intercultural communication, and specifically in the field of intercultural communication. To be sure, intercultural communication research has been less laboratory-based than the subjects surveyed by Henrich et al. (2010). But an English/Western emphasis nonetheless persists and pervades, though in the context of other (read usually: non-Western) cultures (Kuo and Chew 2009). Hofstede's (1984, 1986, 1997) suggested parameters of cultural differences, for instance, were in principle "culture-neutral", though in practice they had a strong anchor in Western countries and values. The initial four were

- individualism-collectivism;
- uncertainty avoidance;
- power distance (strength of social hierarchy); and
- masculinity-femininity (task orientation versus person-orientation)
  to which two were added later:
- long-term orientation;
- indulgence versus self-restraint.

Critiques of Hofstede's approach have often focused on "individualism–collectivism" and "power distance", especially in the ways in which they have been easy to apply to the juxtaposition of "Confucian Heritage Cultures" ("CHC": principally China, Japan, Korea, Taiwan and Vietnam; see Watkins and Biggs 1996) and non-CHC contexts. There has been a growing body of research demonstrating that such East/West dichotomies are far too simple, and that these properties also occur in the communities on the "other" side of the divide, and in gradients rather than dichotomies. And the perspective has been dominated by conceptual frameworks and values originating in the West.

Two key CHC ideas illustrate this bias, and both stem from the writings of Confucius himself (551 BC-479 BC). Their Chinese names are *guanxi* and *mianzi*. Both are central to a working understanding of interpersonal relations in CHC countries and contexts. *Guanxi* – significantly, there is no simple translation in English – involves the reciprocal, and often hierarchical, relationships between people, especially those outside the family. Each individual is involved in an extended, and often extensive, network of *guanxi,* both personal and professional. *Guanxi* entails mutual obligations, reciprocity and trust, which in turn are central to maintaining social and economic order. At the interpersonal level this is in some respects not too different from a Westerner's network of friends and colleagues: you share things with friends and give them priority in your interpersonal dealings. But when it involves individuals in their institutional, corporate or commercial roles there is an immediate potential clash with Western values, according to which some aspects of *guanxi* can be seen as a form of corruption (Dunfee and Warren 2001). *Guanxi* represents one of the areas of cultural tension in the contemporary CHC world as it moves to incorporate aspects of globalisation, meaning Western values (for more on *guanxi*, see Curtis 2018).

Mianzi is commonly translated as "face", and it is closely involved with the concepts of politeness in different cultures (Brown and Levinson 1987; Cai and Donohue 1997). But Asian stereotypes of self-effacement and especially *mianzi* are not well understood in the West. *Mianzi* is one's sense of self-respect and dignity as we present it to the world, and as we wish to be seen. It is rude and inconsiderate to challenge another person or their competence to their face or in public. *Mianzi* also interacts in a complex way with *guanxi*. In this perspective "face" can be seen as a strategy that individuals use to maintain their identity and self-respect, as well as their social standing in the *guanxi* network. CHC students, for instance, are well known for being chary of taking part in classroom discussions, because being seen to be mistaken in front of others is a threat to one's *mianzi* (Singhal and Nagao 1993). Furthermore, in interpersonal situations it can be acceptable not to tell the truth, so long as this is understood by the interlocutor. According to *mianzi* and *guanxi,* personal dignity and social harmony take precedence over truthfulness, which is the reverse of what is common in Western interactions.

Issues such as these raise a series of questions in which a coherent focus on language and cultural communication outside the Western context assumes particular importance (see Bryant and Yang 2004; Chen 2009; Wang and Kuo 2010). That is one of the rationales for the present volume (Ito 1992; Kim 2002). As we have seen, the literature on intercultural communication still perpetuates the Western bias in several ways. It is overwhelmingly written and discussed in English. And where contrastive studies of languages and cultural practices have been involved, they have predominantly involved contrasts of English with another language.

The present volume unashamedly continues the first of these biases by publishing in English. We do so for the pragmatic, but also selfish, reason of reaching as many readers as possible. But we also move some distance towards a more Asia-centric perspective. The majority of the contributors to this volume are either Asian, or based in Asia, or both. The Asian-based contributors come from the PRC, Hong Kong, Japan, Macau, Thailand and Vietnam. Two chapters (by Curtis, and Lian & Sussex) propose theoretical models based on Asian contexts, concepts and data. House (2018) treats English as a lingua franca within Asian frameworks. And the chapter by Sussex on pain brings an emerging domain of scholarship into Asian contexts.

5 The Present Book

The book has three points of departure:

Q1. What are the challenges of intercultural communication vis-à-vis these invisible (or partly visible) constructed boundaries that intersect society, even in today's increasingly fluid, dynamic, hybridised and globalised world?

Q2. What challenges to intercultural communication, as individuals/cultures/groups interact with each other, are posed by considerations of ideology and values, which may not always be fully conscious or explicitly articulated, but which are nevertheless powerful forces affecting decision-making behaviour?

Q3. What are the challenges facing, on the one hand, governments and educational institutions, and, on the other hand, individual educators and students, in adapting to an increasingly internationalised educational environment?

We begin, in one sense, with a paradox. The title of this book refers boldly to "Asia". And yet Asia is a fiction, or at best a loose geographical way of referring to a heterogeneous collection of countries, languages, cultures and practices. In this respect it is not unlike the use of "European" or "Western". For those outside Asia, referring to it in this way seems natural and unproblematic. For those within, the term obscures a rich structure of differences:

> An ungainly conglomeration ranging from Siberia to Saudi Arabia and Japan to Turkey, containing 60% of the world's population, the implausible notion of "Asia" is itself Eurocentric, being merely a label of convenience for non-European areas of the Eurasian continent (Kim 2010, 167).

And yet there is a sense in which speaking of "Asia" in this way does make sense. Not only do the countries of Asia form a coherent landmass; that they have also, in various ways, shared some key trends in their histories, and particularly in their recent developments. We do not imply that there is some higher-level entity called "Asia" with a supra-national reification. But we do use the term "Asia" as a convenient shorthand for a conceptual, cultural and geographical space within which lie the issues which this book addresses.

Fundamental to those issues is the presence and status of English, squarely in the middle of the map of intercultural communication in Asia. This was the focus of the first Macao International Forum in 2010 (Kirkpatrick and Sussex 2012). The penetration of English into the fabric of Asian societies, initially after the end of the Second World War, but with astonishing acceleration since the advent of the Internet in the 1980s, has been unique and deeply resonant. With the possible exception of North Korea, all the countries of Asia, and certainly those covered in this book, bear indelible and possibly permanent imprints of English (Wee et al. 2013). In this book, the bridge between English and intercultural communication is covered in the chapter on English as a lingua franca by House; and in the chapter by Snow on the realisation of these issues in an English-language syllabus. English, without a doubt, is undoubtedly a challenge. It presents opportunities and threats, as well as temptations, to the languages in countries who are hosting its not always gentle invasion.

But the challenges are not always concerned with English as a linguistic or semiotic system. They can equally involve ideological values systems. And here there are indeed some commonalities which make some sense of the term "Asia". This is Kim again:

> While differences do exist between nations in Asia, their similarities, due to the influence of Confucianism, Buddhism, Taoism, or Hinduism, are also undeniable (Kim 2010, p. 167).

These issues are also distinctively Asian, in that, while these value systems are found outside Asia, it is only in Asia that they are found together and to this depth.

In the literature on intercultural communication, ideologies and values have probably been represented most often in the form of stereotypes: typical patterns of beliefs which align with different contrasting cultural behaviours. These questions in turn demand an institutional response, both by governments and specifically by education systems, if the people for whom they are responsible are not to be left behind, as other countries ramp up their efforts to make their citizens interculturally and communicatively competent. The proposed changes have mostly related to English, often in conjunction with specialisations like business studies.

6   Overview of the Chapters

The chapters in the volume[1] form five thematic sections. They are all concerned with intercultural communication, as we defined it at the start of the Introduction: with either the act of communicating across cultural boundaries, or with the properties of the cultures at either end of that act of communication, or both.

6.1   Section 1: Models, Intercultural Competence and Education

Andy CURTIS ("Individual, Institutional and International: Three aspects of intercultural communication"), building on the earlier work of Hinde (1998) and others, develops the idea of the "Individual as cultural artifact", which is in opposition to many of the most widely accepted definitions of "culture", which are premised on the notion of large numbers of people sharing beliefs, customs and values. This chapter considers the question: What would happen to our definitions of "culture" if each of us constituted an entire culture within our individual selves? That would be the first "I" in this three-part conceptualisation of intercultural communicative competence.

The second part of this chapter looks at the relationships between individuals and institutions, the ways in which individuals create institutions as extensions and manifestations of societal cultures, and the ways in which those institutions, as artifacts, reflect the cultural values and beliefs of the individuals and groups who created them. This part of the chapter also discusses what can happen when the culture of an individual clashes with the culture of an institution, and looks at the importance of social connections and social networks known as *guanxi*.

The third part of the chapter considers the possibility that "Internet culture" constitutes an emerging form of "international culture". If so, there are at least two opposing positions possible here: that the Internet has No Culture or No Cultures, or that the Internet is All Cultures. Internet addiction is also explored, as a new clinical phenomenon, which raises the question of what other cultures, if any, have generated their own particular pathologies.

Andrew LIAN and **Roland SUSSEX** ("Towards a critical epistemology for learning languages and cultures in 21st-century Asia") start from the enormous social and economic changes currently under way in Asia, especially those involving China, India and the Association of South-East Asian Nations (ASEAN), and the adoption of English as the common language of the region. Growing personal mobility will bring about rapidly increasing demands linguistically and culturally. Traditional national and cultural boundaries will be less distinct, and learners will

---

[1] The Forum contribution by MAO Sihui, "Bon appétit: A critical reflection on some of the new challenges of Chinese culinary tradition in/as intercultural communication in the digital age", was not available for inclusion in this volume.

need a new set of tools which go beyond the traditional structured language class. This chapter offers flexible and dynamic alternatives to current pedagogic models which are more suited to the conditions of twenty-first century Asia, and in particular, models which allow individuals to explore and develop knowledge and understanding on their own initiative and for their individual purposes. It begins by seeking ways to challenge the learner's "operational histories", or habitual patterns of understanding established by experience, and then helps them to develop new learning strategies, where students navigate at will through networks of knowledge representations and other helpful (ideally optimised) resources to meet their needs as perceived by themselves or by advisers – human members of their personal learning environments.

This model is developed and illustrated further with a detailed example drawn from a recent empirical study on the learning of English pronunciation by Chinese EFL students (He and Sangarun 2015) based on verbotonal theory (Guberina and Asp 1981; Guberina 1972).

For **Don SNOW** ("Intercultural communication in English courses in Asia: What should we teach about?)" increasing globalisation means more intercultural encounters, especially in Asia. Societies and educational institutions are therefore faced with the question of which intercultural factors they should teach?

Intercultural communication training is principally provided in courses in English and other foreign languages. But there is only limited space for teaching the key concepts of intercultural communication, and among these a key issue is when speakers attempt to interpret the words and actions of someone from a different culture. This chapter therefore focuses on three factors: ethnocentrism, in-group bias and stereotyping. These three factors are important in "attribute substitution", and can interfere with the process of interpretation. By teaching these factors explicitly we can help learners better understand how interpretation works in intercultural contexts.

6.2 Section 2: Values and Communication in Cultural Contexts

Thi Hong Nhung PHAM ("Confucian values as challenges for communication in intercultural workplace contexts: Evidence from Vietnamese – Anglo-cultural interactions") poses the question: to what extent are insights into Confucian values able to describe and elucidate intercultural communication in Asia, especially where misunderstandings and frustrations arise? A corpus of Vietnamese self-reported incidents and follow-up in-depth interview data on English language interactions between a Vietnamese and an English speaker was used to investigate three factors, modified from Spencer-Oatey (2002) – Face, Equity Rights, and Association Rights.

The behaviour and concerns of the Vietnamese speaker show a fundamental influence from Confucian values. Many Vietnamese people place a high value on

Anglo-cultural behaviour which is consistent with the Vietnamese Confucian concern for Face, especially individual Quality Face, and for Empathy. The data show that the Vietnamese concern for their personal Face, and to have full freedom of action, is secondary to their wish for solidarity with their co-worker.

6.3 Section 3: English as a Lingua Franca in Asia

Juliane HOUSE ("English as a global lingua franca: The threat to other languages, intercultural communication and translation?") sees English as the first truly international global language, and that includes Asia. But the success of English has given rise to criticism about its alleged cultural neutrality, about its role as an elitist language, and about its alleged tendency to have a negative effect on local languages. Other critiques focus on the insufficient competence of people using English as a lingua franca, which will inhibit its success; and on claims that using English heavily will have a negative impact on other languages, not to mention the speakers' ability to think in their mother tongue.

House reviews these arguments in the light of recent research, including that of her own research group in Hamburg, Germany. Her conclusion is that English can be absolved of these criticisms, in that ideological objections against English as a lingua franca do not stand up to scrutiny. The use of English as a global language offers enormous opportunities for international intercultural communication. And the growth of English as a language of instruction at various levels will change international education scenarios in Asia and elsewhere.

6.4 Section 4: Focal Areas of Intercultural Communication

Istvan KECSKES ("How does intercultural communication differ from intracultural communication?") takes a socio-cognitive approach to intra-cultural and inter-cultural communication. His key concept is that these form not a dichotomy but a continuum.

Speakers who share a high level of language proficiency operate closer to intracultural communication. If speakers come from different ethnic backgrounds, they shift progressively towards inter-cultural communication: the common ground on which they negotiate is emergent rather than "core" – frameworks derived from assumed and shared values. In such contexts they build their frames of communication bottom-up, there is more reliance on the language which they create in the course of the interaction (rather than pre-existing language and frames), and they rely more on context, paying more conscious attention to what is said and its implications. This analysis allows us to see that the conventional opposition of intra- and intercultural communication, which has dominated the literature so far, in fact obscures a number of important insights.

Joanna RADWAŃSKA-WILLIAMS ("The linguistic landscape of Macao") sees the geosemiotics of Macao as a special case of intercultural communication (Scollon and Scollon 2003). Public signs in Macau are typically at least trilingual, involving Chinese, Portuguese and English. This fact reflects the distinctive historical and cultural composition of a city which was once a Portuguese colony, and was only relatively recently returned to China in 1999. Her chapter is a case study of the main street of Macau, and its "geosemiotic" meanings of objects which are physically situated in the spaces of urban agglomerations. Her analysis of the data lead to two important conclusions relating to ethnicity and ideology. Ethnicity is seen from the perspective of multilingualism in the signage, both formal and informal. And ideology is principally involved in the interpretation of spatial and visual semiotics. These meanings show how Macao reflects dynamic tensions in its role as a tourist hub and a Special Administrative Region of China.

Roland SUSSEX ("Pain as an issue of intercultural communication") addresses the unusual topic of pain in intercultural communication. Pain talk – the way patients and health care professionals talk about pain – is of fundamental importance to diagnosis and treatment. Pain talk is crucially mediated by cultural values and conventions. These conventions include the persistent negative associative networks of pain words, including *pain, hurt, ache* and *sore*, and as pain is the body's early-warning system that something is amiss, it is a vital clue to diagnosticians and therapists. And yet there is only a modest literature about pain talk within cultures, let alone across cultures. The dominant cultural paradigms are based on English, with some attention to Spanish, especially in the USA.

Pain talk analysis is not only a matter of English-based word-semantics. This is shown in use of metaphors and metonyms for medical conditions in French, and pain vocabulary in Japanese, both of which are substantially different from English. More widely, pain talk is also realised in discourse. And it is susceptible to complex potential misunderstandings of value systems, interpersonal dynamics, pragmatics, sociolinguistics and cultural linguistics, and specifically in intercultural pragmatics in conversational contexts involving patients and health care professionals. These factors are not only of great inherent intellectual interest, but they are becoming increasingly relevant in an applied and practical sense in the globalising world of the twenty-first century, including medical tourism, especially in Asia.

Kimie OSHIMA ("Functions of humor in intercultural communication: Disarm, tolerance, and solidarity") argues that having a sense of humour helps one to think "outside the box". It helps people overcome their social and cultural preconceptions. Humour is therefore, in its own way, similar in its role as a skill in intercultural understanding and communication. People with a well-developed sense of humour are often more skilful as intercultural communicators, as can be seen in Hawaii, a notably successful and peaceful interethnic society.

The classroom use of jokes to create a humorous environment has been shown to help students learn more effectively and positively. It can foster analytical, critical and divergent thinking. On the other hand, humour which transcends cultural and linguistic boundaries can reveal what speakers have in common. The chapter draws on a course "Intercultural communication (Rakugo in English)", which shows how a traditional Japanese genre of performance can be delivered in English to reveal common values and humour.

6.5 Section 5: Identity

Doreen WU and **Chaoyuan LI** ("Emotional branding on social media: A cross-cultural discourse analysis of global brands on Twitter and Weibo") show that new communication technologies, far from being "culturally neutral", reveal cultural influences related to communication circumstances and outcomes. Most of the literature is couched in terms of contrastive nation-state cultures (Hofstede 1984, 1986, 1997), or cultural variability in communication (Gudykunst and Kim 1997; Gudykunst and Mody 2002), or Triandis' horizontal/vertical individualism/collectivism model (1995).

The chapter goes behind pre-determined cultural categories and examines the nature of virtual language, culture and ideology, from the point of view of their implications for the internationalisation of education. The data are taken from Twitter and Weibo, including examples of the World's Top 10 Best Brands (including Google, Microsoft, IBM, Coca Cola, GE, McDonald's, Samsung and Toyota). The advertisements on Twitter show less variation than on Weibo, and there is a degree of cultural hybridity in the mixing of the three appeals of emotional branding: pragmatist, evangelist and sensualist. The conventional analyses of face and politeness in Chinese (Gu 1990, 1992) may no longer apply.

Finally, **Yihong GAO** ("China's fluctuating English education policy discourses and continuing ambivalences in identity construction") shows how China is restructuring its linguistic and cultural identities in a globalising world, and in the process reorganising linguistic resources. Attitudes towards the teaching of English in China varied from uncritically enthusiastic (the late 1970s to the mid-1990s), to anxiety over the quality of outcomes *versus* the amount of effort expended (mid-1990s to the first decade of the new millennium), and currently to a fear, especially in the important debates between 2013 and 2014, that English may interfere with Chinese language proficiency and cultural identity.

This accelerated re-evaluation of ideas about the West, which has involved national policy makers, educational institutions, educational experts, learners and netizens, can be seen as a recapitulation of Chinese attitudes over the last 150 years. Unlike most other Asian countries, China did not have a history of British colonialism. In contrast, its monistic view of its language and identity have become a "habitus" (Bourdieu 1991).

7   Envoi

Intercultural communication, then, is on a strong upwards trajectory. It is perhaps not surprising that Kim should claim, though perhaps with some hyperbole, that:

> Intercultural communication is arguably the most serious of all the problems confronting humankind, and is the single most vital domain in social science. (Kim 2010, p. 177)

References

Alptekin, C. (2002). Towards intercultural communicative competence in ELT. *ELT Journal, 56*(1), 57–64.

Arasaratnam, L. A. (2015). Research in intercultural communication: Reviewing the past decade. *Journal of International and Intercultural Communication, 8*(4), 290–310.

Arnett, J. (2008). The neglected 95%: Why American psychology needs to become less American. *American Psychologist, 63*(7), 602–614.

Baker, W. (2011). Intercultural awareness: Modelling an understanding of cultures in intercultural communication through English as a lingua franca. *Language and Intercultural Communication, 11*(3), 197–214.

Barker, G. G. (2015). Cross-cultural perspectives on intercultural communication competence. *Journal of Intercultural Communication Research*, 1–18. https://doi.org/10.1080/17475759.2015.1104376.

Bourdieu, P. (1991). *Language and symbolic power.* (Trans: Thompson, J. B. (Ed.), Raymond, G. & Adamson, M.). Cambridge: Cambridge University Press.

Brown, P., & Levinson, S. C. (1987). *Politeness. Some universals in language usage.* Cambridge: Cambridge University Press.

Bryant, J., & Yang, M. H. (2004). A blueprint for excellence for the Asian communication research. *Asian Communication Research, 1*, 133–151.

Byram, M. (1997). *Teaching and assessing intercultural communicative competence.* Bristol: Multilingual Matters.

Byram, M. (2010). Linguistic and cultural education for *Bildung* and citizenship. *Modern Language Journal, 94*(2), 317–231.

Byram, M., Nichols, A., & Stevens, D. (2001a). Developing intercultural competence. In D. K. Deardorff (Ed.), *The Sage handbook of intercultural competence* (pp. 321–332). Thousand Oaks: Sage.

Byram, M., Nichols, A., & Stevens, D. (Eds.). (2001b). *Developing intercultural competence in practice.* Cleveland and Buffalo: Multilingual Matters.

Cai, D. A., & Donohue, W. A. (1997). Determinants of facework in intercultural negotiation. *Asian Journal of Communication, 7*(1), 85–110.

Canagarajah, S. (2007). Lingua Franca English, multilingual communities, and language acquisition. *Modern Language Journal, 91*, 932–939.

Chen, G.-M. (2009). Beyond the dichotomy of communication studies. *Asian Journal of Communication, 19*(4), 398–411.

Cheong, P. H., Martin, J. N., & Macfadyen, L. P. (2012). *New media and intercultural communication: Identity, community, and politics.* New York: Peter Lang.

Chitty, N. (2010). Mapping Asian international communication. *Asian Journal of Communication, 20*(2), 181–196.

Curtis, A. (2018). Individual, institutional and international: Three aspects of intercultural communication. In A. Curtis & R. Sussex (Eds.), *Intercultural communication in Asia: Education, language and values.* Cham: Springer.

Deardorff, S. K. (Ed.). (2010). *The SAGE handbook of intercultural competence*. Thousand Oaks: Sage.

Dunfee, T. W., & Warren, T. D. (2001). Is guanxi ethical? A normative analysis of doing business in China. *Journal of Business Ethics, 32*(3), 191–204.

Gu, Y. (1990). Politeness phenomena in modern Chinese. *Journal of Pragmatics, 14*, 237–257.

Gu, Y. (1992). Politeness, pragmatics and culture. *Foreign Language Teaching and Research, 4*, 10–17.

Guberina, P. (1972). *Restricted bands of frequencies in auditory rehabilitation of deaf*. Zagreb: Institute of Phonetics, Faculty of Arts, University of Zagreb.

Guberina, P., & Asp, C. W. (1981). *The verbo-tonal method for rehabilitation people with communication problems*. http://www.suvag.com/ang/histoire/autrestextes.html. Retrieved 17 Feb 2017.

Gudykunst, W., & Kim, Y. Y. (1997). *Communicating with strangers* (3rd ed.). Boston: McGraw Hill.

Gudykunst, W. B., & Mody, B. (Eds.). (2002). *Handbook of international and intercultural communication*. Thousand Oaks: Sage.

Halualani, R. T. (2008). How do multicultural university students define and make sense of intercultural contact? A qualitative study. *International Journal of Intercultural Relations, 32*, 1–16.

He, B., & Sangarun, P. (2015). Implementing autonomy: A model for improving pronunciation in Chinese EFL university students. *Rangsit Journal of Arts and Sciences, 5*(1), 1–12.

Henrich, J., Heine, S. J., & Norenzayan, A. (2010). The weirdest people in the world? *Journal of Behavioral and Brain Sciences, 33*(2–3), 61–135.

Hinde, R. A. (1998). *Individuals, relationships and culture. Links between ethology and the social sciences*. Cambridge/New York: Cambridge University Press.

Hofstede, G. (1984). *Culture's consequences: International differences in work-related values* (2nd ed.). Beverly Hills: Sage Publications.

Hofstede, G. (1986). Cultural differences in teaching and learning. *International Journal of Intercultural Relations, 10*, 301–320.

Hofstede, G. (1997). *Cultures and organizations. Software of the mind*. New York: McGraw Hill.

House, J. (2018). English as a global lingua franca: A threat to other languages, intercultural communication and translation? In A. Curtis & R. Sussex (Eds.), *Intercultural communication in Asia: Education, language and values*. Cham: Springer.

Ito, Y. (1992). Theories on intercultural communication styles from a Japanese perspective: A sociological approach. In J. Blumler, J. McLeod, & K. Rosengren (Eds.), *Comparatively speaking: Communication and culture across space and time* (pp. 238–268). Thousand Oaks: Sage.

Kim, M. S. (2002). *Non-Western perspectives on human communication*. Thousand Oaks: SAGE Publications.

Kim, M. S. (2010). Intercultural communication in Asia: Current state and future prospects. *Asian Journal of Communication, 20*(2), 166–180.

Kirkpatrick, A., & Sussex, R. (Eds.). (2012). *English as an international language in Asia: Implications for language education*. Berlin/London: Springer-Verlag.

Kuo, E. C. Y., & Chew, H. E. (2009). Beyond ethnocentrism in communication theory: Towards a culture-centric approach. *Asian Journal of Communication, 19*(4), 422–437.

Lian, A., & Sussex, R. (2018). Toward a critical epistemology for learning languages and cultures in 21st century Asia. In A. Curtis & R. Sussex (Eds.), *Intercultural communication in Asia: Education, language and values*. Cham: Springer.

Martin, J., & Nakayama, T. (2012). *Intercultural communication in contexts* (6th ed.). New York: McGraw-Hill.

Morris, P. K. (2014). Comparing portrayals of beauty in outdoor advertisements across six cultures: Bulgaria, Hong Kong, Japan, Poland, South Korea, and Turkey. *Asian Journal of Communication, 24*(3), 242–261.

Nakayama, T. K., & Halualani, R. T. (Eds.). (2011). *The handbook of critical intercultural communication*. Oxford: Wiley-Blackwell.

Neuliep, J. W. (2014). *Intercultural communication: A contextual approach* (6th ed.). Thousand Oaks: SAGE Publications.

Ono, K. A. (2010). Reflections on "problematizing 'nation' in intercultural communication". In T. K. Nakayama & R. T. Halualani (Eds.), *Handbook of critical intercultural communication* (pp. 84–97). Chichester: Blackwell Publishing.

Samovar, L. A., Porter, R. E., McDaniel, E. R., & Roy, C. S. (2014). *Intercultural communication: A reader* (14th ed.). Boston: Cengage Learning.

Sar, S., & Rodriguez, L. (2014). The effectiveness of appeals used in Cambodian and Vietnamese magazine ads. *Asian Journal of Communication, 24*(6), 529–548.

Scollon, R., & Scollon, S. W. (2003). *Discourses in place: Language in the material world.* London: Routledge.

Singhal, A., & Nagao, M. (1993). Assertiveness as communication competence a comparison of the communication styles of American and Japanese students. *Asian Journal of Communication, 3*(1), 1–18.

Snow, D. (2018). Intercultural communication in English courses in Asia: What should we teach? In A. Curtis & R. Sussex (Eds.), *Intercultural communication in Asia: Education, language and values.* Cham: Springer.

So, C. Y. K. (2010). The rise of Asian communication research: A citation study of SSCI journals. *Asian Journal of Communication, 20*(2), 230–247.

Spencer-Oatey, H. (2002). Managing rapport in talk: Using rapport sensitive incidents to explore the motivational concerns underlying the management of relations. *Journal of Pragmatics, 34*, 529–545.

Sussex, R., & Kirkpatrick, A. (2012). A postscript and a prolegomenon. In A. Kirkpatrick & R. Sussex (Eds.), *English as an international language in Asia: Implications for language education* (pp. 223–231). Berlin/London: Springer-Verlag.

Triandis, H. C. (1995). *Individualism and collectivism.* Boulder: Westview Press.

Wang, G., & Kuo, E. C. Y. (2010). The Asian communication debate: Culture-specificity, culture-generality, and beyond. *Asian Journal of Communication, 20*(2), 152–165.

Watkins, D. A., & Biggs, J. B. (Eds.). (1996). *The Chinese learner: Cultural, psychological, and contextual influences.* ERIC Document ED405401. https://eric.ed.gov/?id=ED405410

Wee, L., Goh, R. B. H., & Lim, L. (Eds.). (2013). *The politics of English: South Asia, Southeast Asia, and the Asia Pacific.* Amsterdam: John Benjamins.

Willink, K. G., Gutierrez-Perez, R., Shukri, S., & Stein, L. (2014). Navigating with the stars: Critical qualitative methodological constellations for critical intercultural communication research. *Journal of International and Intercultural Communication, 7*(4), 289–316. https://doi.org/10.1080/17513057.2014.964150.

Zhang, W. (2012). The effects of political news use, political discussion and authoritarian orientation on political participation: Evidences from Singapore and Taiwan. *Asian Journal of Communication, 22*(5), 474–492.

Zhang, D., Shoemaker, P. J., & Wang, X. (2013). Reality and newsworthiness: Press coverage of international terrorism by China and the United States. *Asian Journal of Communication, 23*(5), 449–471.

Part I
Models, Intercultural Competence and Education

Individual, Institutional and International: Three Aspects of Intercultural Communication

Andy CURTIS

Abstract This chapter starts by revisiting the three main sets of overarching questions that guided the Macao International Forum out of which grew this book. The second part, "Individual Cultures and the Individual as Cultural Artifact", focuses on the first corner of a three-part triangular perspective, and begins by considering the original meanings of "individual" and "artifact", and how those meanings have developed and expanded over time. To some extent reversing the idea that artifacts are, by definition, things made by humans, I propose that each of us is as much an artifact as the objects we make.

In the third part of the chapter, Institutional Cultures, I contrast the relatively new idea of individuals as cultural artifacts, with institutional cultures, which have a long-documented history, even though individuals have been around for far longer than the institutions they eventually created. I also consider how such institutions, as extensions and manifestations of societal cultures, reflect the cultural values and beliefs of the individuals and groups who created them. The fourth section explores the amorphous idea of "International Culture", using the concept of "Internet Culture" as a way of concretizing the notion of "International Culture". The chapter concludes by connecting the three corners of the triangle – Individual, Institutional, and International/Internet Cultures – to the three main sets of overarching questions that guided the Forum.

1 Introduction

As we saw in the Introduction chapter of this volume, the international conference out of which this volume grew focused on three main questions:

Q1. What are the challenges facing, on the one hand, government and educational institutions, and, on the other hand, individual educators and students, in adapting to an increasingly internationalized educational environment?

A. CURTIS (✉)
Graduate School of Education, Anaheim University, Anaheim, CA, USA
e-mail: andycurtiswork@gmail.com

© Springer International Publishing AG, part of Springer Nature 2018
A. CURTIS, R. SUSSEX (eds.), *Intercultural Communication in Asia: Education, Language and Values*, Multilingual Education 24,
https://doi.org/10.1007/978-3-319-69995-0_2

Q2. What are the challenges of intercultural communication vis-à-vis these invisible (or partly visible) constructed boundaries that intersect society, even in today's increasingly fluid, dynamic, hybridized and globalized world?

Q3. What challenges to intercultural communication, as individuals/cultures/groups interact with each other, are posed by ideological considerations, which may not always be fully conscious or explicitly articulated, but which are nevertheless powerful forces affecting decision-making behaviour?

These are complex questions, which, together, cover an expansive area of theory and practice, in relation to intercultural communication in Asia, revolving around the three central themes of Education, Language and Values. An overarching question then emerges: How can such broad and deep questions be connected? One way of doing that is to employ another set of three-part relationships, which I will do in this chapter, between the Individual as Artifact, Institutions as Cultural Artifacts, and the Internet as a form of "International Culture".

What follows, then, is a three-part conceptualization of intercultural communication, based on the notion of Three Is: Individual, Institutional and International. The first "I" stands for "Individual", and is based on the idea that each of us is a cultural artifact, which challenges the notion that artifacts are things made by humans, as I claim that humans are as much cultural artifacts as the things they make. The second "I" is for "Institutional Culture", as all institutions have not only an overarching culture, but also myriad sub-cultures. The third "I" makes the amorphous notion of "International Culture" more concrete by focusing on "Internet Culture", starting with two competing propositions: The Internet has No Culture vs. The Internet is All Cultures.

There are several ways in which Internet Culture(s) could relate to International Culture(s). For example, the claim could be made that Internet Culture embraces all other cultures, and so is inclusive in the broadest possible sense, or that the Internet captures, albeit eclectically and in an ad hoc manner, enough individual and international cultures to be a viable platform for global communication, across space and time, in ways that were not possible before. Similar claims could be made that Internet Culture is somehow "neutral", in the sense that it "neutralizes" cultural differences across the board, thereby creating a level playing field, and/or that Internet Culture may in some sense "homogenize" difference, so that people can communicate across the Internet, in spite of external regular cultural differences, making the Internet a "culture-free" zone. It may be too soon to say which of these two claims could be more or less true than the other, as it may depend on the country, context and culture being used as the reference point when considering the two claims.

We can use this triangular perspective as a way of connecting recurring themes regarding intercultural communication in Asia, in relation to Education, Language and Values. It should also be pointed out that each of these concepts – Individual Culture, Institutional Culture, and International/Internet Culture – could be a chapter, or a book, in their own right. Indeed, a large number of large volumes have been written on Institutional Culture and Internet Culture. However, as the purpose of this chapter is to present these three concepts as concisely as possible, each of the three main "I"s will be explored in a preliminary manner (with more on this relationship to come in following publications).

2 Individual Cultures and the Individual as Cultural Artifact

Looking into the origin of words is something of an occupational hazard for those of us who do language for a living. And if we are going to consider this concept of the "Individual as Artifact", then it helps to understand what we mean. According to Harper (2016), the word "individual", as an adjective, comes from the early fifteenth century, with the original meaning being "one and indivisible, inseparable" with reference to the Holy Trinity of the Father, the Son and the Holy Spirit, reflecting perhaps the male bias in words and their meanings at that time (and some would say, still today). By around 1610, the meaning had become somewhat more gender-neutral, defined as "single, separate, of but one person or thing" and by 1889, "individual" also meant "intended for one person", as in an "individual portion".

The meanings of "individual" as a noun followed a similar semantic and syntactic trajectory, but its original meaning, in 1600, was "a single object or thing", which grew to mean "a single human being, as opposed to a group, etc." by the 1640s, with the colloquial sense of "person" attested from 1742. It is also worth noting that the Latin "individuum" as a noun meant an atom, or indivisible particle, and in early fifteenth century Middle English "individuum" meant "individual member of a species". The educational implications of such meanings are alluded to in the example statements given in the online *Cambridge advanced learner's dictionary*: "We try to treat our students as individuals", and "If nothing else, the school will turn her into an individual". Such definitions may reflect a cultural bias towards individuality as an inherently good thing in the countries that used to "own" English, such as the U.K., the U.S., Canada and Australia. As we noted in the Introduction chapter, such biases may be especially important when comparing and contrasting cultures that are characterized as being towards the more Individualistic end of the Collectivistic-Individualistic Cultural Continuum with those at the more Collectivistic end, which includes many Asian cultures, perhaps especially those described as "Confucian Heritage Cultures" (a term contested by, for example, Wang 2013) such as China, Vietnam, Singapore, Korea and Japan (See, for example, Phuong-Mai et al. 2005; Tran 2013).

Moving on to *artifact* (spelled *artefact* in UK English), we find a shorter and more recent history, starting in around 1821, when the word meant "anything made by human art", from the Italian *artefatto*, which was created by combining *arte*, "by skill", with *factum*, "thing made", which in turn came from *facere*, "to make, do". Harper (2016) also notes that the spelling of "artifact" with an "i" came later, in the 1880s, and that the archeological meaning dates from the 1890s. The modern meaning of "artefact" is given in the *Cambridge advanced learner's dictionary* as: "an object that is made by a person, such as a tool or a decoration, especially one that is of historical interest", and the example given of how it is used in a sentence is: "The museum's collection includes artefacts dating back to prehistoric times". One of the consequences of such definitions is that artifacts are seen as things made by people, but the people themselves are not usually seen as artifacts, unless the act of procreation is seen as the making of "human artifacts" or humans *as* artifacts.

This may be one of the reasons why the concept of the "Individual as Artifact" appears to be a somewhat original idea. For example, Google Scholar shows around 4,000,000 hits for "Individual" and around 1.3 million hits for "Artifact" (and, reflecting the dominance of U.S. spelling, only 330,000 hits with the British spelling). But, interestingly, there appear to be no exact matches for the term "Individual as Artifact" in the trillions of pages that Google claims to search. Some research has touched on this concept, for example, in cognitive science, Newman et al. (2014) asked, in their study of "Individual Concepts and their Extensions", in the title of their article: "Are artworks more like people than artifacts?" (pp. 647–662). In answering their own questions about identity, Newman et al. concluded that: "there are important ways in which judgments about ART appear to be more similar to judgments about PERSONS (in their reliance on sameness of substance) than judgments about other kinds of artifacts" (p. 658). However, what we are asking here is: To what extent can a person be considered an artifact?

There have also been explorations of this concept of "Individual as Artifact" in philosophy (see, for example, Errol Katayama's *Aristotle on artifacts: A metaphysical puzzle*, 1999), but few, if any, in education. However, in the broad area of language and meaning, some works have alluded to this concept. For example, Ezell and O'Keeffe's edited collection, *Cultural artifacts and the production of meaning: The page, the image, and the body* (1994), explored such concerns as "the implications of reproduction in manuscript and print cultures, the changing dynamics of print and authorship in the eighteenth and nineteenth centuries, the visual art of post modern books, the psychotechnology [*sic*] of memory in modern fiction, and 'body art' as the concrete expression of the visceral realism of tragedy" (back cover). Whether body art is indeed such an expression of tragedy is open to question. But Ezell and O'Keeffe did see the connection between the human body and cultural artifacts, in which all three – the printed page, the created image, and the human body – can all be reproduced by different means, with varying degrees of sameness or differentness, compared to the original, which echoes the conclusions of Newman et al. (2014). More specifically focused on language, the philosopher Andy Clark argued that language is "in many ways the ultimate artefact" (Clark 1997, p. 218), although this view has been challenged by other philosophers, such as Wheeler (2004).

Having considered the meanings of and relationships between individuals and artifacts, we can now consider what is meant by "cultural artifact", and here we see a wide range of applications and possibilities. For example, 35 years ago, Marsden and Nachbar (1982) wrote about "movies as artifacts" in their cultural criticism of popular film, and from an information sciences and cataloging perspective, Smiraglia (2008) described "documents as cultural artifacts" (pp. 25–37). In *Frames within frames* (2001), Oberhardt described art museums as cultural artifacts, and as a way of teaching theology and religion, Campbell (2014) created activities based on "religious cultural artifacts" (p. 343). Regarding technology and new media, Sterne (2006) reported on the digital music-playing device known as an "mp3" as a cultural artifact. According to the BBC WebWise team, in addition to being a physical object, mp3 is also "a digital music format for creating high-quality sound files" which "transformed the way people buy and listen to music" (2012). Ten years ago, the mp3 player was not only "at the center of important debates around intellectual property and file-sharing" but it was also, according to Sterne, "a cultural artifact in its own right" (Sterne 2006, p. 825). The basis for that claim is that the mp3 is (or was) "an item that 'works for' and is 'worked on' by a host of people, ideologies, technologies and other social and material elements" (p. 826), which highlights a number of important aspects of cultural artifacts.

One of the most interesting areas of study, related to the concept of the Individual as Cultural Artifact, looks at the human body – dead or alive – as a cultural artifact. A study of ritualistic and ceremonial artifacts to do with death was carried out by Curşeu and Pop-Curşeu (2011), who describe their study as "an exploratory cultural artifact analysis" (p. 371–387) of a burial ground in Romania known as the Merry Cemetery of Săpânţa. In terms of what constitutes a cultural artifact and how they come into being, Curşeu and Pop-Curşeu explained that: "Communities, as social groups that share cultural values and engage in joint activity, often develop cultural artifacts which represent patterns of community change, dynamics of interpersonal and inter-group relations, and critical historical and socio-political events" (p. 371), which emphasizes the communal nature of such artifacts.

This tendency to see artifacts as objects made by humans but not to see ourselves as artifacts or "made objects" may reflect a natural human tendency to think of humans as "special" or "different", which goes back at least 2500 years to Aristotle's description of humans as "rational animals". An important aspect of the difference between ourselves and other animals is the brain size of humans, and focusing on that particular organ, archeologist Steven Mithen and cognitive neuroscientist Lawrence Parsons asked, at the beginning of their article on "the brain as a cultural artifact" (2008, pp. 415–422): "Where does biology end and culture begin?" (p. 415). Mithen and Parsons explain that, by describing the brain "as an artefact of culture" they mean that "both its anatomy and function have been unintentionally influenced by the cultural contexts in which it has evolved and in which it develops within each individual" (pp. 415–416).

That approach to the human brain relates to the idea that each of us is a "made object" – shaped as much by the world around us as we shape it, which in turn relates to the Sapir-Whorf Hypothesis. As Whorf wrote, in 1952, language is "not merely a reproducing instrument for voicing ideas but rather is itself a shaper of ideas" (p.5, quoted in Kim 2000, p.100). In the same way that language, as well as being a means of communication, shapes us and the world around us, human beings not only create artifacts, but we ourselves are artifacts. As Mithen and Parsons put it: "The body, whether living or dead, is as much a cultural artefact as a biological entity" (2008, p. 415), and they go further, stating that: "Once human bodies are no longer living, their potential as cultural artefacts becomes even greater" because "Dead brains can also become cultural objects" (p. 415), a famous example of which is the post-mortem brain of Albert Einstein (see, for example, Hao 2014). It is also worth noting that these dead brains, while being a biological relic, also exist in the works that have been produced by those bodies that housed their brains, which are themselves also artifacts.

Commenting on the need for greater interdisciplinary approaches in this area, Mithen and Parsons state that: "historians need to become more scientifically literate, while biologists and physiologists have to become more historically minded and appreciate just how much our brains are products of society and culture" (2008, p. 421). Their comment points to the on-going need for more interdisciplinary studies, not only between archeology and cognitive neuroscience, but also between cultural studies, language studies and education.

That need for greater "inter-disciplinarity" was identified a decade before Mithen and Parsons (2008), by Hinde in his book, *Individuals, relationships and culture* (1987), in which he described the "division between the biological and the social sciences" as "an unfortunate consequence of implying a clear distinction between the biological and social sides of human nature" (p. vii). Thirty years later those divisions are not as great as they used to be, but it appears that we still have some way to go before the gap between these two sciences is fully bridged. And in relation to the bi-directional nature of individual-artifact relations referred to above, Hinde also noted that: "the actual artifacts, institutions, myths, etc. are seen as expressions of the culture" that "may in turn *act back upon* and influence culture in the minds of the individuals" (1987, p. 4, emphasis added).

Having explored the first "I", for Individual", we can now consider the second "I" of "Institutional Culture".

3   Institutional Cultures

In this section, I will look at how the relationships between individuals and institutions are reflected in the ways in which groups of individuals create institutions, as extensions and manifestations of societal cultures, and the ways in which those institutions, as artifacts, reflect the cultural values and beliefs of the individuals who created them. However, in contrast to notions of individuals as cultural artifacts, which appear to be relatively new, institutional cultures have a long-documented history, which may be somewhat surprising, given that individuals have been around far longer than the institutions they eventually created. For example, according to Anne Goldar and Robert Frost (2004), in the introduction to their edited collection, *Institutional culture in early modern society* – by which they mean Europe from around the late fifteenth century to the late eighteenth century: "Institutions have always loomed large in the writing of early modern history" (p. xi). The examples they give of such institutions include parliaments, law courts and the church, as well as guilds, charities and schools, which Goldar and Frost describe as being "essential features of the landscape" (p. xi).

Goldar and Frost also state that: "One of the most important issues for the members of any institution was establishing and maintaining a sense of the institution's identity" (p. xiii), which shows how individual and institutional identities can overlap, in terms of how those are established and maintained. The ways in which individual and institutional identities exist within political contexts was explored by

Bennich-Björkman (2007), who asked: "To what extent do existing institutions particularly determine the political culture of a society, and to what extent does culture exist independently?" (p. 1). However, as we discussed in the Introduction chapter of this book, we question the idea that culture can really exist independently.

Schools were one of the examples given by Goldar and Frost, and much has been written about institutional cultures within educational organizations such as schools, colleges and universities. A dramatic account of a "contested institutional culture" was presented by Morin (2010), who reported on a change of president at The College of William & Mary in Virginia, which was founded in 1693, making it the second oldest tertiary institution in the United States (after Harvard University). In 2005, the College President of 13 years retired, so that the College, which was long known "as a bastion of conservatism" (Morin 2010, p. 93), was now in a position to take the opportunity to change their future, through the appointment of a new president. The College therefore appointed "a liberal democrat and former candidate for political office [who] won over the students, faculty, and Board of Visitors with his larger-than-life presence and impassioned speeches", and who attempted "sweeping changes" at the College "from the very outset of his tenure" (p. 93). However, the new initiatives "were not met with the widespread acclaim many had anticipated" (p. 93) and in the end, the new president served for just two-and-a-half years.

The importance of those in leadership roles understanding the institutional cultures of academic institutions such as universities was the focus of Rita Bornstein's *Legitimacy in the academic presidency* (2003), in which she wrote: "The search for cultural adaptation and acceptance is a mutual process between the new president and the institution's constituents" (p. 45). Borstein went on to note that, although "Most presidents work hard to learn and adapt to their new culture. Some, *generally to their peril*, turn their backs on the institution's history and traditions as they seek to make change" (p. 45, emphasis added). That is exactly what appears to have happened to the new and short-lived President of The College of William & Mary, which is a particularly illustrative example of the kind of upheaval that can take place, when the culture of an institution clashes with the culture of the individual. In that sense, the "Individual as Artifact" is in conflict with the "Institution as Artifact". Although The College of William & Mary may be considered a quintessentially American institution, there may be lessons for universities in Asia. For example, as the vice-president of a university in Hong Kong, Mok (2007) wrote: "One major trend related to reforming and restructuring universities in Asia that has emerged is the adoption of strategies along the lines of the Anglo-Saxon paradigm in internationalizing universities in Asia" (p. 433).

A useful metaphor for considering how individual cultures exist within institutional cultures, and vice versa, is "navigation". For example, Walker (2011) gives advice on "determining and navigating institutional culture" (pp. 113–117), in the context of library management at a university college in Brooklyn, New York. Highlighting the multiplicity of cultures within an institution, Walker points out that: "Often, there is no single culture within an organization – especially if you are in a multi-layered institution", which applied to Walker's college, where she had to take into account the culture of the library, of the College, of the university as a whole, and of the various groups within each of those. It is likely that all institutions, especially larger ones, will be multi-layered, and that the larger and more multi-layered the institution, the more navigation will be needed, as the greater will be the possibilities of getting lost in the maze that can constitute institutional cultures.

In relation to navigating within a particular geographic, linguistic and cultural context, Gold et al. (2002) focused on the ways in which institutional cultures in China are reflected in social connections, specifically the Chinese practice of *guanxi*, which Gold and his co-authors explain is "loosely translated as 'social connections' or 'social networks'" (p. 3). Gold et al. describe *guanxi* as "among the most important, talked about, and studied phenomena in China" (p. i), which "lies at the heart of Chinese social order, its economic structure, and its changing institutional landscape" (p. 3). *Guanxi* is, therefore, "important in almost every realm of life, from politics to business, and from officialdom to street life" (p. 3).

An example of how understanding and acceptance of guanxi has grown in the years since Gold et al.'s *Social connections in China: Institutions, culture, and the changing nature of guanxi* (2002) was a BBC news story titled, "Doing business the Chinese way" (Hope 2014). In that new story, *guanxi* is described as being, "a crucial part of life in China", the roots of which are "tightly bound in history, with the notions of obligation and loyalty going back thousands of years". For the news story, Kent Deng, an associate professor at the London School of Economics, was consulted. He stated that: "The Cultural Revolution of the 1960s and 1970s, when families and friends were encouraged to report on one another in a bid to enforce communism, meant that *guanxi's* importance increased as a way to rebuild trust" (Hope 2014).

In addition to studies of the cultures within educational systems, there have been many studies exploring the cultures of other societal institutions. For example, in their research on institutional culture and regulatory relationships in the Tanzanian health care system, Tibandebage and Mackintosh (2002) defined "institutional culture" in their context as "the norms of behaviour within facilities and in particular of facility staff towards patients and would-be patients" (pp. 271). Tibandebage and Mackintosh also asked the question: "How does the nature of the transaction between patient and facility interact with the facilities' internal institutional culture?" (p. 280). That question highlights the multidirectional and transactional nature of intercultural interaction, as well as the hierarchical aspect of "Individual as Artifacts" in such institutions, depending on, in this case, whether the individual was a patient or a staff member. (For more on the language and culture of patient-doctor interactions see Sussex, this volume.)

Similar questions were asked by Alesina and Giuliano (2015), in their study of how cultural traits affect economic outcomes: "How do culture and institutions interact? Can any causal link between the two be established?" (p. 898). For Alesina and Giuliano: "Culture and institutions are endogenous variables determined, possibly, by geography, technology, epidemics, wars, and other historical shocks" (p. 898), which would include the Cultural Revolution in China in the 1960s and 1970s, referred to above. Drawing on a medical metaphor, in which "endogenous" is used to refer to a disease that is not caused by external, environmental factors, Alesina and Giuliano's position is that institutional cultures have internal origins, which, organically speaking, grow from within an organism. Alesina and Giuliano also discuss different types of institutions, such as political and legal institutions, regulations, and the welfare state, as well as different cultural traits, including trust, family ties, and individualism, which reiterates the idea of the "Individual as Artifact".

In their rejection of the notion of culture as "informal institutions" (2015, p. 902), Alesina and Giuliano draw on a number of definitions of "institution" from other researchers, including North (1990), according to whom, institutions are

> [...] the humanly devised constraints that structure human interactions. They are made up of formal constraints (rules, laws, constitutions), informal constraints (norms of behavior, convention, and self-imposed codes of conduct), and their enforcement characteristics (cited in Alesina and Giuliano 2015, p. 901).

North's definition highlights a number of important cultural aspects of institutions, including their "artifactual" nature, as they are created by humans, and the role of these particular artifacts as necessary structural "boundaries", enforced in ways that are both explicitly written and implicitly understood.

For Acemoglu et al. (2006) the two main types of societal institutions are economic and political, and they define such institutions as "mechanisms through which social choices are determined and implemented" (cited in Alesina and Giuliano 2015, p. 902). That raises the important question of *who* determines and implements those societal choices, which are, in general, decided by a small group of individuals and then applied to everyone else in that society, who may or may not accept them, often with negative consequences for those who reject the choices imposed upon them.

The relationships between medieval trade (from the fifth to the fifteenth century) and modern economies were explained by Greif 2006a, b, p. 30), who defined an institution as "a system of social factors that conjointly generates a regularity of behavior". By "social factors", Greif was referring to "man-made, nonphysical factors that are exogenous to each person they influence," including "rules, beliefs, norms, and organizations" (Greif 2006a, p. 30). As we can see, this contrasts with Alesina and Giuliano's position that "Culture and institutions are endogenous variables" (p. 898), and the reference to "man-made" again recalling the notion of the "Individual as Artifact".

Alesina and Giuliano conclude their 50-page paper by returning to their original question: "What roles do culture and institutions play in determining the wealth of nations?" (p. 938). They reject the idea that either one is causally superior to the other, because: "Culture and institutions interact and evolve in a complementary way, with mutual feedback effects" (p. 938), which is similar to the bi-directional, human-artifact interaction discussed above.

After our brief consideration of the concepts Individuals as Cultural Artifacts, and Institutional Cultures, we can continue on our journey, into the virtual world of Internet Culture.

4 Internet Culture as "International Culture"

As noted in the introduction to this chapter, at least two opposing positions are pos-sible here. One is that the Internet has No Culture or No Cultures. The other is that the Internet is All Cultures. Deciding on which position to take would include, for example, the fact that, for the latter position to hold true, all the countries of the world would need to have access to the Internet. In a 2014 BBC news story titled "The last places on Earth without the internet", Rachel Nuwer (2014) asked: "Is there anywhere left on Earth where it's impossible to access the internet?" She con-cluded that: "There are a few places, but you have to go out of your way to find them", with North Korea possibly being one such place. However, that is at the level of countries, not individuals, and Nuwer pointed out that, in 2014, it was "a well-established problem that many of the world's poorest people do not have the means or technology to log on", with less than one third (31%) of people in the "develop-ing world" using the Internet, compared to more than three-quarters (77%) in the "developed countries".

Whether the World Wide Web is now truly worldwide, in terms of every country having access, is open to question, but it is possible that we may be nearly there. Therefore, in considering the two opposing positions put forward above, it does seem as though we are now much closer to the "Internet is All Cultures" position, than the "Internet has No Culture" position. This is not to suggest that the Internet contains all artifacts from all cultures, but the claim can be made that Internet Culture is now at least one of the major and most influential forms of "International Culture" in the world today.

One of the first books about Internet Culture was the collection edited by Robert Shields, titled *Cultures of the Internet: Virtual spaces, real histories, living bodies*, published in 1996, not long after the World Wide Web had been established, in the early 1990s. The Web grew out of the original version of the Internet, called ARPANET, which came online at the end of the 1960s, as a result of work in the scientific and military fields. That work culminated in the release of the Microsoft Corporation's *Windows 98*, in June of 1998, thereby completing the shift to a commercially-based Internet. As a result, in 1996, Shields stated that: "The Internet is here" but asked: "But have we caught up with all the implications for culture and everyday life?" More than 20 years later, we may still be asking ourselves that same question, and still look-ing for answers, partly because the Internet is constantly growing, and therefore con-stantly changing, which makes "catching up" difficult, if not impossible.

At that time, Shields envisaged the online world as, "a playground for virtual bodies in which identities are flexible, swappable and disconnected from real-world bodies" and "the rise of virtual conviviality" which would supplement "the physical encounters between actors in public spaces" (back cover). This idea of a "virtual conviviality" did catch on in some fields, such as Information and Communications Technologies (ICT). For example, Fainholc (2011) predicted: "a new meaning of the concept of social inclusion for a new conviviality within global social systems traversed by ICT" (p. 47). Fainholc also predicated that this "virtual conviviality" would overcome the "socio-educational exclusion mediated by technology" (p. 47).

However, one of the developments not anticipated by Shields, Fainholc, or others at that time was the Internet as a particularly effective tool for disseminating Hate on a scale not possible before. In *Human rights and the Internet*, Karen Mock, in a chapter titled "Hate on the Internet" (2000, pp. 141–152), pointed out that: "Hate mongers were among the first to realize the tremendous power of the Internet to spread their hateful messages and to recruit members to their hateful causes" (p. 141). That potential appeared to have been harnessed to an unprecedented extent in the U.S. Presidential Elections of 2016, which may constitute one of the most hateful in recent history. For example, in November 2016, the BBC News reported on a sharp increase in the number of "hate attacks" that had been recorded in the US since the election: "A US hate-attack monitoring group has documented 437 cases of intimidation and abuse towards minorities since the general election a week ago [...] It comes after the FBI reported a 67% rise in anti-Muslim bigotry last year". Whatever the reasons for these troubling and marked increases in race-based and religion-based hate attacks, the Internet and online social media platforms, such as Facebook and Twitter, appear to have played a major role.

Following Shields (1996), David Porter, in *Internet culture* (1997), described the Internet as "a cultural phenomenon" (p. xiii), which is "the product of the peculiar condition of virtual acquaintance that prevails online" (p. xi). Some of the challenges of Internet culture and online communication identified by Porter revolved around language, and the communicative contradiction of more people being more connected than ever before, but with the potential for communications breakdowns being that much greater. As Porter put it: "There are words, but they often seemed stripped of context [...] It is no wonder that these digitalized words, flung about among strangers and strained beyond the limits of what written language in other contexts is called to do, are given to frequent misreading" (p. xi). Porter's observations underscore the fact that increased connectivity has been accompanied by greater possibilities for miscommunication. It is here that the Internet – sometimes as a result of the tendency to truncate messages (for example, when using Twitter or other forms of text messaging), and sometimes because of a lack of contextual cues – may be most likely to lead to communication breakdowns in ways that could be hard to imagine in face-to-face, in-person interactions. Porter concluded his Introduction by noting that the Internet had, at that time, "grown in recent years from a fringe cultural phenomenon to a significant site of cultural transformation and production in its own right" (1997, p. xvii). That same year (1997), Sara Kiesler's edited collection, *Culture of the Internet* was also published. Kiesler observed that: "If the Internet is a new domain of human activity, it is also a new domain for those who study humans" (p. x).

Within a few years, by the end of the 1990s, the idea of "cyberspace" had been established, which Jordan (1999), in his introduction to the politics of cyberspace, defined as: "virtual lands, with virtual lives and virtual societies, because these lives and societies do not exist with the same physical reality that 'real' societies do" (p. 1). Such a description is consistent with Walker's (2011) ideas about "navigating institutional culture" (pp. 113). Jordan also stated that: "Virtual societies are marked by political, technological and cultural patterns so intimately connected as to be nearly indistinguishable" (p. 2), and in another tripartite set of connections, Jordan wrote that: "Cyberpower can be broken down into three distinct levels: the individual, the social and the imaginary", which may be somewhat analogous to the relationships between Individual, Institutional and International Cultures.

In discussing the affective dimensions of Internet Culture, King (2001) claimed that: "Internet researchers have long argued that a unique culture underlies online social interaction, a culture similar to but separate from the everyday culture of the offline world" (p. 428). Within such claims we can see a more dichotomous view of the online world versus the off-line world, in which one was either in one or the other, but not both at the same time. While that might have been true in the early 2000's, it is more likely today that many people inhabit both spaces simultaneously. However, the findings of King's study did indicate that Internet users shared "a large set of common affective sentiments toward Internet-related concepts" and that those shared sentiments could be thought of as "cultural sentiments" (p. 428).

Having considered some of the early work on Internet Culture from the mid-1990s to the early 2000's, we can now explore some of the recent work carried out in this area. In terms of changes to the ways in which we communicate and how those can change the way we identify ourselves and others, Tim Jordan (2013) explained that: "With the internet came not just email, electronic discussion boards, social networking, the world wide web and online gambling but across these, and other similar socio-technical artifacts, also came different identities, bodies and types of messages that changes the nature of communication and culture" (p. 1). These changes have had far-reaching effects not only on notions of identity and community, but also on mental health. For example, from the field of Transcultural Psychiatry, Kirmayer et al. (2013) reported that: "The Internet and World Wide Web have woven together humanity in new ways, creating global communities, new forms of identity and pathology, and new modes of intervention" (p. 165). The Kirmayer et al. (2013) paper was part of a special issue of the journal *Transcultural Psychiatry*, based on research presented at a conference on "Cultures of the Internet", which took place in Montreal, Canada, in 2011.

In relation to individual, "artifactual" identities, and the communities that are formed when groups of individuals with shared interests, wants and needs come together, the conference on "Cultures of the Internet" focused on four broad areas, including: "how the Internet is transforming human functioning, personhood and identity" and "how electronic networking gives rise to new groups and forms of community, with shifting notions of public and private, local and distant" (Kirmayer et al. 2013, p. 165). These two spatial pairings, i.e., the public-private and the local-distant, should be seen as continua, rather than as dichotomies.

The other two main areas that the conference on "Cultures of the Internet" focused on were: "the emergence of new pathologies of the Internet, e.g., Internet addiction, group suicide, cyberbullying, and disruptions of neurodevelopment" and "the use of the Internet in mental health care ... as well as for the delivery of health information, web-based consultation, treatment intervention, and mental health promotion" (p. 165). The kind of addiction referred to by Kirmayer et al. (2013) raises the question of what other cultures, if any, have generated their own pathologies. One possible example could be religious cultural crusades, such as the Inquisition, as discussed by Mary Perry and Anne Cruz in their book *Cultural encounters: The impact of the Inquisition in Spain and the New World* (1991).

Since addiction to the Internet was recognized as "a new clinical phenomena" (Young 2004, pp. 402–415) in the mid-2000s, a growing body of work has researched and reported on this emerging health problem. For example, in 2006, in the *International Journal of Mental Health and Addiction*, Widyanto and Griffiths presented a critical review of studies of Internet addiction, and found that "a relatively small percentage of the online population" (p. 31) could be described as being "addicted". However, the number of cases of Internet Addiction has continued to grow, as reported by, for example, Weinstein and Lejoyeux (2010), in *The American Journal of Drug and Alcohol Abuse*, who defined "Internet addiction" as "excessive use of the Internet with resulting adverse consequences" (p. 281). Those consequences include: "arguments, lying, poor achievement, social isolation, and fatigue" (p. 282). Such "social isolation" stands in stark contrast to the earlier (Shields 1996) and more recent (Fainholc 2011) ideas about a new "virtual conviviality", free of the constraints of time, place and space.

One of the most recent works on Internet Culture is titled, rather ominously, *The social media abyss*, with a subtitle of, *Critical Internet cultures and the force of negation* (2016), by Geert Lovink, according to whom we are witnessing: "the drying up of a horizon, from the unbounded space of what was the internet into a handful of social media apps" (p. x). Lovink goes on to claim that: "In this global slump, IT giants such as Google and FaceBook have lost their innocence" (p. x). That comment suggests, some would say rather naively, that those two corporations were ever "innocent", especially given their net worth, in the hundreds of billions of US dollars, at the end of 2017. All culture comes at a cost, and that includes Internet Culture.

In the development of the idea of artifacts as "things made by people" – as well as the people themselves – "The Internet of Things" is emerging as "the rise of a promising new research field" (Bunz 2016, p. 1280), and "the next big thing" (p. 1279) in Media Studies. This new field is the result of books such as *The Internet of Things* (Greengard 2015), *The epic struggle of the Internet of Things* (Sterling 2014) and *Abusing the Internet of Things* (Dhanjani 2015), as well as *How the Internet of Things may set us free or lock us up* (Howard 2015). According to Bunz, the term "Internet of Things": "denotes objects that have become seamlessly integrated into a digital network" (2016, p. 1279). Bunz gives examples of consumer devices and home applications such as lighting systems, loud speakers, and heating systems, "which all have been connected to smartphones and can be manipulated from outside the home" (ibid.).

This third "I" (which may have something to do with "The Third Eye" in Hinduism) is longer than the other two lines of the 3-I triangle, partly because the Internet has grown, in a relatively short time, to be such a pervasive – some would say "invasive" – part of the lives of so many people on the planet, and that is likely to continue to grow.

5 Conclusion

We can now re-visit the three focus questions, at the beginning of this chapter, in light of the discussion of the Three Is:

> What are the challenges facing governments and educational institutions, individual educators and students, in adapting to an increasingly internationalized environment?
> What are the challenges of intercultural communication vis-à-vis these (in)visible constructed boundaries that intersect society, in today's globalized world?
> What challenges to intercultural communication are posed by the kinds of ideological considerations discussed above?

Returning to the idea of the "Individual as Cultural Artefact", we can see that there is a two-way relationship between individuals and their cultures, and it seems clear that individuals are changing the cultures of Asia, and in a more globalizing and Western sense. But it is also clear that these cultural values are, in general, changing individuals, in particular making them more culturally pluralistic than they used to be. Several of the chapters in this volume pick up the sense of identity, for example Wu and Li. But in a wider sense that kind of shift, and the collaboration and/or tension between Individual and Culture, with each being artefacts of the other, runs throughout the chapters in this book.

Regarding Institutional Cultures, the chapter by Snow in this volume is illustrative here, as are the observations by House, and especially Gao, who presents a compelling narrative about the tensions between Chinese education and the imperative of English competence, both linguistically and culturally. It is also possible that geographical spaces can be seen as a special kind of "institution", in a more metaphorical sense, which is the focus of Radwańska-Williams' chapter, and which is an important part of Oshima's chapter, showing how her work with *rakugo* is changing the institution of theatre, performance and humour.

Last but by no means least is the impact of the Internet and its culture in and beyond Asia. For example, in 2015, Cosseboom reported on "How the 'Internet of Things' is poised to boom cross Asia", which shows that the Internet is not only an artefact in its own right in Asia – see, for example, the Japanese influence through the invention and explosion of the emoji – but also an artefact-producing catalytic medium. Between All-Culture and No-Culture, the Internet is also a medium that juxtaposes cultures and prompts its inhabitants to share and exchange thoughts, ideas, feelings, etc. (see the chapters by Wu and Li, and by Lian and Sussex in this volume), making it both active and passive, an agent and a product, a medium and a message.

References

Acemoglu, D., Johnson, S., & Robinson, J. A. (2006). Institutions as a fundamental cause of long-run growth. In P. Aghion & S. N. Durlauf (Eds.), *Handbook of economic growth: Volume 1A* (pp. 385–472). Amsterdam: Elsevier.

Alesina, A., & Giuliano, P. (2015). Culture and institutions. *Journal of Economic Literature, 53*(4), 898–944.

BBC News. (2016, November 15). *Hundreds of hate attacks recorded in US since election*. http://www.bbc.com/news/world-us-canada-37992579.
BBC Webwise Guides: About MP3s. (2012, October 10). http://www.bbc.co.uk/webwise/guides/about-mp3s.
Bennich-Björkman, L. (2007). *Political culture under institutional pressure: How institutional change transforms early socialization*. London: Palgrave Macmillan.
Bornstein, R. (2003). *Legitimacy in the academic presidency*. Westport: Praeger Publishers.
Bunz, M. (2016). The internet of things: Tracing a new field of enquiry. *Media, Culture & Society, 38*(8), 1278–1282.
Cambridge advanced learner's dictionary. (2017). http://dictionary.cambridge.org/dictionary/english/
Campbell, R. S. (2014). Religious cultural artifacts. *Teaching Theology & Religion, 17*(4), 343–343.
Clark, A. (1997). *Being there: Putting brain, body, and world together again*. Cambridge, MA: MIT Press.
Cosseboom, L. (2015). How the 'Internet of Things' is poised to boom cross Asia. *Tech In Asia*. https://www.techinasia.com/internet-of-thingstrends-asia
Curşeu, P. L., & Pop-Curşeu, I. (2011). Alive after death: An exploratory cultural artifact analysis of the Merry Cemetery of Săpânţa. *Journal of Community & Applied Social Psychology, 21*(5), 371–387.
Dhanjani, N. (2015). *Abusing the internet of things: Blackouts, freakouts, and stakeouts*. Sebastopol: O'Reilly Media.
Ezell, J. M., & O'Keeffe, K. O. (Eds.). (1994). *Cultural artifacts and the production of meaning: The page, the image, and the body*. Ann Arbor: University of Michigan Press.
Fainholc, B. (2011). The contribution of virtual education to social inclusion with the consolidation of a new conviviality. *E-Learning and Digital Media, 8*(1), 47–57.
Gold, T., Guthrie, D., & Wank, D. (2002). *Social connections in China: Institutions, culture, and the changing nature of guanxi*. Cambridge: Cambridge University Press.
Goldar, A., & Frost, R. (Eds.). (2004). *Institutional culture in early modern society*. Leiden: Brill Publishing.
Greengard, S. (2015). *The internet of things*. Cambridge, MA: MIT Press.
Greif, A. (2006a). *Institutions and the path to the modern economy: Lessons from medieval trade*. New York: Cambridge University Press.
Greif, A. (2006b). Family structure, institutions, and growth: The origins and implications of western corporations. *American Economic Review, 96*(2), 308–312.
Hao, C. (2014). Revisiting Einstein's brain in brain awareness week. *Bioscience Trends, 8*(5), 286–289.
Harper, D. (2016). *Etymology Online*. http://www.etymonline.com/bio.php.
Hinde, R. A. (1987). *Individuals, relationships and culture: Links between ethology and the social sciences*. Cambridge: Cambridge University Press.
Hope, K. (2014, October 8). *Doing business the Chinese way*. http://www.bbc.com/news/business-29524701.
Howard, P. N. (2015). *Pax Technica: How the internet of things may set us free or lock us up*. New Haven: Yale University Press.
Jordan, T. (1999). *Cyberpower: An introduction to the politics of cyberspace*. New York: Routledge.
Jordan, T. (2013). *Internet, society and culture: Communicative practices before and after the internet*. London: Bloomsbury Academic.
Katayama, E. G. (1999). *Aristotle on artifacts: A metaphysical puzzle*. Albany: State University of New York Press.
Keisler, S. (Ed.). (1997). *Culture of the internet*. New York: Psychology Press.
Kim, Y. Y. (2000). *Becoming intercultural: An integrative theory of communication and cross-cultural adaptation*. Thousand Oaks: SAGE Publishing.
King, A. (2001). Affective dimensions of internet culture. *Social Science Computer Review, 19*(4), 413–430.

Kirmayer, L., Raikhel, E., & Rahimi, S. (2013). Cultures of the internet: Identity, community and mental health. *Transcultural Psychiatry, 50*(2), 165–191.

Lovink, G. (2016). *Social media abyss: Critical internet cultures and the force of negation.* Cambridge: Polity Press.

Marsden, M. T., & Nachbar, J. G. (Eds.). (1982). *Movies as artifacts: Cultural criticism of popular film.* Lanham: Rowman & Littlefield.

Mithen, S., & Parsons, L. (2008). The brain as a cultural artifact. *Cambridge Archaeological Journal, 18*(3), 415–422.

Mock, K. (2000). Hate on the internet. In S. Hick, E. Halpin, & E. Hoskins (Eds.), *Human rights and the internet* (pp. 141–152). London: Macmillan Press.

Mok, K. H. (2007). Questing for internationalization of universities in Asia: Critical reflections. *Journal of Studies in International Education, 11*(3/4), 433–454.

Morin, S. A. (2010). A contested institutional culture. *New Directions for Higher Education, 151*, 93–103.

Newman, G. E., Bartels, D. M., & Smith, R. K. (2014). Are artworks more like people than artifacts? Individual concepts and their extensions. *Topics in Cognitive Science, 6*, 647–662.

North, D. C. (1990). *Institutions, institutional change and economic performance.* New York: Cambridge University Press.

Nuwer, R. 2014, February 14. *The last places on Earth without the internet.* http://www.bbc.com/future/story/20140214-the-last-places-without-internet.

Oberhardt, S. (2001). *Frames within frames: The art museum as cultural artifact.* Berne: Peter Lang.

Perry, M. E., & Cruz, A. J. (Eds.). (1991). *Cultural encounters: The impact of the inquisition in Spain and the New World.* Berkley: University of California Press.

Phuong-Mai, N., Terlouw, C., & Pilot, A. (2005). Cooperative learning vs Confucian heritage culture's collectivism: Confrontation to reveal some cultural conflicts and mismatch. *Asia Europe Journal, 3*(3), 403–419.

Porter, D. (Ed.). (1997). *Internet culture.* New York: Routledge.

Shields, R. M. (1996). *Cultures of the internet: Virtual spaces, real histories, living bodies.* Thousand Oaks: SAGE Publication.

Smiraglia, R. P. (2008). Rethinking what we catalog: Documents as cultural artifacts. *Cataloging & Classification Quarterly, 45*(3), 25–37.

Sterling, B. (2014). *The epic struggle of the internet of things.* Moscow: Strelka Press.

Sterne, J. (2006). The mp3 as cultural artifact. *New Media & Society, 8*(5), 825–842.

Tibandebage, P., & Mackintosh, M. (2002). Institutional culture and regulatory relationships in a liberalizing health care system: A Tanzanian case study. In J. Heyer, F. Stewart, & R. Thorp (Eds.), *Group behaviour and development: Is the market destroying cooperation?* (pp. 271–290). New York: Oxford University Press.

Tran, T. T. (2013). Is the learning approach of students from the Confucian heritage culture problematic? *Educational Research for Policy and Practice, 12*(1), 57–65.

Walker, S. (2011). Determining and navigating institutional culture. *The Bottom Line: Managing Library Finances, 24*(2), 113–117.

Wang, J. (2013). Confucian heritage cultural background (CHCB) as a descriptor for Chinese learners: The legitimacy. *Asian Social Science, 9*(10), 105–113.

Weinstein, A., & Lejoyeux, M. (2010). Internet addiction or excessive internet use. *The American Journal of Drug and Alcohol Abuse, 36*(5), 277–283.

Wheeler, M. (2004). Is language the ultimate artefact? *Language Sciences, 26*(6), 693–715.

Widyanto, L., & Griffiths, M. (2006). Internet addiction: A critical review. *International Journal of Mental Health and Addiction, 4*(1), 31–51.

Young, K. (2004). Internet addiction: A new clinical phenomenon and its consequences. *American Behavioral Scientist, 48*(4), 402–415.

Toward a Critical Epistemology for Learning Languages and Cultures in Twenty-First Century Asia

Andrew LIAN and Roland SUSSEX

Abstract The adoption of English as the working language of Asia and the ASEAN region, together with an increase in the mobility of people and information, are creating new and significant pressures on language and culture education in English, as well as other languages, in the region. It is also bringing about an enormously expanded use of English between speakers for whom English is not a first language, and this expansion includes communication in English between people of different cultural backgrounds. The surge in the use of English highlights a number of current challenges. English language proficiency levels vary widely across Asia. *Communicative competence* in English as a second language is at least equally problematic. The matter is further complicated by the growth of the Internet and other technological progress, which has resulted in the creation of a self-managing, often Do-it-Yourself society engaged in "just-in-time" rather than "just-in-case" activity, as in the past. These considerations call for new learning/teaching approaches which go beyond the conventional classroom and curriculum. The present chapter proposes a generic framework for implementing (language-)learning/teaching structures, with a special focus on challenging learners' "operational histories" – their habitual patterns of understanding stimuli from their experience of the world. The framework is explicitly learner-centred, individual, personalized and adaptive, and is designed to help learners develop mindsets and strategies to tackle learning issues on their own initiative and in their own way. An example is presented of a successful implementation of the framework for the learning of English pronunciation by Chinese university English Majors. This kind of approach, building specifically on challenging learners' "operational histories", has significant potential for developing language and culture teaching and learning, and the acquisition of intercultural communication competence, in Asian contexts.

A. LIAN (✉)
School of Foreign Languages, Suranaree University of Technology,
Nakhon Ratchasima, Thailand
e-mail: Andrew.Lian@andrewlian.com

R. SUSSEX
School of Languages and Cultures, and Institute for Teaching and Learning Innovation,
The University of Queensland, St Lucia, QLD, Australia
e-mail: sussex@uq.edu.au

© Springer International Publishing AG, part of Springer Nature 2018   37
A. CURTIS, R. SUSSEX (eds.), *Intercultural Communication in Asia:
Education, Language and Values*, Multilingual Education 24,
https://doi.org/10.1007/978-3-319-69995-0_3

1 Introduction

The development of Asia in the twenty-first century is marked by the rise of the region socially, economically and politically (Australia in the Asian Century Task Force 2011, p. 4). In particular, the establishment of the AEC (ASEAN Economic Community) will enhance not only the economy in general and help to reduce poverty, but it will also enable controlled yet growing mobility (Koty 2016), leading to overall growth in the region. These changes, so far unprecedented in this part of the world, represent a major step forward in cooperation between countries. They should enrich local labour forces through increased diversity, create opportunities for study across borders, and enable significant cooperation in many hitherto unexplored areas of joint action. However, mobility will also place considerable stress on institutions, facilities and society in general through a de facto reorientation of the composition and practices of groups. And this may well undermine traditional patterns of teaching and learning. We can also expect that diversification of the labour force and any concomitant changes may generate negative reactions in receiving societies and communities of practice. These, in turn, need to find ways of adjusting to new and, so far, unaccustomed challenges to local professional and personal life. And there will be pressure on how citizens of the region construct their identities, deal with diversity, and move together into the future.

Complicating this remodelling of life in the region is the adoption of English, both officially and unofficially, as the common **working** language of South-East Asia and Asia in general (mandatory for ASEAN citizens (Association of Southeast Asian Nations 2008, p. 29) and de facto for the others). The far-reaching policy decision to impose English for all, though designed to set in place a new form of "communicative" unity and to facilitate human contact between the diverse peoples of the region, runs the risk of further undermining linguistic and cultural integrity by introducing new tensions. From now on, instead of learning each other's languages and cultures, people will be importing, from the English-speaking world, new linguistic and, inevitably, new cultural elements that will modify the natural linguistic and cultural landscapes of the region. Even if English were to be used primarily in professional contexts for ostensibly straightforward and relatively unsubtle purposes (which is what experience tells us that people are currently trying to do), in the end experience also tells us that, unless learned to a reasonably high level of proficiency, English will often remain an inadequate, "quick-and-dirty", solution. This will hold even for professional and straightforward contexts where subtle linguistic and cultural interaction is often required for best results and may be of significant benefit. To be sure, using English as a "lingua franca" is much better than nothing. But this is not without a price: the illusion that we are understanding each other "well enough" when in fact this may not be so. This realization will come to users over time and will almost certainly have a potentially far-reaching effect on the ways that they engage in these "professional and straightforward contexts" that are not supposed to require a high level of English proficiency. Thus, the decision to adopt English for the region will have a considerable impact on language and culture learning and teaching, and on communication. High mobility, sometimes at short notice, and the need for speedy response to the pressures of living together in a complex, dynamic and highly diverse community, will challenge the language-learning capacities of traditional providers such as schools and universities, and the kinds of courses which they offer – even when enhanced by contemporary communicative approaches. Further, the conditions of language use, where language-learning needs emerge rapidly and revolve around often unpredicted and unpredictable requirements, may make traditional classroom-based learning systems outdated or, at very least, in need of radical change / improvement. These requirements will involve large numbers of people, all with special requirements and individual learning needs. This will form a mass market of learners with individual communication and personal learning needs requiring rapid solutions, of a size which has never been encountered before. It is no longer a question of catering to the learning elite of a country's population, but also to millions of everyday "average" workers and citizens. And this situation is not limited to English. The demands of mobility will, inevitably, also place greater stress on learning and teaching systems for local languages and cultures. This is partly because there will be a need to valorize non-English languages in an effort to preserve local languages and cultures, and partly because of the real needs of persons travelling to and living in a new country: even English language competence of itself will simply not be enough to meet everyday needs. In short, the internationalization motivated by a drive for English will create new and less controllable language/culture learning/teaching demands that must be met efficiently and effectively, for both short term and longer term needs, for a highly diverse market of people all going about their daily lives in twenty-first century Asia.

To complicate matters further, the levels of English proficiency in Asia vary widely, with Singapore ranked 6/72 in the world (Very High Proficiency Country) in 2016, and Laos ranked 70/72 (Very Low Proficiency Country), according to the EF Proficiency Index. The table below covers a number of Asian nations. The standings reported here are from the EF Proficiency Indexes for 2015 and 2016 (reporting respectively on tests performed in 2014 and 2015) (EF English Proficiency Index 2015 2015; EF English Proficiency Index 2016 2016).

English proficiency standings of selected Asian countries (EF Proficiency Index 2015 and 2016)

2016 Rank (/72)	2015 Rank (/70)	Country	Change in Rank	2016 Score	2015 Score	Change in Score	Proficiency Level
6	12	Singapore	−6	63.52	61.08	+2.44	Very high
12	14	Malaysia	−2	60.70	60.30	+0.40	High
13	N/A	Philippines	N/A	60.33	N/A	N/A	High
22	20	India	+2	57.3	58.21	−0.91	Moderate
27	27	South Korea	−	54.87	54.52	+0.35	Moderate
30	33	Hong Kong	−3	54.29	52.70	+1.59	Moderate
31	29	Viet Nam	+2	54.06	53.81	+0.25	Moderate
32	32	Indonesia	−	52.94	52.91	+0.03	Moderate
33	31	Taiwan	+2	52.82	53.18	−0.36	Moderate

(continued)

2016 Rank (/72)	2015 Rank (/70)	Country	Change in Rank	2016 Score	2015 Score	Change in Score	Proficiency Level
35	30	Japan	+5	51.69	53.57	−1.88	Low
37	N/A	Macau	N/A	51.36	N/A	N/A	Low
39	47	China	−8	50.94	49.41	+1.53	Low
48	N/A	Pakistan	N/A	48.78	N/A	N/A	Low
56	62	Thailand	−6	47.21	43.53	+3.68	Very low
58	N/A	Sri Lanka	N/A	46.58	N/A	N/A	Very low
69	69	Cambodia	–	39.48	39.15	+0.33	Very low
70	N/A	Laos	N/A	38.45	N/A	N/A	Very low

N/A Not available

The EF Index is a well-established test which has systematically collected and reported English proficiency information from around the world since 2011. In 2014 it tested more than 910,000 persons from 70 countries (EF English Proficiency Index 2015 2015, p. 5), and in 2015 it tested more than 950,000 persons from 72 countries (EF English Proficiency Index 2016 2016, p. 3).

The above table is informative in several ways. First, it points to the wide disparity in proficiency levels, especially in the ASEAN countries, which, because they form a close community with high mobility, will have to find ways of dealing with that disparity.

Second, while many countries improved their ranking or their scores, the improvements were usually quite small, e.g. often less than +1.00. There are exceptions, such as Thailand, which increased its score by +3.68, but its score was already very low. At the high end of the spectrum Singapore increased its score by +2.44 to become the first Asian country ever to be classified as Very High Proficiency (comparable to European countries like Finland and Luxembourg). In contrast, Japan and India slipped back. It remains to be seen why this happened and how it could be rectified. "Doing more of the same" in the current educational systems has not brought about the substantial improvements that are needed. Clearly new educational solutions will be necessary to effect some equalization between the different countries.

These critically important linguistic and cultural developments find themselves embedded in a world which is becoming increasingly self-managing, do-it-yourself (DIY) (A.-P. Lian 2011; A. B. Lian 2014), and subject to information overload, largely as a result of the extraordinary growth of technology (A.-P. Lian 2017). In turn, this leads to a general shift away from "just-in-case" learning toward "just-in-time" learning (A.-P. Lian and Pineda 2014; A. B. Lian 2014) in a move which is also de-stabilizing traditional learning and teaching structures in all disciplines, not just languages.

In order to respond to these changes, the needs of twenty-first century Asia specified above require new approaches to learning and teaching. Such an approach, based on theoretical considerations, has been undertaken in detail by A.-P. Lian in previous works (A.-P. Lian 2004, 2011, 2017; A.-P. Lian and Pineda 2014) and is summarized below. While it acknowledges and revolves around the new globalized and globalizing environment, it is based on a general theory of learning (A.-P. Lian 2000), in order to construct a high-level abstract framework capable of application to any learning/teaching context.

2   Conceptual Framework

The conceptual framework for such an extended approach to learning is built on five general Principles:

2.1   Principle 1

We are physiological beings, so that our minds are effectively trapped inside our bodies. Therefore interaction between our minds and the physical world, including the phenomenon that we call "communication", is always indirect, mediated by our perceptual systems: our nervous system and symbolic (i.e. semiotic) systems for making sense of the signals that the nervous system picks up. They also decide which signals are relevant and are selected for further processing. The mechanism for determining which signals should be processed and what meanings they are given is based on each person's past experience, their "operational history", which can be thought of as a meaning-making device or filter which both decides whether a signal is to be processed and, if yes, will help to give meaning to that signal.

But as we have seen, learners' "operational histories" are demonstrably inadequate to support effective learning of English, even based on the needs of contemporary society. And they are very much an outcome of the educational methodologies under which the students have studied. Given the changing social, economic and communicative needs of Asia, the question arises of the capacity of "operational histories" to cope.

The other four Principles are derived from the first Principle:

2.2   Principle 2

Everything that we do is based on acts of meaning-making. Without such meaning-making we would be literally incapable of acting.

2.3   Principle 3

We are not telepaths: the meanings that we create and live by are internal, individual and unknowable by others; all attempts at communication (or what is commonly called "sharing meanings") are themselves mediated by semiotic or symbolic systems that are constructed on the basis of each person's internal logical and representational systems. In this task language is central. We can *talk* about the meanings that reside within us, but the meanings themselves are never visible to the outside world.

2.4   Principle 4

Our internal logical and representational systems are constructed through our interactions with our environment, by our attempts to understand the world in multiple ways through a kind of triangulation process which helps us to verify the validity of our understandings and enables us to have some consistency in making sense of the world around us. In turn, this process enables us to act consistently and with the other people around us in a way which leads to the belief/illusion that we "share" understandings. In fact, we share nothing (in the sense that we might, for instance, share a physical object) but we act as though we do, since our understandings appear to resemble each other at an operational level: in society, we act and react together in similar and consistent ways (a kind of "near enough is good enough" way of working together).

2.5   Principle 5

Our internal logical and representational systems, i.e. the systems that enable us to organize knowledge and the world for ourselves, and to represent knowledge and the world to our-selves, both assist us to make sense of the world and pre-determine how we understand. Any act of learning necessarily implies altering those representations and logical relationships.

There is also growing evidence from psychological studies that signals are not simply accepted "as is". This evidence comes from different sources, e.g. our misperception of sounds, but also in the basic organization of language processing where, in order to understand at all, the stream of spoken language needs to be processed (i.e. understood and organized into higher level units such as "chunks"), as the unprocessed stream would quickly overload our brain's capacity to cope with the sheer volume of incoming signals (Cornish et al. 2017, p. 2). For this to happen, an act of understanding needs to occur. And this, in turn, leads to a gate-keeping function where understood signals are retained and others are rejected (Giedd 2015) in a kind of "use it or lose it" principle. In turn this creates a problem: for new meanings to be accepted, old meanings need to be challenged and refined, possibly replaced, and new neural connections created to replace or modify those that are entrenched. We need to adopt physicist Max Planck's view that "When you change the way you look at things, the things you look at change" (Planck n.d.), and find ways to challenge our operational histories.

So how we understand the world is fundamentally personal. Our understandings are driven by our operational histories, which make each of us different from one another. It is also the distinctive nature of each person's operational history that shows that a one-size-fits-all approach to learning is likely to be counter-productive. This is consistent with the concept of learner-centredness advocated by current language-learning/teaching approaches (as described e.g. in Kumaravadivelu 2012, p. 114), but does not necessarily endorse the detailed application of these approaches.

This, in turn, leads to an argument in favour of autonomy in language-learning defined as the ability to take charge of one's own learning (e.g. Benson 2007; Holec 1981): the myriad needs of learners are unlikely to be fully met by a traditional language-teaching scenario of fixed syllabus, fixed texts and fixed exercises, especially in the current rapidly developing world with its "just-in-time", do-it-yourself (DIY), mass-market language and culture requirements of twenty-first century Asia.

So, learning involves at least a two-step approach. The first is to make the external signals perceptible, i.e. to make them sufficiently meaningful, which entails presenting them as sufficiently different from those that we normally deal with to be noticed, essentially by bypassing existing operational histories. The second is to refine the understandings of these newly-perceived signals so as to enable the construction of new patterns of meaning. Note that the signals referred to here are not necessarily physical, e.g. a sound or a colour, but might include an idea or a way of thinking. Signal-manipulation can take many forms, ranging from discursive approaches like telling the listener to notice something, to actual physical transformation of the signal like digital filtering. This process is a form of awareness-raising (Lian 1987; Mason 1998; Schmidt 2012) and, in this chapter's perspective, it is a central component of the act of learning and, therefore, teaching. Mechanisms for raising awareness include using novel ways of channelling input to defeat the processing habits of our brain. The framework just described is abstract and multidimensional, i.e. it draws simultaneously on a number of different concepts and therefore approaches/techniques. It provides a set of guidelines for thinking about the problems of learning and teaching.

In this light, the framework can be thought of as providing a blueprint for developing (language-) learning/teaching systems which, in turn, will be used as testbeds for the principles contained therein. Furthermore, given the multimodal nature of the framework, the testbeds will also necessarily be multimodal. In summary, the blueprint can be summarized as follows:

Respect the learners' meaning-making mechanisms.
Find ways of making the learners aware of the characteristics of the new signals.
Find ways of refining newly-perceived signals so as to make them usable.

A critically important consequence of this model is the realization of the significance of the meaning-making mechanisms of individuals, the importance of giving these mechanisms the respect that they deserve, and to give them a chance to do their job with few restrictions from the outset and, to the extent possible, avoid imposing other people's ways of understanding. However, the learning of language necessarily requires the learning of the constraints of the linguistic system which need to be understood by the learner. Comprehension and production cannot be random or at the mercy of the learners' meaning-making mechanisms in their current state – that is why the learners' meaning-making mechanisms need to be changed.

3   Learning Framework: Implementation and Testing

The learning framework is based on helping the individual with awareness raising in response to incoming stimuli, to become aware of and to confront their operational histories, to challenge them critically, and to build new representations. It helps them to unpack complex learning tasks, to attend critically to the component parts, and then to reintegrate them.

Since 2013, two doctoral research projects based on the above principles at Suranaree University of Technology in Thailand have confirmed the framework outlined above. Four others are still ongoing but with preliminary indications of similar outcomes. Replication and extended studies will need to be conducted to investigate the framework further.

All projects share the same characteristics:

1. Recognition of and respect for learners' individual meaning-making mechanisms.
2. Awareness-raising activities acting in synchrony with one another.
3. Support for individualization in learning to the extent possible. Students are encouraged to develop their Personal Learning Environments (PLEs)(A.-P. Lian and Pineda 2014; Pineda 2013), with "opportunities to confront, contrast and contest their understandings against observed language phenomena through the feedback provided" (A.-P. Lian 2004, p. 7).

While the framework's conceptual elements are shared, each project implements the framework differently.

The implementation of the framework presented below focuses on the pronunciation of English. It presents ways of challenging learners' operational histories in a context which is individualized, learner-driven and personalized, available on demand and suitable for individual exploration. It is therefore also potentially adaptive, in that the framework could equally be applied to learning other domains of language, as well as culture, communication and intercultural communication. The project described here can therefore be seen as a testbed and a proof of concept, and a prototype of one kind of approach directly aimed at the issues of English language and communication described in the Introduction.

What follows is a summary of one of the completed projects (for details see He and Sangarun 2015; He et al. 2015) conducted in 2013 by Associate Professor He Bi[1]. The methodology was quasi-experimental, comparing the performances of a control group and an experimental group of EFL majors enrolled in two intact classes drawn from a compulsory pronunciation improvement course routinely taught in Xingyi Normal University for Nationalities, PRC. The control group followed the normal program: a typical, commonly-adopted, approach to pronunciation (phoneme-description and production, intonation-description and production,

---

[1] I am grateful to Associate Professor Dr. He Bi for giving me permission to describe and quote the results of her study.

articulatory exercises, minimal pairs and repetition exercises). The experimental group followed a program consistent with the framework outlined above, which combined perception-enhancement synchronized with gesture/body movements, a self-directed autonomous learning system, and minor computer-based assistance. As opposed to the traditional program, the project involved no theoretical descriptions of phonemes or intonation, nor any study of individual phonemes, including minimal pairs. The focus was entirely on the perception and production of the prosodic components (intonation, stress, rhythm, loudness) of English. The program lasted for a total of 14 weeks.

Using a pre-test and post-test and collecting qualitative data too, the experiment compared the pronunciation performances of participants on a number of measures: phoneme-production, word-reading, sentence-reading and free conversation. These were assessed according to a strict set of criteria by a group of expert Chinese university professors not associated with the research project. Additionally, sentence-reading and face-to-face conversation were also assessed by a group of native speakers for pronunciation, comprehensibility and fluency according to a set of rubrics drawn up for that purpose. All testing done by the native speaker raters was blind (i.e. raters did not know who the students were nor if they were listening to a pre-test or a post-test). Importantly, in the pre-test, the control group was significantly ahead of the experimental group in all but one of the measures (free conversation, where there was no significant difference between them). Finally, the teacher for both groups, who was not the researcher, was strongly committed to the traditional approach and did not believe in the experimental system: if there were any teacher bias it would therefore have been in favour of the control group. Both groups underwent substantially identical training in their non-phonetic study of English, and time-on-task for the course was closely monitored to ensure that both groups spent the same amount of time on the study of pronunciation every week.

4   Awareness-Raising Components

4.1   Enhanced Auditory Input – Verbotonalism

Students received awareness-raising input (see below) from a variety of sources, the most important of which were developed on the basis of verbotonalism, a perception-based theory which seeks to rehabilitate the deaf and improve the pronunciation of foreign language learners by helping them to reorganize their perceptual mechanisms (Asp et al. 2012b; Guberina 1972; A.-P. Lian 1980). It considers hearing essentially as an act of meaning-making, and emphasizes the fundamental value of stress, rhythm and intonation in learning pronunciation. The approach uses low-pass filtering, a technique where an audio recording is put through an audio filter which only lets through sounds below a specific "cut-off" frequency, in our case 320 Hz. This preserves the fundamental frequency of the sentences, together with the stress, rhythm, loudness and intonation (the prosody) of the sentences, while removing the higher frequencies which help to define words. The result is a stream of sound like a hummed sentence, where the prosody became salient and available in a way which was both unusual and stimulating.

The procedure raises awareness in two significant ways, essentially by bypassing the operational histories: (a) it is novel and unfamiliar; and (b) it lightens the processing load because the learner does not have to process words and their meanings, which frees up attentional resources for increased processing of the prosodic patterns. The procedure consisted of specific activities.

4.2   Humming and Various Forms of Repetition

Intensive listening to filtered sentences was followed by various forms of repetition linked with body movements (see below). These forms of repetition are sequenced in such a way that they gradually change the perception of the sentences and move from listening toward full articulation of the sentences. They were also designed to reduce the perceptual and articulatory loads in the early stages of the sequencing while moving toward full articulation. The following sequence was used:

- *Humming*: after listening intensively and silently to each filtered sentence, i.e. after becoming accustomed to the intonation of the model sentence, students were asked to hum the intonations. This effectively isolates the articulation of intonation patterns, providing greater focus on them, while relieving students of the load of articulating words and intonations together. At various moments students were asked to state what they believed to be the function of the intonation; e.g. was it a statement, a question, an exclamation or something else.
- *Silent repetition (mouthing of the sentences)*: Following intensive practice of intonation, the students were asked to mouth each sentence, i.e. to repeat each sentence silently, while synchronising with their whole-body movements. This phase acts basically as a prelude to full articulation but without the load of actually producing both intonation and words.
- *Repetition*: Students were asked to repeat the model sentences in the normal way, synchronizing words and intonation with one another. They were helped to achieve this by using the whole-body movements of their choice.

4.3   Whole-Body Exercises and Relaxation – Synchrony

Accompanying the above clearly linguistic aspects of the process, a second major form of awareness-raising was provided by whole-body movement exercises. These are a feature of verbotonal intervention (Asp et al. 2012b), but are also particularly relevant in the context of studies in self-synchrony (Asp et al. 2012a; Condon and Ogston 1971; Condon and Sander 1974). Self-synchrony is a phenomenon whereby the body movements of a person synchronize with or accompany the language that they are producing, e.g. rhythm and stress patterns: "a precise isomorphism (including rhythm features) has been observed across many levels between the speaker's speech and various forms of his own body motion" (Condon and Sander 1974, p. 457). People's body movements are closely coordinated with the production of language. If body movement and language articulation are not antagonistic to one another, then pronunciation will be more satisfactory (Asp et al. 2012a).

In order to enable the new self-synchrony between body and pronunciation, students were encouraged to engage in mind-calming and relaxation exercises in order to break, or at least reduce, the influence of their learnt language-specific Chinese gesture system. They were then invited to listen intensively and to hum, clap, move or dance to the melody and rhythm of the filtered and unfiltered intonation patterns. Students were encouraged to improvise their own patterns so as to generate and display spontaneous *personal understandings* of the studied patterns rather than seeking to conform to an imposed, normative model, while developing an internal representation of the intonation and rhythm patterns of English which need to be internalized for later reuse. This corresponds to the notion that people make sense of things in personally relevant ways. Students were also encouraged to volunteer their interpretations of melodic and rhythmic patterns so as to contrast, confront and contest (Lian 2000 p. 53) their personal understandings with those of others (essentially an exercise in meaning-construction and refinement of meanings). These activities are important awareness-raisers. They connect optimized and non-optimized language signals with articulation and with body movements in order to create new, previously-absent, self-synchrony in learners.

4.4 Manipulation of Spoken Language

Another way of raising awareness is to enable learners to manipulate their own or others' speech for themselves, examine the outcomes, and compare them with other examples. They are thus able to construct more perspicuous internal representations of the language that they are studying. Students worked with their own speech and with every-day, non-classroom, language. Students were provided with a simple free computer-based audio editor, *Audacity* (Ash et al. 2015). They could investigate any spoken text of interest, including their own voice, which they could filter, accelerate or slow down (enabling them to identify features not always discernible in natural language). They could effectively create their own lessons according to their own preferences.

4.5 In-Class Activities

In-class activities involved intensive awareness-raising exercises using both auditory input and whole-body movement: relaxation exercises; sensitization consisting of intensive listening to filtered and unfiltered sentences; followed by structured repetition practice (listening intensively to filtered sentences a minimum of 15 times, humming the sentences, mouthing the sentences and finally repeating the sentences).

4.6 Out-of-Class Activities

Out-of-class activities consisted in listening intensively to any of the materials provided during the course of a class, listening to additional materials of interest discovered by the students themselves, engaging in whole-body exercises individually or in groups, and manipulating audio materials, including making recordings of their own voices. They also had access to a simple, unsophisticated, Computer-Assisted Language Learning system to support practising pronunciation which gave students the ability to listen to any of the filtered and unfiltered recordings used in class, the ability to record their voices, and to compare their voices with the filtered and unfiltered native-speaker models. In addition, they also had the opportunity to choose what, where, when and how they would study and with whom.

4.7 Autonomy

Even though the experiment was conducted in the context of a normal class, students were able to exercise a significant amount of partial autonomy and self-direction. They could decide which activities to engage in after the initial sensitisation period. Out of class, students could choose when, where, how and with whom to engage in learning activities. For instance, they chose to hum, repeat and "dance" their language study "by the fish pond, in the sports ground, and in the garden. One participant even practiced her pronunciation in the gym between work-outs" (He and Sangarun 2015, p. 7). Finally, they did not ignore the teacher, but made better use of her when she was needed (He and Sangarun 2015).

5 Summary Results of the Research Study

The following table summarises the overall results of pre-test and post-test scores (i.e. the sum of the scores for phoneme-production, word-reading, sentence-reading and oral interview).

Group	Test	Mean	Number	Std. Deviation
Experimental group	Pretest	70.89	48	8.38
	Posttest	84.93	48	6.48
Control group	Pretest	75.20	47	8.38
	Posttest	80.94	47	9.45

Statistical analysis showed that while both groups progressed significantly from pre-test to post-test ($p < 0.01$ for both), the experimental group improved significantly more than the control group ($p < 0.01$). In the pre-test, the control group was significantly ahead of the experimental group (exp. = 70.89; ctrl = 75.20), but in the post-test, the experimental group overtook the control group (exp. = 84.93; ctrl = 80.94). In order to reduce within-group error variance and to eliminate confounds caused by any unmeasured variables, an Analysis of Covariance (ANCOVA) was conducted to remove the bias of the variables (after first checking with Levene's test of equality of error variances (Levene 1960)). The same result was true for the analysis of all measures used (whether rated by Chinese raters or by native speakers), with the exception of the pre-test oral interview, where there was no significant difference between control and experimental groups. However, post-test results for the oral interview resembled other results, with the experimental group outperforming the control group significantly ($p < 0.01$).

Thus, the experimental approach for teaching English pronunciation was demonstrated to be more effective than the conventional approach commonly used throughout China and in many other parts of the world.

Interesting points to be noted are:

1. **Phoneme production.** Each student was tested for the production of the 44 phonemes of English. Phonemic scores of the experimental group were significantly higher than those of the control group. This is despite the fact that the control group had a head start and had also received extensive focused instruction and practice on phoneme-production, while the experimental group received no instruction or practice on the pronunciation of phonemes. This means that specific training in individual phoneme production may not be needed, or may be greatly reduced, following the prosodic training described here. While verbotonalism claims that the study of prosody will also adjust pronunciation of individual phonemes (if not all, at least many), this is the first published data-driven study to confirm this phenomenon in the Chinese EFL context. A search of the bibliographic literature shows that it also seems to be the only data-driven study of this question currently available.

2. **Comprehensibility and fluency.** The findings indicate that the experimental group performed significantly better than the control group in both rehearsed settings and, especially, natural unrehearsed settings. The results for comprehensibility and fluency ratings (not reported here in detail) indicate that the experimental group performed significantly better than the control group. The experimental group encoded thought into correct forms rapidly, and therefore was fast in retrieving linguistic items and injecting them into the speech flow, and they did so with greater syntactic accuracy and lexical richness than the control group, resulting in enhanced comprehensibility, fluency and communicative effectiveness. Exactly how a learning activity designed to improve pronunciation could have brought about enhancements in domains outside pronunciation remains to be investigated.

3. The fact that the teacher in charge of the experimental group did not believe in the experimental approach used is relevant. With the experimental group, the nature of the resources and the role occupied by the teacher (which is not that of teaching content but, rather, managing the activities of students engaged primarily in processing signals and self-expression), the implementation of the framework is, at least to some extent, protected from teacher influence. In a sense, it is teacher-neutral. This is worth noting, since there are many teachers in China (primarily in schools, especially rural schools) who are less than optimally qualified and who would not need to develop any special expertise in order for their students to benefit from the framework described above. In that sense, the program can help improve the quality of course offerings without adding significantly to costs. It provides a cheap high-quality solution at no human cost and very little financial cost, while ensuring significant enrichment for the teaching of a critically important part of the English language curriculum in Chinese universities and schools.

Some of the principles or techniques used in this study resemble the "humanistic" approaches like Community Language Learning (Curran 1972, 1976) and The Silent Way (Gattegno 1963), but they are largely based on the principles of the earlier model of verbotonalism (Guberina 1955, 1956). The relaxation techniques adopted here derive from an adaptation of suggestopedic techniques (e.g. Bancroft 1975) supported by research findings from verbotonalism on the relationship between speech and movement (Asp et al. 2012a) as well as on research findings from studies in self-synchrony (see above). The emphasis on learner-centredness and autonomy follows from the internal logic of the five Principles and the framework outlined above. The work described here is therefore largely independent of traditional language teaching approaches. And while verbotonalism provided the trigger for the Structuro-Global Audio-Visual (SGAV) approach to language learning, the latter bears little resemblance to the techniques developed here.

6   The Framework in Asian Contexts

The framework described here is personalised and adaptive: it deals with both formal and non-formal learners with unpredicted and unpredictable needs in unpredicted and unpredictable contexts on unpredicted and unpredictable subjects/topics. It consequently presents as either an alternative or as an extension to fixed, detailed, curricular content or syllabi, or both. It uses a rich, adaptive, student-driven problem-solving pedagogic approach with no pre-determined sequencing. We have shown that this framework is more effective than conventional methods, in a single controlled experiment, for the learning of English pronunciation.

Educational authorities may have difficulty in accepting this approach, because it is open-ended and unstructured. This is at variance with many institutional models' educational policy, which tend to prescribe matters relating to education, ranging from grouping students (usually according to age), to course descriptions to curriculum to syllabus to pedagogy, even down to which books and other resources are permitted (e.g. in the above course, the officially approved textbook was Wang 2005, *English pronunciation & intonation for communication*). Thus, there may be a tension between the above framework, which seeks to mirror and enable the optimal learning processes of individuals who, ideally, study what they need, when they need it, in their own way and according to their own rhythm; and the highly structured, time-controlled curricula and pedagogies of many governing and top-down educational bodies. Therefore, as in the case of other innovative systems, the success of the approach presented here will depend, in part, on the ability of controlling bodies to embrace, accommodate and implement significant change in policy and practices. Until that happens one may be able to implement the framework only as a form of optional enrichment, at least in the short term. Even given the learners' cultural habits relating to education, which are strongly teacher-based in Asia and where students are acculturated to a strong teacher focus, Internet penetration is already high, growing, and changing the way people live and think (Japan 91.1% (0.1% growth p.a.), China 52.2% (+2.2% p.a.), Vietnam 52% (+3.3%o.a.), Philippines 43.5% (+4.4%p.a.), Thailand 42.7% (+6.2% p.a.): see "Internet Users by Country (2016)" 2017). In the long term, the natural pressures of ordinary life, where people's working and leisure habits are changing and where mobility, diversity and transparency grow more rapidly than ever before, are likely to oblige educational authorities to revise their policies so as to allow the development of more flexible, learner-centred structures as more and more citizens embrace Internet activity as well as life-long learning. In the meantime, systems like this one can still be useful in the context of any administrative/educational system, especially the non-formal areas of learning, where they could play a valuable, though more restricted, role. In other words, it is not an all-or-nothing framework, in the sense that it can be used in a limited way within specific sections of a course where students might benefit from greater personalization and autonomy without undermining administrative policies or directives.

7   Conclusion

Overall, and with some exceptions like Singapore, contemporary Asian populations show relatively low levels of English proficiency. But this population is becoming far more mobile than at any time in human history, creating a massive market of people who will need enhanced capacity in intercultural communication. They will need to speak both English as a Lingua Franca (ELF), and local languages, and will need to acquire a functional competence in understanding both English culture and local-language cultures, and how to communicate in different codes and value-systems with people from different language and cultural backgrounds. These needs are being largely driven by real life concerns which substantially exceed the reach of conventional formal classes and pedagogies. In the face of these developments and the growing "do-it-yourself" attitude to learning and communication in societies throughout the world in general, educational organizations are likely to struggle when confronted by these needs of language- and culture-learners, who will experience unpredicted and unpredictable needs requiring resolution in real time. On the evidence of surveys of English competence, their "operational histories" are not handling the demands of contemporary English in Asia. An alternative model is proposed in this chapter, built on the needs of a learning framework. Its goal is to support the individual learner to achieve heightened critical awareness to incoming stimuli, so challenging their operational histories, and to help them construct new understandings and representations. While the framework has had only restricted testing on learning tasks in the sound pattern of English, it potentially has explanatory value in terms of learning, and organizational value in terms of the generation of learning environments. The emerging educational needs for English are so dynamic and open-ended that they challenge educators to test new points of view.

References

Ash, R., Crook, J., Dannenberg, R., et al., (2015). Audacity. Retrieved Feb 5 2017, from http://audacity.sourceforge.net

Asp, C. W., Kline, M., & Koike, K. J. (2012a). Verbotonal body movements. In R. Goldfarb (Ed.), *Translational speech-language pathology and audiology: Essays in honor of Dr. Sadanand Singh* (pp. 137–147). San Diego: Plural Publishing.

Asp, C. W., Kline, M., & Koike, K. J. (2012b). Verbotonal worldwide. In R. Goldfarb (Ed.), *Translational speech-language pathology and audiology: Essays in honor of Dr. Sadanand Singh* (pp. 319–326). San Diego: Plural Publishing.

Association of Southeast Asian Nations. (2008). *The Asean Charter*. Jakarta: Association of Southeast Asian Nations. https://doi.org/10.1017/S0020589308000882.

Australia in the Asian Century Task Force. (2011). Australia in the Asian century, (December). Retrieved 3 July 2017 from http://www.defence.gov.au/whitepaper/2013/docs/australia_in_the_asian_century_white_paper.pdf

Bancroft, W.J. (1975). The Lozanov language class. In *International Symposium on Suggestology* (pp. 1–51). Washington, DC: ED 108 475. Retrieved 3 July 2017 from http://files.eric.ed.gov/fulltext/ED108475.pdf

Benson, P. (2007). Autonomy in language teaching and learning. *Language Teaching, 40*(21), 21–40.

Condon, W. S., & Ogston, W. D. (1971). Speech and body motion synchrony of the speaker-hearer. In D. L. Horton & J. J. Jenkins (Eds.), *Perception of language* (pp. 150–173). Columbus: Charles E. Merrill.

Condon, W. S., & Sander, L. (1974). Synchrony demonstrated between movements of the neonate and adult speech. *Child Development, 45*, 456–462.

Cornish, H., Dale, R., Kirby, S., & Christiansen, M. H. (2017). Sequence memory constraints give rise to language-like structure through iterated learning. *PLoS One, 12*(1), e0168532. Retrieved 3 July 2017 from http://dspace.stir.ac.uk/bitstream/1893/24869/1/journal.pone.0168532.pdf.

Curran, C. A. (1972). *Counseling learning: A whole person model for education*. New York: Grune and Stratton.

Curran, C. A. (1976). *Counseling-learning in second languages*. Apple River: Apple River Press.

EF English Proficiency Index 2015. (2015) (Fifth). EF Education First Ltd. Retrieved 11 July 2017 from http://media2.ef.com/__/~/media/centralefcom/epi/downloads/full-reports/v5/ef-epi-2015-english.pdf

EF English Proficiency Index 2016. (2016). Retrieved 11 July 2017 from http://media2. ef.com/__/~/media/centralefcom/epi/downloads/full-reports/v6/ef-epi-2016-english.pdf

Gattegno, C. (1963). *The silent way*. New York: Educational Solutions Worldwide.

Giedd, J. N. (2015). The amazing teen brain. *Scientific American, 312*(6), 32–37.

Guberina, P. (1955). Tonal audiometry and vocal audiometry in the light of the Verbotonal audiometry. In *Proceedings of the 2nd meeting of the World Association for the Deaf* (pp. 186–199). Zagreb.

Guberina, P. (1956). L'audiométrie verbo-tonale. *Revue de Laryngologie, 1–2*, 20–58.

Guberina, P. (1972). *Restricted bands of frequencies in auditory rehabilitation of deaf*. Zagreb: Institute of Phonetics, Faculty of Arts, University of Zagreb.

He, B., & Sangarun, P. (2015). Implementing autonomy: A model for improving pronunciation in Chinese EFL university students. *Rangsit Journal of Arts and Sciences, 5*(1), 1–12.

He, B., Sangarun, P., & Lian, A.-P. (2015). Improving the English pronunciation of Chinese EFL university students through the integration of CALL and verbotonalism. In J. Colpaert, A. Aerts, M. Oberhofer, & M. Gutiérez-Colón Plana (Eds.), *Seventeenth international CALL research conference: Task design and CALL* (pp. 276–285). Conference Presentation, Tarragona, Spain: University of Antwerp. Retrieved on July 3, 2017, from http://wwwa.fundacio.urv.cat/congressos/public/usr_docs/call_2015_conference_proceedings.pdf

Holec, H. (1981). *Autonomy and language learning*. Oxford: Pergamon Press.

Internet Users by Country (2016). (2017). Retrieved February 5, 2017, from http://www.internetlivestats.com/internet-users-by-country/

Koty, A. C. (2016). Labor mobility in ASEAN: Current commitments and future limitations. Retrieved November 26, 2016, from http://www.aseanbriefing.com/news/2016/05/13/asean-labor-mobility.html

Kumaravadivelu, B. (2012). *Understanding language teaching: From method to postmethod*. New York: Routledge.

Levene, H. (1960). Robust tests for equality of variances. In I. Olkin & H. Hotelling (Eds.), *Contributions to probability and statistics: Essays in honor of Harold Hotelling* (pp. 278–292). Palo Alto: Stanford University Press.

Lian, A.-P. (1980). *Intonation patterns of French (Teacher's book)*. Melbourne: River Seine Publications Pty Ltd..

Lian, A.-P. (1987). Awareness, autonomy and achievement. *Revue de Phonétique Appliquée, 82–84*, 167–184.

Lian, A.-P. (2000). Keynote address: From first principles: Constructing language learning and teaching environments. In M.-S. Lin (Ed.), *Selected papers from the ninth international symposium on English teaching* (pp. 49–62). Taipei: Crane Publishing. Retrieved 3 July 2017 from http://www.andrewlian.com/andrewlian/prowww/first_principles/index.html.

Lian, A.-P. (2004). Technology-enhanced language-learning environments: A rhizomatic approach. In J.-B. Son (Ed.), *Computer-Assisted Language Learning: Concepts, contexts and practices* (pp. 1–20). New York: iUniverse.

Lian, A.-P. (2011). Reflections on language learning in the 21st century: The rhizome at work. *Rangsit Journal of Arts and Sciences, 1*(1), 3–15. Retrieved from http://rjas.rsu.ac.th/article.php?id=10.

Lian, A. B. (2014). "New Learning" and CALL: A DIY paradigm. *AsiaCALL OnLine Journal, 9*, A14–A26. Retrieved 3 July 2017 from http://asiacall.info/acoj/wp-content/uploads/2014/05/Lian_AB_ACOJv09_final.pdf.

Lian, A.-P. (2017). The inexorable rise of the proletarian autodidact. In A. B. Lian, P. Kell, P. Black, & K. Y. Lie (Eds.), *Challenges in global learning* (pp. 282–313). Cambridge: Cambridge Scholars.

Lian, A.-P., & Pineda, M. V. (2014). Rhizomatic learning: "As… When… and If…": A strategy for the ASEAN community in the 21st century. *Beyond Words, 2*(1), 1–28. Retrieved 3 July 2017 from http://journal.wima.ac.id/index.php/BW/article/view/508/487.

Mason, J. (1998). Enabling teachers to be real teachers: Necessary levels of awareness and structure of attention. *Journal of Mathematics Teacher Education, 1*, 243–267. https://doi.org/10.1023/A:1009973717476.

Pineda, M. V. (2013). Open teaching and personal learning networks (PLNs) as avenues of enhanced participation and reflection. *Rangsit Journal of Arts and Sciences, 3*(2), 99–112.

Planck, M. (n.d.). When you change the way you look at things, the things you look at change. Retrieved from http://www.goodreads.com/quotes/1246159-when-you-change-the-way-you-look-at-things-the

Schmidt, R. (2012). Attention, awareness, and individual differences in language learning. In W. M. Chan, K. N. Chin, S. K. Bhatt, & I. Walker (Eds.), *Perspectives on individual characteristics and foreign language education* (pp. 27–50). Boston: Mouton de Gruyter.

Wang, G. Z. (2005). *English pronunciation & intonation for communication.* Beijing: Higher Education Press.

Intercultural Communication in English Courses in Asia: What Should We Teach About?

Don SNOW

Abstract When intercultural communication skills are taught in foreign language courses, three high priority factors to address are (1) ethnocentrism, (2) stereotyping, and (3) ingroup bias. These factors are important to understand not only because they can bias interpretations, but also because they can potentially short-circuit the interpretation process through a mechanism known as "attribute substitution."

Dual process views of thinking hold that the human mind has two basic thinking processes, an intuitive process often called System 1 and a reflective process called System 2. Most interpretive judgments are made rapidly and intuitively by System 1, and in its rush to make rapid interpretive judgments System 1 will often replace a relatively difficult question with one for which easier answers are more readily accessible. Ethnocentrism, stereotypes, and ingroup bias offer highly accessible substitute questions that make it easier for System 1 to make automatic, unreflective judgments.

Teaching explicitly about these factors in foreign language courses helps learners better understand how the interpretation process works and what factors affect it in intercultural encounters. Furthermore, teaching about these factors helps build learners' conscious awareness of the interpretation process itself, which may ultimately be the most valuable contribution to their intercultural communication skills.

1 Introduction

Teacher Li is a young English language teacher at a university in China. One day her department asks her to go to the airport to pick up a professor who is visiting from Canada to give a workshop. When she meets him at the airport, she sees that he is an older man, perhaps in his sixties, and he also has quite a lot of luggage - two large suitcases and several smaller bags. They aren't able to find a luggage cart, so Teacher Li offers to carry one

D. SNOW (✉)
Language and Culture Center, Duke Kunshan University,
Kunshan, Jiangsu Province, People's Republic of China
e-mail: don.snow@dukekunshan.edu.cn

© Springer International Publishing AG, part of Springer Nature 2018
A. CURTIS, R. SUSSEX (eds.), *Intercultural Communication in Asia:
Education, Language and Values*, Multilingual Education 24,
https://doi.org/10.1007/978-3-319-69995-0_4

*of the large suitcases, but he insists that he is able to carry all of his luggage by himself.
However, as they head toward the car, he seems to be having some trouble moving all the
baggage, so at a point when they are stopped in an elevator and he has put down the suitcases, Teacher Li simply picks one of them up. The professor says "I can handle these by
myself," but Teacher Li assumes he is just being polite, and when the elevator door opens
she heads off with the suitcase. Soon they reach the car, but now the professor seems quite
annoyed with Teacher Li, and hardly speaks with her at all when she tries to make conversation during the ensuing ride to the university.*

This story is an example of a critical incident, so called because it is likely to be
both noticeable and memorable for those involved, a point captured in the term used
by Pham – "most noticeable positive and negative incidents" (2018). Critical incident exercises are frequently used in intercultural competence training workshops
(Brislin and Yoshida 1994; Albert 1995; Wight 1995; Cushner and Brislin 1996;
Cushner and Landis 1996; Fowler and Blohm 2004; Apedaile and Schill 2008), and
the basic format of the activity is that trainees are first presented with a critical incident, and then asked to discuss possible explanations for what happened. Critical
incident activities are also sometimes used in English language courses because
they provide both language practice opportunities and an opportunity to build intercultural communication skills (Corbett 2003; Snow 2015). In fact, the incident
above is taken from a textbook for learners of English (Snow 2014). While this
particular incident is fictionalized to some degree for teaching purposes, it is closely
based on an actual experience related to me by an English teacher in China, and I
have included it here as an example of a kind of interaction that is increasingly common not only in China but throughout Asia and indeed the rest of the world.

As a result of globalization, ever larger numbers of people around the world will
have intercultural encounters like Teacher Li's, and this is particularly true in the
Asian region where one of the most dramatic examples of the magnitude of the
changes taking place is provided by China. It was only a few short decades ago that
most people in China would live out their entire lives without ever meeting anyone
from a foreign country. However, now it is not at all unusual for Chinese people to
have face-to-face encounters with foreigners, either because of the increasing number of foreigners streaming into China, or the similarly substantial outpouring of
Chinese who go abroad for schooling, employment, conferences, or tourism.
Similarly, whereas it was not long ago that Chinese were almost entirely cut off
from indirect intercultural encounters of the kind that take place through the media,
now a great number of Chinese have easy and regular access to the rest of the world
via media and the Internet. This leads to a dramatic increase in intercultural encounters in which Chinese people see powerful and sometimes disturbing images of
other cultures, and also have the opportunity to see how people from other cultures
perceive China. The growing frequency of encounters like those illustrated by the
story of Teacher Li raises the question of what can and should be done to better
prepare the people of Asia – and the rest of the world – for interaction across cultural lines. At the individual level, the question would be one of how Teacher Li
prepares herself – and presumably also her students – for effective interaction in
such encounters. At the international and institutional level, the question is what

governments and educational institutions should incorporate in teaching curricu-lums to ensure that more people are well-equipped to interact effectively with peo-ple from different cultural backgrounds.

Clearly the definition of what constitutes effective intercultural communication is quite complicated. For example, in the case of Teacher Li, whether or not her interaction skills were "effective" in this case is probably a matter of more than just her personal satisfaction with the outcomes of the encounter. She probably also needs to consider the expectations of her university and department, and whether or not they will be happy with her interaction. There may even be a national level for her to consider. After all, it is quite possible that in this encounter, to some degree, she perceived herself as an ambassador and representative for China (Chen 1998), and wanted to create a good impression of her country. However, as China's world role grows, the traditional Chinese desire to be a good host may also be tempered by a sense that pleasing foreign guests is not necessarily always desirable, particularly if those foreigners behave in ways that seem unreasonable. In short, the issue of what constitutes effective intercultural interaction is quite complex, and goes well beyond what is possible to deal with here. So, for the purposes of this chapter, we will use a relatively simple definition of "effective" interaction as striking a reason-able balance between achieving one's own goals in the situation and also achieving the goals of others who have a stake in the encounter.

This chapter considers the issue of **what** aspects of intercultural communication should be taught in foreign language courses, especially English language courses, and what should be taught about those aspects. Of course, the question of **how** to teach intercultural communication skills is also very important. However, I have recently addressed this question elsewhere (Snow 2015), so here I will simply note that there are a number of activities which can be used in English classes that build both language skills and also intercultural communication skills; the critical inci-dent activity above is but one of many possible examples. Rather than focusing on method, this chapter will focus on the question of content, of what we should teach learners about intercultural communication.

This chapter will discuss the role played in intercultural communication by three factors: ethnocentrism, ingroup bias, and stereotyping. The idea that these three fac-tors play a substantial role in intercultural communication will not come as a sur-prise as these are all well-established "usual suspects" found in any discussion of intercultural communication, so there is little need to argue their importance. The goal of this chapter is to explore what should be taught about them, and what the goals of teaching about these factors should be.

My argument will be that in intercultural communication training in English language courses, our primary focus should not be on teaching about British and American cultures, which is the approach often taken when issues of culture are addressed in ELT materials in Asia. Instead, I will argue that our goal is to prepare learners for what Kecskes (2018) refers to as a success approach in intercultural communication, and that one way we can do this is by helping learners gain a better understanding of the processes by which they go about interpreting – making sense of – intercultural encounters. I will also argue that one good way to do this is by teaching learners about the three factors identified above, and helping teachers and learners develop a mental intercultural encounter checklist that will help them attend to these factors during problematic, challenging or difficult intercultural encounters.

A secondary goal of the chapter is to argue that our understanding of the interpretive process in intercultural communication will be enhanced if we draw on recent findings from the field of psychology, particularly what are known as dual-process views of human thinking, and if we explore the implications that a concept called "attribute substitution" has for intercultural communication. However, before exploring these issues, it is necessary to first explicitly discuss several assumptions that underlie the arguments in this chapter.

2 Working Assumptions

I have discussed these four working assumptions in more detail elsewhere (Snow 2015), but brief re-statement of them here will help set the stage for points to be made below.

2.1 Incorporating Intercultural Communication into English and Other Foreign Language Courses

The first assumption is that foreign language courses should be an important vehicle – perhaps the most important vehicle – through which people receive basic training in intercultural communication. Of course, people receive intercultural communication training in many different kinds of settings, including not only courses in universities but also various kinds of workshops in businesses, hospitals, and the hospitality industry. However, in many countries foreign language study is required for all students, especially at the secondary and tertiary levels, and for many of these students foreign language courses are the main form of preparation they receive for dealing with people from other countries and cultures.

I would argue that intercultural communication training should be a part of all foreign language courses, but I feel it is especially important in English language courses, not only because English is the foreign language most widely taught in Asia, but also because "English as Lingua Franca" (House 2018) is the language most frequently used in intercultural communication, even in encounters where no participants speak English as their first language. Why should English courses become a major site for intercultural communication training? The answer is simple – English courses provide the only formal training for intercultural encounters that most learners ever get. It is easy to lose sight of this fact in a world where intercultural communication courses are gradually becoming more common on university campuses and curriculums. However, for the foreseeable future, the kind of pre-intercultural encounter training which reaches the most learners in Asia – and in which they invest the most time – consists of English language courses.

Of course, many English language courses already have a culture component of some kind, often focused on British and American cultures. However, learning basic facts about British and American cultures is not at all the same thing as gaining a working knowledge of intercultural communication, and the latter is actually more valuable in a world where many or most of the people from other cultures that learners will need to interact with are from countries other than Britain and the US. What learners need most is an understanding of the basic dynamics of communication with people whose culture is unfamiliar to them, and the factors that affect such communication.

2.2   Limiting the Number of Intercultural Communication Concepts Addressed

A second working assumption is that, if we incorporate intercultural communication training into English and other foreign language courses, it is neither possible nor desirable to try to cover all the topics and concepts that would normally be included in a typical intercultural communication course or textbook. One reason is that intercultural communication is a very broad and complex field of study, and even an introductory textbook will normally cover dozens of major concepts. Taking just one relatively recent textbook as an example (Liu et al. 2011), we find more than 50 different topic areas listed in the table of contents, and under each of these multiple concepts are introduced, explained, and illustrated. Clearly, there simply is not enough extra time in English language courses – which obviously need to focus first and foremost on language skills – to cover so many different concepts, and attempting to cover them all would make it very difficult to address any of them in any depth.

Furthermore, not all English teachers have had training in intercultural communication, and it seems somewhat unreasonable to expect that English teachers – who are often busy people facing large numbers of students and heavy workloads – will add mastery of so many new concepts to their teaching repertoire. While it is reasonable and desirable for language teachers to develop some understanding of intercultural communication, it also seems more practical and reasonable that they familiarize themselves especially with a limited number of key concepts which are likely to affect many kinds of intercultural encounters. In other words, when considering how to best incorporate intercultural communication training into English language courses, we need a short list of high priority items.

2.3   Focusing on the Interpretation Process

My third working assumption is that, as we look for a short list of high priority items, it is desirable to focus particularly on the issue of interpretation, in other words, the process by which one goes about making sense of the words and actions of "strangers". (Here and below, I use the word "strangers" to refer to people who are from other and unfamiliar cultural backgrounds.) By way of example, in the case of Teacher Li, interpretation would be the process by which she generates one or more explanations for why the Canadian professor seems to be unhappy, and by which she decides which possible explanation to adopt. This interpretation, in turn, will influence how she proceeds in her further interactions with the Canadian professor.

Why focus on the interpretation process? The first reason is that it plays an important role in all intercultural encounters (Chen and Starosta 1998; Gudykunst and Kim 1997; Scollon et al. 2012). Here it may help to contrast an interpretation-focused approach with approaches that emphasize teaching students information about the cultures of English-speaking countries, usually Britain and the US. For example, teaching students proper table manners for a dinner in a British or American home may help students if they are ever invited to such a meal. However, this approach has two major limitations. The first is that such information is only useful if the strangers with which a student needs to interact are British or American, and – as noted above – this will often not be the case. The second is that such culture teaching generally consists largely of broad generalizations that may well not apply to many actual situations where one is dealing with individual British or Americans; for example, the norms of politeness that hold sway at a formal family dinner in the US would not be quite the same as those that would apply among college students at a fast food restaurant – or for that matter, in some respects, at a formal dinner in the UK.[1] In short, in many intercultural encounters, much of what students learn about British and American culture will not really help them very much, and attempts to apply whatever limited culture information they have learned may actually do more harm than good, leading to inappropriate interpretations or behaviors.

The second reason to focus on the interpretation process is that interpretation is the basic starting point of virtually all communicative acts. A common sense description of a communicative act might look more or less like the following:

I have idea → I encode idea into message → I transmit message →You receive/interpret message

However, as reasonable as this formula seems, it is misleading in that it may suggest the chain of events begins with the generation of an idea, and that interpretation only enters the process later on. In reality, the chain actually begins with interpretation because, in the chain of communication moves, most moves are impacted by

---

[1] I am keenly aware that concepts and terms such as "British culture" or "American culture" – not to mention "Western culture" or "Asian culture" – are not only extremely broad, but also potentially dangerous, especially if they lead us to believe that all of the people in these huge categories are essentially the same. I use such terms in this chapter only for the sake of expediency, and also because they to reflect how people often talk and think about cultural groups.

one's interpretation of whatever move came before. For example, most if not all of the communication moves made by Teacher Li in the story above are responses to things the professor said or did, and are based on her interpretation of those things. Even when she appears to be the one who initiates the chain of communication acts, as she presumably did when she first spoke upon meeting him, her choice of words and actions will be shaped by her interpretation of the general situation and what she feels is expected of her in the situation (Scollon et al. 2012).

Of course, interpretation is not the only aspect of a communicative act that is worthy of attention; for example, learners could also benefit from training in how to generate and evaluate response strategies. However, interpretation is worthy of particular attention in intercultural training because one's interpretations have such a significant impact on responses. My argument below will be that, as we consider how best to incorporate intercultural communication training into English language courses, one of our main goals should be to help learners gain a better understanding of the interpretation process and the factors that affect it in intercultural encounters.

3   Interpretation and Dual Process Views of Thinking

To understand how factors such as ethnocentrism, stereotyping, and ingroup bias affect interpretive judgments in intercultural encounters, we need to first make a quick detour into the field of psychology, and what are known as dual processing views of thinking. Many psychologists subscribe to some version of the idea that the human mind takes two basic approaches to thinking (e.g. Wilson 2002; Kahneman 2011; Evans 2010; Evans and Stanovich 2013). While there is not yet complete consensus as to the terms that should be used for these two approaches, many scholars use the terms "System 1" and "System 2".

System 1 consists of those human thinking processes which function instinctively and generally below the level of conscious awareness. These processes are largely or entirely automatic, and are often described as a kind of automatic pilot. They function very rapidly and efficiently, and involve relatively little effort or conscious control. Interaction and communication require that we make a large number of rapid interpretative decisions, as often as once every second (Scollon et al. 2012), so by necessity System 1 handles most interpretive judgments and is our default system for dealing with such judgments (Evans 2010). For example, from the moment Teacher Li meets the Canadian professor, her mind is constantly making interpretive decisions such as:

Should I speak first, or wait for him?
Should I shake his hand? How long? How hard do I squeeze?
Do I look him directly in the eye? How long?
What do I talk about first? Should I ask about his trip? Should I introduce myself? Should I ask how he is feeling?
What do I think of him? Does he seem reasonably friendly or not? Does he seem to be relatively formal or informal?
How tired does he seem to be? How physically able does he seem to be?

These are all interpretive decisions Teacher Li's mind is likely to be dealing with even in the first minute of her acquaintance with the professor, and it would be impossible for her to consider all of these issues – and no doubt more – deliberately and consciously. However, rather than being overwhelmed, Teacher Li is able to deal with all of these issues because her mind (System 1) deals with most of them automatically and often without the need for conscious attention and awareness.

In contrast, System 2 is the term used for the kinds of thinking we are more consciously aware of, the conscious application of reasoning to judgments and decisions. In fact, System 2 is essentially what we think of when we use the term "thinking". System 2 requires much more investment of mental effort than System 1, and as a result it functions much more slowly. However, it is also more careful and thorough, and we are more likely to engage this system when we feel that an issue demands deliberate thought. For example, the Canadian professor's unexpectedly negative response to Teacher Li's attempts to help may cause her to make a conscious effort to ponder the question of why he responded as he did – at least if the intervention of System 2 is not pre-empted in some way by the faster and more efficient System 1.

Even though System 1 functions very rapidly and automatically, its judgments tend to be fairly accurate, and there is a growing literature, both scholarly and popular, that encourages us to "go with our gut" more often when confronted with problematic decisions (e.g. Gerdzinger 2007; Gladwell 2007). The reason System 1 tends to be fairly accurate, especially when dealing with familiar tasks in familiar settings, is that it has been honed and trained through previous exposure to similar situations (Evans 2010). However, in less familiar settings with which our minds have less experience, System 1 is prone to certain kinds of errors; one of these is the attribute substitution error which we will discuss in more detail below. When dealing with novel situations, what Evans and Stanovich (2013) refer to as "hostile environments" for System 1 processing, System 2 is generally more reliable because it is more painstaking and thorough, and better at noting and processing new clues from the situation, rather than relying on past experience. But it is also more effortful and time-consuming, so the natural tendency is to employ it as little as possible (Kahneman 2011). The trick, therefore, is to make good choices about when to trust fast and efficient System 1, and when to engage the more effortful but more reliable System 2. As Kahneman puts it, "System 2 is much too slow and inefficient to serve as a substitute for System 1 in making routine decisions. The best we can do is a compromise: learn to recognize situations in which mistakes are likely and try harder to avoid significant mistakes when the stakes are high" (2011, p. 28; see also Evans and Stanovich 2013; Portnoy 2012).

In general, intercultural encounters such as that of Teacher Li with the Canadian professor involve interaction with someone whose culture is relatively unfamiliar, and in such situations it is generally desirable to have more conscious control over the interpretation process than is necessary when interacting with people from a familiar cultural background. This suggests not only that System 2 should be engaged more often, but also that learners should have a better understanding of how the interpretation process works and what factors are likely to affect it in intercultural encounters. For this reason I suggest that an important aspect of building effective intercultural communication skills in English courses is enhancing conscious awareness of the interpretation process, and also enhancing understanding of the factors that often affect interpretation in intercultural encounters, factors such as ethnocentrism, stereotypes, and ingroup bias. These factors not only have the potential to bias interpretive judgments made in intercultural encounters; they also have the potential to short-circuit the interpretation process, allowing it to function at an unconscious (System 1) level when it would be better to engage System 2 more and interpret more consciously. This happens particularly because of one of the systematic errors to which System 1 is prone – attribute substitution.

Attribute substitution is probably best described as a short cut that System 1 takes when it is confronted with a complex or difficult problem. As Kahneman puts it: "If a satisfactory answer to a hard question is not found quickly, System 1 will find a related question that is easier and will answer it" (Kahneman 2011, p. 97; see also Kahneman and Frederick 2002). Because System 1 needs to make judgments very rapidly, it often deals with difficult questions by replacing them with similar but simpler questions, and then answering those. For example, when confronted with a difficult question like "How popular will the president be six months from now?" System 1 may replace it a simpler question involving fewer unknown variables, such as "How popular is the president now?". Similarly, confronted with a complex question like "How should financial advisors who prey on the elderly be punished?", System 1 may suggest a similar but much simpler question like "How much anger do I feel when I think of financial predators?" (Kahneman 2011, p. 98).[2]

Such substitutions are most likely to be made when two conditions are met: (1) the original question is relatively difficult to deal with, and no satisfactory answer is readily accessible; (2) a similar but easier question is readily accessible. Under these conditions, System 1 is likely to replace the more difficult "target question" with a simpler "rule of thumb" (heuristic) question (Kahneman and Frederick 2002). Of course, as Kahneman notes, "[…] System 2 has the opportunity to reject this intuitive answer, or to modify it by incorporating other information. However, a lazy System 2 often follows the path of least effort and endorses a heuristic answer without much scrutiny of whether it is truly appropriate" (Kahneman 2011, p. 99).

This is all highly relevant to intercultural encounter situations because they almost inevitably constitute hostile environments for the operation of System 1, in other words, environments which offer few familiar clues that would aid System 1 in rapidly making accurate judgments, and which instead confront System 1 with interpretation questions that are generally more difficult than those faced when interacting with people from one's own culture. For example, even though Teacher Li presumably knows something about Western culture, accurately interpreting the behavior of the Canadian professor will still be more difficult for her than assessing the behavior of a Chinese person would be. She may find it difficult to determine whether his behavior is normal for a Westerner, or the result of individual personal-

---

[2] Substitute questions suggested by System 1 often have a significant affective component, as is the case in the second example here (Snow 2016).

ity features. She may not know whether there are Western cultural rules that she inadvertently broke and, if so, what they were. She may not even be sure of the degree to which his silence represents displeasure with her, rather than grumpiness after a long flight. When dealing with someone from her own culture, there would be a rich body of shared norms, values, and knowledge that would help her rapidly and accurately assess the situation; without this shared fund of cultural knowledge, interpreting his behavior becomes much harder. As Teacher Li struggles to make sense of the Canadian professor's behavior, the three factors discussed below – ethnocentrism, stereotypes, and ingroup bias – offer temptingly easy substitute questions and answers.

4 Ethnocentrism

Ethnocentrism should quite clearly be included on any short list of topics for intercultural training in English language courses. It plays a role in the great majority of intercultural encounters, and is one of the most frequent sources of problems because, as we attempt to make sense of the stranger's behavior, it is virtually certain that our thoughts will be shaped to a considerable degree by the norms and values into which we have been socialized from childhood (Brislin and Yoshida 1994; Triandis 1995; Chen and Starosta 1998).

The most obvious problem caused by ethnocentrism is bias. The very essence of ethnocentrism is the human tendency to assume that the norms of our own culture are universal and should apply just as much to other cultures as they do to our own. While this tendency is quite natural, it also causes problems in intercultural communication because it tempts us to view any behavior that deviates from the norms of our own culture as at least abnormal, and often simply wrong or bad. This is a widely discussed feature of ethnocentrism which does not require further elaboration here (Brislin 1993; Gudykunst and Kim 1997; Ting-Toomey 1999).

My focus here is on a second way ethnocentrism causes intercultural communication problems – it is a fertile source of substitute questions on which System 1 can draw when confronted with difficult interpretation questions. To illustrate this point, let's go back to Teacher Li's encounter. As Teacher Li attempts to interpret the behavior of the Canadian professor, it will be relatively difficult for her to see the situation from his perspective, and to know with any certainty the norms by which he would judge the appropriateness of his behavior in this situation. In contrast, the norms of her own culture, learned through years of experience, are quite readily available to her. Keep in mind that System 1 works precisely because people learn through repeated exposure to situations, and the main reason System 1 is often quite accurate when it makes rapid and automatic judgments is that it draws on lessons learned through similar previous experiences. It is quite likely that Teacher Li has previously had multiple experiences with hosting situations (which is probably how she frames this particular encounter), and through these she has internalized a set of norms that are now familiar to her and readily accessible as she attempts to interpret the situation.

"Accessability" is a concept from psychology that relates to how easily and quickly an idea comes into one's mind. As Wilson (2002) notes, one important factor determining accessibility is:

> how often a concept has been used in the past. People are creatures of habit, and the more they have used a particular way of judging the world in the past, the more energized the concept will be. Our unconscious minds develop chronic ways of interpreting information from our environments; in psychological parlance, certain ideas and categories become chronically accessible as a result of frequent use in the past (Wilson 2002, p. 32).

Naturally, as Teacher Li reacts to the Canadian professor's behavior, the ideas which are most accessible to her System 1 and which most automatically come to mind will generally be based on her previous experience, most of which probably took place in a Chinese setting and cultural context.

So, as Teacher Li confronts the relatively difficult and complex target question "Why didn't this particular Canadian professor in this particular situation respond positively to my efforts to be a good host?", ethnocentrism offers System 1 a tempting heuristic – a simple rule of thumb – that facilitates quick, easy and even automatic interpretive judgments: "Use the norms of your own culture". In this situation, such substitute questions might be:

> (According to my cultural standards), did the Canadian respond appropriately?
> Why might a normal (Chinese) person respond negatively to my efforts to help?

We want to teach students about ethnocentrism not only because it may bias interpretive judgments, but also because it offers a tempting short-cut which may pre-empt more careful and mindful interpretation. Students should actively be on the lookout for ethnocentrism, and one of the questions on their mental intercultural encounter checklist should be: Am I judging based on the norms of my own culture, or trying to consider the norms of the stranger's culture?

5   Stereotypes

A second phenomenon that definitely belongs on any short list of topics to be addressed in intercultural communication training is the tendency to stereotype. Like ethnocentrism, this is a very natural tendency, based on the need to learn and manage information by categorizing and generalizing (Hall 2002). However, it can also cause problems in intercultural communication (Bar-Tel 1997; Scollon et al. 2012).

One way stereotypes influence interpretation is through bias. Of course, not all stereotypes are negative, and positive stereotypes at times cause people in intercultural encounters to interpret the behavior of strangers in ways that err on the positive side (though this can also be a source of problems if it creates overly high expectations that are later dashed). However, as Brewer notes: "Stereotypes about out-groups most often are predominantly negative and consequently lead to expectations that are likely to organize our interaction with a previously unknown member of the out-group in ways that promote hostility, rejection, or conflict" (2003, p. 72).

A second important way stereotypes affect interpretation is by offering readily accessible substitute questions for interpretative judgments. In fact, we could say that stereotypes are pre-packaged judgments, learned from the media, from direct contact, or from stories we have heard others tell, that are ready and waiting to be applied in intercultural encounters. For example, Teacher Li may be influenced by stereotypes that portray Westerners as rather demanding and difficult to deal with, as very concerned about privacy, or perhaps as generally being rather suspicious toward Chinese. Then, when confronted with the relatively difficult question of what the intentions of a particular stranger are in a particular situation, System 1 substitutes an easier rule-of-thumb question – what are people from that group generally like? In the case of Teacher Li, easy and tempting substitute questions would include:

What are Westerners/foreigners like?
How do Westerners/foreigners normally act?

These are questions to which stereotypes offer convenient ready-made answers – all that is necessary is to identify the group to which the stranger belongs and then apply the relevant stereotype. (Of course, the very broad nature of categories like "Westerners" and "foreigners" facilitates the attribute substitution process.) Such stereotype-driven substitutions are especially likely when someone faces time pressure or is distracted; as Evans (2010, p. 115) notes, "if people are required to respond very quickly or while carrying out a second mental task [...] the intuitive belief-based response is more likely to dominate" (see also Triandis 1994).

One would think that in an actual encounter situation visible clues would serve as an effective check on System 1's tendency to find easy answers in stereotypes, either by calling attention to discrepancies between the stereotype and the reality before our eyes, or by reminding us that not all members of a group are necessarily the same. To some extent this does happen, especially if contact with the stranger continues over time and there is opportunity for learning more about the stranger's culture – as well as the extent to which particular strangers are typical of their cultures. However, it is also important to recognize that once a stereotype-based judgment is made, it is often quite resistant to modification. In fact, through a mechanism called the anchoring effect (Kahneman 2011), System 1 often tends to shape evidence to fit conclusions. In other words, if Teacher Li decides that the professor's reaction is due to the fact that Westerners are very suspicious of Chinese people, her judgment will tend to guide her interpretation of new evidence that emerges later. Essentially, she is now primed to look for evidence that will confirm her judgment, and is likely to interpret any further evidence in ways that that confirm the original judgment. This makes it easier for stereotype-based judgments generated by System 1 to survive any scrutiny System 2 may offer, and decreases the chance that System 2 will feel compelled to intervene. As Kahneman notes: "System 2 is more of an apologist for the emotions of System 1 than a critic of those emotions – and an endorser rather than an enforcer. Its search for information and arguments is mostly constrained to information that is consistent with existing beliefs, not with an intention to examine them" (2011, pp. 103–4).

To sum up, teachers and students should be aware of the tendency to draw on stereotypes when making interpretive judgments, and of the potential for bias that this introduces. People are more likely to question or reject interpretations if they are consciously aware these interpretations are based on stereotypes (Evans 2010). They should also be aware of how stereotypes may facilitate attribute substitution, replacing difficult interpretive questions with easier "what are they (generally) like?" heuristics. For their intercultural encounter checklist, the question students should develop the habit of asking is: Am I judging the stranger based on evidence in this person's actual behavior, or based on things I have previously heard about the stranger's group?

6 Ingroup Bias

A third factor which often impacts interpretive judgments in intercultural encounters is ingroup bias. This tendency to categorize people as either ingroup members or outsiders is deeply rooted in human nature, and creates a degree of natural bias against outsiders. This is not to say that we are always negatively disposed toward outsiders and strangers. But, in general, we are less concerned about their welfare, have less sense of obligation toward them, and are somewhat less willing to trust them than would be the case for ingroup members (Brislin 1993; Triandis 1994; Gudykunst and Kim 1997).

As with ethnocentrism and stereotyping, ingroup bias not only has obvious potential to bias our interpretation of the behavior of strangers, but also affects interpretation by offering substitute questions that may allow System 1 to make relatively fast and easy interpretive judgments. When dealing with strangers from unfamiliar cultures, it is often difficult to make reliable interpretive judgments about how much they can be trusted, how well disposed they are toward us, and so forth. It is far simpler to answer the basic ingroup/outgroup question. Thus, when confronted with the puzzling behavior of the Canadian professor, rather than engaging System 2 to consciously go through the effort of trying to sort out his intentions and motivations, it is possible that Teacher Li's System 1 will offer an easier question:

Should I treat him as one of us or one of them?

The danger, of course, is that Teacher Li's System 1 will have asked and answered this question before System 2 even becomes engaged, much less before Teacher Li has opportunity to gain a better understanding of what happened, for example, by talking with the professor. If the professor has been assigned to the "them" category, any subsequent conscious thinking Teacher Li engages in may take on something of a negative tint.

However, the other problem created by ingroup bias-driven attribute substitution is that it may well discourage any engagement of System 2 at all. As mentioned above, when we are trying to interpret the actions of a stranger, System 2 does have opportunity to review substitutions offered by System 1, and does not always accept them. However, because engaging System 2 requires extra time and effort, we tend to be reluctant to use it – unless there appears to be especially good reason. When we are interacting with ingroup members, if they do or say something that is puzzling or problematic, we have a relatively high level of vested interest in working out the problem; in other words, there are good reasons to go through the effort of engaging System 2. However, one of the core characteristics of the in/outgroup dynamic is that we tend to have less sense of obligation toward outgroup members than we do toward ingroup members. When dealing with strangers we have categorized as outgroup members, it seems likely that we would be somewhat more likely to accept automatic System 1 substitutions because we would feel less obligation to invest the time and effort to engage System 2 in a more careful review of the situation.

In summary, we want students to be consciously aware of the role the ingroup/outgroup dynamic may play in intercultural encounters, not only its potential to bias judgments against the stranger but also its potential to facilitate automatic System 1 processing and discourage more deliberative System 2 processing. Learners should actively look for this factor, using an intercultural encounter checklist question like: Am I judging the stranger differently – more harshly – than I would judge a member of my own group?

7 Teaching Goals

As Teacher Li attempts to figure out the behavior of her Canadian guest, there are two reasons why it would be good for her to be consciously aware of the three factors discussed above and to understand how they might affect her interpretation process. The first is that awareness of these factors in and of itself may be helpful (Lian and Sussex 2018). There is some evidence that attribute substitution is less likely to take place when people are consciously aware of factors that may influence interpretative judgments (Kahneman and Frederick 2002), so a higher level of awareness of these factors and the role they play may be useful in managing them.

The second is that by studying these factors and gaining a better understanding of them, attention is called to the interpretation process itself, and to the need to engage System 2 more often during intercultural encounters. It is possible for System 2 to monitor judgments suggested by System 1, which it may then "endorse, correct, or override" (Kahneman and Frederick 2002, p. 51). Put another way, Teacher Li is more likely to handle the situation well if she is thinking about an encounter consciously and carefully, and making a deliberate attempt to manage the factors that are relatively likely to short-circuit the process and lead her to easy but less reliable interpretations.

For Teacher Li – and for all of us – we are more likely to attend to these factors and manage them appropriately if we have a short intercultural encounter checklist of potentially problematic factors, and develop the habit of consciously running through it when in confronted with puzzling or problematic behaviors during intercultural encounters. By way of review, the checklist questions I would suggest are as follows:

Am I judging the stranger based on the norms of my own culture?
Am I judging the stranger based on things I have previously heard about the stranger's group?
Am I judging the stranger by different rules than I would use to judge a member of my own group?

These three questions do not call attention to all of the factors that may influence our interpretive judgments when problems arise in intercultural encounters. However, they do call attention to three factors that are very likely to be at play in virtually any intercultural encounter, that have high potential to bias judgments against the stranger, and that have high potential to short-circuit the interpretation process if we don't consciously manage them and engage System 2.

8 Conclusion

As we consider how to build the intercultural communication skills of learners in Asia – and the rest of the world – we should give serious attention to the role that English language courses can and should play. As its lingua franca role grows, English is increasingly the language that is used when people from different countries and cultures interact with each other. Therefore, for learners of English, building effective intercultural communication skills is at least as important as building linguistic accuracy, if not more so. By addressing concepts such as ethnocentrism, stereotyping, and ingroup bias in English language courses, we have the opportunity to build students' awareness and understanding of the role these factors play in intercultural communication. We also have the opportunity to help students develop the habit of consciously checking for these factors when they encounter problems in intercultural encounters. Learners will be more able to fairly and effectively manage the influence of these factors if they are consciously on the lookout for them and understand how they may affect interpretive judgments made during encounters with strangers.

References

Albert, R. (1995). The intercultural sensitizer/culture assimilator as a cross-cultural training method. In S. Fowler & M. Mumford (Eds.), *Intercultural sourcebook* (Vol. 1, pp. 157–167). Yarmouth: Intercultural Press.

Apedaile, S. & Schill, L. (2008). *Critical incidents for intercultural communication: An interactive tool for developing awareness, knowledge, and skills.* Retrieved on 1 July 2017 from http://www.norquest.ca/NorquestCollege/media/pdf/centres/intercultural/Critical IncidentsBooklet.pdf.

Bar-Tel, D. (1997). Formation and change of ethnic and national stereotypes: An integrative model. *International Journal of Intercultural Relations, 21*(4), 491–523.

Brewer, M. (2003). *Intergroup relations* (2nd ed.). Buckingham: Open University Press.

Brislin, R. (1993). *Understanding culture's influence on behavior*. San Diego: Harcourt Brace.

Brislin, R., & Yoshida, T. (1994). *Intercultural communication training: An introduction*. Thousand Oaks: Sage Publications.

Chen, X. (1998). *Lujuzhe he "waiguoren": Liu Mei Zhongguo xuesheng kuawenhua renji jiaowang yanjiu (Sojourners and "foreigners": A study on Chinese students' intercultural interpersonal relationships in the United States)*. Changsha: Hunan jiaoyu chubanshe.

Chen, G. M., & Starosta, W. (1998). *Foundations of intercultural communication*. Boston: Allyn and Bacon.

Corbett, J. (2003). *An intercultural approach to English Language Teaching*. Clevedon: Multilingual Matters.

Cushner, K., & Brislin, R. (1996). *Intercultural interactions: A practical guide* (2nd ed.). Thousand Oaks: Sage Publications.

Cushner, K., & Landis, D. (1996). The intercultural sensitizer. In D. Landis & R. Bhagat (Eds.), *Handbook of intercultural training* (2nd ed., pp. 185–202). Thousand Oaks: Sage Publications.

Evans, J. (2010). *Thinking twice: Two minds in one brain*. Oxford: Oxford University Press.

Evans, J., & Stanovich, K. (2013). Dual-process theories of higher cognition: Advancing the debate. *Perspectives on Psychological Science, 8*(3), 223–241. https://doi.org/10.1177/17456912460685.

Fowler, S., & Blohm, J. (2004). An analysis of methods for intercultural training. In D. Landis, J. Bennett, & M. Bennett (Eds.), *Handbook of intercultural training* (pp. 37–84). Thousand Oaks: Sage Publications.

Gerdzinger, G. (2007). *Gut feelings: The intelligence of the unconscious*. London: Penguin.

Gladwell, M. (2007). *Blink: The power of thinking without thinking*. New York: Back Bay Books.

Gudykunst, W., & Kim, Y. Y. (1997). *Communicating with strangers* (3rd ed.). Boston: McGraw Hill.

Hall, B. (2002). *Among cultures: The challenge of communication*. Belmont: Wadsworth.

House, J. (2018). English as a global Lingua Franca: A threat to other languages, intercultural communication and translation? In A. Curtis & R. Sussex (Eds.), *Intercultural communication in Asia: Education, language and values*. Berlin: Springer Verlag.

Kahneman, D. (2011). *Thinking, fast and slow*. New York: Farrar, Straus, & Giroux.

Kahneman, D., & Frederick, S. (2002). Representativeness revisited: Attribute substitution in intuitive judgment. In T. Gilovich, D. Griffin, & D. Kahneman (Eds.), *Heuristics ad biases: The psychology of intuitive judgment* (pp. 49–81). Cambridge: Cambridge University Press.

Kecskes, I. (2018). How does intercultural communication differ from intercultural communication? In A. Curtis & R. Sussex (Eds.), *Intercultural communication in Asia: Education, language and values*. Berlin: Springer Verlag.

Lian, A., & Sussex, R. (2018). Toward a critical epistemology for learning languages and cultures in 21st century Asia. In A. Curtis & R. Sussex (Eds.), *Intercultural communication in Asia: Education, language and values*. Berlin: Springer Verlag.

Liu, S., Volčič, Z., & Gallois, C. (2011). *Introducing intercultural communication: Global cultures and contexts*. Los Angeles: Sage.

Pham, T. H. N. (2018). Confucian values as challenges for communication in intercultural workplace contexts: Evidence from Vietnamese-Anglo-cultural interactions. In A. Curtis & R. Sussex (Eds.), *Intercultural communication in Asia: Education, language and values*. Berlin: Springer Verlag.

Portnoy, F. (2012). *Wait: The art and science of delay*. New York: Public Affairs.

Scollon, R., Scollon, S., & Jones, R. (2012). *Intercultural communication: A discourse approach* (3rd ed.). Oxford: Wiley-Blackwell.

Snow, D. (2014). *Encounters with Westerners* (2nd ed.). Shanghai: Shanghai Foreign Language Education Press.

Snow, D. (2015). English teaching, intercultural competence, and critical incident exercises. Language and Intercultural Communication. DOI:https://doi.org/10.1080/14708477.2014.98 0746.

Snow, D. (2016). Affective factors and interpretive judgments in intercultural encounters. *Intercultural Communication Studies, 25*(3), 19–32.

Ting-Toomey, S. (1999). *Communicating across cultures.* New York: Guilford Press.

Triandis, H. (1994). *Culture and social behavior.* New York: McGraw Hill.

Triandis, H. (1995). *Individualism and collectivism.* Boulder: Westview Press.

Wight, A. (1995). The critical incident as a training tool. In S. Fowler & M. Mumford (Eds.), *Intercultural sourcebook* (Vol. 1, pp. 127–140). Yarmouth: Intercultural Press.

Wilson, T. (2002). *Strangers to ourselves: Discovering the adaptive unconscious.* Cambridge: Harvard University Press.

Part II
Values and Communication
in Cultural Contexts

Confucian Values as Challenges for Communication in Intercultural Workplace Contexts: Evidence from the Motivational Concerns in Vietnamese Politeness Behaviour

Thi Hong Nhung PHAM

Abstract The present chapter explores salient issues regarding Confucian values that occupy politeness behaviour of the Vietnamese in Vietnamese – Anglo-cultural interactions in intercultural contexts in Vietnam. We will present an analysis of the literature on the impact of Confucian values on Asian communication and Vietnamese politeness, broadly interpreted, and then describe the empirical data of how Confucian values have an impact on the fundamental motivational concerns underlying politeness behaviours of Vietnamese working in intercultural contexts. From the findings, relevant implications for the teaching of English as a foreign language in various Asian Confucian cultures in general and in Vietnam in particular are suggested in order to prepare English language learners better for intercultural communication contexts.

1 Introduction

Politeness has a central role in interpersonal communication and intercultural communication. The concept of politeness helps explain the way people communicate not only in one language and culture, but also between languages and cultures. Although the concept of politeness and its linguistic representation (i.e. linguistic politeness) have been extensively investigated, the literature on politeness has so far failed to present conclusive outcomes on the definition of the term.

The Western theories are language-based and have emphasized how politeness is linguistically realized. This language-based approach is also shown in the extensive discussion of rules, maxims, principles (Grice 1975; Lakoff 1990), and the concept

T. H. N. PHAM (✉)
English Department, University of Foreign Languages, Hue University, Hue, Vietnam
e-mail: n.pham@hueuni.edu.vn

© Springer International Publishing AG, part of Springer Nature 2018
A. CURTIS, R. SUSSEX (eds.), *Intercultural Communication in Asia: Education, Language and Values*, Multilingual Education 24,
https://doi.org/10.1007/978-3-319-69995-0_5

of Face (Brown and Levinson 1987), which, these researchers believe, determine politeness strategies. These theories also suggest the existence of politeness formulae (Schlund 2014), which point out factors and elements dictating politeness strategies. However, linguistic politeness is realized not only by the use of language. On the contrary, it is a complex phenomenon that extends well beyond its linguistic manifestations (Bargiela-Chiappini 2003). As Locher (2004) maintains "[p]oliteness cannot be investigated without looking in detail at the context, the speakers, the situation and the evoked norms" (p. 90) and culture is a particular salient factor influential in the enactment of politeness (Schnurr and Chan 2009, p. 132).

Research on politeness in major Asian cultures has revealed that the Western individual-oriented model of politeness, as presented in Brown and Levinson (1987), is problematic and fails to explain politeness phenomena in many major Asian cultures (Gu 1990; Ide 1989; Mao 1994; Matsumoto 1989). Substantial contributions have shown that the Asian Confucian notion of *Face* and politeness differs significantly from the conceptualization of these notions in the Western theories of politeness. These studies suggest that the heavy reliance on linguistic means, the lack of insights into culture-specific characteristics of politeness, and the overemphasis on individual wants, have all hindered the process of establishing and validating a universal model of politeness, and of testing culture-specific models of this phenomenon.

It is widely agreed that the reason for the penetration and spread of Confucianism in Vietnam is that the Vietnamese found in it an effective ideological tool to organize and manage their society (Dam 1994). Different Confucian-based expressions can be observed in the way Vietnamese behave and communicate with each other in daily life (Marr 2000). The common consensus in research on Vietnamese communication and politeness is that the Vietnamese concept of *lịch sự* 'politeness' is deeply rooted in Confucianism. Taking the position that central to communication, as a fundamental social linguistic and non-linguistic process, politeness is influenced by the philosophical foundations and value systems of the cultures in which it is found (Yum 1988), and that Confucianism is a common cultural heritage in many major Asian cultures (Chang and Holt 1994; Xiaohong and Qingyuan 2013), the present chapter explores salient issues regarding Confucian values that occupy politeness behaviour of the Vietnamese in Vietnamese – Anglo-cultural interactions in intercultural contexts in Vietnam. We will present an analysis of the literature on the impact of Confucian values on Asian communication and Vietnamese politeness, broadly interpreted, and then describe the empirical data of how Confucian values have an impact on the fundamental motivational concerns underlying politeness behaviours of Vietnamese working in intercultural contexts. From the findings, relevant implications for the teaching of English as a foreign language in various Asian Confucian cultures in general and in Vietnam in particular are suggested in order to prepare English language learners better for intercultural communication contexts.

The Confucian *Analects,* a key treatise of Confucianism believed to have been written by Confucius (551-479 BC) (Lee 2012), together with Confucianism-related materials on communication and politeness in Asian Confucian cultures, are "documentary materials" (Atkinson and Coffey 2004, p. 59), which provide the conceptual basis for our critical analysis of Vietnamese communication and politeness. The specific data for the present study consists of written documents in the form of diary-type record sheets and oral data from interviews with Vietnamese working in intercultural contexts. These provide authentic incidents of the Vietnamese motivational concerns in interactions with Anglo-culturals, i.e., those of Anglo origin, mainly Australians, British and Americans.

2   Confucian Communication

A critical analysis of the *Confucian Analects* and related recent literature on Confucianism has revealed five main characteristics of communication from the Confucian framework. These 5 characteristics are: (1) speech is consistent with virtue; (2) attitudes and actions are more important than words; (3) communication is harmony-oriented; (4) communication is based on the rule of reciprocity; and (5) language use is based on the rules of *lẽ* (propriety, rituals, and righteousness). Related literature on Vietnamese politeness has also revealed the connection between these characteristics and Vietnamese politeness (Pham 2007a).

2.1   Speech-Virtue Correspondence

The Confucian concern that speech and virtue should faithfully reflect each other is highlighted in the five principles: speech is trustworthy; speech is modest; speech is sincere, especially in expressions of emotions; one should avoid using plausible but insincere words; and one should be able to judge others' morality through their modest speech. Trustworthiness in speech is repeatedly emphasized in the *Analects* (I, 5; I, 13; I, 6; VII, 25; XV, 18),[1] because "to be trustworthy in words is close to being moral in that it enables one's words to be repeated" (I, 13). The insistence on the speech-virtue correspondence also involves talking modestly about oneself (I, 13; XV, 18; XIV, 21). Lack of modesty, in the Confucian view, shows moral deficiency (Chang 1997). The Confucian practice of speaking modestly about oneself is often referred to in the literature as the understatement of one's own success (Gao 1998), a reluctance in taking pride in one's personal achievements, a tendency to self-denial, and a preference for humble or self-effacing expressions over self-enhancing ones (Mao 1994). In Vietnamese culture, *khiêm* 'modesty', or *khiêm tốn* 'modesty and self-restraint' has become one of the most important virtues that a

---

[1] The Confucian *Analects* consists of 26 chapter-length books. Each book consists of a number of Confucius' teachings. The book is referred to by the Roman numerical system and the specific teaching by the Arabic system. For example, "I, 13" refers to the teaching documented in Section 13 of Book I.

Vietnamese should acquire, and is taught to young children of school age. The emphasis on the correspondence between speech and virtue leads to the Confucian avoidance of plausible but insincere words, because "plausible [but insincere] words confound virtue" (XV, 26). Over-elaborate expressions are immoral, and hence shameful (V, 25; XV, 24).

The Confucian-based concern for the speech-virtue correspondence requires the Vietnamese to be sincere in their expressions of emotions. The Confucian concern for sincere speech is shown in the avoidance of insincere expressions when they do not reflect the speaker's true feelings and emotions. The linguistic use of politeness in conformity with this line of thinking is seen in expressions of invitations, compliments and apologies. In contrast to Americans' extensive use of compliments, especially compliments containing strong positive adjectives and many superlatives such as "superb", "brilliant" or "fantastic", the Vietnamese pay compliments much less frequently, and use less extreme adjectives like "nice" or "good" (Pham 2014).

2.2 Attitudes and Actions Being More Important Than Words

The Confucian concern for attitudes and actions is shown in three main characteristics of communication: one's internal sincere attitude is more important than one's speech; one should do what one says; and one should be hesitant in speech. What people say about a matter is not as important as their sincere attitudes toward it. Having internally appropriate attitudes suffices, regardless of whether the attitude is verbalized or not. This explains why Vietnamese in particular, are uncomfortable with foreigners' excessive use of thanks and apologies (Nguyen 1990). They tend to thank only when they genuinely acknowledge the hearer's debt to them, and to apologize only when they believe that an apology is specifically required. As a result, they tend to feel that their Anglo-cultural counterparts are hypocritical when thanking and apologizing frequently, whereas the English speakers complain about Asians' coldness and rudeness in not thanking warmly and not apologizing often enough. Even when the Vietnamese do acknowledge the hearer's help or support, they do not tend to verbalize it as frequently as their Anglo-cultural counterparts. To the Vietnamese, what matters more is their internal attitudes and reflections (e.g. the sense of gratitude).

This emphasis on the speech-action correspondence, (i.e., the match between one's speech and one's actions) is central to Confucianism: "The gentleman is ashamed of his word outstripping his deed" (XIV, 27). The significance of action is indicated in Confucius' teachings about giving and taking advice. It is easy to give good and persuasive advice. However, the advice is meaningful only when the person to whom the advice is directed acts on it (IX, 23). In other words, the act of applying the advice to the reality makes the offering of the advice meaningful: only when one "brings words to completion" and does what one says, are one's words valued (XV, 18). Confucius' appreciation of action is also indicated in his emphasis on hesitancy in speech. First, action is given priority over speech. One should, therefore, take action before one makes claims about it. The attention paid to being "halting in speech but quick in action" (IV, 24) is also due to the belief that it is not always easy to live up to one's claims (XIV, 21). Accordingly, if people do not want to feel ashamed when they cannot live up to what they say (XIV, 27), they should be hesitant in their speech. What can be inferred from these teachings is that actions are more important than words, and that Confucius emphasizes that we should ensure that our words are consistent with our behaviour. The Confucian concern for speech-action correspondence is also seen in the Vietnamese insistence on the hearer's acceptance of the offer/ benefit to the point where this can be interpreted as an imposition. Pham (2007a) has illustrated this type of imposition in the Vietnamese act of food/drink serving, inviting, and offering, where the host tries to realize *his/her* politeness by insistence on the guest's acceptance of the invitation or offer. Similar Confucian-derived practice is also observed in Chinese (Mao 1994) and Korean cultures (Yu 2003).

2.3   Harmony-Oriented Communication

Central to Confucianism is social harmony and face, which should always be maintained in relationships (Chang 1997). The concern for mutual harmony and face, which functions as a guide for social conduct and helps shape people's behaviour and harmony, is maintained when face is respected. The concern for harmony and face is reflected in Confucian communication through the mastery of emotions, the preference for an indirect communication style, the preference for responsiveness rather than assertiveness, and the avoidance of conflict and confrontation (Pham 2007b). In Vietnamese politeness, the orientation toward harmony and face is unambiguously expressed in the notion of *quan hệ* 'relationship', which is derived from the Confucian concept of *guanxi* in Chinese. Semantically, *quan hệ* (lit., bi-lateral relation) emphasizes the balanced co-existence of two sides in a relationship. *Giữ quan hệ* and *thể diện* 'maintaining/keeping *relationship* and *face*' is an important task in Vietnamese social interactions. A Vietnamese person's life is said to be bound in different *quan hệ*, from blood ties to social relationships. This is seen both in traditional Vietnamese communities and in modern social practice (Marr 2000).

The Vietnamese concern for mutual harmony and face is also reflected in their elusive and ambiguous use of "yes" and "no" (Katalanos 1994). The following example from Katalanos' (1994) study illustrates the transfer of this type of language use in the mother tongue into the intercultural context (the text in square brackets explains the communicative intention):

Physician's assistant	"Did you take your medicine?"
Vietnamese patient	"Yes [I hear you]. No [I did not take it]."
Physician's assistant	"You did not take your medicine?"
Vietnamese patient	"Yes [I hear you]. Yes [I did not take it. The medicine is too strong]."
Physician's assistant	"Ah, so you did not take it!"
Vietnamese patient	"Yes. No." (Katalanos 1994, p. 31)

In this example "yes" is used to mean "I hear you", "I understand what you say", or "I am attending to you and what you are saying", and also "I agree with your saying that I did not take the medicine". A similar use of "yes" is also found in other Confucian cultures such as Chinese (Lii-Shih 1994) and Korean, where Park and Kim (1992) claim that the use of "yes" is to avoid being negative and disruptive to interpersonal harmony, and to maintain face, rather than to express the speaker's explicit confirmation of what is being asked.

Confucian politeness shows one's consideration for others in communication. This consideration is expressed in one's sensitivity to the other's feelings which can lead to speech modifications in order to avoid hurting another's feelings in a relationship (Vu 1997). The alteration of one's speech as a result of one's concern for others' feelings does not necessarily mean that Confucianism encourages lying. Nevertheless, there is a tendency to water down the truth in order to preserve good mutual feelings of communication (Robinson 2003). This can be seen in extract 7 below.

2.4 Communication by the Rule of Reciprocity

The Confucian orientation towards the hearer in communication is well represented in the rule of reciprocity. By the rule of reciprocity, which is considered to be among important Confucian ethics (King 1985), Confucius emphasizes the practice of using oneself as a measure in gauging the wishes of others. In Confucius' view, one word that can guide people's conduct through their life is reciprocity (XV, 24). With the emphasis on feelings and emotions, the practice of putting oneself in the other's situation reflects the Confucian sensitivity toward the hearer. The Confucian empathetic capacity to put oneself in the other's position also involves the anticipation of others' feelings and their possible reactions in communication. This is consistent with the Vietnamese anticipation of others' feelings and their possible reactions, as expressed in 'suy bụng ta ra bụng người' (lit. Guessing others' minds based on our mind). It is also present in the common concept of "anticipatory communication" (Lebra 1976, p. 123) expressed in kan in Japanese, noon-chi in Korean (Lim 2002), and pao in Chinese (Chang and Holt 1994). Markus and Kitayama (1991) argue that this anticipatory communication is clearly indicated in the Japanese practice of serving food or drink to the guest. A likely Japanese response to the question "Hey, Tomio, what do you want?" would be a short moment of bewilderment and a noncommittal utterance such as "I don't know". Under the assumptions of the anticipatory communication approach, it is the host's responsibility to be able to "read" the guest's mind and offer what the guest perceives to be appropriate (Markus and Kitayama 1991). One also tends to alter the way one speaks as a result of one's anticipation of others' feelings and possible reactions.

2.5 Language Use Conforming to the Rules of lễ (Righteousness)

As the moral order of human beings reflects the natural order of the cosmos, the Confucian concept of *li* as expressed in the Vietnamese notion of *lễ,* therefore, regulates ethical relations in society, and maintains differentiations among people. Central to *li* is the emphasis on social hierarchy, ritual practices, and conformity to social rules (Vu 1997). As a result, *li* is often translated into English as rituals, ceremony, appropriateness, righteousness, and propriety. The impact of *li* on East Asian language behaviour can be observed in the following aspects: ritual communication, differentiated and respectful speech, and role-directed communication.

Li, translated as "rituals", emphasizes the rites of speech (i.e., patterned familiarized discourse). In order to speak appropriately, people are expected to follow the rituals of speech. Appropriate speech is speech directed properly to a specific person in a specific situation at a specific time, and it involves suitable ritualized language forms. Ritualized discourse is seen in Confucius' teaching of how to receive, entertain, and to bid farewell to one's guests. When receiving guests, one must not appear reluctant or to be holding back; and when the guests leave one must wait at the doorstep until the guests are out of sight and no longer looking back (X, 3). Similarly, the ritualized discourse of offer-decline-offer-decline-offer-acceptance of giving and receiving gifts or invitations is widely practised in many Confucian cultures (Lim 2002). It reflects the Confucian ritual process of communication in which major phases of the conversation are prescribed from the moment one enters a conversation to the time one finishes it. The failure to follow this prescribed process of communication breaches the rule of *li/lễ,* and hence invokes social sanctions.

Confucian communication in general, and Vietnamese politeness in particular, require role mastery. Because the practice of communication in the rule of *lễ* must respond to the hierarchical nature of social structures, politeness as a central part of communication should also address this nature. People are different in terms of their role(s), and their role(s) differ across situations, so that the amount and kind of politeness manifested to them by others, and by them to others, also differs accordingly. Role mastery requires that one should successfully know one's roles and others' in a specific situation, and converse in accordance with those roles. This entails that people should be polite as dictated by their role(s). The Vietnamese polite way of saying "feel at home" to their guest, *đừng làm khách* with its literal meaning as "don't be a guest", reflects their perception of the role of a guest as an out-group member in interpersonal communication. "Don't be a guest", meaning "you don't have to act like a guest, please feel at home", is polite in the sense that one is extending one's in-group membership to others. On the one hand, "don't be a guest" expresses the host's acknowledgement of the different roles and hence different rights s/he and his/her guest have in interaction. On the other hand, it indicates the permission for the guest to override the conventional rule of guest behaviour, to act in a more comfortable way. Likewise, the practice of asking about another's age and job in Korean, Chinese, and Vietnamese cultures, at the very beginning of a conversation, is the first step in getting to know someone's role, to make clear who a person is and how s/he fits into one's overall framework of society, and hence how s/he should be appropriately addressed. In other words, people's perception of their role(s) and those of others' helps decide their language use of politeness. A failure to recognize one's role(s) prevents one from using suitable linguistic forms to convey politeness.

The Confucian insistence on social hierarchy is manifested in its focus on five main hierarchical relationships, and its code of ethics for each relationship. An examination of the Confucian codes of ethics (originally *wu* [five] *lun* [ethic]) shows that the most salient characteristic in interpersonal relationships is hierarchical power (i.e., one always has more power than the other in a relationship, except for friendship). In the five codes of ethics, subjects are loyal to the king, children are obedient and filial to their parents, wives are dutiful to their husbands, the younger are obedient to the older, and friends are faithful to each other (Cheng 1990). What all of these relationships share is the power of one person over another in each relationship, where the request or expectation from the one with more power becomes a command to the other, who serves the former unconditionally and dutifully. Research has also provided evidence to suggest that power is the most powerful factor in deciding the language use of politeness, at least in Confucian cultures (e.g., Scollon and Scollon 1995).

2.6   The Study

Based on the understanding about the impact of Confucian values on Asian communication and Vietnamese politeness, we now present the empirical evidence of how such an understanding can help us better comprehend the fundamental motivational concerns for politeness behaviour of Vietnamese people working in intercultural contexts. Incidents described as noticeable are provided by 24 Vietnamese speakers of English who work full-time with native speakers of English (specifically British, Americans and Australians) in various offices of non-government-organizations' (NGO) foreign-funded projects in Vietnam. They comprised 15 males and 9 females, aged from 28 to 46 and each had at least 5 years of work experience at the time of the study. They are in different positions in their jobs, ranging from secretary, officer and consultant to programme/project coordinator or director. As a requirement of their jobs, they must be able to use English to communicate competently.

A diary-type record sheet adapted from Spencer-Oatey (2002) was used to collect the most noticeable events to explore the Vietnamese motivational concerns underlying the Vietnamese politeness behaviour in their interaction with Anglo-culturals. Each participant was asked to complete at least two record sheets, one to describe the most noticeable event with a particularly negative effect, explicitly explained as interactions with Anglo-cultural native speakers of English that made him/her feel particularly annoyed, insulted, embarrassed and/or humiliated; and the other to record the most noticeable event with a particularly positive effect, explicitly explained as interactions that made him/her feel particularly happy, proud and/or satisfied. As a popular means of generating information in research dealing with personal experiences and perspectives (Holstein and Gubrium 2004), interviews in this study are used to explore further the fundamental concerns of Vietnamese politeness behaviour in the incidents reported. After the data collection process was completed, 135 incidents were collected via the record sheet instrument, and 69 more were elicited during the follow-up interviews, which resulted in a total of 204 incidents reported in Vietnamese. Of these, 3 did not involve direct interactions with Anglo-culturals, but rather the participants' feelings about their Anglo-cultural counterparts' general behaviour, and so they were discarded. This left 201 incidents for analysis. Taking the position that Confucian face may not be the same as face in Brown and Levinson's (1987) politeness model (Haugh and Hinze 2003), and that politeness is not just driven by the need to protect one's face (Hinze 2012), the incidents collected were analysed following Spencer-Oatey's (2002) framework of concerns. These are the concern for *Face*, the concern for *Equity*, and the concern for the *Association Principle*.

In Spencer-Oatey's framework, *Face* has two interrelated aspects:

1. *Quality Face*, referring to peoples' desire to be evaluated positively in terms of their personal qualities like competence, abilities and appearance.
2. *Social Identity Face*, referring to the desire for people to acknowledge and uphold our social identities or roles, e.g., group leader, valued customer, close friend.

We added the concern for *Between-Group Face* to the original list in order to better capture the Vietnamese sense of the cultural and/or ethnic difference between them and their Anglo-cultural counterparts, and hence their sense of their national/ethnic face in intercultural communication. This is the sense of country face as seen in extracts 4 and 5 below.

The concern for *Equity* consists of:

1. *Cost-Benefit considerations*, which refer to people's concerns that they should not be exploited or disadvantaged. That is why a "costly" request (e.g. borrowing money) should be worded in a different (i.e., more polite) way compared with a less costly request.
2. *Fairness and Reciprocity*, which refers to people's concern that cost-benefit should be fair and kept thoroughly in balance. For instance, a favour should be reciprocated.
3. *Autonomy-Control*, which refers to people's concern that they should have full freedom in their actions and should not unduly controlled or imposed upon. For example, in the workplace the boss should only make "work-related" demands on employees.

The *Association Principle* is comprised of three components:

1. *Involvement*, the concern that one should have appropriate amounts and types of activity involvement with other people. For instance, colleagues should socialize with each other apart from work matters (e.g., visiting or telephoning each other socially on a regular basis).
2. *Empathy*, referring to the concern that people should share appropriate interests, feelings and concerns with others. For example, existing staff should show concern for new staff, or the boss should show concern for subordinates.
3. *Respect*, referring to the concern that people should show appropriate respect for each other. For instance, younger people should pay respect to elders.

3   Findings

An examination of the total data set demonstrates that 79 out of the total of 201 incidents contain events which relate to two or more codes of concerns. There are 168 identified by the participants as negative incidents and 33 as positive incidents. The participants' typical comment was that generally they had many favourable impressions of their Anglo-cultural counterparts' behaviour, but they found it harder to recall positive incidents than negative ones. Similarly, many more frequent negative incidents than positive ones were reported in Spencer-Oatey's (2002) research. This confirms that politeness is more noticed in its absence (i.e., politeness is anticipated) (Haugh 2003) and/or when it is different from what is expected.

3.1   Dominant Concern for Association Rights

The incident data reveal that among the three groups of concern for *Face*, *Equity Rights* and *Association Rights*, it is *Association Rights* that are the most dominant driver in Vietnamese politeness in Vietnamese-Anglo-cultural interaction. This is in line with the Confucian-based interdependent self, which is oriented toward harmony and solidarity with the group. The concern for *Empathy*, i.e., for showing concern and sympathy with other people, prevails most strongly not only within the group of *Association Rights* concerns, but also across the nine sub-concerns investigated. As seen in the following case, the Vietnamese expression of consideration for others may cause some misunderstanding in intercultural communication:

> *Extract 1*: The Vietnamese participant's gender: male; age range: 31–40; the nationality, gender, and age[2] of the Anglo-cultural compared with the Vietnamese: Australian, male, older).
>
> I used to get on well with my former boss but because of his inflexible viewpoints our good relationships did not last long. Once on the way to a village for a fieldtrip, while we [I, my Anglo-cultural boss and the driver] were talking about woman and child things, I suggested that he should get married. He was my older brother's age, 42. In Vietnam men at that age will worry their parents if they are not married yet. Generally, I was suggesting in a friendly way because I was concerned about him, who I considered my brother. I said my brother was of his age but already had two children. He said he was too independent to get married. I asked him why he did not try because if he did not try how he could know he was not suitable for family life. However, he did not seem to take my advice seriously [...] he just laughed. I was hurt and felt a loss of face in front of the driver. Everybody knew that we were close, so I was just caring about him but he did not appreciate that. I think, for Anglo-cultural colleagues we [the Vietnamese staff] should not be too close to them or one day we will be hurt.

Apart from the concern for *Social Role Face,* the motive behind the act of the subject's strong suggestion about the Australian personal life is his concern for the Australian, whom he considered a virtual family member. As seen from the incident

---

[2] As described in the record sheet by the Vietnamese participants.

described above, the Vietnamese insisted on the Australian acceptance of his suggestion that the Australian should get married, which was meant to be understood as an expression of care, concern, closeness, and hence politeness. The case of his brother was even quoted by the subject in order to persuade the Australian with whom he was interacting: "I said my brother was of his age but already had two children". However, from the Anglo-cultural perspective, such an act is probably viewed as impolite in the sense that it directly interferes with one's wish to have full freedom in one's personal life (Brown and Levinson 1987), and so the Australian in this situation might have taken his Vietnamese colleague's comment as a criticism.

The consideration of association-driven incidents has shown that, influenced by the Confucian emphasis on the emotional exchange in interpersonal interaction, Vietnamese have a high tendency to value the need to associate with others over the need to save time. In the following example, two *Association Rights* sub-concerns were identified:

> *Extract 2*: The Vietnamese participant's gender: male; age range: 41–50; the nationality, gender, and age of the Anglo-cultural compared with the Vietnamese: American, male, about same age.
>
> I and Mr. A [American] used to work in the same office and we got on well with each other then. After that I was transferred to another section of the project. I was appointed to be in charge of district level and therefore, for quite a long time we did not see each other. We just talked on the phone or emailed each other since he works in the main office in the city centre and I am based in the district office. Just last week I had to work with some staff of the main office so I dropped by his office to say hello. […] When I came in he seemed to be glad and we asked about each other's things such as work and family. I felt very good catching up with him after such a long time. However, while we were talking he suddenly said he had an appointment in 10 minutes and then had to look at some related documents before that. Therefore, I said goodbye and left his office. I came to see the [Vietnamese] secretary of the programme to say hello since we did not meet for a long time too. About 20 minutes later on my way out of the building I passed his office again and accidentally saw him working alone with a cup of coffee or tea on his desk. Obviously there was nobody there. I was hurt. I dropped by just to see how he was. We were close friends and I was just caring about him [that was why I came to talk to him and to see how he was] and clearly he did not have any appointment but he values working time more highly than my consideration for him. It was very frustrating.

First, the motive for the Vietnamese paying a visit to his American colleague was that he was concerned about the American after a long period when they had not met (i.e., *Empathy*), and he expected a similar concern in return. The second concern underlying the subject's judgment of the American early withdrawal from the talk with the Vietnamese is that people should take part in an activity with other people (i.e., *Involvement*). The main Vietnamese criticism in this case is that the American involved in interaction with him valued working time over the need to associate and to share feelings with other people. As Pham (2007a) points out, Vietnamese hold quite different views about the concept of time from that of Anglo cultures, and this can cause misunderstandings in intercultural communication. Specifically, most Anglo-culturals consider time as a scarce and valuable commodity (Lakoff and Johnson 1980). Once time passes, we lose it. Consequently, from an Anglo-cultural viewpoint, timetables, work schedules and plans are very important, and it is essential to do things "as planned". In contrast, Vietnamese have a more relationship-oriented view of time in which time does not necessarily never return, and can be described as a multi-directional concept, as seen in *ngày rộng tháng dài* (lit., days wide year long) and *ngày tháng thênh thang* (lit., time spacious), implying time can be multi-dimensional and return.

In extreme cases, the high level of concern for showing consideration (i.e., *Empathy*) and *Involvement* with others over the concern for time loss can even cause serious misunderstandings in interactions with Anglo-culturals:

> *Extract 3*: The Vietnamese participant's gender: female; age range: 31–40; the nationality, gender, and age of the Anglo-cultural compared with the Vietnamese: Australian, male, older.
>
> [...] my [Anglo-cultural] boss asked me to work over time. I was not well at that time so at first I was unwilling to do extra work apart from what I was assigned to do. However, finally I accepted his request because of my sense of responsibility and concern for work. Nevertheless, when that period [of working over time] finished, instead of thanking me and appreciating my cooperation, my boss came to my room asking me if I would like to take money [for working over time] or have some days off. I was shocked. I knew that he was fair to me and wanted to compensate for the time I lost but he was too inconsiderate of the emotional aspects ["cái tình"] of my being devoted to my job. I burst into tears and came back to my room. After that he sent the money into my account and said that he did not mean to embarrass or insult me and that was what he would do in his [Anglo-cultural] culture. [...] I just wanted him to understand that I did not work over time for that money. I lived enough on my salary and at the beginning I did tell him that working overtime would not be my preference since I was not in good health. Therefore, he should not and could not think that money could be compared with my responsibility for my job and my devotion in it. Money cannot buy my effort and the sacrifice of my health for work. He should at first be caring about my health and should acknowledge my good will and responsibility instead of paying me some money and getting away with that.

The description cited suggests that the Vietnamese act of accepting the Australian request to work overtime is driven by the need to be involved in and to share activities, as required by the group (i.e., *Involvement*). The Vietnamese criticism of the Australian act of directly offering payment, in addition, reveals her concern for *Quality Face* ("He should [...] acknowledge my good will and responsibility [for work]" and "I did not work over time for money") and the concern for showing consideration for the other interactions (i.e., *Empathy* concern), when the Vietnamese expects her Australian boss to be considerate of her well-being. The Australian offer of extra money as compensation for the time lost can be seen as a consequence of his views of fairness and of time as a valuable commodity for which one should be compensated (or paid, in this case) for the time one has spent in an activity. O'Hara-Devereaux and Johansen (1994) recommend that in intercultural communication contexts, teams from diverse cultures should put money into face-to-face interaction early on to establish trust as Western emphasis on individual initiative, contribution, and rewards. However, as inferred from the interpretation of the Vietnamese in the incident, it is not considerate, and hence not polite, just to pay somebody for their work, since underlying one's work is one's responsibility and good will and even sacrifices (e.g., health risk). This interpretation is closely connected to the Confucian-based concept of *tình người* or *nhân/ân tình* (compassion) in Vietnamese, which originates from the Chinese concept of *renqing* referring to emotional debt (Hwang 1987), where one can completely pay a debt materially but one can never fully return it emotionally. Specifically, in the incident cited, one's contribution, support and favours cannot be compensated with money; rather the expression of the Australian consideration for the Vietnamese well-being during the period she worked overtime would be more appreciated than a direct offer of money for compensation. Either or both the Australian unawareness of the Vietnamese concern for *Association Rights* in interaction, or the Vietnamese ignorance of Australian view of time values, in this case, may damage their interpersonal relationship.

3.2   Concern for Different Aspects of Face

A scrutiny of incidents which were identified as being motivated by concerns for different aspects of *Face* has revealed major tendencies in Vietnamese behaviour which is influenced by *Face* attendance. The emphasis on attending to face contributes to the fact that Vietnamese often give information which is irrelevant when compared to Anglo norm, as seen below:

Extract 4: The Vietnamese participant's gender: male; age range: 31–40; the nationality, gender, and age of the Anglo-cultural compared with the Vietnamese: American, male, older.

This American man from the provincial US-Vietnam bridging project came to ask me for some statistics about victims of bombs and mines who are being covered by the government healthcare policy. I tried to be helpful and gave him all information I thought was useful to him. One of the important pieces of information he wanted was how the criteria for the victim of a bomb and mine were set up. That type of information is beyond my knowledge since normally the ministry of health decides the policy and we are to carry it out. It sounds a bit bureaucratic but I don't want him to think about our [Vietnamese] government that way. However, although I could not say exactly how the criteria were set up, I did provide him with the content of the criteria in detail since I thought they might be helpful to him. We had a very interesting talk too. [...] Later on my boss said in his [the American colleague's] feedback to him [my boss] he said, the information I gave him was not relevant and he could not get all of the information he wanted. I was disappointed.

From the description above it could be imagined that when asked how the criteria were set up, the Vietnamese did not want to say either (a) "I don't know." or (b) "The Ministry of Health dictated the policy". In (a), to the Vietnamese involved in the encounter above, saying "I don't know" might reveal his ignorance, and so his lack of competence/expertise in the field could damage his *Quality Face* accordingly. However, this concern is not explicitly expressed in his description, so it was not coded as concern for *Quality Face*. In (b), saying "The Ministry of Health dictates the policy" in his view may threaten the positive image of the Vietnamese government in the eyes of the American. As a result of his consideration for this collective aspect of *Face*, i.e., the *Between-Group Face*, the subject did neither (a) nor (b). Instead he gave details about the content of the criteria as a way of compensating for his not giving direct information in response to the question raised. An observer of this interaction could infer that the information given was related but not relevant to the question asked. By responding to the question in that way, the Vietnamese still could both "appear to answer" the question and save face. This face-driven practice of "answering X-related to X question" violates Grice's Relevance Maxim (i.e. the information provided is not relevant to the question asked), which requires that the interlocutor gives relevant and logical information in interaction.

The Vietnamese concern for *Face* can also lead to their decision to offer part of the information requested rather than complete information:

Extract 5: The Vietnamese participant's gender: male; age range: 31–40; the nationality, gender, and age of the Anglo-cultural compared with the Vietnamese: British, male, about same age.

I had an appointment with an English project maker, who has helped us write many good proposals. Before we met, as usual he sent [me] the main questions that he wanted me to answer. When we met I did go through all of the questions with him. Among his supplementary questions there was one question which for some reason I think was quite sensitive from the Vietnamese administrative point of view and might be unbeneficial to the [Vietnamese] collective image, so I did not give him all of the information I had. However, when I had just finished he raised the unanswered question again but expressed it differently to suggest that [he thought] I would not recognize that the question was asked before and would give him the information he wanted. He should have understood that when I do not answer a question that means I do it deliberately and that there are some reasons for me not to answer the question. However, in this case my role did not seem to count to him. He was rude and I felt my face was not respected.

The Vietnamese reluctance to give a full answer to the supplementary question from the English counterpart was meant to be considered as an expression of face concern, specifically *Role Face* and also *Between-Group Face* consideration. The message is "in my role, I am the one to decide which of your questions I will answer and which part of the information should be given to you". The act of holding back some "sensitive information from the Vietnamese point of view" indicates the Vietnamese concern at the possible negative consequences (e.g., a negative judgment by the English colleague on the Vietnamese administration of the project) which can arise from the release of the information. The English person's paraphrasing of the question was viewed as a challenge to the *Social Role Face* of the Vietnamese in the incident above.

In contrast, in the following situation, the Vietnamese tend to give more information than is required as a result of concern for their *Quality Face*:

Extract 6: The Vietnamese participant's gender: male; age range: 31–40; the nationality, gender, and age of the Anglo-cultural compared with the Vietnamese: American, male, older.

When my [American] boss just started to take over his present job we [supporting staff] had a general meeting to welcome him and to give him a brief idea about what was going on in the programme. The next day we [the Vietnamese head of each section of the project] each had a separate meeting with him to report to him the current situation of the section we are in charge of. When my turn came I told him a bit more detail to provide him with some background knowledge about the project and the staff who are directly involved in the project I was in charge of. [...] However, he was not very polite. He impatiently interrupted me and asked me to talk briefly. I felt hurt. I knew that Anglo-culturals are frank and direct. Having been working with them for years, I am also straightforward and do not often beat about the bush. I have been rated as a competent employee with many years of working experience. As a group leader, I knew my staff well and given that he was a newcomer, I was just concerned that he may not know who [among the project staff] was good at what, so I took time to explain things to him enthusiastically, but he was very impatient and jumped to a conclusion too quickly.

The interaction visualized from the description above was: the American boss asked about the project; the Vietnamese gave information about the project and the staff members' competence. The additional information about the staff members offered by the Vietnamese was meant to provide the American new-comer with general knowledge about the weaker and stronger points of staff members, but the underlying message is that, as a group leader, the Vietnamese wanted to show that he knew the staff members very well and that he was a committed person. The implied message "I know more than I am required to know" is meant to enhance the *Face* of the Vietnamese. Although the subject did mention his role when reporting the incident ("as a group leader"), the follow-up interview data do not show his concern for *Social Role Face*. The motivation behind the act of volunteering extra information is a result of the Vietnamese attendance to the expression of his quality and/or work competence, i.e., his *Quality Face* towards his Anglo-cultural new boss. In other words, the concern for *Face* is one of the motivational forces that can make the Vietnamese either hold back part of the information requested, or offer more information than needed. In both cases, he violated Grice's Quantity Maxim, which requires interlocutors to give no more and no less information than requested.

Data analysis also shows a prevalence of *Face* attendance over truth, i.e., the Vietnamese concern for *Face* can lead them to lie and/or give incorrect information.

Extract 7: The Vietnamese participant's gender: male; age range: 41–50; the nationality, gender, and age of the Anglo-cultural compared with the Vietnamese: American, male, older.

As a Vietnamese planning advisor of the programme I am always busy with too many things to do. What I dislike about my Anglo-cultural counterparts is they always try to get information they want at any price regardless of whether the person they are working with is ready to answer or not. The other day in a bilateral meeting [Vietnamese and Anglo-cultural sides in an ODA {official development assistance} project], they asked me certain questions about the plan to support our new project from the administrative [office] of the province. […] as a co-leader of the programme I always have heavy workload. All questions take time if they are meant to get answered properly. That is why we often ask them to send us the questions in advance. However, they just do not always understand and sympathize with us. Last week, during our meeting Mr. E [the Anglo-cultural representative of the sponsor in the project] asked me for estimated time for the implementation of X&Y project. That type of question […] is not easy to answer. However, you cannot not answer, since they [Anglo-culturals] ask you officially in the meeting with the presence of many people, and they are all waiting for your answer. […] Anglo-culturals, they always get what they want [when they want it]. I told them that I was not quite sure yet but it may take about 3 months. They said that they wanted to see our detailed proposal. However, after that when I worked thoroughly with my [Vietnamese] staff we [I and my Vietnamese colleagues] all thought it must be 5 months at least since it consists of many phases. Just yesterday we [I and my Vietnamese colleagues] got the feedback from them [Anglo-culturals] which says that our plan is not convincing enough and they do not see why the time to implement the

project must be prolonged 2 months longer than initially suggested. [...] They must understand that when I said 3 months I did also say I was not quite sure yet so I did not quite mean
3 months. There are situations when you cannot not answer although you are not so sure.
As a planning advisor, I would have no face left if I did not answer. I know that the shorter
the time to implement a project the better it is since it saves us budget and labour but [...]
Now we have to prepare another proposal. They [Anglo-culturals] just don't understand.

Contrary to Tsui's (1991) statement that the Anglo-cultural motivation for uttering the English "I don't know" is often to save face of self and other, the extract
above shows the Vietnamese view that saying "I don't know exactly how much time
the project may take yet" can suggest to the Anglo-culturals a lack of competence in
the workplace, and hence may damage the *Quality Face* of the speaker accordingly.
This consideration for *Face* and the awareness of others' expectation, as shown in
"and they are all waiting for your answer", prompted the Vietnamese to make a
statement of the estimated time of the project which was outside his knowledge. The
clear difference between this estimated time (i.e., 3 months) and the actual feasible
time for the implementation of the project (i.e., 5 months) shows that the Vietnamese's
claim of the estimated time in the meeting was not based on serious previous considerations or specific plans for future; rather it was provided simply for the protection
of the speaker's *Face*. In his research on intercultural workplace contexts, Clyne
(1996) has a similar observation: to the Chinese and Vietnamese, it is important to
express a commitment linguistically if it appears that others expect or desire it, and
that contrary to the European (including Anglo) cultures, where as a requirement of
being polite, the commissive and future action are meshed and combined, South-
East Asian "politeness is determined not so much by the future action to which a
commitment has been made but rather by the commissive" (p. 191). This is clearly
expressed in the subject's interpretation of his act of providing information beyond
certainty: "That type of question [...] is not easy to answer. However, you cannot not
answer, since they [Anglo-culturals] ask you officially in the meeting with the presence of many people, and they are all waiting for your answer"; and "They must
understand that when I said 3 months I did also say I was not quite sure yet so I did
not quite mean 3 months. There are situations when you cannot not answer though
you are not so sure". In other words, the concern for *Face* protection and the awareness that others are expecting his answer compelled the Vietnamese to provide information outside his knowledge. Whether the X&Y project could be completely
implemented within 3 months or not is not as important as the protection of the *Face*
of the speaker. The subject's claim of the estimated time of the implementation of
the project was not meant to be understood as a commitment that the project would
be implemented within 3 months. Additionally, the presence of other people who
were not asking the question, but official members of the meeting, also had an
impact on the Vietnamese decision to provide incorrect information. As analysed
above, the data of actual experiences of Vietnamese participants with Anglo-culturals
has revealed that concern for *Face* is one of the fundamental motivational forces for
Vietnamese violating Grice's Relevance, Quantity and Quality Maxims.

Our analysis has shown that, on the one hand, insights into Confucian values help
us understand more clearly Vietnamese politeness behaviour in intercultural

communication. On the other hand, it provides evidence that, as an ancient philosophy, Confucian values can bring new challenges to intercultural communication, where they can cause misunderstandings, frustrations and even communication breakdowns in Vietnamese – Anglo-cultural interactions. While language proficiency plays an important role in intercultural communication (Peltokorpia and Clausen 2010), cultural values such as Confucian values should be taken into account to better understand the politeness behaviour of those coming from Asian Confucian contexts.

4 Implications for English Language Education

The analysis and data of Vietnamese – Anglo-cultural interactions presented in this chapter have shown that even when they use the same language code to communicate, people in different cultures may not necessarily be oriented towards exactly the same values. If they are, these values may still prevail to different degrees in different cultures and within different people. Differences either in cultural values or in their levels of dominance may shape expectations and beliefs with which they enter intercultural communication contexts, make judgments and evaluation of the behavior of those they communicate with, and shape their own behaviour. In intercultural contexts where the interlocutors cannot always rely on common ground and shared knowledge (Kecskes 2017) and when the culture-driven expectations are not met, these discrepancies may cause misunderstandings and even conflicts, prejudices, and frustrations. Foreign language education therefore, should raise learners' awareness of this possible source of misunderstandings in intercultural communication. The language teacher needs to teach learners to be good observers of culture and familiar with common cultural scripts. They need to be given examples of language use which indicate that language competence alone cannot guarantee the effect of communication. Similarly, Anglo-culturals who are going to enter communication with those of Asian Confucian cultures need to be aware of the common values influential to Confucian communication.

Among various activities, noticeable authentic incidents as collected and described above should be used as engaging stimulus for classroom discussions on intercultural communication so as to better prepare language learners for intercultural encounters. Providing scenarios where different factors including cultural differences can be useful in explaining possible misunderstandings, frustrations or communication breakdowns creates opportunities for language learners to put themselves in the position of the people involved and use their own experience and knowledge of both home culture and of the intermediate culture (i.e. the culture of the person described in the scenario) to make sense of the situation. As such it helps them understand how people using the same language involved in communication may own different culture-driven expectations and have these expectations shape their way of judging others and of behaving towards others. This understanding will then develop their tolerance and acceptance for cultural differences, and prepare them better for challenges in intercultural communication.

References

Atkinson, P., & Coffey, A. (2004). Analysing documentary realities. In D. Silverman (Ed.), *Qualitative research: Theory, method and practice* (2nd ed., pp. 56–75). London: Sage Publications.

Bargiela-Chiappini, F. (2003). Face and politeness: New (insights) for old (concepts). *Journal of Pragmatics, 35*, 1453–1469.

Brown, P., & Levinson, S. (1987). *Politeness: Some universals in language usage.* Cambridge: Cambridge University Press.

Chang, H.-C. (1997). Language and words: Communication in the analects of Confucius. *Journal of Language and Social Psychology, 16*(2), 107–131.

Chang, H.-C., & Holt, G. R. (1994). Debt-repaying mechanism in Chinese relationships: An exploration of the folk concepts of *pao* and human emotional debt. *Research on Language and Social Interaction, 27*(4), 187–351.

Cheng, S. (1990). Understanding the culture and behaviour of East Asians – A Confucian perspective. *Australian and New Zealand Journal of Psychiatry, 24*(4), 510–515.

Clyne, M. (1996). *Inter-cultural communication at work: Cultural values in discourse (reprint).* Cambridge: Cambridge University Press.

Dam, Q. (1994). *Nho giáo xưa và nay (Confucianism: Past and present).* Hanoi: Nhà Xuất Bản Văn hóa thông tin (Culture and Information Publishing House).

Gao, G. (1998). Don't take my words for it-understanding Chinese speaking practices. *International Journal of Intercultural Relations, 22*(2), 163–186.

Grice, H. P. (1975). Logic and conversation. In P. Cole & J. Morgan (Eds.), *Syntax and semantics, Speech acts* (Vol. Vol. 3, pp. 107–142). New York: Academic Press.

Gu, Y. (1990). Politeness in modern Chinese. *Journal of Pragmatics, 14*(2), 237–257.

Haugh, M. (2003). Anticipated versus inferred politeness. *Multilingua, 22*(4), 397–413.

Haugh, M., & Hinze, C. G. (2003). A metalinguistic approach to deconstructing the concept of 'face' and 'politeness' in Chinese, English and Japanese. *Journal of Pragmatics, 35*, 1581–1611.

Hinze, C. G. (2012). Chinese politeness is not about 'face': Evidence from the business world. *Journal of Politeness Research, 8*, 11–27.

Holstein, J. A., & Gubrium, J. F. (2004). The active interview. In D. Silverman (Ed.), *Qualitative research: Theory, method and practice* (2nd ed., pp. 140–161). London: Sage Publications.

Hwang, K. K. (1987). Face and favor: The Chinese power game. *American Journal of Sociology, 92*, 944–974.

Ide, S. (1989). Formal forms and discernment: Two neglected aspects of universals of linguistic politeness. *Multilingua, 8*(2–3), 223–257.

Katalanos, N. K. (1994). *When yes means no: Verbal and non-verbal communication of Southeast Asian refugees in the New Mexico health care system.* Unpublished MA thesis, University of New Mexico, Albuquerque.

Kecskes, I. (2017). Context-dependency and impoliteness in intercultural communication. *Journal of Politeness Research, 13*(1), 7–31.

King, A. Y. (1985). The individual and group in Confucianism: A relational perspective. In D. J. Munro (Ed.), *Individualism and holism: Studies in Confucian and Taoist values* (pp. 57–84). Ann Arbor: The University of Michigan.

Lakoff, R. (1990). *Talking power: The politics of language in our lives.* New York: Basic.

Lakoff, G., & Johnson, M. (1980). *Metaphors we live by.* Chicago: University of Chicago Press.

Lebra, T. S. (1976). *Japanese patterns of behavior.* Honolulu: The University Press of Hawaii.

Lee, C. L. (2012). Self-presentation, face and first-person pronouns in the Analects. *Journal of Politeness Research, 8*, 75–92.

Lii-Shih, Y. E. (1994). What do "yes" and "no" really mean in Chinese? In B. Kachru (Ed.), *Georgetown University round table on languages and linguistics* (pp. 128–149). Washington, DC: Georgetown University Press.

Lim, T. (2002). Language and verbal communication across cultures. In W. B. Gudykunst & B. Mody (Eds.), *Handbook of international and intercultural communication* (2nd ed., pp. 69–87). Thousand Oaks: Sage.

Locher, M. (2004). *Power and politeness in action: Disagreements in oral communication.* Berlin/New York: Mouton de Gruyter.

Mao, L. R. (1994). Beyond politeness theory: 'Face' revisited and renewed. *Journal of Pragmatics, 21,* 451–486.

Markus, H., & Kitayama, S. (1991). Culture and the self: Implications for cognition, emotion, and motivation. *Psychological Review, 98,* 224–253.

Marr, D. G. (2000). Concepts of "individual" and "self" in twentieth-century Vietnam. *Modern Asian Studies, 34*(4), 769–796.

Matsumoto, Y. (1989). Politeness and conversational universals – Observations from Japanese. *Multilingua, 8*(2), 207–221.

Nguyen, P. L. (1990). Why they rarely say "thank you"? *Journal of Vietnamese Studies, 1*(3), 42–44.

O'Hara-Devereaux, M., & Johansen, R. (1994). *Global work: Bridging distance, culture and time.* San Francisco: Jossey-Bass.

Park, M., & Kim, M.-s. (1992). Communication practices in Korea. *Communication Quarterly, 40*(4), 398–404.

Peltokorpia, V., & Clausen, L. (2010). Linguistic and cultural barriers to intercultural communication in foreign subsidiaries. *Asian Business & Management, 10*(4), 509–528.

Pham, N. (2007a). Áp đặt trong lời mời của văn hoá Á đông là hành động đe doạ thể diện âm tính hay chiến lược lịch sự dương tính: Tiếp cận từ góc độ Nho giáo (Imposition in Asian-Confucian politeness is a negative face threatening act or positive face enhancing act? A Confucian perspective). *Tạp chí Ngôn ngữ (Journal of Linguistics), 3*(214), 69–82.

Pham, N. (2007b). Xu hướng giải quyết mâu thuẫn trong môi trường giao tiếp đa văn hoá tại các văn phòng dự án phi chính phủ (Tendency of solving conflicts in NGO intercultural offices). *Tạp chí Tâm lý học (Journal of Psychology), 2*(95), 56–63.

Pham, N. (2014). Strategies employed by the Vietnamese to respond to compliments and the influence of compliment receivers' perceptions of the compliment on their responses. *International Journal of Linguistics, 6*(2), 142–165.

Robinson, J. H. (2003). Communication in Korea: Playing things by eyes. In L. Samovar & R. Porter (Eds.), *Intercultural communication: A reader* (10th ed., pp. 57–64). Belmont: Thomson Wadsworth.

Schlund, K. (2014). On form and function of politeness formulae. *Journal of Politeness Research, 10,* 271–296.

Schnurr, S., & Chan, A. (2009). Politeness and leadership discourse in New Zealand and Hong Kong: A cross-cultural case study of workplace talk. *Journal of Politeness Research, 5,* 131–157.

Scollon, R., & Scollon, W. S. (1995). *Intercultural communication.* Cambridge: Blackwell Publishers.

Spencer-Oatey, H. (2002). Managing rapport in talk: Using rapport sensitive incidents to explore the motivational concerns underlying the management of relations. *Journal of Pragmatics, 34,* 529–545.

Tsui, A. (1991). The pragmatic functions of *I don't know. Text, 11*(4), 607–622.

Vu, T. T. H. (1997). *Politeness in modern Vietnamese: A sociolinguistic study of a Hanoi speech community.* Unpublished doctoral dissertation. University of Toronto, Toronto.

Xiaohong, W., & Qingyuan, L. (2013). The Confucian value of harmony and its influence on Chinese social interaction. *Cross-Cultural Communication, 9*(1), 60–66.

Yu, M. (2003). On the universality of face: Evidence from Chinese compliment behavior. *Journal of Pragmatics, 35,* 1679–1710.

Yum, J. O. (1988). The impact of Confucianism on interpersonal relationships and communication patterns in East Asia. *Communication Monographs, 55,* 374–388.

Part III
English as a Lingua Franca and in Inter/Intra-cultural Communication

The Impact of English as a Global Lingua Franca on Intercultural Communication

Juliane HOUSE

Abstract This chapter first examines the concept "lingua franca", moving from an historical overview to the present status of English as a lingua franca (ELF). English as a lingua franca is today used in many domains across many different ethnic groups, nation states and regions, and it is steadily becoming more important as a default language in many parts of Asia. As a lingua franca, English is also the first truly global language in history. And it is this unrivalled position of English today which has thrown up massive criticism – criticism directed at the assumption of the cultural neutrality of English as a lingua franca, at the elitist nature of English in many parts of the world, and at its potential for harming local languages in Asia. These points of criticism will be examined in the chapter from a socio-cultural and economic perspective.

The growing use of English as a lingua franca is further often critiqued on ideological grounds by so-called "liberation linguists" such as e.g. Phillipson (2009) who maintain that every human being has the right to speak their own native language in every situation of their choice. This pro-mother tongue ideology will be confronted in the chapter with the reality of language use, the consequences of language choice, and the suggestion that English as a lingua franca is merely a language of communication, and as such poses no real threat to native and other languages that will continue to be used as languages for identification (cf. House 2003 for a detailed explanation).

In the second part of the chapter, other major arguments against the use of one dominant language will be problematized. The first can be summarized as follows: intercultural communication in English as a lingua franca is bound to fail because of users' deficient lingua-cultural competence. This allegation will be examined with reference to an extensive body of research on the nature of English as lingua franca interactions, which clearly documents that such interactions are both successful and systematically different from native English use in certain linguistic domains. Another

J. HOUSE (✉)
Applied Linguistics, University of Hamburg, Hamburg, Germany
e-mail: jhouse@fastmail.fm

© Springer International Publishing AG, part of Springer Nature 2018
A. CURTIS, R. SUSSEX (eds.), *Intercultural Communication in Asia:*
Education, Language and Values, Multilingual Education 24,
https://doi.org/10.1007/978-3-319-69995-0_6

97

attack against the use of English as a lingua franca relates to the claim that its heavy use negatively impacts on other languages, a claim that can also be relativized through reference to relevant research such as that described below in this chapter.

Apart from these ideologically fuelled pessimistic views of the linguistic side of the use of English as a lingua franca, there is also an often-heard criticism from a psycholinguistic viewpoint. Here it is claimed that the frequent use of a dominant language negatively impacts on speakers' ability to think and conceptualize in their mother tongue. This claim, too, will be reviewed on the basis of existing research.

Finally, the chapter briefly discusses the growing spread of English as a language of instruction at various educational levels, and how this will change international education scenarios in the future in Asia.

1 What Is English as a Lingua Franca?

Let us first consider the concept of a "lingua franca" to find out what one might mean when one refers to "English as a lingua franca". A lingua franca – the term is often said to derive from Arabic LISAN AL FARANG (which originally meant "the Italian language") – in its original meaning was simply an intermediary or contact language used, for instance, by speakers of Arabic with travellers from Western Europe. In this original meaning, a lingua franca was a contact or vehicular language that consisted of elements and structures of diverse origins. Its meaning was later extended to describe a language of commerce in general, a rather stable variety with little room for individual variation (cf. House 2003) As a mixed contact language, a lingua franca would be more or less neutral, since it does not belong to any national language, any national language community or any national territory – concepts that arose much later.

More recently, lingua francas were also based on certain territories or speech communities, but from these they tended to be locally adapted accordingly, as their radius of influence expanded. One of the historically most important lingua francas is Latin during the Roman Empire, which also survived for a long time afterwards as a language of Science and Religion. In more modern times, it was French that was elevated to lingua franca status as the language of European royalty, aristocracy and diplomacy. Other kinds of lingua francas are artificially constructed systems, the most well-known being Esperanto.

English is also without doubt the most important lingua franca in Asia (Kirkpatrick 2007; Tsui and Tollefson 2007), despite the fact that in different parts of Asia there are many other commonly spoken languages such as Chinese, Arabic or Hindi-Urdu, languages that are used on a world-wide scale. The use of ELF in Asia is enormous, and the number of ELF users in India and China alone are today over half a billion (Kirkpatrick 2003, 2016; Kachru 2005), which makes them the largest ELF group in the world. As Baker (2009) points out, in many South and East Asian countries, ELF is widely used as a language of tourism and trade and as the language of the elite. ELF has thus often replaced French. The wide-spread recognition of the importance of ELF in the region is documented in the adoption of English as the working language of ASEAN (Kirkpatrick 2012, 2016), thus cementing its important political role in South and East Asia – a role which has led McArthur (2003) and Kachru (2005) to propose that English is in fact more than a lingua franca, but an Asian language in its own right. In Asia, English is used extensively both at local levels for local needs within countries, and at the global level as a lingua franca, i.e. an instrument of communication across regions, and of course internationally.

English is therefore without doubt the currently most wide-spread and most widely used lingua franca in the world – a truly global phenomenon that cuts right across the well-known Kachruvian (Kachru 1982) circles (inner, outer and expanding circles): it can occur anywhere and in any constellation of speakers, and can also integrate native speakers of English, though they tend to play a minor role. ELF is characterized by a great variability: it is NOT a fixed code, and it cannot be defined by certain formal characteristics such as specific sound patterns, preferred syntactic structures or simplified vocabulary. Rather, it is an 'open-source phenomenon', a resource available for whoever wants to take advantage of the virtual English language. ELF is negotiated AD HOC varying according to context, speaker constellation and communicative purpose. It is individually shaped by its users and can fulfil many different functions ranging from simple small talk to sophisticated arguments. While of course based on English, ELF is also full of interlingual and intercultural adaptations, such that it typically contains elements from different linguacultures (see e.g. Ji 2016).

Pennycook (2012) makes a plea for conceptualizing ELF not simply in terms of removing it from native English norms, but, more importantly, as a linguistic practice that emerges from a local context. ELF is closely tied to language in use, to discourse practice in an on-going, ever-changing social process, continuously reshaped from the linguistic repertoires available to its users, who are embedded in locally occurring interactions (cf. Canagarajah 2007, who also makes an interesting distinction between LFE (negotiated on the fly) and ELF.

Since the prime aim of any lingua franca communication from the time of the Crusades, the first of which began in 1095, to the present day has been mutual intelligibility and efficient communication, correctness tends to be not very important. This means that intelligibility and comprehensibility is considered more important than phonetic, or lexico-grammatical accuracy. Equally unimportant for ELF is what generations of learners of English have dreaded and often unsuccessfully imitated: typically English forms such as idioms or other phrases referring to insider cultural phenomena.

Taken together, we can say that the most important features of ELF are its enormous functional flexibility, its variability and spread across many different linguistic, geographical and cultural areas, as well as its openness to foreign forms. Internationally and intra-nationally, ELF can thus be regarded as a special type of intercultural communication, because speakers of many different languages and cultures come into contact. Since the number of non-native speakers of English is now substantially larger than its native speakers (the ratio is about 4:1), English in its role as a global lingua franca can be said to be no longer owned by its native speakers, the inner circle of native speakers is no longer the centre of the English speaking world, rather a type of "pluricentricity" seems to have occurred.

ELF is not a language for specific purposes, because it is not used exclusively for any "specific purpose", but can be used for an unlimited number of purposes. Nor is it a sort of pidgin or creole. Nor is it some species of "foreigner talk" or learner language. And it is certainly not Nerriere's "Globish" or BSE – Bad Simple English, as I have heard some people say. The interlanguage paradigm (cf. Selinker 1972 who initiated a long tradition of research into the characteristics of learner language) with its focus on deficits of learners' competence in a foreign or second language measured against a native norm, is also clearly no longer valid here. Instead of comparing ELF speakers' competence with a hypothetical native speaker competence, it is rather the multilingual individual and his or her "multicompetence", that is a speaker's competence in different languages, (Cook 1992) that should be taken as a norm for describing and explaining what ELF speakers typically do when they are engaged in ELF communication. Here we can find support from the rich literature on bilingualism and multilingualism, where proficiency in more than one language is generally seen as beneficial and enriching.

ELF Speakers are per se multilingual speakers, and ELF is a language for communication, i.e. a medium which can be given substance with different national, regional, local and individual cultural identities. ELF does not carry these identities; it is not a language for identification (Hüllen 1992; House 2003), i.e., not a language for which speakers are emotionally committed, as speakers often are with their mother tongue in which they were socialized. However, recent studies do show that ELF can indeed assume emotive values and may thus be used for 'identity regionalism' (Hashim et al. 2016). When English is used as a language for communication, it is, in principle, neutral with regard to the different socio-cultural backgrounds of its users. It has thus great potential for international understanding – precisely because there is no pre-fixed norm, and because ELF speakers must always work out anew – in different communities of practice (cf. the application of this concept into ELF research by House 2003 – a joint linguistic, intercultural and behavioural basis for their communication).

It may be legitimate to ask why it should be English, and not for instance Spanish or Arabic, or any other widely spoken language, that has developed into today's major lingua franca. The answer is simple: this is due to the former world-spanning British Empire, which was swiftly replaced after the Second World War by the United States and its current dominant political and economic status. Another facilitating factor is contemporary technological progress propelling a demand for fast and efficient international communication – preferably in one language which obviously speeds up communication. Other explanatory suggestions of the folk wisdom kind point to the supposed simplicity of the English language – a rather dubious explanation. There may also be another rather banal reason for the continuous growth of ELF: once a language has reached such a global spread and such a high degree of availability and frequency of use, it might simply keep growing. This growth, however, may well come to a halt, once the support by the current world power is waning – but I do not want to speculate about this at the present time.

The role of ELF as a means for worldwide communication has of course not been welcomed unanimously. On the contrary, there has been a lot of controversy surrounding the use of ELF. We will therefore now consider this controversy from a number of different perspectives.

2 Is ELF a Threat to Multilingual Communication or Simply a Useful Tool for Global Communication?

One of the strongest oppositional stances vis-à-vis the use of ELF is the propagation of "Linguistic Human Rights" coupled with the idea that, if these rights are denied, many languages are doomed to die (Phillipson 2009). The widespread use of ELF – seen as embodying "linguistic imperialism" – is considered a powerful threat to linguistic human rights and to people's unfettered use of their mother tongues. De Swaan has commented on this view in the following way:

> Recently, a movement has spread across the Western world advocating the right of all people to speak the language of their choice, to fight "language imperialism" abroad and "linguicism" at home, to strengthen "language rights" in international law. Alas, what decides is not the right of human beings to speak whatever language they wish, but the freedom of everybody else to ignore what they say in the language of their choice. (De Swaan 2001, p. 52)

Given the influence of the linguistic rights movement, the use of English in certain contexts may indeed prove problematic for speakers, not least because of the still prevailing myth of the superiority of native English speakers still prevailing in language learning and teaching context, their control over the norms and conventions of language use in the practice of English teaching, and the English language study materials used across Asia. While in some parts of countries like India English has grown to be a recognized and generally accepted nativized instrument for expressing local identities, in other expanding circle Asian countries such as China there is a much greater ambiguity and insecurity about which norms to follow and teach, and possibly a growing acceptance of ELF rather than native English norms (cf. Wang 2015). In view of the ever-growing numbers of ELF used for communication in Asia, it should really be expert ELF speakers as norm setters rather than native English speakers (see the references above).

ELF is a useful language for communication, not necessarily a language for affective and emotional identification (Hüllen 1992; House 2003), and the difference between a language for communication and a language for identification is subjectively felt by many language users. Languages for communication and languages for identification are not in competition, rather they supplement each other or they might overlap. This does not mean, however, that ELF users cannot develop an affective identification with ELF, but the point I am trying to make here is that this need not necessarily be the case.

The opposition against the use of English in multilingual contexts has recently found a new voice propagating the use of a "lingua receptiva" or "parallel talk", promoting what has been called "receptive bilingualism" (Ten Thije and Zeevaertt 2007). The idea is that in multilingual constellations each speaker uses his or her native language. Interactants will then infer the meanings of others' talk and understand what has been said. While this is an interesting attempt to avoid ELF, it is obviously meant to function first and foremost with groups of people who speak typologically close languages, such as languages belonging to the Scandinavian, Romance or Slavic language families. In the case of typologically distant languages, however, communication following this model would be difficult to put into practice. Here the use of gestures and other body languages might prove to be more useful.

That English will be responsible for sweeping away other languages may be unlikely, despite the depressing predictions of language death over the next century of 50–90% of the world's languages (cf. e.g. Krauss 1992). In fact, one can often observe that widespread use of English tends to also strengthen the use of indigenous languages for identification purposes, and that these languages can then also be employed as vehicles of protest against English. For example, in the German pop music scene, the use of dialects such as Bavarian is very popular, and acts as a protest against the dominance of English in this genre. And in the INTERNET, long thought to be the prime killer of languages other than English, a profusion of many different languages has come to be used. So what we may have here is a healthy co-existence of English and native languages, which has, in some cases, stimulated the emergence of new "mixed" varieties characterized by code-mixing and translanguaging (cf. House 2016a). As a case in point, the contemporary music scene features more and more productions in local languages and dialects, and the Internet – long assumed to marginalize all languages other than English – now boasts a growing number of different languages and also features ELF with admixtures of other languages (cf. e.g. Bloch 2004; Lam 2004).

I will now look at several more specific arguments against the use of ELF in Asia and elsewhere. I will discuss these arguments and try to relativize them by drawing on the results of empirical research.

3   Are ELF Users as Non-native English Speakers Disadvantaged Vis-à-Vis Native English Speakers?

From a linguistic perspective, one often hears statements such as the following: The use of ELF in multilingual constellations is unfair to all those who are non-native speakers of English, because however advanced their command of English may be, it will never be as differentiated and sophisticated as their L1 competence. As anecdotal evidence, I would like to point to the numerous cases where users of an L2 successfully overcame the putative 'non-native handicap', and turned out to be content in their use of a new language, despite the fact that they may never have been as differentiated and sophisticated in their use of this L2as they are in their L1. Recent approaches to second or third language acquisition no longer focus on its shortcomings, but they emphasize instead the positive sides of multilingualism for individual speakers (Kramsch 2009). With regard to the way users of ELF are affected by the fact that English is not their L1, much recent research has shown that interactions in the medium of ELF clearly work, thus contradicting the claim that they are inherently problematic and precarious (cf. e.g. House 2002, 2009a, 2010, 2011; Firth 2009; Jenkins 2009; Baumgarten and House 2010; Seidlhofer 2011). ELF use seems to work surprisingly well, not least thanks to the "Let it pass" principle, an interpretive procedure where interactants tolerantly wait for problematic utterances to become clearer as the discourse proceeds (Firth 2009). Further, many studies of ELF talk (cf. e.g. Firth 1996; Knapp and Meierkord 2001; Seidlhofer 2011; House 2014) found that few misunderstandings, corrections or other-repairs occur in ELF talk – a stark contrast to non-native-native talk examined in classic interlanguage studies (cf. Selinker 1972).

In what follows I will describe some of the results of my own work on the pragmatics of ELF interactions in a project funded by the Volkswagen Foundation at Hamburg University from 2008 to 2011. Here we have compiled a corpus of institutional and every-day interactions between ELF users with many different mother tongues, complemented by retrospective interviews with these users about "rich points" in the interaction as these emerged from our analyses. The four most interesting findings can be characterized as follows.

3.1   Recourse to Speakers' Mother Tongues

Such recourse was, for instance, found to occur in this data in the form of transfer. The following extracts show cases of transfer from speakers' L1. The extracts are taken from the Hamburg ELF conversational data.[1]

3.1.1   Examples of Transfer

One such case of transfer from speakers' L1 is Asian ELF users' tendency to engage in a kind of cyclical topic management (cf. Kaplan 1966; Connor 1996; House 1999, and others) which leads to a number of non-sequitur turns. These often puzzling non-sequiturs are however consistently ignored by other participants, such that the discourse remains "normal" and "robust". Here is an extract listing two short exchanges which feature such non-sequitur sequences. They are taken from an

---

[1]The transcription conventions in all examples presented in this paper are simplified for better readability. The length of pauses (in seconds) as well as participants' non-verbal actions are indicated by round brackets, emphasis by capital letters, laughter by @, overlapping speech and translations by square brackets, and latching by =. All names of interactants are anonymized.

every-day ELF conversation on the role of English in the world enacted by students at the university of Hamburg (Geli: German; Joy: Korean; Wei: Chinese). In this conversation, one interactant, Wei, relentlessly pulls back the discourse to the topic he happens to favour.

EXTRACT 1
Geli: If we if everybody spoke one language maybe let's say English it would be boring very boring and why is it English is it so wonderful
Wei: In China many dialects many languages erm eh Chinese people speak maybe a little different Cantonese Yunnan province

----

Joy: But is English really so strong in the world so all the people want to speak it in France for example I know people do not
Wei: China is a big area and big diversity

Another form of referring to a speaker's L1 is Code Switching.
Analyses of how speakers use code-switching in our Hamburg ELF office-hours interactions show that this device is not necessarily a sign of incompetence, but can also be taken as an indication of speakers' subjective identification with their linguistic origins. Here is an example, again featuring A, an assistant, and S, an international student from Spain.

EXTRACT 2
A: Also jetzt koennen wir dann ja mal anfangen (So now we can start) yeah okay so now let's start
S: erm I want to ask you erm some questions about the new semester

Extract 2 shows how the assistant A automatically launches into German at the very beginning of an advising session, but in the middle of his turn he switches into ELF, dutifully following the institutionally prescribed code.

Code-switching showcases the fact that ELF users are multilingual speakers, who do not lose their loyalty to their L1. The normality of code-switching in ELF discourse, whenever this is possible given the constellation of speakers on hand, has also been amply documented by other ELF researchers using different data (Pölzl and Seidlhofer 2006; Jenkins 2009).

3.2   Accommodation: Frequency of the Multi-Functional "Represent" Gambit

In the Hamburg data there is a high incidence of speakers' deliberate accommodation to other participants' ELF competence via the use of a certain gambit, which Edmondson (1981) called a "Represent". A Represent is a meta-communicative procedure and a useful and versatile discourse marker with which a speaker re-presents (parts of) a previous speaker's move in order to: 1. strategically support his own and his interactants' working memory, 2. create coherence by constructing lexical-paradigmatic clusters, 3. signal receipt and confirm understanding, and 4. strengthen awareness of the ongoing talk and monitor its progress. Other researchers have confirmed such uses of Represents, albeit using different terms (Cogo and Dewey 2006). Here is a simple example of such a Represent taken from an every-day conversation between university students (A: Korean; C: Danish; L: Chinese):

EXTRACT 3
A: When I first started here all the courses seemed erm too difficult too complex to understand for me
L: Too difficult and complex to understand yes
C: I think so too

Represents – also referred to in the literature as echo-signals, mirror elements or shadow-elements – are typical of psycho-therapeutic interviews, instructional discourse ("teacher talk"), and air traffic control (ATC) discourse – genres where information is deliberately and routinely re-stated to ensure understanding. That ELF users frequently resort to this procedure (cf. House 2013, 2014) can be taken as proof of their well-developed strategic competence and their meta-communicative awareness.

3.3   Co-constructing Utterances to Show Solidarity and Consensus

In the face of manifold cultural and linguistic differences, ELF users demonstrate their solidarity with each other by co-constructing utterances whenever necessary – a clear sign of a feeling of group identity that develops in the community of practice in which ELF speakers find themselves. One might say that ELF users view ELF as an egalitarian tool ("We're all in the same boat"), and there seems to be an underlying determination and consensus about making the discourse work. Here is an example of German speaker B's readiness to come to the rescue of co-interactant J (Korean), who is patently at a loss for words, which makes her pause for a very long time:

EXTRACT 4
J: I recently read an article in a Korean erm (2sec) Moment (4sec)
B: Newspaper, Internet?
J: Yes thank you (laughs) erm the article is about new foreign language education in Japan.

3.4   Re-interpreting Gambits: You Know, Yes/Yeah; So, Okay, I Think, I Don't Think, I Mean

In our analyses of the Hamburg data, ELF users tended to use certain gambits in a way which systematically differs from the way native English usage is described in the literature. For instance, the analysis of the behaviour of the gambit *you know* in our data (see House 2009a for a detailed discussion) shows that *you know* is predominantly used in this ELF data as a routinized self-supportive strategy whenever speakers want to make salient coherence relations or bridge word-finding difficulties ("fumbling"). *You know* in ELF discourse is thus NOT used primarily as a polite hedge or an interpersonal expression appealing to knowledge shared with address-ees, as it has often been described in the literature on native English usage (e.g. by Östman 1981). In our ELF interactions, *you know* collocates very frequently with the conjunctions *but/because/and* and, just like these conjunctions, it highlights discourse-external (i.e., real world) relations. And in its function as a routinized fumble, *you know* was found to help ELF users structure their output and monitor the progression of their talk. So *you know* in ELF talk is clearly a speaker strategy, NOT a sign of a "restricted code" or proof/evidence of some underdeveloped com-petence in English. When employing the gambit *you know*, a speaker primarily demonstrates that her strategic competence is intact, and that she is capable of exploiting the resources of the English language. Here is one typical example of the use of *you know* by speaker M (Taiwanese):

EXTRACT 5
M: so we should care about us ourself and and and not er somebody you know outside us should say how w we have to look like because if we if w w were you know those models they are idols they are

Analyses of other discourse markers such as *I think, I don't think* and *I mean* (Baumgarten and House 2010) show that ELF speakers prefer using these gambits in their prototypical semantic meanings, i.e., *I think* is not used as a rather empty routine but as a collocation that refers to the speaker's mental process, rather than as routinized de-semanticized phrases common in native English speakers' usage. And ELF users' employment of the gambits *yes/yeah, so,* and *okay* (House 2011) seems to also deviate from native speaker usage, in that in ELF, speakers tend to creatively modify their L1 use for self-support, monitoring and coherence-creation. When using the gambits *yes/yeah/ja,* for instance, ELF speakers formally and functionally vary their usage, preferring the token *yes* for agreement, *yeah* for signalling compre-hension, and the equivalent German token *ja* for back-channelling, i.e. the produc-tion of hearer-signals such as 'hmm' etc., where the hearer does not intend to take over the speaker role. This interestingly variable use is illustrated in the following extracts where P is a German professor, and S a student from Spain:

EXTRACT 6
P: Next thing you know on the fourteenth of Ju June there is a German AUtag just for your information
S: AUtag nee
P: It's where you are coming here
S: It's here at the TU?
P: Yes yes yes once a year there is a so-called AUtag

Extract 6 shows that the token *yes* is used by P to show agreement with S's state-ment when answering his question:

EXTRACT 7
S: Because then it will be a very heavy heavy weight producer
P:@ @ erm yeah but erm you mentioned before a four level bridge
S: no that wasn't me
P: yeah no what what you mentioned erm what subject in the past you have erm had in mind...

In Extract 7 P signals uptake of S's utterance by using the token *yeah*:

EXTRACT 8
S: I have currently I have prepared them in English=
P=ja
S: and I also want send them too in German which I've not yet sent anywhere cause I've just
prepared them with help of some [friends]
P: [ja]
S: and colleagues=
P:=[ja]
S: I should give a copy of that copy
P: yes

In Extract 8, P does not challenge S's turn but just signals to S that he should continue talking. In doing so he automatically reverts to his German mother tongue.

Taken together, the results of analyses of ELF interactions in our Hamburg data show that ELF talk does/can work surprisingly well, because ELF speakers are able to make good use of the English language for their own purposes, exploiting its potential to suit their own particular needs.

4   Does the Wide-Spread Use of English as a Lingua Franca "Contaminate" Other Languages?

Another often heard argument against the widespread use of ELF is that it "contaminates" other languages. Purists and prescriptivists have long worried about English as the world's foremost language "invading" other languages in the form of Anglicism, more often than not compiling "black lists" of those foreign bodies and providing readers with native alternatives. Such an argument against ELF can be relativized on the basis of another research project – a project that went beyond examining those rather obvious and, I believe, essentially harmless lexical importations from English. I am referring to the project "Covert translation" which I directed at the German Science Foundation's Research Center on Multilingualism from 1999 to 2011. The initial assumption of this project was that ELF changes the communicative norms in other languages via massive unidirectional translations from English into these languages. In this study, we mainly examined whether and how translations change the German language – German being the most popular target language for the translation of English texts in our sample – but we also considered some translations into French and Spanish. And I believe that the results may also be of relevance to translations from English into other languages, and also Asian languages (cf. here in particular the study by Amouzadeh and House 2010 on the influence of English on Persian).

The project work is based on previous extensive German-English contrastive research (House 2006) on communicative conventions, which were hypothesized to vary along a number of parameters in German and English. German texts in many genres were found to be more direct, more explicit, more oriented towards the content of the message, and thus generally more transactional and detached than comparable English texts that tend to be more interactional and involved. In the past, translations of texts from English into German were routinely subjected to a "cultural filter" in order to adjust them to the new audience's expectation norms (House 1997). Given the dominance of ELF, we assumed that these differences in communicative conventions would no longer be heeded, with the result that English communicative conventions would now be superimposed on German texts.

These considerations led to the formulation of two hypotheses: 1. In translations from English into German, a cultural filter will be less consistently applied over time such that English-German translations increasingly follow Anglophone text conventions; and 2. Anglophone text conventions will spread from English-German translations to German original texts. These hypotheses were operationalized as follows: the frequency and usage patterns of certain linguistic items (resulting from detailed qualitative analyses of some 80 textual exemplars) change over time. Two time frames were examined: 1978–1982 and 1999–2002 (2006 for economic texts). The hypotheses were tested using a multilingual, one million word corpus that contained texts from two genres: popular science and business texts – genres which we assumed to be particularly vulnerable to Anglophone influence. The texts were drawn from popular science magazines (*Scientific American* and *Spektrum der Wissenschaft*), and letters to shareholders in globalized companies' annual reports. The corpus contains English texts, their German translations (parallel texts), German originals (comparable texts), some translations and original texts into French and Spanish, as well as translations in the opposite direction (i.e. into English). The method used in this project combines qualitative and quantitative approaches progressing from detailed text analyses and comparisons on the basis of a translation evaluation model (House 1997, 2009b) to a quantitative phase involving frequency counts, and finally to a re-contextualized qualitative phase, where we investigated how certain linguistic items and patterns were translated, and how these compared with original texts. The qualitative analyses revealed differences in the linguistic realization of subjectivity and addressee-orientation, i.e. the expression of author identity and addressee-orientation in simulated author-reader interaction in written discourse.

Here is an example highlighting English-German differences in the expression of addressee-orientation. The extract is taken from an article in the *Scientific American*, July 1998 and its German translation in *Spektrum der Wissenschaft*, October 1998.

EXTRACT 9
English Original: Suppose you are a doctor in an emergency room and a patient tells you she was raped two hours earlier... Can you in fact do anything? ...
German Translation: In der Notfallaufnahme eines Krankenhaus berichtet eine Patientin, sie sei vor zwei Stunden vergewaltigt worden... Kann der Arzt überhaupt irgendetwas tun?
...
[Backtranslation into English: In the emergency room of a hospital a patient reports that she was raped two hours ago...Can the doctor do anything at all? ...]

The English text draws readers into the text by inviting them to identify with the doctor, whereas the German translation keeps readers at a distance by maintaining a factual reporting style, leaving the doctor in the text, as it were, and using the third person. The translator clearly applied a cultural filter adapting the original text to German readers' expectation norms.

The results of the project studies show that there is indeed an English influence in the translations for all phenomena investigated, but the hypothesized influence on original German texts is only documented for *but-aber/doch*. Over time, the frequency of all other phenomena associated with interactionality in written discourse was found to remain consistently higher in the English originals than in the German originals, i.e. the English texts remain more personal, more dialogic and more interactional than the corresponding German texts. In other words, Anglophone influence via translation seems to be a marginal phenomenon: it did not affect original mainstream text production. The influence of English on other languages is probably more indirect: it may have to do with a current trend towards colloquiality fuelled by general contemporary processes such as the democratization of knowledge and the growing acceptance of informality not only in oral, but also in written interaction, particularly in the social media, e-mail, SMS, blogs, Wikis etc. (cf. Crystal 2006).

So the hypotheses underlying this project were essentially not confirmed. No wonder, you might think, since these hypotheses are typically mono-causal ones of the kind: "the bigger the prestige of a language – ELF in this case – the bigger its influence". Such a simplistic assumption, you might say, needs to be rejected. Instead we should assume a complex interaction of many different factors in language change, such as e.g. linguistic economy and intelligibility, standardization of genres in the target language (both popular science texts and letters to shareholders were new genres in German in the seventies of the last century!), as well as jargonization and popularization. (cf. Kranich et al. 2011). We might therefore conclude that German translations do not simply adopt Anglophone text conventions, rather translators may have set out to creatively achieve their own communicative goals responding to a need in German for expressing interpersonality, addressee orientation, and jargonization by exploiting the existing interpersonal and interactive Anglophone model for their own benefit.

5   Can Thinking and Conceptualization in L1 Be Damaged by "Anglicisms"?

Here I refer to the popular claim that large-scale importation of English words and phrases into another language influences thinking and concept formation in that language, and that the constant stream of English words and phrases damages a person's L1-mediated knowledge. Such a claim is, in my opinion, compatible with the strong version of the Humboldt-Sapir-Whorf hypothesis (cf. Whorf 1956) – a version which was refuted a long time ago and was subsequently replaced by a weak version (cf. Lucy 1992, 1996) for at least the following three reasons: (1) the universal possibility of translation; (2) the fact that all languages in use are in a sense "anachronisms", i.e., linguistic forms in the flow of natural language use rarely rise to a speaker's conscious awareness (at least in the case of ordinary language users, not linguists!) (Ortega y Gasset 1960); and (3) the converging evidence that multilinguals – such as ELF users – possess a "deep" common conceptual store to which "lower level" language-specific systems come to be attached (cf. e.g. Paradis 2004). With competent multilinguals, which many ELF speakers are, processing often remains "shallow", i.e. there is no semantic-conceptual processing at all (Sanford and Graesser 2006). And neurolinguistic studies of translation and language switching (Price et al. 1999) show that multilinguals move flexibly and smoothly between their languages, the two systems being distinct but permeable. There is thus no proof of a direct link of only one particular language to thinking and conceptualizing.

In other words: speakers' increased use of ELF worldwide need not necessarily inhibit concept formation in their mother tongues.

6 Is the Increasing Use of ELF a Threat to Translation?

This seems unlikely. The very same phenomena that have caused ELF use to surge have also influenced translation, i.e. globalization processes that boosted ELF use have also led to a continuing increase in translations worldwide. Alongside the impact of globalization on the world economy, on international communication and politics, translation has also become more important than ever before.

Information distribution via translation today relies heavily on new technologies that promote a worldwide translation industry. Translation plays a crucial and ever-growing role in multilingual news writing for international press networks, television channels, the Internet, the World Wide Web, social media, blogs, Wikis etc. Whenever information input needs to be quickly disseminated across the world in different languages, translations are indispensable. Translation is for instance essential for tourist information worldwide and for information flows in globalized companies, where ELF is now often replaced by native languages to improve sales potentials.

Further, there is a growing demand for translation in localization industries. Localization is a procedure with which translated texts are adapted to the new users' expectations. Software localization covers diverse industrial, commercial and scientific activities ranging from engineering and testing software applications, to managing complex team projects simultaneously in many countries and languages. Translations are needed in all of these. Indeed, translation is part of almost all localization and glocalization processes. In order to make a product available in many different languages it must be localized via translation. This process is of course similar to what was described above as "cultural filtering" (cf. most recently House 2016b). Producing a localized, i.e. culturally filtered and translated, version of a product is essential for opening up new markets, since immediate access to information about a product in a local language increases its demand. An important offshoot is the design of localized advertisements, again involving worldwide translation activity.

Translation is also propelled by the World Wide Web, the development of which has spread the need for translation into e-commerce globalization. And the steady increase of non-English speaking Web users also boosts translation.

Another factor contributing to the growing importance of translation is e-learning. The expansion of digital industries centred on e-learning and other education forms spread over the Web in many different languages again shows the intimate link between translation and today's global economy.

In sum, we can say that globalization has led to an explosion of demand for translation. And translation is not simply a by-product of globalization, but an integral part of it. Without it, the global capitalist, consumer-oriented and growth-fixated economy would not be possible. Therefore, not only has ELF not threatened translation, but quite the reverse.

7   Is the Wide-Spread Use of English as a Lingua Franca in Education a Threat to the Development of Speakers' Mother Tongues?

ELF used as a medium of instruction in non-Anglophone educational contexts is increasing exponentially all over the world – including Asia. Here we find programs with English as the sole or predominant medium of instruction (cf. e.g. the programs at UIC (United International College) in Zhuhai, PRC) as well as some mixed forms of instruction. Worries about the potentially damaging effects of such programs have led to an increase in programs that offer instruction in students' L1 alongside ELF. In general, we can say that in Asia, as elsewhere in the world, there is a widespread awareness of ELF as the single most important medium of international recognition in the academy, especially in business studies and the sciences (cf. Terauchi and Maswana 2015).

The perceived usefulness of competence in ELF in the education sector means also that ELF is often regarded as culturally neutral (cf. the detailed empirical study by Soltau 2007 for a German context), which confirms the "cultural irrelevance" hypothesis of ELF proposed early on by House (1999). The cultural irrelevance hypothesis suggests that there is no direct/one-to-one link between the ELF and native Anglophone cultures; rather culture emerges only when made relevant by interactants in situations of intercultural communication.

According to Soltau, native speakers of English are still widely admired, but they are no longer seen as guardians of an intimidatingly superior and essentially non-reachable standard. The native speaker model, i.e. that learners of English should aim at native or near-native competence, is outdated in any non-Anglophone educational context, although it is unfortunately still too often followed across the world and in particular in Asia (cf. Kirkpatrick 2003). Rather than adhering to a native English speaker model, teachers of English should be aware of the hybridity and dynamism of the use of ELF in the world, including Asia, and the importance of teaching for competence in intercultural communication with a focus on strategies, accommodation and negotiation. (cf. the detailed suggestions for improving oral intercultural competence in House 2012).

8 Conclusion

ELF is a useful tool for intercultural communication, as an additional language, but never as a substitute for other languages, as these fulfil different, often affective and identificatory, functions. When using ELF in multilingual constellations, speakers are found to frequently have recourse/revert to their L1 s via transfer and code-switching, thus documenting that other languages are well and alive, beneath the ELF surface. ELF users also creatively appropriate the English language for their own strategic purposes. The influence of ELF on communicative conventions of other languages via a plethora of translations from English turns out to be marginal in the case of German. Psycho-and neurolinguistic studies of bilingualism and translation disconfirm the view that the heavy use of one language (ELF) inhibits conceptualization in another. Finally, translation is not threatened by worldwide use of ELF. Globalization, which has boosted ELF, has also led to an explosion of demands for translation. In fact, translation lies at the heart of the global economy. For educational contexts, it is necessary to abandon native English speaker norms, and to overcome an automatic linking of language and culture, particularly in an Asian context where the use of ELF in many scenarios is continuously growing. A more useful and realistic aim is to teach intercultural communication focussing on communicative strategies and negotiation.

References

Amouzadeh, M., & House, J. (2010). Translation as a language contact phenomenon: The case of English and Persian. *Languages in Contrast, 10*, 54–75.

Baker, W. (2009). Language, culture and identity through English as a lingua franca in Asia: Notes from the field. *The Linguistics Journal. Special Issue: Language, Culture and Identity in Asia.* pp. 8–35.

Baumgarten, N., & House, J. (2010). Stance-taking through high-frequency I plus verb collations in native and non-native English. *Journal of Pragmatics, 42*, 1183–2001.

Bloch, J. (2004). Second language socialization in a bilingual chatroom: Global and local considerations. *Language Learning and Technology, 8*(3), 44–65.

Canagarajah, S. (2007). The ecology of global English. *International Multilingualism Journal, 1*(2), 89–100.

Cogo, A., & Dewey, M. (2006). Efficiency in ELF communication: From pragmatic motive to lexico-grammatical innovation. *Nordic Journal of English Studies, 5*(2), 59–93.

Connor, U. (1996). *Contrastive rhetoric*. Cambridge: Cambridge University Press.

Cook, V. (1992). *Linguistics and second language acquisition*. New York: St. Martin's Press.

Crystal, D. (2006). *Language and the internet* (2nd ed.). Cambridge: Cambridge University Press.

De Swaan, A. (2001). *Words of the world*. Cambridge: Polity Press.

Edmondson, W. J. (1981). *Spoken discourse. A model for analysis*. London: Longman.

Firth, A. (1996). The discursive accomplishment of normality: On conversation analysis and 'lingua franca' English. *Journal of Pragmatics, 26*(2), 237–259.

Firth, A. (2009). The lingua franca factor. *Intercultural pragmatics*. In J. House (Ed.), *Special issue on English as a lingua franca* 6(2), 147–170.

Hashim, A., Kaur, J., & Kuang, J. S. (2016). Identity Regionalism and English as an ASEAN lingua franca. *Journal of English as a Lingua Franca, 5*(2), 229–247.

House, J. (1997). *Translation quality assessment. A model revisited*. Tübingen: Narr.

House, J. (1999). Misunderstanding in intercultural communication. Interactions in English as a lingua franca and the myth of mutual intelligibility. In C. Gnutzmann (Ed.), *Teaching and learning English as a global language* (pp. 245–267). Frankfurt/Main: Lang.

House, J. (2002). Communicating in English as a lingua franca. In *EUROSLA yearbook* (Vol. 2, pp. 243–261).

House, J. (2003). English as a lingua franca: A threat to multilingualism? *Journal of SocioLinguistics, 7*(4), 556–578.

House, J. (2006). Communicative styles in English and German. *European Journal of English Studies, 10*(3), 249–267.

House, J. (2009a). Subjectivity in English as lingua franca discourse: The case of *you know*. In J. House (ed.), *Special issue, intercultural pragmatics*, 6(2), 171–193.

House, J. (2009b). *Translation*. Oxford: Oxford University Press.

House, J. (2010). The pragmatics of English as a lingua franca. In A. Trosborg (Ed.), *Handbook of pragmatics* (Vol. vol. 7, pp. 363–387). Berlin: Mouton de Gruyter.

House, J. (2011). Global and intercultural communication. In K. Aijmer & G. Andersen (Eds.), *Handbook of pragmatics* (Vol. vol. 5, pp. 363–390). Berlin: Mouton de Gruyter.

House, J. (2012). Teaching oral skills in English as a lingua franca. In L. Alsagoff, S. Lee, G. H. McKay, & W. A. Renanda (Eds.), *Principles and practices for teaching English as an international language* (pp. 186–205). New York: Routledge.

House, J. (2013). Developing pragmatic competence in English as a lingua franca: Using discourse markers to express (inter)subjectivity and connectivity. *Journal of Pragmatics, 59*, 57–67.

House, J. (2014). Managing academic institutional discourse in English as a lingua franca. *Functions of Language, 21*(1), 50–67.

House, J. (2016a). Own language use in academic discourse in English as a lingua franca. In K. Murata (Ed.), *Exploring ELF in Japanese academic and business contexts* (pp. 59–70). Amsterdam: Benjamins.

House, J. (2016b). *Translation as communication across languages and cultures*. London: Routledge.

Hüllen, W. (1992). Identifikationssprachen und Kommunikationssprachen. *Zeitschrift für germanistische Linguistik, 20*, 298–317.

Jenkins, J. (2009). Exploring attitudes towards English as a lingua franca in the East Asian contexts. In K. Murata & J. Jenkins (Eds.), *Global Englishes in Asian contexts* (pp. 40–56). Houndsmill: Palgrave Macmillan.

Ji, K. (2016). The linguistic features of ELF by Chinese users in China-ASEAN communication contexts. *Journal of English as a Lingua Franca, 5*(2), 273–290.

Kachru, B. (1982). *The other tongue: English across cultures*. Urbana: University of Illinois Press.

Kachru, B. (2005). *Asian Englishes: Beyond the canon*. New Delhi: Oxford University Press.

Kaplan, R. (1966). Cultural thought patterns in intercultural education. *Language Learning, 16*(1), 1–20.

Kirkpatrick, A. (2003). English as an ASEAN lingua franca: Implications for research and language teaching. *Asian Englishes, 6*(2), 82–91.

Kirkpatrick, A. (2007). *World Englishes: Implications for international communication and English language teaching*. Cambridge: Cambridge University Press.

Kirkpatrick, A. (2012). English in ASEAN: Implications for regional multilingualism. *Journal of Multilingual and Multicultural Development, 33*(4), 331–344.

Kirkpatrick, A. (Ed.) (2016). *Special Issue of the Journal of English as a lingua franca: The Asian Corpus of English.*

Knapp, K., & Meierkord, C. (Eds.). (2001). *Lingua franca communication.* Frankfurt/Main: Lang.

Kramsch, C. (2009). *The multilingual subject.* Oxford: Oxford University Press.

Kranich, S., Becher, V., & Höder, S. (2011). A tentative typology of translation-induced language change. In S. Kranich, V. Becher, S. Höder, & J. House (Eds.), *Multilingual discourse production* (pp. 11–44). Amsterdam: Benjamins.

Krauss, M. (1992). The world's languages in crisis. *Language, 68*(1), 4–10.

Lam, W. S. E. (2004). Second Language cyber rhetoric: A study of Chinese L2 writers in an on-line Usernet group. *Language Learning and Technology, 8*(3), 66–82.

Lucy, J. (1992). *Language diversity and thought: A reformulation of the linguistic relativity hypothesis.* Cambridge: Cambridge University Press.

Lucy, J. (1996). The scope of linguistic relativity: An analysis and review of empirical research. In J. Gumperz & S. Levinson (Eds.), *Rethinking linguistic relativity* (pp. 37–69). Cambridge: Cambridge University Press.

McArthur, T. (2003). English as an Asian language. *English Today, 19*(2), 19–22.

Ortega y Gasset, J. (1960). *Miseria y esplendor de la traducción. Elend und Glanz der Übersetzung.* München: Langewiesche-Brandt.

Östman, J.-O. (1981). *You know – A discourse-functional approach.* Amsterdam: Benjamins.

Paradis, M. (2004). *A neurolinguistic theory of bilingualism.* Amsterdam: Benjamins.

Pennycook, A. (2012). Lingua Francas as language ideologies. In A. Kirkpatrick & R. Sussex (Eds.), *English as an international language in Asia: Implications for language education* (pp. 137–154). Berlin/New York: Springer.

Phillipson, R. (2009). *Linguistic imperialism continued.* London: Routledge.

Pölzl, U., & Seidlhofer, B. (2006). In and on their own terms: The 'habitat factor' in English as a lingua franca interactions. *International Journal of the Sociology of Language, 177,* 151–176.

Price, C., Green, D., & Studnitz, R. v. (1999). A functional imaging study of translation and language switching. *Brain, 122,* 2221–2235.

Sanford, A., & Graesser, A. C. (2006). Shallow processing and underspecification. *Discourse Processes, 42*(2), 99–108.

Seidlhofer, B. (2011). *Understanding English as a lingua franca.* Oxford: Oxford University Press.

Selinker, L. (1972). Interlanguage. *IRAL, 10*(3), 31–54.

Soltau, A. (2007). *Englisch als lingua franca in der wissenschaftlichen Lehre: Charakteristika und Herausforderungen englischsprachiger Masterstudiengänge.* Dissertation Universität Hamburg.

Ten Thije, J., & Zeevaertt, L. (2007). *Receptive multilingualism.* Amsterdam: Benjamins.

Terauchi, H.. & Maswana, S. (2015). Essential English for business meetings: Responses from 909 businesspersons' scaled survey. In K. Murata (Ed.), *Waseda working papers in ELF, 4,* pp. 89–107.

Tsui, A. B. M., & Tollefson, J. W. (2007). *Language policy, culture and identity in Asian contexts.* London: Erlbaum.

Wang, Y. (2015). A case study of the role of English in a Chinese University. In K. Murata (Ed.), *Waseda working papers in ELF, 4,* pp. 209–219.

Whorf, B. L. (1956). *Language, thought and reality: Selected writings of Benjamin Lee Whorf. Edited by J. B. Carroll.* Cambridge, MA: MIT Press.

How Does Intercultural Communication Differ from Intracultural Communication?

Istvan KECSKES

Abstract The chapter discusses the differences between intracultural communication and intercultural communication from a socio-cognitive perspective that treats this issue as a continuum rather than a dichotomy. Variation on the continuum and differences between the two phenomena are affected by different factors. While discussing those factors I will refer to issues that are relevant to the three focus points of this volume: internationalization of education, ethnicity, and ideology with special attention to Southeast Asia.

1 Introduction: Understanding Culture

Theoretically, human verbal communication can be considered a process with two extreme end points: the intracultural at one end, and the intercultural at the other. However, practically, communicators are always in between, closer or further to one of the ends, creating and interpreting meaning by using their existing linguistic tools. So it would be a mistake to talk about a dichotomy. There is nothing like pure intracultural or intercultural communication. What we have is something in between on a continuum between the two end points.

Before we explain how the continuum works we need to define culture as understood in this chapter. We adopt Bates and Plog's definition according to which culture is a system of shared beliefs, norms, values, customs, behaviors, and artifacts that the members of society use to cope with their world and with one another (Bates and Plog 1980, p. 6). However, culture cannot be seen as something that is "carved" in every member of a particular society or community. It can be made, changed, manipulated and dropped on the spot. In fact, it is not culture that can be changed, manipulated and dropped in talk but its manifestation (Kecskes 2014, p. 86).

Gumperz (1982) and Gumperz and Roberts (1991) called our attention to the fact that "culture" is not present in communication in the "old" sense of a transcendent identity which is composed of values and norms and linearly related to forms of

I. KECSKES (✉)
Educational Theory, State University of New York, Albany, NY, USA
e-mail: istvan.kecskes@gmail.com

© Springer International Publishing AG, part of Springer Nature 2018
A. CURTIS, R. SUSSEX (eds.), *Intercultural Communication in Asia:*
Education, Language and Values, Multilingual Education 24,
https://doi.org/10.1007/978-3-319-69995-0_7

behavior. Cultural phenomena in speech are contingent, situational, and emergent in nature. Blommaert (1998, p. 4) claimed that what we can observe and analyze in intercultural communication is "different conventions of communication, different speech styles, narrative patterns, in short, the deployment of different communicative repertoires. As far as 'identity' is concerned (cultural, ethnic identity), it can be an inference of these speech styles: people can identify selves or others on the basis of such speech styles. But in actual fact, not 'culture' is deployed, but communicative repertoires."

The main argument of the research line represented by researchers such as Gumperz, Hymes, Blommaert, Rampton and others is that there is no single language, culture, or communicative style. What we have is language, culture, and communicative style instantiated in different group and individual varieties. In intercultural communication, speakers have a "repertoire" of varieties of styles and a combination of styles, which are deployed according to the communicative needs in the changing context. The nationality or ethnic membership of people may suggest the possibility of ethnic or cultural marking in communicative behavior. However, the interplay of several different factors affects the emergence of "ethnically" or "culturally marked" aspects of communicative behavior, which is most frequently dominated by factors that are not necessarily cultural. Some of them will be discussed in this chapter.

Blommaert (1998), following the line of argument developed by Gumperz, Hymes and others, claimed that culture is rarely unified, and new contexts generate new cultures and new forms of intercultural communication. Rampton's research (1995) provided empirical substance for the old Sapirian claim that one society can hide many societies, one culture can hide many cultures, and one language can hide many others.

This, however, does not mean that there is nothing relatively stable and unifying in culture. On this issue there is a significant difference between the constructivist view represented by Blommaert, Gumperz and Rampton, and the socio-cognitive approach (see Kecskes 2010, 2014). The difference between the constructivist view and the socio-cognitive approach lies in the understanding of the nature of existing "communicative repertoires", and the ways these repertoires are deployed. In intercultural communication, existing communicative repertoires have been developed from prior experience and communicative encounters in a language or languages other than the common language of communication (Kecskes 2014). What the online[1] creation of culture means is similar to what online, actual meaning construction means: the process brings about something relatively new that is needed in the actual situational context. This process relies on existing repertoires and newly emergent elements. Culture, just like meaning, is characterized by both regularity and variety. It certainly is more than just an online-created and co-constructed phenomenon. In communication, interactants can rely mainly on two types of repository of prior experience and encounters: lexical units and communicative styles.

---

[1] "online" here refers to creation of culture in the moment of speech.

Like lexical items, cultural patterns (often expressed in different communicative styles) code prior experience and encounters, i.e., relatively standard cultural behavior models and expectations, which are activated in a given situational context. Here is, for instance, an exchange between a librarian and a student:

(1)
Student: - I'm returning these books.
Librarian: - Can I see your library card, please?
Student: - Here you are.
Librarian: - Do you want to extend the due date of any of these books?
Student: - No, thank you.
Librarian: - Here's your card. You're all set.

In the course of interaction, these existing models are modified and blended with situationally emergent new elements. This process of blending, that relies both on existing and emerging factors, constitutes the communicative encounter. Blending means joining existing and emerging elements/factors into new "intercultures" (see Kecskes 2013, 2014) So in the interaction, the communicative repertoires of speakers are not just deployed but they are actually modified and blended with emerging elements as the process develops. The socio-cognitive approach emphasizes that this "third culture" creation means not just putting together what we have, and bringing about a third phenomenon which is neither this or that/neither one nor the other, but actually giving sense to the communicative repertoires and changing them by relating them to the actual situational context, that also adds to or takes away something from what is existing. Cultural constructs and models change diachronically, while cultural representation and speech production by individuals change synchronically.

Durkheim (1982) argued that culture is distributed. Cultural norms and models gain individual interpretation in concrete social actions and events. People have collective norms and standards but they use them individually. The core of these norms and standards is the same but its actual use may differ depending on individual wish, need and desire. People both produce culture and are governed by it. Because of people's ability to reify social reality, the socio-cultural world comes to have a life of its own and can dominate the actors who create them (e.g. Simmel 1972).

Culture is a dynamic phenomenon. Existing, relatively definable models are modified and blended with situationally emergent new elements. As we discussed above, there is a major difference between the socio-constructivist view and the socio-cognitive approach. While social constructivists argue that models and frames have to be rebuilt again and again, so it is just our impression that they exist outside language, the socio-cognitive approach claims that cultural models have some kind of psychological reality in the mind, and when a situation occurs the appropriate model is recalled, and adjusted, which supports the appropriate verbalization of triggered thoughts and activities. This socio-cognitive approach is the view that this chapter adopts because it considers people not only social beings but also individuals with their particular individual experience and interpretation as will be explained below.

2   The Difference

The dominant view is that there is no principled difference between intracultural communication and intercultural communication (e.g. Winch 1997; Wittgenstein 2001). This is true as far as the purpose and mechanism of the communicative process is concerned. However, according to Gumperz and Gumperz (2005) monolingual people and multilingual people do not differ in what they do with language, but in how they do what they do. So when we intend to explain the relationship between intracultural and intercultural interaction our focus should be on the "how".

We can now present a working definition of the two phenomena in the socio-cognitive approach. *Intracultural communication* occurs in interactions between members of a relatively definable L1 speech community following conventions of language and conventions of usage with individual choices and preferences. *Intercultural communication* refers to interactions between speakers who have different first languages, communicate in a common language, and, usually, represent different cultures. So how is this difference reflected in language use?

From a pragmatic perspective, the main difference between intracultural communication and intercultural communication appears to be that the latter, to some extent, shifts the emphasis from the communal to the individual. Kecskes (2014) argued that what standard pragmatics assumes about how things work in communication depends on there being commonalities, conventions, standards and norms between speakers and hearers. This, however, may not be exactly so in intercultural communication. Commonalities, conventions, common beliefs, norms, shared knowledge and the like all create a core common ground on which intention and cooperation-based pragmatics is built. (Of course, there are plenty of varieties within those commonalities.) However, when this core common ground appears to be limited, as is the case in intercultural communication, interlocutors cannot take it for granted; rather they need to co-construct it, at least temporarily. So what is happening here is that there appears to be a shift in emphasis from the communal to the individual. It is not that the individual becomes more important than the societal. Rather, since there is limited common ground, it should be created in the interactional context in which the interlocutors function as core common ground creators, rather than just common ground seekers and activators, as is the case in intracultural communication. So the nature of intersubjectivity, the way rapport is established between interlocutors, seems to be being changed.

In intercultural communication, there is more reliance on language created ad hoc by individuals in the course of interaction, than on prefabricated language and pre-existing frames. In the case of interlocutors who use a common language and whose L1s differ (intercultural communication or/and lingua franca communication), the lack of full control over language skills (L2) and full knowledge of conventions, beliefs and norms in the target language (L2) used as the medium of communication may lead to a more conscious approach to what is said, and how it is said. This should certainly affect the way we evaluate speaker production, hearer comprehension and implicatures in intercultural interactions. Furthermore, in intercultural communication, a more conscious recipient design, a more careful attention to the audience may be involved than in intracultural communication, in which interlocutors do not have to deal with language skill issues, and may rely on more spontaneous, (partly) prefabricated speech and less monitoring. This more conscious recipient design is especially well-observable when Chinese people communicate with other nationalities in English as a lingua franca, as the example below demonstrates:

> (2) A Chinese student is talking with a Japanese student:
> CH: So glad to meet you. Let me ask you how long you have been here?
> JA: - Two and a half month
> CH: - Two and a half months. Ok yeah
> JA: - I start this August
> CH: - August. Right. We have the same time. I'm only two months. I came here… right here … on august… also… yeah
> JA: - When you … stay [word]
> CH: - Oh … one year. One year … yeah … at program. So you … what's your purpose of … intention of coming here?
> JA: - Intention
> CH: - Yah intention.
> JA: - Intention
> CH: - For what purpose?
> JA: - Ah I'm exchange student.
> CH: - Oh exchange student.
> JA: - My Japanese university has exchange program
> CH: - Oh yeah
> JA: - This program
> CH: - So that is … so now you want to get to a degree of bachelor or master … master degree or bachelor….

There are two strategies of the Chinese student that show careful recipient design. Occasionally she repeats what the Japanese student says to make sure that she heard properly what the Japanese partner said. When she notices that the Japanese student has difficulties in understand the word "intention", she gives it up and uses "purpose" instead.

Given the described mindset of nonnative speakers, there seems to be reason to take up the question of how people go about formulating utterances and interpreting them when they cannot count on, or have limited access to, those commonalities, conventions, standards and norms, so they are, in a sense, expected to create and co-construct them in/during the communicative process. Kecskes (2014) claimed that what people depend on that makes pragmatic meaning reliable within a speech community – the focus of standard pragmatic theories – becomes more visible when we see the troubles, misunderstandings and also different routes to success that may arise when those commonalities and/or conventions are missing or limited cross-culturally. This means that while working on intercultural pragmatics and analyzing language use in intercultural communication, we may be able to see and notice things that standard theories of pragmatics may miss or just take for granted. For instance, in the Gricean paradigm cooperation is considered to be a rational behavior exhibited by all human beings. It is essential that human beings are cooperative in the course of communication subconsciously and automatically. In intercultural communication, however, this rational and subconscious behavior is enhanced with a conscious, often monitored endeavor of interlocutors to be cooperative and make deliberate efforts to comprehend others and produce language that is processable and understandable by others. So in intercultural communication, it is even more emphasized that the goal of coming to an understanding is "intersubjective mutuality – shared knowledge, mutual trust, and accord with one another" (Habermas 1979, p. 3).

3   The Success Approach

If we accept that what we do in any kind of communication is similar but how we do it is different, then we should focus on the different or modified routes to success when those L1 commonalities and/or conventions are missing or are limited, as is the case in lingua franca exchanges/interactions/discourse.

There have been several attempts (e.g. Samovar and Porter 2001; Ting-Toomey 1999; Gudykunst and Mody 2002; Nishizaka 1995) to explain the difference between intracultural and intercultural communication. Samovar and Porter (2001, p. 63) argued that "intracultural communication" is the type of communication that takes place between members of the same dominant culture, but with slightly different values, as opposed to "intercultural communication" which is the communication between two or more distinct cultures.

Many scholars argued that interculturality is the main reason for miscommunication (e.g. Thomas 1983; Hinnenkamp 1995; Ting-Toomey 1999). Intercultural communication as a field of inquiry was basically constituted as an analysis of understanding troubles (e.g. ten Thije 2003; Gumperz 1982; Gudykunst and Kim 1992), on the presumption that "during intercultural communication, the message sent is usually not the message received" (Neuliep 2006, p. 1).

When understanding troubles that occurred in intercultural interactions, analysts typically searched cultural differences for a cause, without considering other factors, or more importantly, without examining what non-native and native speakers might be doing to overcome them.

The deficit view was best summarized by Varonis and Gass (1985, p. 340):

> NSs and NNSs[2] are multiply handicapped in conversations with one another. Often they may not share a world view or cultural assumptions, one or both of which may lead to misunderstanding. In addition, they may not share common background [...] that would permit them to converse with shared beliefs about what Gumperz and Tannen (1979) call the 'semantic content' of the conversation. Furthermore, they may have difficulty with speaking and interpreting an interlocutor's discourse as a result of a linguistic deficit.

However, some researchers' findings show the opposite (e.g. House 2002, 2003; Kecskes 2007). The use of semantically transparent language by non-native speakers

---

[2] NS: Native Speaker, NNS: Non-Native Speaker.

results in fewer misunderstandings and communication breakdowns than expected. The insecurity experienced by lingua franca speakers makes them establish a unique set of rules for interaction which may be referred to as an "interculture", according to Koole and ten Thije (1994, p. 69) a "culture constructed in cultural contact". Several authors (e.g. Kaur 2010; Deterding 2013) using ELF datasets from Southeast Asia report relatively low level of misunderstandings, mainly as a consequence of careful recipient design described above.

What we need is a success approach to intercultural encounters. Those who adopt that view tacitly regard people interacting as passive victims of their differences. However, people generally produce language as participants in interaction, and in interacting they actively engage in making it work, in achieving understanding and being understood. This is congruent with Kidwell's (2000) proposal that we use a "success approach" in the study of intercultural, cross-linguistic communication that has as its aim explicating the resources that enable participants to accomplish their communicative tasks successfully.

The "success approach" has a profound effect on international education. Students using not their L1 for education but another language such as English are not considered deficient learners but learners in their own right. These learners are perfectly capable of expressing themselves through L2 and negotiate meaning by creating "intercultures" that can be considered as unique tools of creating meaning as, for instance, in the following sequence (3) in which a Polish woman is speaking about housing with a man from Hong Kong:

HKM: - How about you? …circumstances…Where do you live? You rent…or?
PAF: - Mmm…I am live…not so far from the university.
HKM: - Hmm.
PAF: - It is a college…you don't know… It is not so far. It's Albany.
HKM: - Hmm.
PAF: - But I have 3 minutes…errh… to go to my work.
HKM: - Hmm.
PAF: - And this house is…errh… on our own so my husband and I….
HKM: - Hmm.
BIF: - Doesn't have any kids?
PAF: - No. don't have….
BIF: - No?
PAF: - Yeah.
BIF: - Errh…Are your husband American or…?
PAF: - Errh…Actually he is…he is Polish. He is American but….
BIF: - OK.
PAF: - …because he came into the United States when he was a child.
HKM: - Hmm.
PAF: - He was something like twelve.
BIF: - All right.

Intercultures are co-constructed common ground elements that rely both on relatively definable cultural models and norms as well as situationally evolving features (Kecskes 2010, 2012, 2014).

In this conversation the following elements can be considered intercultures: a Polish woman rents a house with her husband; they live close to work and university;

the husband is a Polish-American. These are like talking points that are unfolded and co-constructed in the course of interaction between the two parties.

When talking about intercultures and the process of co-contructing them we should mention that when English as a lingua franca is used in the Southeast Asian region interlocutors' linguistic behavior and the way they use English have quite a lot in common. This is an important fact because the shared core common ground and way of thinking between an interlocutor with a Mandarin L1 and a Vietnamese L1 is much closer than is the case between a Mandarin L1 speaker and a German L1 speaker. Co-constructing intercultures may be a smoother process in the first case.

4   Factors Defining Movement Along the Continuum

4.1   Language Proficiency

Relatively high proficiency in language use allows the speaker to pay more attention to the communicative process itself rather than just to language use issues (word choice, fluency, correctness, etc.). There is hardly any proficiency issue affecting intracultural communication.

So the higher the language proficiency of the interlocutors is, the more the intercultural communicative process resembles intracultural communication. Of course we recognize that there are individual differences in L1 use too. However, those affect language use in a different way than in intercultural encounters, where looking for words and building meaningful utterances may require more significant effort than in L1 communication.

This has special importance for education because the language of instruction requires high proficiency no matter in what internationalized environment the education takes place. Language proficiency tests (TOEFL, IELTS, etc.) serve to identify the proficiency levels of students, and academic discourse is highly dependent on language skills. It is, then, often the case that international students have the necessary academic content knowledge, but do not always have the required language skills to let others in the educational environment know that they really know what they know. This is especially true for students coming from the Southeast Asian region including China, Malaysia, Hong Kong, Singapore, etc.) Proficiency like this may cause serious frustration in the language behavior of some international students. Most universities introduce special programs to address this issue and give their international students all the language support they need.

High proficiency in English is a major issue in Southeast Asia as well because English plays the role of lingua franca in that part of the world. The countries that belong to the Association of Southeast Asian Nations (ASEAN) make special attempts to promote the use of English as a lingua franca and make it available for students in the region. They recently ratified ASEAN charter enshrines the position of English as the sole working language of the organization. English is also the working language of the extended grouping known as ASEAN +3, which includes the ten states of ASEAN plus China, Japan and Korea. Kirkpatrick (2010, 2014) argued that in spite of these developments little research has been done into English as a lingua franca in Asia. He described the Asian Corpus of English (ACE) project in which a number of teams across East and Southeast Asia are collaborating. Their aim is to compile a million-word corpus of naturally occurring, spoken, interactive English being used as a lingua franca in Asia. This is a very important step forward to find out something about the real English language use of people living in that area. Co-constructing intercultures as explained above is best demonstrated in the use of English as a lingua franca, and corpus studies will significantly enhance our knowledge about the nature of the "interculture" creating processes that constitute the main part of English language proficiency in ELF.

4.2   Preferred Ways of Saying Things and Preferred Ways of Organizing Thoughts

Intracultural communication is dominated by preferred ways of saying things and preferred ways of organizing thoughts within a particular speech community (see Kecskes 2008, 2014, 2011). This is not the case in intercultural communication, because the development of "preferred ways" requires time and conventionalization within a speech community.

Kecskes (2007) argued that using a particular language and belonging to a particular speech community means having preferred ways of saying things and preferred ways of organizing thoughts. This is expressed in a well-balanced blend of prefabricated language with ad hoc generated language. Preferred ways of saying things are generally reflected best in the use of formulaic language and figurative language. Selecting the right words and expressions in communication is more important than syntax. Americans *shoot a film, run a business, make love, do the dishes* and *put out the fire*. The TV anchor asks you to *stick around*, and the shop assistant tells you at the end of the transaction that *you're all set*.

Language socialization, to a great extent, depends on the acquisition of what is expected to be said in particular situations, and what kind of language behavior is considered appropriate in the given speech community. For instance:

(4) Husband and wife are talking.
Are you OK, Mary?
I am fine, Roy.
I would have believed you if you hadn't said "Roy".

"I am fine" is a formulaic expression. But Mary added "Roy", the name of the husband to the expression, which, with this action, ceased to have its usual function, and implied the opposite meaning: "No, I am not fine." As his response shows, the husband recognized that his wife was feeling bad about something.

Formulaic language is the heart and soul of native-like language use. In fact, formulaic language use makes language use native-like. Pawley and Syder argued that "it is knowledge of conventional expressions, more than anything, that gives speakers the means to escape from the one-clause-at-a-time constraint, and that is the key to native-like fluency" (Pawley and Syder 1983, p. 164). Sometime before Pawley and Syder, Dell Hymes wrote that "a vast proportion of verbal behaviour consists of recurrent patterns, ... [including] the full range of utterances that acquire conventional significance for an individual, group or whole culture" (Hymes 1968, pp. 126–127). Coulmas (1981, pp. 1–3) also argued that much of what is actually said in everyday conversation is by no means unique. Rather, a great deal of communicative activity consists of enacting routines making use of prefabricated linguistic units in a well-known and generally accepted manner. Successful coordination of social interactions depends heavily on standardized ways of organizing interpersonal encounters, because conventional ways of doing things with words and expressions are familiar to everyone in the speech community, so speakers can be expected to be understood according to their communicative intentions and goals. Wray and Namba (2003, p. 36) claimed "[...] speech communities develop and retain common ways of expressing key messages". What they meant by "key messages" is expressions that are expected to be used in certain reoccurring situations that Kecskes called "Situation-Bound Utterances" (Kecskes 2002, 2013). For instance: "what can I do for you?" in service encounters, "you are all set" at the end of a payment transaction, "welcome aboard" to a new employee, etc. Or in Chinese: Hěn gāoxìng rènshi nǐ [Very nice to meet you], Dào nǎli qù ya? [Where are you heading?].

Several studies have referred to the low rate of formulaic language in intercultural communication (Prodromou 2008; Kecskes 2007). Researchers argued that the main reason for this is that interlocutors prefer semantically analyzable units, because they cannot be sure of how much of formulaic language their partners can process the way they do. Discrepancy in formulaic language use in intercultural communication can lead to serious misunderstandings, as the following example shows:

(5) A Korean student is talking to the clerk in the university's Human Resources office.
Lee: - Could you sign this document for me, please?
Clerk: - *Come again...?*
Lee: - Why should I come again? I am here now.

Although the clerk used an interrogative intonation with the expression "come again", the Korean student still misunderstood her because she did not know the formulaic function of that particular expression in that particular context.

The use of formulaic expressions, especially Situation-Bound Utterances, means a special problem for Asian students whose culture is usually very different from American, Australian or British culture. As SBUs reflect preferred ways of saying things in a language, they reflect the way of thinking of members of a speech community. English language learners are expected to understand and accept the way language is used in reoccurring situations. If one knows an SBU that the other interlocutor is not familiar with, that may cause serious problems in the interaction, which is the case in the following example:

(6) Sally and Xiaolu are standing at the door of Human Resources:
Sally: - Here is the door.
Xiaolu: - Who should go in first?
Sally: - Be my guest.
Xiaolu: - We are not guests here.

Xiaolu completely misunderstood the expression "be my guest" that is often used by native speakers of American English in similar situations. The reason of misinterpretation was that Xiaolu processed the utterance literally, not as an SBU. She probably never met the expression used in that sense.

4.3   Reliance on Emergent Common Ground Rather than on Core Common Ground

Common ground refers to the "sum of all the information that people assume they share" (Clark 2009, p. 116), which may include world views, shared values, beliefs, and situational context. What standard pragmatics assumes about how things work in communication depends on there being commonalities, conventions, standards and norms between speakers and hearers (Kecskes 2014, 2015). This, however, may not be exactly so in intercultural communication. Commonalities, conventions, common beliefs, norms, shared knowledge, etc. all create a core common ground on which intention and cooperation-based pragmatics are built. (Of course, there are plenty of varieties within those commonalities). However, when this core common ground appears to be limited, as is the case in intercultural communication, inter-locutors cannot take them for granted; rather they need to co-construct them, at least temporarily. So *there appears to be a shift in emphasis from the communal to the individual.* As noted above, it is not that the individual becomes more important than the societal. Rather, since there is limited common ground, it should be co-created in the interactional context in which the interlocutors are functioning at that moment, with the interlocutors as core common ground creators, rather than just common ground seekers and activators, as is the case in intracultural communication.

We need to make a difference between core common ground and emergent common ground (see Kecskes and Zhang 2009). Core common ground refers to prior experience of individuals within a speech community. People usually infer this "common ground" from their past conversations, contacts, encounters, their immediate surroundings, and their shared cultural background and experience within the speech community. People belonging to a speech community share much core common ground, which makes communication relatively smooth between members of the speech community.

Emergent common ground is the result of creating and co-constructing intercul-tures in intercultural communication. It is important to underline that this co-construction is not separated from core common ground. Co-construction, which is the co-creation of emergent common ground, builds not only on actual situational needs and context, but also existing shared knowledge and information. During this process new and old are blended into a synergistic whole. This phenomenon also exists in intracultural communication. However, while intracultural communication builds on existing core common ground that is the result of relatively similar prior experience of interlocutors and less on emergent common ground, intercultural communication relies more on emergent common ground, because of the limited availability of core common ground resulting from little or no mutual prior experience. So again, what we see as difference between intracultural communication and intercultural communication is the degree of reliance on core common ground and emergent common ground.

Creating common ground is also important from the point of view of ideology. Emerging co-constructed common ground ensures mutual understanding not only in the communicative process, but also for tolerance for/of different ethnicities and ideologies. Woolard and Schieffelin (1994, p. 63) define language ideology as:

> the networks of beliefs that language users hold, either tacitly or overtly, about language and its assumed relation to other aspects in their environments, especially other individuals and social groups, which stem either from explicit teaching or implicit socialization. Owing to their connections between language and language users or social groups, language ideologies are intimately connected to macro-structures of power and privilege.

Woolard and Schieffelin (1994, p. 65) highlighted the fact that: "In particular, language ideologies are often used as an interpretive lens to explain the ways in which language varies across social groups in a society and to draw connections between specific aspects of language and the identities, moral goodness, or worth of those using particular features of language". In a recent study, Subtirelu (2015) analyzed the complaints of native speaker students against non-native speaker teaching assistants. He argued that the study of language ideology offers a way of viewing complaints about accents, ostensibly an issue of language, as connected to broader issues of political power and social exclusion through their intersection with other oppressive ideologies, such as racism. Lippi-Green (1994) suggested that the term "accent" commonly makes reference to the way the Other speaks. She also wrote that an accompanying ideological phenomenon is the assertion or assumption that one's own speech is without accent. Lippi-Green stated that "when people reject an accent, they also reject the identity of the person speaking: his or her race, ethnic heritage, national origin, regional affiliation, or economic class" (1994, p. 165). Lippi-Green viewed undergraduate students' complaints as an act of social exclusion; as a means of denying meaning to the communicative attempts of the NNS instructor as Other. I believe Lippi-Green went too far with this conclusion, but it is true that willingness to try to create common ground in communicating with "people of accent" as Lippi-Green refers to them, can be considered as an attempt to include those people into the given speech community.

4.4   Change in the Nature of Intersubjectivity

Cognitive-oriented approaches to intersubjectivity have focused on the process of cooperative meaning-making (Habermas 1979), with a focus on a shared meaning as an end goal. Similarly, the psychologist Rommetveit (1992, p. 58) viewed intersubjectivity as an end goal within social understanding, framing it as "reciprocal perspective setting and perspective taking" within the pursuit of a "state of intersubjectivity", which refers to the development of a shared understanding and/or focus on particular elements of the communicative process between speaker(s) and hearer(s).

In intercultural communication the nature of intersubjectivity seems to be being changed. There is more reliance on language created ad hoc by individuals in the course of interaction than on prefabricated language and pre-existing frames. In the case of interlocutors who use a common language and whose L1s differ (intercultural communication), the lack of full control over language skills (L2) and full knowledge of conventions, beliefs and norms in the target language (L2) used as the medium of communication, may lead *to a more conscious approach to what is said, and how it is said.* This should certainly affect the way we evaluate speaker production, hearer comprehension and implicatures in intercultural interactions. Furthermore, in intercultural communication more conscious recipient design may be involved than in intracultural communication, in which interlocutors do not have to deal with L2 language skill issues and may rely on more spontaneous, (partly) prefabricated speech and less monitoring.

All this results in a shift from the societal to the individual. It is the responsibility of the participating individuals to develop their socio-cultural frame for the conversation, create common ground, and find linguistic elements that are mutually understandable in the actual situational context. So the basic difference between intracultural communication and intercultural communication from the perspective of intersubjectivity is that while participants in intracultural interactions can rely on existing frames that affect them top-down, in intercultural interactions participants must build up those frames bottom-up while negotiating meaning with their interlocutors. Diversity of individuals participating in the communicative process will result in social frames that are built on mutual understanding of different ethnicities, rather than just on the experience of one particular speech community. Rampton's data (1995) showed that, depending on who is addressed, when, and in what particular type of activity (e.g., playing, discussing, listening to music), the role and function of ethnically marked communication styles may change.

In her study, Strickland (2010) described the process of developing intersubjectivity between teachers and newcomer students with a diverse background. In the shared classroom experience, the native speaker teachers and immigrants constructed multiple meanings and invoked multiple voices to make sense of what they experienced in their interactions. The study examined each voice, both those present voices of the participating teachers and newcomers, as well as the traces of voices from their past social and cultural contexts, which are brought into the intersubjective process in each classroom. Strickland pointed out that a teaching-learning process may provide the opportunity for intercultural dialogue that is beneficial for all participants in the culturally diverse classroom.

4.5 Context-Sensitivity

Kecskes (2008, 2014) argued that context-sensitivity works differently in intracultural and intercultural communication. In linguistics, context usually refers to any factor – linguistic, epistemic, physical, social, etc. – that affects the actual interpretation of signs and expressions. This is too broad a definition, and it does not reflect the complexity of the issue of context. The socio-cognitive approach calls for the revision of how we understand the role of context in communication in general and in intercultural communication in particular. This revision is needed because context does not exactly affect meaning production and comprehension in the way it does in intracultural communication. There are several reasons for this.

One reason is that actual situational context cannot play the role of catalyst in intercultural communication in the way it does in intracultural communication, because the participants' different socio-cultural background ties them to culturally different L1 communities, where both prior context and actual situational context function in a variety of ways. Also, context-sensitiveness may work differently because of the increasing number of "interpretation sensitive terms". Cappelen argued that: "[N]atural languages contain what I'll call *interpretation sensitive terms*: terms the correct interpretation of which varies across interpreters (or, more generally, contexts of interpretation). An interpretation sensitive sentence can have one content relative to one interpreter, and another content relative to another interpreter" (Cappelen 2008, p. 25). When Cappelen writes about "interpretation sensitive terms", he does not think about nonnative speakers of a natural language, as he refers only to native speakers of a natural language. However, he is right that this notion is important in natural languages, no matter whether the given language is used by a native speaker or a nonnative speaker.

What these *interpretation sensitive terms* are, and how they function for nonnative speaker language users, is an important matter in intercultural interaction as we will see in the examples below. The content of an utterance should be understood relative to a speaker and a hearer. The same utterance can express several distinct propositions depending on who the hearer/s is/are. The question is what makes those "terms" interpretation sensitive in intercultural interactions, and how the nature of interpretation sensitive terms may depend on the culturally diverse background of interlocutors.

The following excerpt is an interaction between an African French speaker and a Korean speaker. The common context is that they both live in Albany, NY but have different cultural backgrounds. The interlocutors appear to jump from one topic to another, seemingly changing their intention and interrupting the flow of communication. However, a closer look shows that they think along similar topic-comment lines, and co-construct a coherent narrative in which emergent intention and common ground play an important role. The topic-comment lines are as follows: living in Albany – likes/dislikes – likes: quiet, nice neighbors - dislikes: offices and forms. Their prior context gives different understanding to terms such as school, driver station, manager, etc. The actual situational context does not help them much to specify the meanings of those key expressions (interpretation sensitive terms) so they need to negotiate their meanings in the course of their interaction;

(7)
K: - I like living in Albany. Because the Albany is the... especially I [word] almost two months... it's quiet ... nice people ... neighbor...
AF: - Yeah you have nice neighbors.
K: - Yeah, yeah.
AF: - The manager in the apartment is good?
K: - Yeah good.
AF: - ah ... so you have good neighbors ... it's quiet ... good ... so everybody has difficulties where they live so since you came from Korea what kind of difficulties you ... what are the problems that you have to live in Albany?
K: - Ah I came ... when I came here ... the first time about ... I applied the driver's license and you go to there
AF: - Yeah.
K: - DMV ... yeah yeah ... driver station
AF: - Yeah.
K: - And then they require so many documents
AF: - I see.
K: - So I had to go another office.
AF: - To apply to school.
K: - Yeah social number or ... officer ... anybody ... anyway I had to go there and then ... receive the document I gave them ... so long time I ... take a long time.

Context-sensitivity, which in the socio-cognitive paradigm means *actual situational context-sensitivity*, works differently in intercultural encounters and intracultural encounters. There are universal contextual factors that affect language processing similarly, no matter what language is actually used. These factors are connected with general knowledge of the world, such as weather, landscape, human relations, etc. When I say "have a good one", it is not necessary to name/specify whether I mean day, night, afternoon or morning, as the actual situational context does that. Or in Russian, when we say Саша и Света поженились (*Saša i Sveta poženilis',* Sasha and Sveta got married), we do not have to refer to the fact that they got married to each other (example from Kecskes 2014).

However, most actual contextual factors are language- and culture-specific. Each language has interpretation-sensitive lexical items, expressions and utterances, where a part or all of the knowledge that is necessary for processing is taken for granted in the given culture. No wording is needed because actual situational context does the rest. For instance, when in Russian we say "Как дела?" (*Kak dela?* How are things?), speakers know what the word "дела" (*dela,* things) refer to. Basically, the closest equivalent of this expression in English is "how are you doing?". This is where the major problem of intercultural communication with context occurs. *Whose context are we talking about in a communicative encounter?* The prior context of the L1, or the prior context of the L2, or the actual situational co-constructed context, or all three?

If we go back to the definition of interculturality then our answer should be "all three". However, we should know that the lower the target language proficiency of speakers is, the more they will be affected by the prior context of the L1 and ignore or pay little attention to the actual situational context. So context-sensitivity in these cases cannot work the way it does *in intracultural communication, where salience and common ground are governed by the relatively more homogenous culture.* However, this does not mean that there is much more misunderstanding in intercultural communication than in intracultural encounters. Interlocutors negotiate meaning, and relying more on semantics than context, they work out their differences as in the example below, in which a Japanese student and an American student are talking through Skype (data collected by Emiko Kamiya):

```
(8)s
A: You know (.) I used to play tennis myself
J: Oh really
A: Yeah I (..) I just I used to play (      ) the first serve? ((gesture))
J: [Mm hm?
A: [You know? then (.) you know? (      ) a couple of (      ) [(      )
J:                                                         [Ahhhhhh
A: I never (      ) but played a little bit (here and there?)
J: Ahahaha
J: [I
A: [Hahaha
J: I can just play (0.3) SOFT tennis?
A: Sof (..) now soft tennis (.) you play with a racket and a tennis ball though right?
J: Ah (1.2) white ball↑
(1.4)
A: White ball↓
J: Yeah (.) gom? (.) gom ball?
(1.4)
A: gom ball
J: a (.) I don't know
A: HAHAHA
J: ((laugh))
A: Are you using a (gumball?)? to play tennis? hehehe
J: Mmm (..) Yyeah (.) maybe hahaha
A: I use my (      ) hehe=
J: =fffff
```

The Japanese student is explaining to the American student that she also played some game similar to tennis. However, she does not know the right word in English for *softball* so she uses the ad hoc constructed phrase "soft tennis" and tries to explain to the American student what she really means by talking about the ball they used. However "gom ball" (instead of "rubber ball") does not help her make her partner understand what she wants because of the two things: (1) wrong pronunciation, and (2) wrong choice of word ("gum" instead of "rubber"). She uses "gom" (gum) because she has prior experience with that word rather than with "rubber". Actual situational context does not help the interlocutors much in this situation.

What they rely on is their prior context and prior experience. However, there is a/ some discrepancy between those experiences that is worked out after all in the actual situational context.

5   The Linguistic Context of Education

The issues discussed above about intercultural communication are relevant to education. The linguistic context in education is rapidly changing all over the world. The context-sensitivity issue is directly connected to what is called "plurilingual usage" and "plurilingual education", especially in Europe and partly in South East Asia (Taiwan and Japan). Multilingualism and plurilingualism are supposed to be different notions. "Multilingualism" refers to the co-existence of different languages, whether in the mind of an individual or a society, and represents a diversification of available languages. Plurilingualism, on the other hand, underlines that a person's languages and cultures are not kept in strictly separated mental compartments, but that the languages in a person's mind will interrelate and interact to contribute to the growth of communication skills as a whole (see, for instance, Canagarajah 2009). This is basically not much different from Kecskes and Papp's (2000) approach to bi- and multilingualism. They emphasized that a common underlying conceptual base (CUCB) operates two or more language channels (systems of linguistic signs). Communicative "repertoires" and strategies that are the reflections of blended skills and knowledge are parts of the CUCB and they are deployed no matter what language the speaker uses.

Plurilingual education is a more liberal approach to language learning, because it emphasizes that you are not expected to reach native-like mastery of a foreign language. Even a bit/small amount/piece of a new language would build your abilities to communicate by providing you with more tools to do so, even if these tools are rudimentary and context-specific. If you learned just the basics of, say, Chinese, your abilities to survive in China will have increased to some extent, even though you are not fluent at all. Plurilingual education is a more enlightened approach to language learning, taking much of the pressure off of you, the language learner, in trying to achieve nativelikeness.

As the Council of Europe in its Common European Framework of Reference for Languages (CEFR) puts it: "From this perspective, the aim of language education is profoundly modified. It is no longer seen as simply to achieve 'mastery' of one or two, or even three languages, each taken in isolation, with the 'ideal native speaker' as the ultimate model. Instead, the aim is to develop a linguistic repertory, in which all linguistic abilities have a place" (2001, p. 15). Overall, this approach is based on a higher awareness of students' varied backgrounds, recognition of the linguistic rights of speakers of languages and language varieties other than the main language of the community, and the recognition of the many benefits of a plurilingual education.

6 Conclusion

The chapter has promoted the idea that the relationship between intracultural communication and intercultural communication can be explained by a continuum whose two ends represent the two "types" of interaction. Movement on/along the continuum, and differences between the two phenomena, are affected by different factors.

As noted above, the main difference between intracultural and intercultural communication is that in intercultural communication there is a shift from the communal/societal to the individual, because conventions, common beliefs, norms, shared knowledge, etc. that constitute a core common ground in L1 are quite limited in intercultural interaction, so the participants should/need to co-construct them. The socio-cognitive approach emphasizes that this shift does not mean that the individual is more important than the societal. What it means is that both are important, but language use frames should be co-constructed by individuals who participate in the process, because language use frames and contextual support do not work the way they do in intracultural communication. It was emphasized that research should use a "success approach" to describe how this co-construction takes place.

The socio-cognitive approach as described in this chapter looks like the opposite of the socio-cultural view that is based on Vygotsky's ideas (1978). Socio-cultural theories require a shift from "the individual human mind" as the single unit of analysis in understanding human thought, to the recognition of the socially and culturally constituted practices through which human thinking and behavior develop (Scribner 1997). Informed by such a theoretical perspective, language learning by students is viewed as a process of changing participation in the socio-cultural activities of students' communities, where identity development is conceptualized as socially, culturally and historically constructed (Rogoff 2003).

There are two problems with the socio-cultural approach. First, it puts emphasis on the actual situational experience of the students, but does not mention how important their prior experience is. Second, the socio-cultural approach has led to the plurilingual view of language proficiency that de-emphasizes languages as separable and discrete entities, and instead focuses attention on the individual's ability to move between and across languages in contextually appropriate ways.

Unlike the socio-cultural approach, the socio-cognitive approach emphasizes that both the actual situational experience and context, and prior experience and context, are important in meaning construction and comprehension, but to varying degrees. This is how we can make sense of the differences between intracultural and intercultural communication.

It would be a mistake to de-emphasize languages as separate and discrete entities as the socio-cultural approach tends to do. Vygotsky (1978) wrote that when we enter school, language becomes the main regulator of thinking. If there is no language per se, what is the "regulator" that we can rely on? This has immediate relevance to the language situation in Southeast Asia where the goal should be multilingualism and not necessarily plurilingualism, which refers to an individual's or a society's ability to speak at least two languages and switch between languages according to the circumstances at hand. There is less emphasis on language boundaries. Multilingualism means something different. It refers to a society in which different languages coexist side by side but are used separately. Multilingualism may mean that some people speak only one language and other people speak several languages. What really matters is that there are several languages being spoken. English as a lingua franca can serve as a common language in the region and a facilitator of intercultural communicat(ion.)

References

Bates, D. G., & Plog, F. (1980). *Cultural anthropology* (2nd ed.). New York: Alfred A. Knopf.

Blommaert, J. (1998). Different approaches to intercultural communication: A critical survey. Plenary lecture, *Lernen und Arbeiten in einer international vernetzten und multikulturellen Gesellschaft, Expertentagung.* Universität Bremen, Institut für Projektmanagement und Witschaftsinformatik (IPMI), 27–28 February. Retrieved 27 July 2017 from http://www.cie.ugent.be/CIE/blommaert1.htm

Cappelen, H. (2008). Content relativism and semantic blindness. In M. García-Carpintero & M. Kölbel (Eds.), *Relative truth* (pp. 265–286). Oxford: Clarendon Press.

Clark, H. H. (2009). Context and common ground. In J. L. Mey (Ed.), *Concise encyclopedia of pragmatics* (pp. 116–119). Oxford: Elsevier.

Cnagarajah, A. S. (2009). The plurilingual tradition and the English language in South Asia. *AILA Review, 22,* 5–22.

Coulmas, F. (Ed.). (1981). *Conversational routine: Explorations in standardized communication situations and prepatterned speech.* The Hague: Mouton.

Deterding, D. (2013). *Misunderstandings in English as a Lingua Franca: An analysis of ELF interactions in South-East Asia.* Berlin/Boston: DeGruyter Mouton.

Durkheim, E. (1982). *The rules of sociological method* (W. D. Halls, Trans.). New York: Simon and Schuster.

Gudykunst, W. B., & Kim, Y. Y. (1992). *Communicating with strangers: An approach to intercultural communication.* New York: McGraw-Hill.

Gudykunst, W. B., & Mody, B. (Eds.). (2002). *Handbook of international and intercultural communication.* Thousand Oaks: Sage.

Gumperz, J. J. (1982). *Discourse strategies.* Cambridge: Cambridge University Press.

Gumperz, J. J., & Roberts, C. (1991). Understanding in intercultural encounters. In J. Blommaert & J. Verschueren (Eds.), *The pragmatics of intercultural and international communication* (pp. 51–90). Amsterdam: John Benjamins.

Gumperz, J., & Gumperz, J. C. (2005). Making space for bilingual communicative practice. *Intercultural Pragmatics, 2*(1), 1–25.

Gumperz, J. J., & Tannen, D. (1979). Individual and social differences in language use. In C. J. Fillmore, D. Kempler, & W. S.-Y. Wang (Eds.), *Individual differences in language ability and language behavior* (pp. 305–325). New York: Academic Press.

Habermas, J. (1979). *Communication and the evolution of society.* Toronto: Beacon Press.

Hinnenkamp, V. (1995). Intercultural communication. In V. Jef, Ö. Jan-Ola, B. Jan, & C. Bulcaen (Eds.), *Handbook of pragmatics* (pp. 1–20). Amsterdam: John Benjamins.

House, J. (2002). Developing pragmatic competence in English as a lingua franca. In K. Knapp & C. Meierkord (Eds.), *Lingua Franca communication* (pp. 245–267). Frankfurt am Main: Peter Lang.

House, J. (2003). Misunderstanding in intercultural university encounters. In J. House, G. Kasper, & S. Ross (Eds.), *Misunderstanding in social life: Discourse approaches to problematic talk* (pp. 22–56). London: Longman.

Hymes, D. H. (1968). The ethnography of speaking. In J. A. Fishman (Ed.), *Readings in the sociology of language* (pp. 99–138). The Hague/Paris: Mouton de Gruyter.

Kaur, J. (2010). Achieving mutual understanding in world Englishes. *World Englishes, 29,* 192–208.

Kecskes, I., & Papp, T. (2000). *Foreign language and mother tongue.* Mawah: Lawrence Erlbaum.

Kecskes, I. (2002). *Situation-bound utterances in L1 and L2.* Berlin: Mouton De Gruyter.

Kecskes, I. (2007). Formulaic language in English lingua franca. In I. Kecskés & L. R. Horn (Eds.), *Explorations in pragmatics: Linguistic, cognitive and intercultural aspects* (pp. 191–219). Berlin/New York: Mouton de Gruyter.

Kecskes, I. (2008). Dueling context: A dynamic model of meaning. *Journal of Pragmatics, 40*(3), 385–406.

Kecskes, I. (2010). The paradox of communication: A socio-cognitive approach. *Pragmatics & Society, 1*(1), 50–73.

Kecskes, I. (2011). Interculturality and intercultural pragmatics. In J. Jackson (Ed.), *The Routledge handbook of intercultural communication* (pp. 67–84). London: Routledge.

Kecskes, I. (2012). Is there anyone out there who really is interested in the speaker? *Language and Dialogue, 2*(2), 285–299.

Kecskes, I. (2013). Why do we say what we say the way we say it? *Journal of Pragmatics, 48*(1), 71–83.

Kecskes, I. (2014). *Intercultural pragmatics.* Oxford: Oxford University Press.

Kecskes, I. (2015). Is the idiom principle blocked in bilingual L2 production? Chapter 2. In R. Heredia & A. Cieslicka (Eds.), *Bilingual figurative language processing* (pp. 28–53). Cambridge: Cambridge University Press.

Kecskes, I., & Zhang, F. (2009). Activating, seeking and creating common ground: A socio-cognitive approach. *Pragmatics & Cognition, 17*(2), 331–355.

Kidwell, M. (2000). Common ground in cross-cultural communication: Sequential and institutional contexts in front desk service encounters. *Issues in Applied Linguistics, 11*(1), 17–37.

Kirkpatrick, A. (2010). Researching English as a lingua franca in Asia: The Asian Corpus of English (ACE) project. *Asian Englishes, 31*(1), 4–18.

Kirkpatrick, A. (2014). English in SEA: Emergent concepts: Pedagogical and policy implications. *World Englishes, 33*(4), 426–438.

Koole, T., & ten Thije, J. D. (1994). *The construction of intercultural discourse: Team discussions of educational advisers.* Amsterdam/Atlanta: RODOPI.

Lippi-Green, R. (1994). *Language ideology and language change in early modern German: A sociolinguistic study of the consonantal system of Nuremberg.* Amsterdam/Philadelphia: John Benjamins.

Neuliep, J. W. (2006). Editorial welcome. *Journal of Intercultural Communication Research, 35*(1), 1–2.

Nishizaka, A. (1995). The interactive constitution of interculturality: How to be a Japanese with words. *Human Studies, 18,* 301–326.

Pawley, A., & Syder, F. H. (1983). Two puzzles for linguistic theory: Nativelike selection and nativelike fluency. *Language & Communication, 5*(5), 191–226.

Prodromou, L. (2008). *English as a Lingua Franca: A corpus based analysis.* London: Continuum.

Rampton, B. (1995). *Crossing: Language and ethnicity among adolescents.* London: Longman.

Rogoff, B. (2003). *The cultural nature of human development.* New York: Oxford University Press.

Rommetveit, R. (1992). Outlines of a dialogically based social-cognitive approach to human cognition and communication. In A. H. Wold (Ed.), *The dialogical alternative: Towards a theory of language and mind* (pp. 19–44). Oslo: Scandinavian University Press.

Samovar, L. A., & Porter, R. E. (2001). *Communication between cultures* (4th ed.). New York: Thomas Learning Publications.

Scribner, S. (1997). A sociocultural approach to the study of mind. In E. Tobach, R. J. Falmagne, M. B. Parlee, L. M. W. Martin, & A. S. Kapelman (Eds.), *Mind and social practice: Selected writings of Sylvia Scribner* (pp. 266–280). Cambridge: Cambridge University Press.

Simmel, G. (1972). *On individuality and social forms* (D. N. Levine, Ed.). Chicago: University of Chicago Press.

Strickland, M. J. (2010). Are they getting it? Exploring intersubjectivity between teachers and immigrant students in three culturally diverse classrooms. *The International Journal of Learning, 17*(6), 197–214.

Subtirelu, N. C. (2015). "She does have an accent but…": Race and language ideology in students' evaluations of mathematics instructors on RateMyProfessors.com. *Language in Society, 44*(1), 35–62.

Ten Thije, J. D. (2003). The transition from misunderstanding to understanding in intercultural communication. In L. I. Komlósi, P. Houtlosser, & M. Leezenberg (Eds.), *Communication and culture: Argumentative, cognitive and linguistic perspectives* (pp. 197–214). Amsterdam: Sic Sac.

Thomas, J. (1983). Cross-cultural pragmatic failure. *Applied Linguistics, 4*(2), 91–112.

Ting-Toomey, S. (1999). *Communicating across cultures*. New York: Guilford Press.

Varonis, E. M., & Gass, S. M. (1985). Miscommunication in native/nonnative conversation. *Language in Society, 14*(3), 327–343.

Vygotsky, L. S. (1978). *Mind in society*. Cambridge: Harvard University press.

Winch, P. (1997). Can we understand ourselves? *Philosophical Investigations, 20*(3), 193–204.

Wittgenstein, L. (2001). Philosophical investigations (3rd ed.). Oxford/Malden: Blackwell.

Woolard, K. A., & Schieffelin, B. B. (1994). Language ideology. *Annual Review of Anthropology, 23*, 55–82.

Wray, A., & Namba, K. (2003). Formulaic language in a Japanese-English bilingual child: A practical approach to data analysis. *Japanese Journal for Multilingualism and Multiculturalism, 9*(1), 24–51.

Part IV
Focal Areas of Intercultural Communication

Reading the City: The Linguistic and Semiotic Landscape of Macao's San Ma Lo (新馬路)

Joanna RADWAŃSKA-WILLIAMS

For my colleague Mao Sihui, who taught me to think visually about culture.

Abstract Macao is a city of six hundred thousand inhabitants, but it receives 30 million visitors per year. Together, they constitute the public that interacts with public space. In distinction from bilingual Hong Kong (Chinese and English), the public signage in Macao is at least trilingual: Chinese, Portuguese and English, reflecting the unique historical and cultural makeup of the city as a former Portuguese colony that has recently (1999) been returned to China. This paper explores the linguistic landscape of Macao from the perspective of a case study of the main street of the historic city center.

The study of linguistic landscape can be considered part of what Scollon and Scollon (Discourses in place: language in the material world. Routledge/Taylor and Francis, London, 2003) term "geosemiotics", referring to the analysis of meanings that are materially situated in the space of urban agglomerations. Adapting a phenomenological approach to data collection, the researcher photographed every aspect of Macao's main street, including public signage in its linguistic aspect, as well as architectural spatial semiotics and the visual semiotics of advertising and shop fronts. The data were classified into three broad categories of spatial, visual and linguistic semiotics, as well as sixteen detailed subcategories. The author's analysis of the data is informed by Chmielewska's (Semiosis takes place or radical uses of quaint theories. In Jaworski A, Thurlow C (eds), Semiotic landscapes: language, image, space. Continuum International Publishing Group Ltd, London/New York, pp. 274–291, 2010) insight into the subjectivity of the process of semiotic interpretation. The semiotic analysis of situated meanings reveals the linguistic and socioeconomic challenges Macao faces as a tourist hub, gaming (gambling) centre and Special Administrative Region of the People's Republic of China.

J. RADWAŃSKA-WILLIAMS (✉)
MPI-Bell Centre of English, Macao Polytechnic Institute, Macao, People's Republic of China
e-mail: onhajrw@ipm.edu.mo

© Springer International Publishing AG, part of Springer Nature 2018
A. CURTIS, R. SUSSEX (eds.), *Intercultural Communication in Asia: Education, Language and Values*, Multilingual Education 24,
https://doi.org/10.1007/978-3-319-69995-0_8

139

1 Introduction

The Special Administrative Region of Macao (Macao S.A.R.) is a former Portuguese colony (since 1557) which was handed back to the People's Republic of China on December 20th, 1999 under the "one country, two systems" formula that guarantees the territory a special degree of autonomy until 2049. The official languages of the territory are Chinese and Portuguese, and the legal system continues to be based on Portuguese law. Government documents are prepared bilingually in Chinese and Portuguese, and sometimes in English translation, as a non-binding ancillary language. With its geographical location approximately forty miles across the Pearl River Delta from the territory of Hong Kong, English has long been an ancillary part of the linguistic make up of Macao, but has arguably become more widespread since 1999 because of Macao's socioeconomic transformation into a gaming (gambling) boomtown. This paper explores Macao's sociolinguistic make up, as well as aspects of its socioeconomic transformation, through a case study of the linguistic landscape of the historic main street of Macao, Avenida de Almeida Ribeiro, popularly called San Ma Lo or 新馬路.

Macao is a fascinating instance of "glocalization", the intersection between globalizing tendencies and local specificities. One could expect that with the return of sovereignty to China, there would be increased visibility of communist ideology, and also, a tendency for Chinese to supplant Portuguese. However, the development of Macao since 1999 has been driven by several vectors. The most visible of these is what could be termed "blatant capitalism" (Mao Sihui, personal communication), as a consequence of the expansion of the gaming industry. The gaming monopoly (single concession) of Societade de Jogos de Macao, headed by the local tycoon Stanley Ho, was broken up in 2002 by the granting of two more gaming concessions, to Sands China (headed by the American tycoon Sheldon Adelson) and to Wynn Macao (headed by the American Steve Wynn). Because of an allowance for subconcessions, instead of three competing casinos this resulted, within the space of 15 years, in over thirty newly built casinos and gigantic resort hotels, with revenue by far exceeding that of Las Vegas. The population of Macao increased by approximately 50%, from four to six hundred thousand; wages rose substantially (between twofold and fourfold depending on the type of work); residential real estate prices rose tenfold; and the number of tourists per year, at 30 million, is fifty times the size of the population. Besides gambling, tourists come to enjoy the beauty of the Portuguese-style architecture; a diversity of restaurants with all of the world's cuisines; high-end brand-name shopping; and services ranging from (semi-legal) prostitution to luxury spas, swimming pools and golf courses. Macao has also become a popular MICE (Meetings, Incentives, Conferences and Exhibitions) destination for concerts, weddings and conventions, bringing in additional private and business tourism that is not exclusively gaming oriented. Thus, the most powerful socioeconomic vector in Macao is the ideology of capitalism (capital development) and globalization (internationalization of the economy), paradoxically promoted by the (local and national) government since the reunification with China.

The second possible expectation since the return of sovereignty to China could be that Chinese would replace Portuguese. However, Portuguese, as text, continues to be widely visible around the city, if not to the same extent audible. Although the number of Portuguese-speaking inhabitants is relatively small (several thousand), Macao is being promoted by the local and national governments as a gateway for trade with Lusophone (Portuguese-speaking) countries, such as Brazil, Angola, Mozambique, São Tomé and Príncipe, East Timor, and Portugal. Visitors and migrant workers and expats from these countries are visible; e.g., there is an African presence in Macao; and, partly because of the Eurozone crisis, there are newly arrived expats from Portugal as well as Portuguese who have resided in Macao for many years. Moreover, the small but influential community of mixed-heritage "Macanese" (colonial families who settled in Macao since the sixteenth century and intermarried with local Chinese and with people from other Portuguese colonies and points of contact) constitute the core identity of Macao's cultural uniqueness (Carvalho 2015). Thus, the sociolinguistic status of Portuguese is open to investigation.

The other prominent variables in Macao's sociolinguistic make up are the use of English as an international language, and the choice between Cantonese and Mandarin Chinese. English is widely visible, and audible (probably) to a larger extent than Portuguese. To enable interaction with international tourists, hotels and restaurants, especially at the high end, favour the hiring of English-speaking staff. Despite preferential policies for hiring local staff (mandatory in the case of casino croupiers), this results in the hiring of non-local staff who can demonstrate fluency in English, e.g., from mainland China, the Philippines and Malaysia. English has a privileged although not exclusive status in the educational system, with the top schools and university programmes being offered in the English medium. However, local supply of English speakers into the labor force does not keep up with demand, resulting in the importation of English speakers. Many of these imported workers are bilingual or multilingual, bringing other languages into the social mix, e.g., Mandarin, Tagalog, Malay.

In terms of varieties of Chinese, Macao (as well as Hong Kong) has the local specificity of being predominantly Cantonese-speaking, with local in-group solidarity, while Mandarin is recognized as the standard national language. Textually, Chinese in Macao (as well as in Hong Kong and Taiwan) is written with traditional characters, while mainland China and Singapore use simplified characters (promoted as the official script in mainland China after the communist revolution of 1949). In addition, there are speakers of other Chinese dialects in Macao, e.g., a large community from Fujian. To various extents, most people in Macao are bidialectal in Cantonese and Mandarin (or multidialectal if originating in a non-Cantonese community) and may also be biliterate in traditional and simplified characters, depending on their degree of exposure to mainland texts. However, I can illustrate the local preference for Cantonese with the following anecdotal evidence. In a second-year university course on Intercultural Communication that I was teaching in English to Chinese-English Translation and Interpretation majors in the spring semester of 2015, the students were not paying close attention to the details of a case study we were discussing. As a comprehension check, my teaching assistant, a young American Fulbrighter, asked one of the students sitting in the front row (who was from mainland China) to summarize the details to the class in Chinese. The student did so in Mandarin. Not convinced that the students in the back of the class were paying attention, the TA asked a student in the back row (who was a local Macao Chinese) to repeat what her classmate had said. The student asked for permission to use Cantonese rather than Mandarin, then repeated the summary. From the above interaction, I had the impression that the active use of Mandarin was as difficult for the local student as the use of English, i.e., that the exercise had been perceived by the student as more of an interpretation task than a simple comprehension check. In this particular class, the Mandarin speakers had chosen to sit in the front row; the middle row consisted mostly of local students and included a local Filipina who spoke Cantonese but whose native language was Tagalog; and the back row consisted entirely of local Macao students.

Intercultural communication can be defined as "communication between individuals from different cultural or ethnic backgrounds, or between people from subculture groups" (Liu et al. 2011, p. 287). In the public space of Macao, intercultural communication takes place on a daily basis, mediated through several languages (Portuguese, English, Cantonese, Mandarin, and others). Individuals and cultures are in contact in this tourist city – local post-colonial Portuguese, Macanese, Cantonese Chinese, and Chinese of other subgroups; expats and migrant workers from English-speaking countries, Lusophone countries, mainland China and Southeast Asia; businessmen and visitors from all over the world (mainland China, East and Southeast Asia, South Asia, Russia, Australia, etc.). The study of linguistic landscape – language visible in public space – can reveal the extent to which different languages and visual codes are present in the sociolinguistic make up of Macao. Based on the above overview of the sociolinguistic and socioeconomic situation of Macao, the following research questions are formulated:

RQ1. Which languages are present on public signs in Macao, and what (if anything) can be inferred from the linguistic landscape about the sociolinguistic situation of Macao?

RQ2. What (if anything) can be inferred from the linguistic (or geosemiotic) landscape about the socioeconomic situation of Macao?

This formulation is intentionally vague, because the extent of inference depends partly on the methodology, and partly on the researcher's subjectivity, as will be explained below in the discussion of linguistic landscape research and its extension into the framework of geosemiotics (Scollon and Scollon 2003; Jaworski and Thurlow 2010).

2   The Study of Linguistic Landscape: LL as Evidence of Social Change

2.1   Sociolinguistic Data: Naturalistic Data

The linguistic landscape provides a window on the sociolinguistics of a locality through naturalistic data that are entirely unelicited. The data are authentic in the same sense that "authentic text" is used in Communicative Language Teaching – i.e., the text is not originally written with an academic purpose in mind (whether teaching or research). Unlike either quantitative research design (e.g., factorial analysis) or qualitative methodology (e.g., questionnaires, interviews, focus groups), these written discourse data are already present in the environment, and thus are not skewed *a priori* by the researcher's expectations. The linguistic landscape provides field data that are more static than the typically oral data of a journalistic report, yet show dynamism over a longer course of time, comparable to the time strata of archaeology, although revealing the stratum of the present rather than of the past.

The study of linguistic landscape was first defined as pertaining to urban settings, perhaps because that is where the major part of publicly displayed written discourse can be found:

> The language of public road signs, advertising billboards, street names, place names, commercial shop signs, and public signs on government buildings combines to form the linguistic landscape of a given territory, region, or urban agglomeration (Landry and Bourhis 1997, p. 25, cited in Garter 2013, p. 190).

Since Macao is an urban setting, I will not concern myself with other possible sources of data to which LL methodology has been applied, such as road signs and billboards in rural settings, postings in cyberspace, etc. Generally speaking, however, the idea of "linguistic landscape" pertains to any kind of discourse displayed in public space. Moreover, it could be extended to oral discourse and mixed media (e.g., typically a political demonstration takes place for the purpose of displaying discourse in public space, the temporal frame is transient rather than fixed, and the message is conveyed in both oral and written form), as well as to other kinds of purposive symbolic activity in public space. Below, I will comment on some aspects of an extended construal of "linguistic landscape".

2.2   Temporal Dynamism

Linguistic landscape studies have dealt predominantly with affixed signs rather with "transgressive" (Scollon and Scollon 2003, pp. 147–151) discourse that is unsanctioned by the authorities of a given locality, such as graffiti, randomly affixed individual advertising, or discarded print matter. While affixed signs are also the focus of this study, it should be noted that even sanctioned signs are often more temporary in nature than the buildings to which they are affixed. For example, if a shop changes ownership, so will its signs and other aspects of its decoration. If regulations concerning language policy are changed, the signs may be revised. Advertising campaigns may prompt the appearance and disappearance of billboards and other displays. Some displays may be seasonal in nature. Upon the glass-and-concrete canvass of the city, its commercial and administrative signage reveals a temporal dynamism. Thus a city's linguistic and semiotic landscape can provide evidence of change on a faster scale than its buildings do, but on a slower scale than the day-to-day media of newspapers, brochures and other unaffixed matter.

2.3 Geosemiotic Indexicality

In their book *Discourses in place: Language in the material world*, Scollon and Scollon (2003) explore and classify the types of discourse data provided in the linguistic landscape of an urban context. They define their approach as "geosemiotics", thus offering an extended understanding of linguistic landscape in which the meaning of signs and other kinds of symbolic activity is seen as situated in the locality and its cultural milieu. Geosemiotics is "the study of social meaning of the material placement of signs and discourses and of our actions in the material world" (Scollon and Scollon 2003, p. 2).

A key concept in Scollon and Scollon's (2003) study of "geosemiotics" is "emplacement". They extend the framework of linguistic landscape beyond "decontextualized" discourse such as brand names that could appear similar in any locality, and beyond a focus solely on language within the "frame" of the sign, to consider the meaning of the placement of the sign. A sign's placement is indexical of its contextual referent, above and beyond its textual referent:

> Whether or not a sign is an icon, a symbol, or an index [cf. Peirce 1955, cited in Scollon and Scollon 2003, p. 3], there is a major aspect of its meaning that is produced only through the placement of that sign in the real world in contiguity with other objects in that world. This is the focus of the field of geosemiotics (Scollon and Scollon 2003, p. 30).

In addition, various aspects of a sign's design, beyond the words themselves, can be analyzed semiotically as indexing the cultural context. For example, within Chinese written language, a choice is possible between traditional characters (used in Hong Kong, Macao and Taiwan) and simplified characters (used in mainland China and Singapore). In their research, Scollon and Scollon (2003, p. 133) found that they and their research assistants were able to find only one shop "in the year following the political change in Hong Kong [i.e., 1997] which was using simplified writing. […] [T]raditional Chinese writing in Hong Kong indexes Hong Kong – that is the way Chinese is written here." Finding simplified characters on signs in Hong Kong was somehow anomalous, out of the local cultural context, even though Hong Kong had returned to (mainland) Chinese sovereignty.

In this study, I adopt Scollon and Scollon's (2003) insight of geosemiotics, that the interpretation of signs is contextualized within their locality. Moreover, I adopt their framework in order to study and gain insight into the locality, rather than into the signs themselves; in this regard I differ from the purpose of Scollon and Scollon's study, which was to construct a system of classification for discourses present within an urban landscape. I also differ from Scollon and Scollon, as discussed below with reference to Chmielewska (2010), in that I am acutely aware of the subjective nature of the process of interpretation, as that of interaction between reader and text. I therefore do not discard the authorial "I" from the researcher/reader's eye.

2.4   Reading the City: Semiotic Analysis as Interactive Interpretation

In the closing chapter of a collection of studies of semiotic landscapes (Jaworski and Thurlow 2010), Chmielewska (2010) points to the subjective nature of the process of interpretation, as a reader (whether local or tourist) navigates the texts of a city. With reference to the semiotics of Karl Bühler (1934/1990, cited in Chmielewska 2010, p. 276), Chmielewska points out that the process of interpretation is a semiotic triad which crucially involves the reader, rather than a flat decoding of a Saussurean signifier-signified dyad. She compares her own readings in two vastly different but comparable contexts: on the one hand, visiting post-communist Poland as a returnee from abroad, finding strange what once was familiar, and on the other hand, visiting neo-capitalist China as a European tourist entirely unfamiliar with the context, who encounters telling markers of globalization, such as billboards and brand names, against a backdrop of undecipherable Chinese characters. In this way, "[t]he image and its reading rely on the reader's knowledge of the context outside the frame, the specific spatial, material and cultural array as well as the language and the setting of the display" (Chmielewska 2010, p. 286). Whether local or tourist, naïve viewer or researcher, each person brings his or her own subjectivity to reading the discourse of the city:

> If we understand an object merely through its images (representation) we inevitably lift it from its context and abstract its surface(s), consequently disregarding a possibility of meaning present in the very attachment of the sign to place [...]

> To consider meaning *in situ* we need to [...allow] for our distinct positions, discourses surrounding the particular locale and their specific linguistic and symbolic contexts, the singularity and subjectivity of the place (Chmielewska 2010, p. 289).

3   Methodology

3.1   Delimiting the Data

One methodological problem which presents itself in linguistic landscape studies is the choice of data set. In some instances in existing studies, data are chosen impressionistically, i.e., when a particular sign makes an impression on the researcher as

being worthy of observation and commentary. In other instances, data sets are chosen systematically so as to enable some sort of comparison. For example, Scollon
and Scollon (2003) compare signs found on major street intersections in different
parts of the world (a systematic comparison that yields their "grammar" of classification), but also include impressionistically chosen signs, e.g., with right-to-left
writing, when relevant to the analysis (Scollon and Scollon 2003, p. 5). In the case
of my study of Macao, I wanted the data set to be representative of the city, to be
"social" as well as "linguistic". One complication is that Macao has changed so
much recently that it is difficult to delimit what can be considered most representative. Nevertheless, the main street of the historic city centre seemed a logical place
to start. In future studies, other streets or other parts of the city could be compared
to it as a kind of yardstick. Future studies could also take a longitudinal approach by
comparing different points in time on the same street, to document its sociolinguistic change.

The street, Avenida de Almeida Ribeiro, officially named after the Portuguese
Minister for the Colonies (1928–1935) Artur Rodrigues de Almeida Ribeiro (1865–
1943), is nicknamed "San Ma Lo", which means "New Avenue" (Wordie 2013,
p. 351). It was constructed in the 1920s to open up the traffic flow through the city
centre, connecting the shoreline of Avenida da Praia Grande (which at present, since
the city's land reclamation, is no longer the prime waterfront) with the Inner
Harbour, which was at that time the major commercial waterway. To this day, it is
one of the two major tourist destinations of Macao (the other being the huge resort-
casinos on the reclaimed land of the Cotai Strip, which rivals the Las Vegas Strip in
global importance). Any tourist who is still interested in Macao's history first heads
to San Ma Lo and its adjoining Largo do Senado ("Senado Square"), which is a
beautiful pedestrian area with many historic buildings that have been inscribed onto
the UNESCO World Heritage List. Because of its attractive shopping, romantic
ambience and sentimental value, local residents also flock to this area.

The street sign of San Ma Lo is worthy of commentary in itself (Fig. 1). On the
sign, we see the name inscribed three times: above, in traditional Chinese characters; below, in Portuguese; and in parentheses, the popular short name "San Ma Lo"
in traditional Chinese characters, with no Western transliteration and no Portuguese
equivalent. The colour, style and material of the sign are Portuguese tiles called
azulejos, referencing both Portuguese and Portuguese colonial culture. In Lisbon,
the capital of Portugal, there is a museum of azulejos (Museu Nacional do Azulejo),
which are a ubiquitous architectural motif in Portugal; the origins of blue-and-white
ceramic glaze date back both to the (Arab) Moorish influence on the Iberian
Peninsula and to the Maritime Silk Road of trade with China and the Orient, which
was conducted in large part by the Portuguese in colonial times (Azulejo n.d.). In
Macao, azulejos street signs are also ubiquitous – not as an import and not for the
tourists' benefit alone, but as a cultural marker of the Portuguese-Chinese hybridity.
At the same time, it is noteworthy that the ultimate cultural appropriation of this
sign is the parenthetical local Chinese nickname of the street with no equivalent in
Portuguese.

Fig. 1   Street sign of Avenida de Almeida Ribeiro on Portuguese-style blue tiles (azulejos)

3.2   Data Collection

I gathered the data in the manner of a naturalistic participant-observer, over a short time tranche of December 9th-10th, 2014, by snapping pictures with my (Sony Experia) mobile phone just as the hundreds of tourists do every day. I aroused no curiosity, commentary or security concerns whatsoever, except in one instance when taking a picture of an ATM by a bank, when a man who may or may not have been a security guard looked amused, said something and moved out of my way. On another instance, a street vendor waved to me and encouraged me by gesture to buy his product. Indeed, I think there may not be another city in the world where a person taking hundreds of pictures would be so unnoticed as in Macao. It is a photographer's and researcher's paradise.

Originally, I intended to take pictures only of street signs, but finding myself entirely undisturbed, I adopted a phenomenological approach and took approximately 1900 photographs of everything, going up and down the street several times. The street is approximately 620 m long and lends itself well to this kind of phenomenological approach. I did this because, with my researcher's "gaze" turned to attention mode, I immediately began to notice semiotic details beyond the purely linguistic, having to do with visual aspects of advertising, architecture and urban design. Hence, while I originally intended to document the sociolinguistic situation in Macao (Research Question 1), the broader second research question of Macao's socioeconomic situation emerged from the data.

I uploaded the photographs into a computer and coded them by recursively sorting emergent patterns and categories, using the alphabetical and numerical automatic sorting function of file names in Windows 2007. The resulting categories are discussed under their respective headings and subheadings in the Results section below, which offers a thick description of the data.

4   Results

The data are broadly categorized as illustrating spatial semiotics, visual semiotics and the linguistic landscape of multilingualism, with subcategories corresponding to the subheadings below.

4.1   Spatial Semiotics

4.1.1   Historical Layering

In architectural design, some of the old buildings show historical layering. Figure 2 shows the façade of the headquarters of the Portuguese bank Banco Nacional Ultramarino, dating back to 1926, with an add-on high-rise tower constructed in 1997. The original name of the bank on the rose-coloured colonial-style façade is in Portuguese only, while the signs of the BNU logo are in Portuguese and Chinese. In the windows, scrolling digital displays alternately show advertising in Portuguese, Chinese and English. Thus, the Portuguese past – architecturally and linguistically – is fully preserved, while overlaid with the present modern construction and trilingual communication.

Figure 3 shows an example of architectural detail from the inside of the Leal Senado ("Loyal Senate") building (now housing the Civic and Municipal Affairs Bureau). The original building, dating back to the late sixteenth century, was reconstructed more than once in its history (in 1784, 1876, 1887 and 1940), and is presently one of the structures inscribed onto the UNESCO World Heritage List of Macao's twenty-five most important historical monuments. The name "Leal Senado" ("Loyal Senate"), derives from the title "City of the Holy Name of God Macao, there is none more loyal" "Ciudad del Santo Nombre de Dios de Macao, no hay otra más leal", bestowed upon Macao by Portuguese King D. João IV in 1654 after Portugal regained independence from Spanish rule (1580–1640) to reward Macao's loyalty to Portugal (Cultural Affairs Bureau n.d.). Architectural details such as this bas-relief are incorporated into the building's present construction from earlier periods in its history.

Fig. 2 The façade of Banco Nacional Ultramarino with new glass high-rise add-on tower

4.1.2   Layout

Open Store Fronts

Most of the shops on the street have store fronts that are either entirely open or partially open directly onto the street, as shown in Fig. 4. At night, when shutting up shop, the store fronts are screened off with pull-down scrolling steel shutters that look rather like a garage door but may be further sectioned as shown a little later in Fig. 9. The open store fronts create a sense of immediacy and invitation to potential customers passing by.

Arcades

The sense of invitation and comfort when shopping is also sustained by the arcades, which in a hot and humid subtropical climate protect pedestrians from both rain and sunshine, as shown in Fig. 5. The sidewalks are paved with Portuguese-style small irregularly shaped stone tiles, sometimes arranged into marine-themed design motifs, which add aesthetic attractiveness to the walking experience. The street adjoins at a right angle to the main historic square of the city, Largo do Senado (popularly known as Senado Square), which is similarly paved and entirely pedestrian, and inscribed onto the UNESCO World Heritage List. Thus the street, despite being a vehicle traffic thoroughfare, has a pleasantly welcoming pedestrian feel to it.

Fig. 3 Old bas-relief and
azulejos built into the walls
inside Leal Senado

Hawker Stands

Figure 6 shows an example of a hawker stand, this particular one, with a
chestnut-roasting machine, being located approximately 15 m off the main street on
the historic Largo do Senado itself, at the corner of the square and a side-street
which serves as an open-air market. Although not as conspicuous as the distinctive
architecture or well-decorated store fronts, there are many hawker stands on street
corners and side streets. They each seem to be a permanent business with a fixed
location, even though the location is a small stand. At night, they are neatly closed
off or shuttered.

Fig. 4 Glassed-in open store front of a traditional Chinese pharmacy

4.1.3　A Tale of Two Streets

Despite the historic appeal and commercial attractiveness of Avenida de Almeida Ribeiro, there is a marked contrast between the two ends of the street, even though they are only 620 m apart. The BNU headquarters (Fig. 2) is at the heart of the central business district, at an intersection where other banks, lawyers' offices and travel agents are located. The opposite end of the street forms a T-junction intersection with the Inner Harbour area. On this corner, in poignant contrast to the well-preserved BNU building, is the gutted and dilapidated skeletal structure of the former 1920s Grande Hotel Kuoc Chai (Fig. 7), with no architectural indication of

Fig. 5 Pedestrians walk
comfortably under arcades

the original identity of the building as erstwhile "one of Macao's premier places to
stay" (Wordie 2013, pp. 268–269). There are signs of much renovation and construction at this more dilapidated end of the street, but this particular building seems
not yet to have been reclaimed. The feel of this end of the street is of an old neigh-
bourhood in decline, or in transition from old to new.

Across the T-junction, there is a new five-star Sofitel Macau At Ponte 16 hotel
and casino facing the Inner Harbour. In contrast, the shops that are open for business
are decidedly more traditional, such as the dried-seafood store approximately ten

Fig. 6 A hawker stand of roasted chestnuts in Largo do Senado

metres off on a side-street (Fig. 8). Many shops are shut off in a manner that makes it difficult to tell whether the owners are away on vacation or the business has closed down (Fig. 9).

In the chinks between the boards and shutters, one can in places glimpse construction and renovation work, such as that indicated by the hand-painted construction permit notice (in Portuguese and Chinese) in Fig. 10. Fewer pedestrians walk on this end of the street compared to the central business district, although the street is by no means deserted. Along a couple of blocks at this end of the street, there is a community centre, a budget long-stay hotel, and a busy Chinese noodle café. Despite the presence of the luxury Sofitel Macau At Ponte 16 in the Inner Harbour, this end of the street is much less glamorous than the BNU end.

4.2   Visual Semiotics

4.2.1   Reduplication

One interesting design feature that emerged from the data is reduplication. This is a twin repetition or multiple repetition of the same item in the arrangement of advertising or shop display. For example, many shops feature their logo or name-sign repeated two or more times on their store front. Figure 11 shows reduplication in the symmetrically recursive display of cookie gift boxes in a bakery.

Fig. 7 The gutted
dilapidated Grand Hotel

4.2.2 Opulence

At the high end of the economic scale, the street features many expensive jewelry
stores, selling gold, jade, precious stones and luxury watches. These stores utilize
brand-name advertising, and crowded displays to create a sense of opulence and
desire, as shown in Fig. 12.

Fig. 8 Traditional Chinese dried seafood store on a side-street close to Inner Harbour

4.2.3   Economy

On the lower end of the economic scale, some shops seem deliberately to be promoting a sense of economy, even though they may be next door to an expensive brand-name store. Figure 13 shows clothes rather haphazardly displayed, with no advertising other than the name of the shop (in transliterated Cantonese) and prominently attached price-tags.

4.2.4   Use of Posters

The amount of information on display is visually and linguistically dense. The display of products and advertising is often enhanced by the use of posters which most probably are supplied by the product manufacturers, such as the advertising of brand-name watches shown in Fig. 14. In a business environment that caters to tourists, but where not all managers may be fluent in English (or in Chinese, for that matter, given the diverse ethnic mix of Macao), the widespread use of brand-name advertising creates an international aura. At the same time, it has tremendous status appeal to Chinese consumers, who are the drivers of this market even more than international tourists are. The brand-name posters bombard the eyes, vying for attention. In the Chinese context, the crowded aesthetic feels joyful and inviting, in an iconic parallelism to the often crowded nature of this street, where the flow of pedestrians can be elbow-to-elbow at peak times.

Fig. 9 A store front that is shut for business

4.2.5 Use of Notices

In contrast to posters, which are probably mass-manufactured without regard to the particular store that might display them, notices tend to be much more specific to a particular location or circumstance. The manner of their display, however, can be similarly attention-grabbing as posters. Figure 15 shows a relocation notice prominently displayed across the entire front window of a store. Ironically, the notice appears to have been posted in June 2011, and was still in place in December 2014, without a replacement business having occupied the same premises. This seems to be indicative of the economic problems that some businesses experience as the price

Fig. 10 Hand-painted
construction works permit

of buying or renting commercial premises has skyrocketed in the 15 years since the
handover of Macao to China in 1999.

4.3   The Dynamism of Semiotic Landscaping

As noted by Moriarty (2014), the study of linguistic landscape captures dynamic
aspects of language use and social change. An example of visual dynamism occurred
on December 9th-10th, 2014, as shown in Figs. 16 and 17. As part of the

Fig. 11 Reduplication as a design feature of a bakery gift box display

celebrations of the Christmas season and the 15th anniversary of the handover of Macao to China (December 20th, 2014), a giant digital display screen was erected in Largo do Senado, approximately ten metres away from the main street, to advertise the festive "Parade through Macao Latin City – Celebration of the 15th Anniversary of Macao's Handover to China" to be held on December 14th (a Sunday). The advertisement was in Chinese, Portuguese, and English. This was a temporary installation, to be taken down after the event; and it was obviously a government-sanctioned advertisement in the heart of the city's tourist area.

4.4 Multilingualism

A large part of the study of linguistic landscape is the evidence it provides of societal multilingualism, including language policy, language attitude and language shift. In the data description below, the extent of multilingualism in Macao is examined from the evidence of the presence of languages on street signs.

4.4.1 "English Only" Signs

Other than the frequently occurring prominently displayed brand-name logos, which could be termed as "international" rather than "English" in terms of linguistic classification (e.g., Omega, Gucci, Tissot, Doxa, Seiko, etc.), there are very few instances of English-only signs. Figure 18 shows an English-only decorative

Fig. 12 Brand advertisement in a jewelry shop

display of menu items in the interior of a sit-down, somewhat upscale branch of Pizza Hut, located on the 1st (rather than ground) floor of a commercial office building near the BNU end of the street.

4.4.2 "Portuguese Only" Signs

Equally scant is the presence of Portuguese-only signs, the emplacement of which indicates that they are vestigial of the colonial era, such as the original sign on the BNU façade (Fig. 2). Figure 19 shows a stone plaque built into the outside wall of

Fig. 13 An inexpensive
clothing store

the Leal Senado building, commemorating the latest major renovation of the building which took place in 1939–1940.

4.4.3   English and Portuguese

Although the data showed no affixed signs which would include both English and
Portuguese but exclude Chinese, this possible language combination, shown in
Fig. 20, is on display by an enterprising newsstand hawker advertising the three
daily Portuguese and three daily English newspapers published in Macau. The

Fig. 14 Posters advertising expensive watch brands

Fig. 15 A relocation notice posted in a shop window in 2011 is still present in 2014

display is in Largo do Senado, facing out from the store front of a small shopping mall and into the square, and serves to attract the attention of passers-by. The Chinese-language publications are on the other side of the stand, facing inward into the store to catch the gaze of shoppers leaving the shopping mall.

Fig. 16 The scaffolding for a giant digital display screen being erected on Dec 9th, 2014

Fig. 17 On Dec 10th, 2014, the giant digital screen advertises a festival to take place on Dec 14th

4.4.4 "Chinese Only" Signs

Somewhat surprisingly, the data from this street did not show many instances of Chinese-only signs, perhaps because it is the main street in the tourist-frequented historical heritage area of the city. One surmises that side-streets would have a higher frequency of Chinese-only signs, such as the store front of the dried seafood shop in Fig. 8. Below, Fig. 21 shows a "closed" sign across the door of a small

Fig. 18 An English-only sign advertising the menu inside Pizza Hut

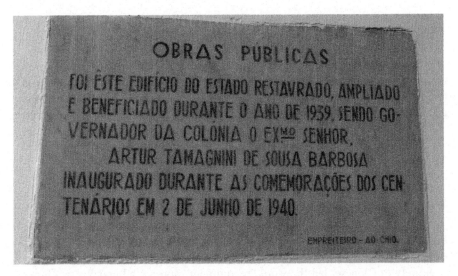

Fig. 19 A Portuguese-only sign dating to 1940 commemorates the renovation of Leal Senado

restaurant. Figure 22 shows an ICBC (Industrial and Commercial Bank of China) poster advertising the sale of coins commemorating the 15th anniversary of the handover of Macao to China. The poster is in Chinese only, even though international tourists to Macao might be potential customers interested in buying such a coin set. At the bottom of the poster, next to the ICBC logo, the name of the bank appears in simplified Chinese characters, but otherwise, the poster uses traditional characters.

Fig. 20 A newsstand hawker display showing Portuguese and English daily newspapers

4.4.5   English/Chinese (English-Prominent) Signs

The majority of signs on the main street include more than one language from the trilingual mix of Chinese, Portuguese and English, in various proportions and combinations. Figure 23 shows a bakery on the corner of Avenida de Almeida Ribeiro and Largo do Senado, advertising its success prominently in English, while its name and logo appear above the shop in transliterated Cantonese and in Chinese characters, with the English translation "Koi Kei Bakery" less prominent under the Chinese logo.

4.4.6   Chinese/English (Chinese-Prominent) Signs

Figure 24 shows a staff recruitment poster for a jewelry chain store, with encouraging graphics showing a career ladder and photographs of staff training. The poster is entirely in Chinese, but the word "recruitment" appears bilingually, in Chinese and English. The inclusion of the English word suggests professionalism, as the local workforce is expected to have some knowledge of English to be able to deal with international customers.

Fig. 21 A "closed" sign in Chinese only

4.4.7   Mixed Code

In the names of businesses that appear on street signs, sometimes mixed code is used. Figure 25 shows a sign displaying the name and logo of a pharmacy, with Chinese characters prominent, then the name in transliterated Cantonese, the word "farmacia" in Portuguese and "Chinese Co." in English.

Fig. 22 A bank poster advertising commemorative coins

4.4.8 Chinese/Portuguese Signs

In terms of language policy, the official languages of Macao are Chinese and Portuguese. Figure 26 shows this policy being implemented inside the window of a bus, displaying the sign meaning "exact fare" in Chinese and Portuguese, but not in English, despite the fact that tourists would benefit from English signage on the transport system. It is not the case that English signs are prohibited in municipal services; rather, they are not required, and thus are often absent. The bus system is run by several private companies contracted and regulated (even subsidized) by the government of Macao (Lai 2015).

Fig. 23 A bakery
advertising sign in English

Fig. 23 A bakery
advertising sign in English

Figure 27 shows what is in fact a very attractive stamp collection display at the
General Post Office on Largo do Senado, which would be of interest to international
tourists, as the stamps are beautifully presented in commemorative envelopes and
albums. However, the sign on the window is in Chinese and Portuguese only, and
English speakers would have to rely on the visual sign of the logo, the stamp artifacts themselves, and their knowledge of the similar English word "philately" signi-
fying stamp collecting.

Fig. 24 A Chinese-
prominent staff recruitment
poster

4.4.9 Chinese/Portuguese/English Signs

Despite a plethora of bilingual signs in Chinese and English or Chinese and
Portuguese, the data show surprisingly few signs featuring all three languages. The
signs that do contain all three languages are somewhat top-down in nature, indicating a high level of professionalism and effort in their manufacture. The two main
instances are given below in Figs. 28 and 29, as discussed below.

Fig. 25 A Chinese-prominent sign showing name in Chinese-Portuguese-English mixed code

Government Signs

Outside the General Post Office in Largo do Senado, there is a prominently displayed large map of the city, obviously intended to be helpful to tourists. The map is trilingual in Chinese, Portuguese and English. Interestingly, the Chinese text contains both traditional and simplified characters. Traditional characters are used in Macao, Hong Kong and Taiwan; elsewhere on this street, Chinese is written using traditional characters. Simplified characters are used in mainland China and Singapore; since a large part of the tourists to Macao are from mainland China, this would be very helpful to them. Figure 28 shows the text at the bottom of the map, which advertises four different historical walking tours arranged by the Macau Tourism Board.

Commercial/Regulatory Signs

Another example of a trilingual sign is shown in Fig. 29. This is an official certificate issued by a commercial regulatory body, the Macau Goldsmith's Guild, to ensure the compliance of the jewelry shop with professional regulations.

4.4.10 Signs in Other Languages

Besides the trilingual mix of Chinese, Portuguese and English, there is limited evidence of the presence of other languages on public signage. The choice of additional language appears to be at the discretion of business owners, according to their own

Fig. 26 "Exact fare" bus
window display in Chinese
and Portuguese

linguistic competence and their target clientele. Fig. 30 shows a sign advertising a
private medical office. The sign is in mixed code transliterated Cantonese and
Portuguese ("Dr. Fong Mei Ha Medica", where Fong Mei Ha is the name of the
doctor), Chinese characters and Thai script. It is posted twice – on the building and
above the street – and the second instance also contains a phone number. The original painted phone number has been pasted over with a newer phone number, probably indicating that the business has existed for a long time, and is still operational.
The medical doctor's office is not on street level; presumably it is within the building itself, or in the vicinity, and patients can contact the doctor by phone to make an
appointment.

Fig. 27 Post office commemorative stamps display in Chinese and Portuguese

Figures 31 and 32 show the signage on an Islamic restaurant, the owners of which are a Han-Uyghur mixed couple from Xinjiang Uyghur Autonomous Region in northwestern China. Above the store front and in the window, the restaurant advertises in traditional Chinese characters, Arabic script and English, and includes the words "Islam" and "Halal". There are Islamic graphic motifs, showing desert sands, a camel caravan, and pointed arches characteristic of Islamic-style architecture. Prominently displayed in the window, there are also pictures of some of the dishes on offer on the menu. The door to the restaurant is located in a side street approximately eight metres from the main street. A second sign above the street faces the main street, and features the word "Halal" (prominently), Chinese

Fig. 28 Macau Tourism Board information about historical walking tours

Fig. 29 Jewelry shop window display of Macau Goldsmith's Guild certification for 2014

characters (prominently), Arabic script (at the bottom of the sign, non-prominently) and the name of the restaurant in run-on Portuguese (with no spaces between words), "Estabelecimento de Comidas Lou Lan Islãmico", the equivalent of the English wording "Lou Lan Islam Restaurant" that appears on the store front. A phone number is also given on the street sign.

Fig. 30 Medical doctor advertising in Chinese and Thai

5   Discussion

5.1   Archeology of the Present: Time Strata and Evidence of Change

The historical layering of past and present in the spatial layout, architectural detail and visual design create an archaeology of the present. On the one hand, the past is brought into the present moment – for example, the building of Leal Senado, now renamed the Civic and Municipal Affairs Bureau, hearkens back, through several

Fig. 31 Shop front of Lou Lan Islam Restaurant including Arabic script, Chinese and English

renovations, to the very beginning of the history of the city. It stands in the place it has historically stood; incorporated into its walls are vestiges of its past. On the other hand, the present moment extends into the uncertain future. There will be new buildings, shops and signs, as the city is developing dynamically. The public signage and the street's spatial and visual semiotics are in dynamic "motion" through time. At any particular point (day) in time, a slice of time is captured like a geological or archeological stratum. Since the slice is temporal, there is no literal archeological excavation; only photography captures the moment.

The "slice of time" methodology does have some drawbacks. Only a longitudinal comparison would produce firm evidence of change. Statements about trends, e.g., the movement towards a greater presence of English in Macao's multilingual mix, are conjectural unless supported by longitudinal data. With this caveat, my conjecture is that my data supports a trend towards multilingualism, with English as a lingua franca firmly a part of the mix, rather than simply a shift away from Portuguese. On the public signage, there is a visible and widespread presence of Portuguese in a bilingual or trilingual context, even though very few Portuguese-only signs remain. There are also visible efforts at maintenance and promotion of Portuguese language and Lusophone culture, as evidenced by Portuguese daily newspapers and Lusophone cultural festivals. Also, surprisingly, at least on the main street, there are few Chinese-only signs, indicating a preference for bilingualism/multilingualism rather than monolingualism. Commercial signage is mostly bilingual in Chinese and English, while government-produced informational and regulatory signs are either bilingual in Chinese and Portuguese, or trilingual in Chinese, Portuguese and English. Here and there, in a commercial (bottom-up) context, other languages appear, as in the case of Thai and Uyghur in my data.

Fig. 32 Restaurant sign includes Portuguese, Chinese and Arabic script (Uyghur)

5.2 Material Semiotics: Indexicality Pointing at Socioeconomic Megatrends

If I had not adopted a phenomenological approach of taking snapshots of all details of the street – textual, spatial and visual – I might have missed the big picture of materially emplaced semiotics. I started out being interested in the multilingual mix of Macao and its tendencies, but I ended up also becoming more deeply aware of the architectural and commercial transformations of the city. Following Scollon and Scollon's (2003) idea of emplacement, I started out looking at the main street as being a place that must by assumption be quite representative of the city as a whole.

However, I found some anomalies, or data contrary to my expectations of representativeness, such as the boarded up shops on the less frequented end of the street, which piqued my interest in the significance of the total layout of the street and the types of shops and advertising displays. Macao is a city that is reinventing itself, and the imbalance between the different ends of the street is, on a micro-scale, indicative of the megatrends of the city's socioeconomic transformation.

San Ma Lo was originally built in the 1920s as an artery through the heart of the city. Before the land reclamation that added substantially to the area of Macao Peninsula (Kvan and Karakiewicz n.d.), this street connected its two most active shores – Praia Grande and the Inner Harbour. To this day, it is an important artery, with many bus routes going through it. However, it is not the only main street any more, and moreover, the entire centre of gravity of the city within the past few years (since the opening of the Venetian Hotel Resort and Casino in 2007) has been shifting towards the Cotai Strip, an area that rivals the Las Vegas Strip and that is being built entirely on reclaimed land on a land bridge connecting the islands of Coloane and Taipa, far away from the historic city centre. In a sense, the Cotai Strip has no history – it has only the present and the future. San Ma Lo, by contrast, is the epitome of history. Thus, its present reveals tensions between the historical past and the pull of fast-paced change.

To appreciate how semiotics can help us to understand socioeconomic change, let us examine the concept of indexicality. In Scollon and Scollon's (2003, pp. 2–6) conception, emplacement embodies indexicality, with reference to Peirce's tripartite semiotics of icon, index and symbol. Originally, in Peirce's (1955, pp. 102–103, 107–111) semiotics, an index points to something beyond itself to which it has a physical causal relationship. For example, a painted portrait of a person is an icon because it resembles that person; but a photograph of a person in addition to being an icon is an index, because light waves physically travelled (by reflection rather than emanation) from the person's face to the photograph in the instant that it was taken, their impact producing the image on the film or digital imprint. Because of the quality of physical connection, an index can come into being without direct intentionality or even without human agency. Smoke is an index of fire; but fire can sometimes be caused by lightning without human agency. Likewise, fire can result from a faulty short circuit, which is due to human agency farther back in the causal chain, but not to the direct intention of causing fire. In such a case, smoke is an index, indicative of a fire taking place; it can be recognized as a sign of fire, i.e., communicate the fact of fire to a receiver, even though the sender of the sign, i.e., the fire itself, has no direct intentionality of communication. Applying the above explication of the nature of an index to the idea of emplacement, we can distinguish between intentional vs. unintended signification. The latter in turn becomes helpful in the analysis of the big picture of socioeconomic megatrends.

Let us take as an example the relocation notice in Fig. 15. The communicative intention of the sign by the people who put it up was to inform customers of the relocation of the premises of the business and to attract them to the new location by giving obvious and accurate information. The obviousness of the information is iconically represented by the large size of the sign, which occupies the entire store window. However, the material placement of the sign – both spatial and temporal – indexes a significance beyond the conscious communicative intent of the sender. The sign had been put up in June 2011 and had not yet been taken down in December 2014 at the time of the data collection. This means that the owner of the commercial premises where the sign was displayed had not yet found a new tenant, even in the space of more than 3 years. One would expect that a main street location is a fantastic one for a business, and yet the overly lengthy duration of the placement of the sign – more than 3 years, which surely was originally unintended – indicates that it is difficult, at the present time (and continuing into the uncertain future), for this location to be financially viable for both owner and tenant, otherwise the premises would already be re-occupied. The physical location on the main street is somehow causally connected to the loss of economic viability, as evidenced by the length of time the sign has been in the window. This is what I mean by the semiotic indexing of socioeconomic megatrends. A semiotic analysis has the potential to inferentially reveal the significance of various kinds of symbolic human activity, including not only intentional meanings, but also those meanings and consequences that lie beyond the intention of the original sender-communicator.

6   Conclusion

The small but vibrant territory of Macao, a Portuguese colony since 1557, has seen many changes since its handover to mainland China in 1999. Macao is multicultural in its heritage, and its economy relies on tourism. Its socioeconomic transformation since the handover has been meteoric, with unprecedented GDP growth. At the same time, the city has painstakingly preserved its quaint and unique heritage, especially in the architectural aspect of the historic city centre, with twenty-five buildings inscribed onto the UNESCO World Heritage list. The city's population has grown by at least 50%, absorbing human resources attracted by the burgeoning casino gaming industry. These two vectors of conservation and globalization pose challenges to the communication and livelihood needs of its inhabitants.

In this study, I have used linguistic landscape methodology, with a single-street data collection design, to research the sociolinguistic situation (RQ1) and socioeconomic situation (RQ2) of Macao. The inferences gained therefrom are limited by the data set and by my own subjectivity and background knowledge as a researcher. Nevertheless, my classification and interpretation of the data has allowed for some generalizations. In my "reading of the city", in response to the first research question, the following generalizations can be made. Firstly, there is a ubiquitous multilingualism, incorporating English as a Lingua Franca (ELF)/ English as an International Language (EIL) and Mandarin, in addition to Cantonese and Portuguese. While my methodology is from a slice of time, from my background knowledge I would posit that this is evidence of additive multilingualism, with an increase in English and Mandarin since the handover, no decrease in Cantonese, and a slight decrease in Portuguese. Secondly, there is maintenance/reappropriation of Lusophone/Macanese/Portuguese culture as a "glocal" (global/local juncture) identity marker. The official promotion of Macao as a "Latin City" (displayed on the video screen in Senado Square on 10th December, 2014, Fig. 17) as part of the 15th anniversary of the handover to the mainland was particularly striking, because it stands in contrast to the disavowals of the colonial heritage of Hong Kong by mainland authorities in the wake of the pro-democracy Occupy Central demonstrations occurring simultaneously (28th September – 15th December, 2014). This promotion of Portuguese by the authorities counteracts the decline in the use of Portuguese by the population. Evidently, the preservation of Portuguese language and culture is seen as one of the communicational challenges for Macao, as part of its identity and also its contribution to China as a whole, with Macao acting as a gateway between China and Portuguese-speaking countries.

In response to the second research question, my reading is that the megatrends of tourism/gaming/capitalism are impacting the socioeconomic microtrends at different ends of the historic main street, as inferred from the indexicality of the spatial and visual semiotics. Against the backdrop of government policies, such as the promotion of the gaming industry and the conservation of Portuguese heritage, individual business owners, architects, designers and decorators make their own choices. The sum of these choices is evident in the look of the city, its layout, advertising, and the presence or absence of various businesses. Over some length of time, this aggregate of choices changes dynamically. The economic demands of tourists and locals influence the supply of goods and services. In this regard, and somewhat serendipitously, I found that small businesses are struggling to make ends meet at the less frequented end of the street. This is evidence of a socioeconomic challenge for Macao, despite its impressive prosperity.

In recent history, with the growth of urbanization, cities have increasingly become the prime human habitat. As Chmielewska (2010, p. 289) points out, signs are affixed onto the city's "surfaces". These surfaces, the city's buildings and spaces, are its material texture, like the pages of a book, upon which the signs are affixed or written. However, unlike a book's flat blank pages, the city's surfaces are in and of themselves integrally constitutive of the meanings and functionalities indexed by the signs. Moreover, in extending the scope of investigation to spatial and visual semiotics, I have also endeavoured to show that the non-verbal aspects of the city's indexicality are to some extent self-referential. The boarded-up shops signify their own demise. The opulence vs. economy attract different market segments of customers. Historical layering of architectural features encodes cultural time. The plethora of meanings embodies the cityscape and is constitutive of it. Among the surfaces and signs, human bodies wander, eyes gaze, minds wonder. In the cubist world of today's space and time, the webs of our contemporary existence are defined.

References

Azulejo. (n.d.) Accessed on 12 Nov 2015 from https://en.wikipedia.org/wiki/Azulejo

Bühler, K. (1990). *Theory of language: The representational function of language* (D. F. Godwin, Trans.). Amsterdam: John Benjamins. (Original work published in 1934.)

Carvalho, R. (2015, November 12). *Macau: The rise and fall of an empire? South China Morning Post*. Online multimedia report. Accessed on 12 Nov 2015 from http://multimedia.scmp.com/macau/

Chmielewska, E. (2010). Semiosis takes place or radical uses of quaint theories. In A. Jaworski & C. Thurlow (Eds.), *Semiotic landscapes: Language, image, space* (pp. 274–291). London/New York: Continuum International Publishing Group Ltd..

Cultural Affairs Bureau of the Government of Macao S.A.R. (n.d.) *"Leal Senado" Building*. Accessed on 12 Nov 2015 from http://www.macauheritage.net/en/HeritageInfo/HeritageContent.aspx?t=M&hid=36.

Garter, D. (2013). Linguistic landscape in a multilingual world. *Annual Review of Applied Linguistics, 33*, 190–212.

Jaworski, A., & Thurlow, C. (Eds.). (2010). *Semiotic landscapes: Language, image, space*. London/New York: Continuum International Publishing Group Ltd..

Kvan, T., & Karakiewicz, J. (n.d.). *Regaining the sense of the city: Reclamation in Macau*. Rudi. net, Accessed on 12 Nov 2015 from http://www.rudi.net/books/11653.

Lai, S. (2015, September 7). Gov't to sign public concession contract with TCM soon. *Macao Business Daily*. Accessed on 12 Nov 2015 from http://macaubusinessdaily.com/Society/Gov%E2%80%99t-sign-public-concession-contract-TCM-soon.

Landry, R., & Bourhis, R. Y. (1997). Linguistic landscape and ethnolinguistic vitality: An empirical study. *Journal of Language and Social Psychology, 16*, 23–49.

Liu, S., Volčič, Z., & Gallois, C. (2011). *Introducing intercultural communication: Global cultures and contexts*. London/Thousand Oaks/New Delhi/Singapore: SAGE Publications.

Moriarty, M. (2014). Languages in motion: Multilingualism and mobility in the linguistic landscape. *International Journal of Bilingualism, 18*(5), 457–463.

Peirce, C. S. (1955). Logic as semiotic: The theory of signs. In J. Buchler (Ed.), *Philosophical writings of Peirce* (pp. 98–119). New York: Dover Publications.

Scollon, R., & Scollon, S. W. (2003). *Discourses in place: Language in the material world*. London: Routledge/Taylor and Francis.

Wordie, J. (2013). *Macao: People and places, past and present*. (With photography by A. J. Headley & C. Day.) Hong Kong: Angsana Ltd.

Intercultural Communication About Pain

Roland SUSSEX

Abstract As far as language and communication studies are concerned, pain is barely visible on the radar. It has received even less attention in the context of inter-cultural communication. And yet pain is universal. It is prominent among the causes why we visit the doctor. And its impact on the quality of life of pain sufferers, as well as on national economies, make it a topic of urgent interest: it highlights, in a particularly sharp perspective, some of the key issues currently facing intercultural communication, and specifically intercultural communication in Asia.

The purpose of this chapter is threefold: to present pain as a bona fide area of research in linguistics and communication studies, specifically in intercultural com-munication; to survey the current state of play of research into pain and communica-tion; and to outline the implications of intercultural pain communication for the key themes of this volume, with special reference to Asia. Pain will be seen, as it is communicated by individuals in an internationalizing world, at the intersection of linguistic, cultural and value systems.

1 Introduction

Pain is a universal of the human condition. There is a small number of people who have Congenital Insensitivity to Pain (CIP, congenital analgesia), and who are unable to feel pain. Systematic analgesia can also result from leprosy (Hansen's Disease). People who cannot feel pain often do not live very long, because the feed-back and warning functions of pain are absent: a broken bone, the heat sensation from touching a hot object, the awareness of sharp objects in the eye – all these and similar symptoms are simply not registered, and the person does not take either evasive or remedial action. Pain, in short, is one of our most valuable and necessary survival mechanisms (Biro 2010; Butler and Moseley 2013).

R. SUSSEX (✉)
School of Languages and Cultures, and Institute for Teaching and Learning Innovation,
The University of Queensland, St Lucia, QLD, Australia
e-mail: sussex@uq.edu.au

© Springer International Publishing AG, part of Springer Nature 2018
A. CURTIS, R. SUSSEX (eds.), *Intercultural Communication in Asia:
Education, Language and Values*, Multilingual Education 24,
https://doi.org/10.1007/978-3-319-69995-0_9

Most humans are familiar with a variety of experiences of pain during their lives. They suffer it, live with it, and take action to mitigate or remove it. They communicate about their pain to doctors and healthcare professionals, to experts in traditional medicine, and to their families. And in the globalizing world of the twenty-first century, such pain communication is increasingly crossing cultural boundaries.

The academic study of pain is profoundly interdisciplinary. It includes at least:

basic science
medicine and alternative medicine
neuroscience
areas of biology and microbiology, including stem cell research
allied health, including dietetics
pharmacology
neurology, neuroanatomy
psychology
communication studies and language / linguistics
anthropology and ethnography
philosophy
physical sciences including physics and chemistry as they apply to pain.

In this chapter we concentrate on pain in languages, linguistics, communication studies, and value systems. This discussion is framed by their implications for education, not principally in the sense of formal instruction, but more specifically in terms of the kinds of knowledge about pain and communication which are necessary to the understanding and management of pain in individuals and human societies – and which might, for instance, form part of professional development for healthcare professionals, and general education for people in pain in the broader context of public health.

2   Pain: Definition and Evidence

The standard definition of pain, as approved by the International Association for the Study of Pain, is:

[…] an unpleasant sensory and emotional experience associated with actual or potential tissue damage, or described in terms of such damage. (www.iasp-pain.org/Taxonomy)

(and see Melzack and Torgerson 1971; Merskey and Bogduk 1994). This definition concentrates on physical pain, and leaves aside the very large domain of emotional pain, which may accompany physical pain, or may exist in its own right. In this chapter we will similarly concentrate on physical pain, while bearing in mind that it has close links to non-physical pain and suffering.

Most humans are familiar with "acute" or short-term pain, often in the context of some wound, lesion or medical condition. Acute pain often begins rapidly, and has a specific cause like a wound, damage from an accident, infection or other lesion (known as "nociceptive"). Pain, then, can be an indication of actual or impending threat to the organism, and as such is highly influenced by emotion and the "significance" of the injury to that person. It recedes when the cause is treated or removed. In contrast, "chronic" pain is defined as lasting beyond the resolution of the cause of acute pain, and typically lasts for more than three months. It is possible for pain to persist, and for the body to experience pain without nociceptive cause, and this can happen with pain pathways which have been habituated to transmitting pain signals long after the original nociceptive cause has healed or been removed. Such chronic pain can persist with agonizing intensity for years, and is now recognized as a disease in its own right.

The importance of pain in our medical lives is shown by the fact that it is among the most common reasons why people go to see their doctor or seek medical help. A study in Finland found that 40% of patients visited their doctor because of pain (Mäntyselkä et al. 2001). A large scale investigation by the Mayo Clinic in the USA showed that while skin diseases were the most common single reason why patients visited the doctor, the second and third most frequent causes were osteoarthritis and joint disorders, and back problems, two pain-based groups of medical conditions which together easily outnumbered skin diseases (Sauver et al. 2013). And that is without counting the times we visit a pharmacy, or simply buy painkillers off-the-shelf.

The economic impact of pain has also been calculated in a number of studies. Access Economics in Australia estimated that chronic pain costs the economy approximately 4.4% of GDP every year, or AUD 34 billion in 2007 dollars (Access Economics 2007). Data from the USA (American Academy of Pain; Institute of Medicine 2011) have shown that in the American economy chronic pain costs a similar percentage of GDP, amounting to between USD560 billion and USD635 billion every year, or $2000 for every person living in the United States of America.

These sobering quantitative results are paralleled by important considerations of quality of life. It is estimated that fewer than 50% of cancer patients receive appropriate relief from the pain, in spite of the fact that medical science is able to relieve 90% of that pain. And among chronic pain sufferers, less than 10% receive appropriate pain management, whereas as much as 80% could be alleviated (National Pain Strategy 2011, p. 2).

A major complicating factor is the lack of objective biological or technical proof of the existence, intensity, periodicity or location of pain. Pain is perceived in the brain, even though we may believe that it is localized in parts of the body. "Phantom pain" can occur in parts of the body which are no longer there, for instance after amputation. But a brain scan (electroencephalograph, EEG) does not give decisive results. It can indicate that pain is present when the patient feels no pain at all. Mutatis mutandis, a patient can be in agonizing pain and the EEG will show no evidence of pain. As a result, as was confirmed in correspondence in the leading journal *Pain* in 2015,

> [...] pain is fundamentally subjective with self-report providing the most complete and reliable access to another's pain (Sullivan and Derbyshire 2015, pp. 2119–2120).

If pain is a universal of the human condition, then it is also a universally covert aspect of the human condition. None of us can experience the pain of another. As the philosopher Wittgenstein has argued (1953/1989), pain can be conceived as a beetle in a box. Everybody has a box, but only they can see their beetle, and no-one may ever see anyone else's beetle. The other person's box might indeed be empty. The only way that we can know about the existence of pain is the way in which it is made manifest in body language and in language itself. This leads naturally to a problem of validation. The health care professional, faced with a patient reporting pain, will triangulate many kinds of information in evaluating whether and what kind of pain is present. But it is still possible for people to lie about pain and persuade both health practitioners and the courts, as is evident from some damages claims which have been shown to be fraudulent when the victim is later discovered to be leading a pain-free life.

In other words, the patient's account is the key source of information about their pain – and by "account" we must include all modes of communication, including various metalinguistic factors: swearing, for instance, increases one's tolerance for pain (Stephens 2009), and there is a positive correlation between the intensity of pain and the amount of pain talk (Rowbotham et al. 2014). Pain may be universal, or nearly so. But its expression certainly is not. Pain is deeply embedded in our culture and values, social and personal.

3   Pain as a Component of Culture

There is ample evidence of the ability of how culture and value systems affect the way we experience pain, drawing on the ground-breaking study *People in pain* by Zborowski (1969; and see Fabrega 1976). Some people under torture have deflected their thoughts from the pain by concentrating on Christian values and symbols (Bourke 2012, 2014). Less dramatically, in many cultures children, especially male children, are brought up to believe that acceptable standards of behaviour include not showing pain and not talking about it. This is true for instance of childbirth: in some cultures women are taught to go through labour and childbirth in silence as a matter of cultural practice, as happens among Bariba women in Benin and Nigeria (Sargent 1984), while in other cultures the expression of pain is expected and encouraged (Bourke 2014). The "show no pain" mindset can persist throughout people's lives. In other words, nurture, and the cultural values so instilled, can filter or mask the expression of pain. It can also affect not just the way we express pain, but also the nature of the pain which we feel (Al-Harthy et al. 2015; Butler and Moseley 2013; Kwok and Bhuvanakrishna 2014). To be sure, pain can be blocked by willpower, meditation and medication, and by medical interventions related to neurological systems. But the medical treatment of pain is a relatively recent development, which has arisen as a result of advances in biology, physiology, neurology, pharmacology, and wider areas of medical care. This in turn increases the need for an understanding of how patients express their pain, especially pain which cannot clearly be linked to visible causes like injury.

This can be seen very clearly from some of the key developments in the history of pain over the last 400 years (Rey 1998; Bourke 2014). In the Christian tradition, which covers a wide range of languages and cultures, pain – the word comes from Latin *poena*, meaning "punishment" – was an expected component of human life. Resurrection would relieve the suffering of humans. In the meantime pain was a natural accompaniment of life, illness, childbirth, injury, and also through deliberate infliction in education and religious zeal, where it was thought to make the individual a better person. As Rey puts it, pain was seen as:

[… a] necessary trial, unpleasantness preceding some greater good, punishment, or fate (Rey, p. 2).

Individuals were expected to bear pain with courage and fortitude. Numerous accounts of battlefield surgery without anaesthetics, borne by wounded soldiers with minimal fuss and complaint, show how a system of values can make humans able to tolerate pain in a way which would be unthinkable nowadays. Routine surgery was often performed without analgesics well into the twentieth century. And the church once took the position that pain relief for a dying patient would render them incoherent when they met their Maker (Bourke 2014, p. 288).

The steps by which we have grown through and beyond such mindsets owe most to the impact of scientific discovery on the understanding and treatment of pain. The gradual growth of knowledge about human physiology from the seventeenth century led to a less theological, and more biological and eventually pharmacological, approach to the treatment of pain. In the nineteenth century pain was progressively medicalized, with the discovery of morphine and related opioids, anaesthetics, and painkillers like aspirin. From a fatalistic acceptance of pain as part of a divine plan, we have now moved to a position where we regard pain as removable, and expect our health care professionals to do precisely that. So even within a single cultural tradition, values about pain can change radically over the course of several centuries, driven by science, technology, and social change. An English person of Shakespeare's day would find themselves in an intercultural conversation when talking to us in the twenty-first century about pain and its treatment.

In some respects the Christian view of pain is not too different from what we find in Buddhism, Confucianism and Islam. For the Buddhist, pain and suffering are among the defining characteristics of the human condition. Someone feeling pain has bad karma, as a result of bad acts. This belief is broadly also a feature of Hinduism. The true Buddhist should practice the eight true paths of right speech, right action, right living, right effort, right mindfulness, right meditation, right thought and right understanding in order to achieve a higher state of being without pain. Buddhists therefore tend to be stoical about pain, and are slow to seek medical relief. They may also profit from the reputation and proven efficacy of Western medicine for short-term ailments, but may rely more on traditional medicine for longer term problems (Bourke 2014, 121ff.)

Confucianism is dominant throughout East Asia. Having pain is seen as affirming one's status as a human being, and pain should be endured in silence until it becomes unbearable. It should not be shared with others, a value which is the converse of Western views, after Freud, that "bottling it up" is bad for you. Confucianists respect the harmony of those around them, and so tend to conceal their pain and avoid talking about it to others. They will also postpone seeking help for pain until much later than might be the case in Western countries. In addition, Confucianists respect social hierarchy, and so are subservient and passive to the health practitioner in a medical consultation.

For the Muslim, pain is part of the will of God, and divine predestination. It should be borne patiently. This view is very close to the Christian one. A stoic resignation is a proper attitude to the arrival and existence of pain, and is part of one's religious duty. Painkillers are less readily advocated than in contemporary Western medicine, though the rules about sedation in end-of-life pain contexts may be relaxed with the permission of an Imam.

4   Pain, Communication and Culture

When we place pain in the context of cultures, three questions arise:

How do languages differ in giving us tools to talk about pain?
How do cultural differences themselves relate to these tools?
How do cultural differences within a language, especially English, and most especially
    English as a lingua franca, relate to the tools which we have available to talk about
    pain?

These questions were posed in a somewhat different format as early as 1976 by Fabrega and Tyma, who proposed three key questions about the universal nature of pain vis-à-vis its cultural specificity:

Is there a limited set of semantic categories that people and languages draw on to describe pain?
Do the pain behaviors of a people bear a non-trivial relation to the models of pain which the culture imposes on people or to the grammatical rules and conventions which the language system imposes?
Which facets of a pain experience are communicated verbally, which ones non-verbally, and how do groups differ in the way they use these channels? Are there cultural invariants in any of these channels? (Fabrega and Tyma 1976, p. 336).

And yet there is no headword entry for "pain" in the most recent encyclopaedia of intercultural competence (Bennett 2015).

5   Pain Communication: Language

Scarry (1985) notes that at the elemental level pain cancels language:

Physical pain does not simply resist language but actively destroys it, bringing about an immediate reversion to a state anterior to language, the sounds and cries a human being makes before language is learned (Scarry 1985, p. 4).

We can communicate about pain through body language or vocally. Body language, including movement and touch, is more instinctive but also less rich in information. Vocal communication about pain may involve instinctive responses to the pain stimulus, which are pre-linguistic, and involve groans and exclamations.

 1. elemental: *argh*

There are then three levels of linguistic (verbal) response to pain which are language-specific:

 2. involuntary exclamations: *ouch* (French *aïe,* Russian *okh)*
 3. *awful burning pain*
 4. *overall increases in input through cutaneous and proprioceptive channels*

#4 involves the technical medical descriptions in the language of the healthcare professional. These last three levels can be either spoken or written. But even regulation communication about pain is fraught with difficulties, as Barker et al. (2009) have shown in their analysis of the problems of communicating about back pain, where there is a genuine lack of a common agreed language of pain communication. On the other hand, there is good reason to believe that *pain* is a universal of human languages, and that it is one of perhaps eleven emotional universals (Wierzbicka 1999), which then relate to words like *happiness* (Goddard and Ye 2014) and *suffering* (see Wierzbicka 2012, 2014, for an analysis in the theory of Natural Semantic Metalanguage).

Spoken pain communication (Pauwels 1990) can exploit features of the human voice like tone, volume, pitch and pace. Both spoken and written and communication make use of vocabulary, grammar, metaphor and discourse (Sussex 2009). Of these levels of language the grammar of pain has received some attention, especially from Halliday (1998) on English, and in Lascaratou's (2007, 2008) extended study of pain communication in Modern Greek. There has been some work on pain language and metaphor (Lascaratou and Marmaridou 2005; Kövecses 2000, 2008). But the overwhelming body of research has been based on vocabulary and on English as a means of understanding pain.

The dominant pattern of this work, in one way or another, is based on or derives from the McGill Pain Questionnaire ("MPQ") (Melzack 1975; Wilkie et al. 1990). The MPQ consists of 78 adjectives, in four broad semantic categories: sensory, evaluative, affective and miscellaneous. These four categories are then further broken down to yield a total of 20 groups, each containing between three and six adjectives, ranked from weakest to strongest. A typical set from the sensory category is:

pricking
boring
drilling
stabbing
lancinating

In the pain consultation, patients are shown a picture of the human body and are asked to indicate where the pain is felt. They then fill in the written MPQ questionnaire, selecting a total of 20 adjectives to describe their pain. The results are then scored, with "1" for the weakest adjective in each group up to whatever number corresponds to the highest-ranked item in each group. The 20 scores are then summed to give a pain index (Melzack 1975).

There are many linguistic reservations which can be made about the MPQ (Sussex 2009). All the 78 adjectives, for example, are metaphors: *hot* comes from the vocabulary of heat sensation, while *flickering* comes from the domain of light, and *beating*, which is listed in the same group of "sensory" terms, comes from either sound or tactile sources. It is a valid question whether the semantic disparity of these items, and their different metaphorical interpretations, can be independently justified. There is also the question of scoring. The five terms in the "pricking" group score between 1 and 5 on the grounds of rising intensity. But how could one prove that there is a single unit of intensity between *pricking* and *boring*, and between *boring* and *drilling*? There is also a fundamental objection to some of the 78 adjectives on the grounds of frequency and familiarity. *Lancinating,* the strongest term in the "pricking" group, suggesting the penetration of the skin by a sharp object, is ultimately related to the mediaeval war weapon *lance.* Except among healthcare professionals, however, the use of the word "lancinating" is vanishingly rare: in the 1.9 billion word GLOWbE corpus of English (corpus.buy.edu/glowbe/), it occurs only 15 times, and of those, 12 for some unexplained reason come from India.

The MPQ also makes a simplifying assumption that one diagnostic instrument can be used for all people and all purposes. The example of *lancinating* shows that this assumption is lexically unsound. But there are also strong sociolinguistic reasons why the MPQ does not offer a single undifferentiated flat playing field. Strong et al. (2009), for example, showed that gender plays a major distinguishing role in the pain language use of 232 healthy young undergraduates (Strong et al. 2009; see also Nayak 2000; Wiesenfeld-Hallin 2005). These issues are compounded with speakers whose first language is not English.

For all its imperfections, the MPQ has been undoubtedly successful in clinical practice, where it has dominated the use of word-based diagnostic instruments for pain. Realising that the 78 adjectives had significant problems, Melzack (1987)) produced the Short-Form MPQ, with only 18 terms in more transparent categories (and see Fernandez and Boyle 2001; Fernandez and Towery 1996; Towery and Fernandez 1996). Dworkin et al. (2009) have more recently proposed a further short version, the "Short Form MPQ-2".

The performance of the MPQ as a diagnostic instrument over 40 years of practice has recently been reviewed by Main (2015). He recognizes the utility of the MPQ in the assessment and treatment of pain, and in the way it has helped to at least partly legitimize pain and its qualitative assessment in the context of a growing emphasis on evidence bases and empirical, quantitative data in the practice of medicine. Main is correct in identifying the absence of the social and contextual dimension in the administration of the MPQ, building on suggestions by Craig (2009), Hadjistavropoulos et al. (2011), and Menezes Costa et al. (2009). It is significant that it has taken nearly 40 years for these issues to be raised in a systematic way, which is itself an indication of the lack of involvement of the linguistic, sociolinguistic and cultural linguistic professions in the study of pain talk (Sussex 2009) –

for instance, from the sociolinguistic viewpoint with variables like age, education, socio-economic status and ethnicity (though cf. Zborowski 1969).

6 Pain Communication in Other Languages

The MPQ has been translated into more than 25 languages, with multiple competing versions in both French and Spanish. But here too there have been problems of equivalence of vocabulary, and it has been necessary to adapt the array of adjectives from the MPQ in each language. Here some more linguistic difficulties have arisen. Since the MPQ terms are all metaphors, they come with a variety of attendant semantic information. They are not merely "denotations", referring to some specific property (e.g. "red" as the name of the colour); they also carry connotations (e.g. *red* is the colour of good luck in Chinese, the colour of the Communist party, or the colour associated with political parties, red for the left-leaning Labor Party in Australia, and for the right-leaning Republican Party in the USA).

A specific, and symptomatic, difficulty arose with the translation of the MPQ into Finnish (Ketovuori and Pontinen 1981). One of the MPQ's categories includes the five terms *punishing, gruelling, cruel, vicious* and *killing.* These words in English carry overtones of punishment or retribution. But the equivalents in Finnish were identified by test subjects as being overwhelmingly associated with the intensity of pain. The Finnish version of the MPQ ("FPQ") had to be re-designed and re-structured accordingly, and the words re-located in the "Evaluative" category. A range of other difficulties of translation and interpretation have been found in adaptations of the MPQ into languages like Japanese (Hasegawa 2001; for the MPQ in other languages see e.g. Boyle 2003 for Spanish; Kim et al. 1995 for Norwegian; and Mystakidou 2002 for Greek).

There are also major differences in the arrays of pain terms available in different languages. In English we have four principal terms for physical pain: *pain, hurt, sore* and *ache,* with *suffering* ambivalent but more oriented towards emotional pain. Some European languages make a clearer fundamental distinction between physical and non-physical pain (though metaphors blur the distinction in both directions):

	Physical	Non-physical
French:	*douleur*	*peine*
Spanish:	*dolor*	*sufrimiento*
German:	*Schmerz*	*Leid*

But this semantic specialization is overshadowed by the lexical richness of the terms for physical pain in Japanese. In Japanese, as in many Asian languages, the standard terms for pain are verbs rather than the nouns which we find in English. Japanese has a category of mimetic or reduplicated verbs where the repeating structure intensifies the action or adds information (*kirakira* "to shine sparklingly").

Japanese has a number of specific mimetic verbs to express pain (Iwasaki et al. 2007; Asano-Cavanagh 2014):

gan-gan	pounding headache
zuki-zuki	throbbing pain
shiku-shiku	dull pain
kiri-kiri	sharp continuous pain
hiri-hiri	burning pain
chiku-chiku	prickly pain
piri-piri	pain from scraped skin or electric shock

As the English translations show, it is certainly possible to render these semantic differentiations in English by adding one or more adjectival modifiers. But it is also clear that the conceptual map of pain in Japanese, organized around these specific pain terms, is structurally different from that of English. Certain categories of pain have been reified by the allocation of specific designations.

The Japanese coding of pain expressions as verbs is also found in Thai verbs of pain:

chep	general pain
saep	stinging / smarting pain, usually superficial
yok	sudden piercing / stabbing pain, focused
puet	deep seated aching pain, hot and diffuse
mueai	soreness and aching of joints, muscles, tendons
khlet	dislocation pain
chuk	pain from swelling, blocking, pressure
siat	focused abdominal pain

(Diller 1980; Fabrega and Tyma 1976; for Modern Greek see Lascaratou 2007, 2008; Halliday 1998; Lascaratou and Marmaridou 2005; Sussex 2009). Two features stand out from this array of terms. The first is that the central grammatical expression of pain in these languages is the verb. Pain is not a thing but a process. This presents a fundamental difference of epistemology and understanding (Halliday 1998). And the second is that the first categorization of pain is not like *pain – hurt – sore – ache* in English, but is cast rather in terms of surface *versus* deep-seated pain: *chep* (general and surface) versus *puet* (deep-seated). The same semantic distinction is found in Vietnamese, where pain is initially categorized into *đau* for surface pain, and *nhức* for deep-seated pain (Nguyen 2014).

7   Intercultural Communication and Pain

In one sense it is not necessary to come from a different language background in order to be involved in intercultural communication. There are many sub-cultures within each language, depending on many factors like age, gender, education, socio-economic status, and more. The closest thing to an intra-cultural communication in a medical consultation might be when one medical professional treats another: a doctor treats a doctor, and so on. But even here, socio-linguistically speaking, there are differentials, especially those relating to power and the health practitioner < > patient dyad. As we move further away from a balanced dyad, and the patient becomes less like a doctor and more like a member of the general public, the asymmetry grows. And with it, the differences of culture. These differences can clearly be seen in the way cultural accommodation plays out in the medical consultation (Kim et al. 2000; and for a more general review of Asian health care communication, see Lwin and Salmon 2015).

We can take this a step further. As Kecskes has argued (2018), it is misleading to conceive of the intracultural/intercultural distinction as belonging to two different dimensions. Instead, they can be seen as fitting along a continuum. At one end the cultural values of the participants can be close. At the other end they may diverge radically, a situation which is exacerbated if the health practitioner has never experienced the kind of pain that the patient is presenting with. Participants in conversation therefore have to begin by negotiating exactly where they are in relation to cultural identity and cultural overlap: the health practitioner, for instance, needs to work out how much the patient understands about medical terms and conditions, so that they can achieve the right level of communication. Leaving a wide gap will quite possibly result in lack of communication, as when the health practitioner mistakenly assumes that the patient knows more (or less) than they do. In contrast, assuming a wide gap on the part of the health practitioner may well appear condescending or insulting to a medically well informed patient. The "common ground" (Clark 2009; Kecskes and Zhang 2009) which they negotiate defines a cultural space for effective communication.

Negotiating common ground often takes place quickly, and sometimes under confusing and conflicting circumstances. The medical consultation, for instance, may last eight minutes or less. During that time the health practitioner, who is effectively directing the encounter, has to make rapid judgements about the patient, especially if the patient is on their first visit. Here physical appearance can provide valuable clues: dress, age and presentation. Body language is important, particularly in indicating the patient's degree of comfort. Linguistic competence is highly relevant. Does the patient express themselves fluently and with a sophisticated vocabulary? The lack of these properties may not indicate lack of education or sophistication. In particular, we do habitually rely a great deal on linguistic competence and communicative expertise as an indicator of cultural identity and competence. And yet this may be quite misleading. There are people who are able to express themselves in a language other than their mother tongue with great fluency, but who have never mastered the cultural value systems of that language. And there are others who, while having limited linguistic competence in the foreign language, are in fact culturally well adapted and capable.

The potential complexity of these factors in interpersonal pain communication can be appreciated in an example from French, a language which has had long and continuous contact, both linguistically and culturally, with English. The word *mal* in French has a range of meanings not dissimilar to those of the English word *pain:* pain, difficulty, illness, lack, damage, calamity, ill luck, evil. The standard phraseology for "my X hurts" in French is *j'ai mal à* plus the organ concerned, so literally "I have a pain in the X": *j'ai mal à la tête*, literally "I have (a) pain in the head", means "I have a headache".

Now consider the following scenario. A patient enters the consulting room of an English-speaking health practitioner. The patient speaks English reasonably fluently but with a clearly French accent. He says in accented English: *I have a pain in the heart.*

Is the health practitioner to call a cardiologist? Perhaps. But there is a difficulty of which the health practitioner may not be aware. In French *j'ai mal au coeur* literally means "I have a pain in the heart". But it is also the conventional way of saying "I feel nauseous, I feel off-colour". If the health practitioner calls a cardiologist he may be acting literally, but at least responsibly. However, the Frenchman may not know that English does not have a parallel expression involving the heart when one is feeling off-colour, and is simply translating his idiom literally. Is the health practitioner aware of this? He may be. Then it comes down to a matter of the health practitioner knowing enough about French, and the possible dangers of literal translation into English, to ask the patient to clarify his condition, in order to determine whether in fact the cardiologist is needed, or a routine consultation. What in fact was the patient trying to express in English? As we have seen before, uttering English sentences does not necessarily mean that one is uttering English meanings. And here, before we even get to underlying cultural values, there is a problem of phraseology and idiom to be resolved. There is, incidentally, a parallel problem with the French phrase *j'ai mal aux reins,* literally "I have a pain in the kidneys", which is the conventional phraseology for saying that you have a backache.

A great deal of the talk between health practitioners and patients will not be complicated by such problems of idiom and translation. Routine medical matters, with a clearly identified cause, may be relatively straightforward, since the various factors can be seen and tested by methods that both the health practitioner and the patient can share. Ostensive definitions and regulation investigations will confirm swollen tonsils, an infected finger, a sprained knee. More deeply hidden problems, like damaged disks and tumours, will often yield to the evidence of a CT scan or MRI. But the hidden and subjective nature of pain makes pain communication altogether more complex and uncertain, and intercultural pain communication introduces additional values and interpersonal considerations. Wittgenstein's beetle is not only obscure within its box; the box may itself be obscure behind cultural barriers and distortions which may or may not be evident.

We can capture some of this complexity diagrammatically. This schema is broadly adaptable to non-pain communication, but for pain it serves to highlight the special points of difficulty ("PiP" = Person in Pain, "HCP" = Health Care Professional):

Pain (Beetle in box)	>	PiP (Person in Pain)	>	Pain Message Out	>	Pain Message In	>	HCP Health Care Professional	>	Pip's pain/ beetle?
A		B		C		D		E		

Each of the arrows points to a location where intercultural pain communication may encounter difficulties. The health practitioner is able to see the person in pain, and to perceive their pain message as it is transmitted and received. The health practitioner cannot directly see or verify the existence of the pain, a.k.a. the beetle in the box. The difficulties offered by the points A-E include these:

A. The beetle is invisible, and can only be inferred by the health practitioner from the visible appearance and speech of the person in pain, and the messages that they make. The pain is not empirically verifiable or accessible to ostensive definition.
B. Is the person in pain presenting a full and un-skewed account of their pain, real or imaginary?
C. Is the transmission of the message affected by any factors in the context of the consultation? For example, the power dynamics between the health practitioner and the patient, the formality, constraints of professional contact, stereotypes of behaviour from some culture, visible or presumed?
D. In receiving and processing the incoming pain message, is the health practitioner applying their own cultural habits, or making allowance for the patient's cultural background, or presumed cultural background?
E. In interpreting the pain message, how faithfully and confidently can the health practitioner take the evidence which is offered?

In addition, there are the beliefs of the interlocutors about each other, about each other's cultural frameworks, and about what each thinks about the other. Some healthcare professionals have had wide experience of different cultural backgrounds in communicating with patients, and may understand where the patient's values are situated. The health practitioner will still make a number of inferences about the patient's cultural identity and orientation. But that identity and orientation, as presented by the patient, may be affected by the way the patient believes the health practitioner wants to see them, and perhaps by apprehension or uncertainty at what the health practitioner may feel about the patient if the patient speaks too fully, or perhaps not fully enough, about their pain. In particular, cultural taboos and stereotypes can interfere with the full and frank transmission of information about pain, and with its reception in the way the patient either intended it to be received, or hoped that it would be received, in order to achieve the desired outcome from the health practitioner. And embedded in this complex network of communication is the issue of face (Lim and Bowers 1991), the way we present ourselves to others and want them to see us, together with what we think about them and what we think they think about us. Managing all this in the context of what will probably not be a relaxed interchange in the medical consultation is difficult and sophisticated. And negotiating and clarifying all this common ground (Kecskes and Zhang 2009) and communication in the space of a short consultation, while proceeding with the business of investigation and diagnosis, is a daunting task by any measure, especially with a topic like pain which may carry with it many kinds of social value and even stigma.

Central to the success of the negotiation of common ground is accommodation, or the ways in which interlocutors adapt their behaviour to match and suit that of the other participant (Giles 2016). Becoming a socially competent accommodator is part of our education as competent speakers of our language, and competent representatives of our culture and its values. Communication is aided by accommodation, and people are often comfortable with adapting their behaviour, at least to some extent, to lessen the distance between them and the other person. This is another part of the two-and-fro of negotiation. As it proceeds we ask: is the other person accommodating to me? How do I know? What do they know about my language and culture? What do I know about their language and culture, assuming that I know what it is?

One can accommodate in either language or culture or both (as well as along some other parameters like pragmatics, which we will leave aside here). In practice accommodation is very often asymmetrical between the participants, which means that one will accommodate more than the other. If they accommodate to the point where they overlap, communication may be enhanced. But it is perfectly possible for the participant to be making major concessions in terms of language, but staying within their own cultural frame of reference. In this case, there may be significant difficulties of cultural communication brought about by the gap between the two, even after accommodation has been negotiated and taken place.

A further complication involves the presence of a "third person in the room" in the chain of communication in the medical consultation. Parents are very aware of their role as intermediary and interpreter when they take a young child to the health practitioner, or when we accompany an elderly relative with cognitive impairment. This situation has some parallels with the presence of an interpreter, except that the intermediary is already very well acquainted with the patient. The "third person in the room" phenomenon, however, is a standard feature of the practice of medicine in countries like Vietnam. When a woman goes to see a health practitioner she is routinely accompanied by a relative, who may be male, and may be her husband or even her father. The health practitioner, who until recent times has been most likely to be male, directs most talk to and from this third person, who speaks on behalf of the patient. And as we have seen, since pain is the most likely single reason for visiting a health practitioner, pain communication is centrally involved in this medical consultation (Fan 2011; Sakai and Carpenter 2011; Wolff and Roter 2008, 2011).

8   Contexts of Intercultural Pain Communication

We now turn to concrete contexts of intercultural pain communication, where people from different cultural backgrounds communicate about pain, especially but not only in a medical context. Intercultural pain communication is occurring with increasing frequency as people and messages become more mobile, and English is the dominant lingua franca for communication in these domains. But using English linguistic forms does not necessarily imply making culturally English messages (Sussex and Kirkpatrick 2012; Sussex 2012), especially in contexts like:

1. **Multicultural societies,** prompted both by higher levels of cultural diversity in the homeland, and the freer movement of peoples across geo-political borders, as with the Schengen Agreement in the European Union.
2. **Tourism** involves travellers away from their homeland finding themselves in need of medical attention. Statistica reports 1.186 billion international tourism arrivals in 2015, and the tourism industry is annually worth USD7.27 trillion (https://www.statista.com/ topics/962/ global-tourism/).
3. **Medical tourism,** a category of tourism undertaken specifically to access medical services overseas, is growing dynamically. Medical tourism occurs when people either choose voluntarily, or are unable to afford the cost of certain medical procedures, including elective surgery, in their home country, and travel abroad to seek alternative providers. The principal providers are (in alphabetical order) Costa Rica, India, Israel, Malaysia, Mexico, Singapore, South Korea, Taiwan, Thailand, Turkey, and the USA. More than half the target countries for medical tourism are in Asia. Although no firm figures are available, it is estimated that this industry was used by 11 million cross-border patients in 2014, including 1.2 million Americans (Patients Beyond Borders n.d.). The revenue from medical tourism is estimated at between $38 billion and $55 billion American dollars a year (Patients Beyond Borders n.d.). Medical tourism is particularly relevant to intercultural pain communication because of the prominence of English in the medical consultation, in all its various manifestations. It is quite possible to have professional conversations where none of the participants has English as a native tongue. At a Thai hospital specialising in medical tourism, for example, a Thai health practitioner, a German patient and a Philippino nurse would routinely communicate in English (Lian and Sussex 2018).
4. **Education overseas.** Growing numbers of students study overseas, especially in English-speaking countries, partly because of the quality of education and its prestige, and partly because of the economic and cultural status of the English language. The top four destinations for overseas education are the United States of America, the United Kingdom, France and Australia. The numbers are substantial: in 2014–2015 nearly 975,000 overseas students studied in the United States of America alone, led by China (31.2%) and India (13.6%) (https://en.wikipedia.org/wiki/International_student), and while studying these students experience health care outside their homelands. The students who then return to their homelands are already functionally bilingual and at least partly bicultural.
5. **International business, trade and commerce,** where people, messages and products move around the world with increasing freedom. Sometimes these products and their messages are adapted to the target country, sometimes less so.
6. **Migration,** with people from one language and culture voluntarily take up residence in another, with substantial unmet needs for medical care in general, and pain management in particular (Brady et al. 2016).
7. **In-migration of overseas-trained health care professionals.** In 2011 in Australia, for instance, the Australian Bureau of Statistics (ABS) reported that 56% of GPs and

47% of medical specialists had been born overseas, together with 33% of the nurses. The countries of origin for GPs and specialists were led by the UK, India and Malaysia, with China and New Zealand in fourth and fifth position. While extensive quality controls are applied to incoming health care professionals for medical and communicative competence, there is obvious diversity in the backgrounds of health care professionals, not to mention their contact with the 240 languages spoken in Australia. Again, competence in English may not be matched by intercultural competence.

8. **Refugees.** The enormous numbers of refugees from the Middle East and Africa, and most recently especially from Syria and Iraq, need medical care outside their homeland and home context.

9. **Westernization of medical practice and medical education.** Although the dominance of the Americas and Europe is now starting to be challenged, especially from the leading technological countries of Asia, westernized models of medicine are clearly prominent internationally. In some parts of the world, for example in Asia, traditional medicine continues to flourish in parallel, sometimes with points of contact with Western medicine. But this change creates a situation where not only clinical medicine, but also the social aspect of medicine, bring together homeland and imported practices.

In terms of medical education, younger generations of health practitioners are increasingly being trained overseas, especially in English-speaking countries. They return home with knowledge and principles of practice derived from the places where they have studied, and so become bicultural practitioners in their homeland – and here "bicultural" can include medical practices from different traditions and systems (Chen et al. 2013).

10. **Retiring abroad.** Increasing numbers of retirees from wealthier countries, including those who were badly affected by the Global Financial Crisis of 2008, are deciding to retire in less costly countries. Some of these are in Europe, but others involve countries like Malaysia, which have widespread English language competence, an appropriate standard of living, and – very important for older retirees – quality medical care.

This list is not exhaustive, but is representative and wide-ranging. And the categories of intercultural contact that it defines reveal issues of intercultural medical communication of substantial volume and complexity.

From the sociolinguistic point of view intercultural pain talk can be divided into two broad categories, professional and social-informal. In professional talk between a health practitioner and a patient, typically in a medical consultation, there is an archetypical power differential, where the health practitioner is in a position of power and knowledge, and the patient is seeking help and remedies (Todd and Todd 1993). In many cases the health practitioner will be speaking their first language and activating their first culture, and it will be the patient who accommodates. And if the patient does not have that knowledge and skill, and if the health practitioner is not bilingual and bicultural in the patient's context, then an interpreter will be necessary. The numerous Arabic-speaking refugees arriving in Europe from the Middle East present precisely this kind of situation, and one often exacerbated by medical emergencies as a result of their experiences.

In many other cases, however, and especially in Asia, patients will try to choose medical practitioners who speak their language, or at least a language in which they have adequate competence. That will usually be English, and specifically Lingua Franca English (Canagarajah 2007) in many cases.

9 Implications for Education

The evidence presented in this chapter shows that there is indeed an urgent need for education in the area of the intercultural communication of pain. As we have seen, pain itself is a major burden on economies, and more importantly, on the quality of life, of millions of people world-wide. We have established that current communication about pain is insufficient to correct this situation. To cite one example among many: pain in younger women is under-appreciated and under-reported (Evans and Bush 2016; Perquin et al. 2000), to the extent that 20% of a sample of females aged 16–18 in Canberra, Australia, were shown to have missed school due to menstrual pain (Parker et al. 2010). And when we add the dimension of intercultural communication we find ourselves in an area where disturbingly little has been done, and the nature and extent of the problem are only now starting to be realized.

Rather than beginning from educational principles, let us start by considering an optimal intercultural pain communication, and then reverse-engineer the educational needs from there. Optimal intercultural pain communication would require that the barriers and disruptors to intercultural communication and pain communication should be realized, understood and neutralized. The health practitioner needs clear and complete information from the patient about the location, nature, severity and periodicity of the pain, together with its impact on the patient's quality of life. The patient needs to provide that information without cultural or personal filtering, and to volunteer relevant information if the health practitioner's line of questioning omits it; patients need to feel free to ask the health practitioner unprompted questions, and to provide unprompted information. The two need to be able to negotiate these issues through the consultation to a point where the health practitioner understands all that the patient is able to communicate about the pain, and can make the most reliable possible diagnosis about the pain, its cause, and a subsequent plan of action. For their part, the patient should not be constrained by stereotypical or cultural models of the all-powerful and omniscient health practitioner, and should feel at the end of the consultation that the interactions have led to a full and satisfying, and personally reassuring, outcome.

In educational terms, reaching this position will take a great deal in terms of effort, resources and learning. From the point of view of the training of doctors and healthcare professionals, there is already an emerging view, especially among pain specialists, that medical education about pain is limited and unsatisfactory. In a medical curriculum which is already both full and intense, finding room for training about pain, especially chronic pain, will be difficult. In contrast, training for health practitioner – patient communication is better established, and many medical curricula devote training to this question. However, when we come to intercultural communication as a part of medical training the situation is more serious. There is intercultural communication training for healthcare professionals who have to work with specific ethnic groups, for instance with numerically substantial immigrant communities. The best levels of intercultural communication competence are probably found with health practitioners in countries where English is not a national language, but is increasingly being used as a lingua franca (House 2018) in medical consultations. As we have seen, the situation applies particularly clearly to tourism and medical tourism. But there are also broader needs for training in intercultural communication across the full range of healthcare professions. And healthcare professionals also need training in working with interpreters, in order to achieve a comprehensive understanding of what the patient has to tell them. Interpreters for their part will need special training in the specific difficulties of pain in medical consultations. And there is also the problem posed by the "third person in the room" phenomenon.

If there is already a framework for achieving these goals in the training of healthcare professionals, both before graduation and after it in professional development, the same cannot be said for the patient perspective. Being a helpful and constructive pain patient in the context of intercultural pain communication is not straightforward, even for patients who appear to be competent in the same language as a healthcare professional. As we have seen, linguistic competence is not necessarily accompanied by cultural competence. The situation is compounded if a doctor, a nurse and a patient all come from different linguistic and cultural backgrounds, and are using English as a lingua franca, with indeterminate cultural values operating in the communicating situation. Patients may also be constrained by stereotypes from their homeland culture, including the "omniscient health practitioner", respect for power, and related matters. It is necessary, in other words, to "educate" patients to be full and productive contributors to an intercultural pain consultation. How that could be done is yet to be addressed.

10 Conclusion

Pain is not merely a private part of our personal lives. As acute pain it has an important part in medical diagnosis and treatment, as well as its effect on our quality of life while we are recovering. And as chronic pain it is recognized as a disease in its own right, something requiring sophisticated and specialized attention from healthcare professionals. Pain is expensive, costly, and a burden on the quality of life of those who are unfortunate enough to suffer from it.

As our world becomes increasingly globalized, people from different languages and cultures are finding themselves more and more away from their homeland in places where they need to seek medical help. And pain, because of its covert and difficult existence, presents itself as one of the most difficult aspects of our medical condition to communicate. Pain talk, since pain is the most common reason why people go to the doctor, inevitably dominates talk between healthcare professionals and patients.

This chapter has presented a quantitative and qualitative case for promoting pain as one key aspect of intercultural communication. And within the range of medical conditions which bring us to visit a doctor, pain is among the most difficult and intractable. As we have seen, only a small number of pain sufferers receive appropriate treatment for their pain (National Pain Strategy 2011, p. 2).

Asia, with its dynamic growth of population and its population-movement, is an area where intercultural pain communication will become more frequent and therefore more important. English as a lingua franca will certainly be the dominant language and culture paradigm in this expanded area of intercultural communication (Lian and Sussex 2018). The accelerating influence of China in Asia – the movement of people out of and into China for business, education and cultural goals – means that the Chinese language and values will also become increasingly important players in the communication of pain.

From the linguistic point of view, pain is under-explored territory. The bulk of the work done so far on pain language has been carried out by non-linguists, and has concentrated on vocabulary and the creation of instruments for clinical pain assessment. As we have seen, at least in a brief analysis, these approaches have a number of assumptions which need rigorous testing. The grammar of pain, apart from work by Halliday and Lascaratou, has been hardly touched. The same is true of the conversational analysis of pain talk, especially in the crucial context of the medical consultation between health care professionals and patients. The sociolinguistics (e.g. the role of swearing in pain tolerance: Stephens 2009), sociology and anthropology, as well as the metalinguistics (e.g. tone of voice) and pragmatics, of pain are waiting for investigation.

Pain as a topic of intellectual enquiry in intercultural communication finds a number of points of engagement with the chapter in the present volume. The whole question of English as a lingua franca is central here, both as a code for communication, and as value systems which accompany it, since people using English forms may not be making English messages in the L1 semantic, pragmatic and cultural sense (Sussex 2012).

The issue of the language construction of how people in pain formulate their pain reports, and their interpretation, relate closely to the notion of culture and artefact (Curtis 2018). In a fundamental sense pain IS its constructed report: that is the only way we can get at it, in the absence of independent objective means and representations. But the artefact of the pain report depends in turn on the underlying value systems, both as intended by the speaker, and understood by the hearer. The two may not mesh, and grasping and externalizing pain descriptions may turn out to be a complex matter of negotiation, misunderstanding, repair and renegotiation. Here the Confucian values addressed by Pham (2018) are of central importance. Respect for power figures, including professional power figures, can shape and limit the patient's readiness to speak fully and frankly about their pain. So too are issues of gender, of respect, and of interpersonal roles, whether in the workplace (Pham 2018; and see Nguyen 2014) or in the medical consultation. And, in ways which have not yet been adequately addressed, contexts of pain communication involves issues of intra-and inter-cultural communication (Kecskes 2018). It is relatively straightforward to classify as "intercultural" the communication between a health practitioner and a patient where one of them is speaking a second or foreign language. But when the health practitioner and the patient are speaking the same first language, it is still possible to conceptualize the conversation in terms of inter-cultural communication, as between a professional and a non-pro-

fessional discourse and system of values. Here the gradient which Kecskes proposes between intra-and inter-cultural communication offers opportunities for new
analysis.

References

Access Economics. (2007). *The high price of pain: The economic impact of persistent pain
    in Australia.* http://www.bupa.com.au/staticfiles/BupaP3/Health%20and%20Wellness/
    MediaFiles/PDFs/MBF_Foundation_the_price_of_pain.pdf.
Al-Harthy, M., Ohrbach, R., Michelotti, A., & List, T. (2015). The effect of culture on pain sensi-
    tivity. *Journal of Oral Rehabilitation.* https://doi.org/10.1111/joor.12346.
American Academy of Pain. Retrieved on July 8, 2017, from http://www.painmed.org/
    PatientCenter/Facts_on_Pain.aspx
Asano-Cavanagh, Y. (2014). Japanese interpretations of "pain" and the use of psychomimes.
    International Journal of Language and Culture, 1(2), 216–238. Retrieved on 27 Jan 2017 from
    http://doi.org/10.1075/ijolc.1.2.05asa.
Australian Bureau of Statistics. *IBABS.* http://www.abs.gov.au/AUSSTATS/abs@.nsf/Lookup/410
    2.0Main+Features20April+2013#p7.
Barker, K. L., Reid, M., & Minns Lowe, C. J. (2009). Divided by a lack of common language? A
    qualitative study exploring the use of language by health professionals treating back pain. *BMC
    Musculoskeletal Disorders, 10*, 123. https://doi.org/10.1186/1471-2474-10-123.
Bennett, J. M. (Ed.). (2015). *The SAGE encyclopedia of intercultural competence.* Thousand Oaks:
    Sage.
Biro, D. (2010). *The language of pain: Finding words, compassion, and relief.* New York: W. W.
    Norton.
Bourke, J. (2012). The art of medicine: The language of pain. *The Lancet, 379*, 2420–2421.
Bourke, J. (2014). *The story of pain: From prayer to painkillers.* Oxford: Oxford University Press.
Boyle, G. J. (2003). El cuestionario del dolor de McGill (McGill Pain Questionnaire – MPQ):
    consideraciones lingüísticas y estadísticas. *Revista de Psicología de La Universidad de Chile,
    12*, 111–119.
Brady, B., Veljanova, I., & Chipchase, L. (2016). Are multidisciplinary interventions multicul-
    tural? A topical review of the pain literature as it relates to culturally diverse patient groups.
    Pain, 157(2), 321–328. https://doi.org/10.1097/j.pain.0000000000000412.
Butler, D. S., & Moseley, L. G. (2013). *Explain pain* (2nd ed.). Adelaide: Noigroup Publications.
Canagarajah, S. (2007). Lingua Franca English, multilingual communities, and language acquisi-
    tion. *Modern Language Journal, 91*, 932–939.
Chen, Y.-Y., Tsai, S.-L., Yang, C.-W., Ni, Y.-H., & Chang, S.-C. (2013). The ongoing western-
    ization of East Asian biomedical ethics in Taiwan. *Social Science & Medicine, 78*, 125–129.
    https://doi.org/10.1016/j.socscimed.2012.12.001.
Clark, H. H. (2009). Context and common ground. In J. L. Mey (Ed.), *Concise encyclopedia of
    pragmatics* (pp. 116–119). Oxford: Elsevier.
Craig, K. D. (2009). The social communication model of pain. *Canadian Psychology/Psychologie
    Canadienne, 50*(1), 22–32. https://doi.org/10.1037/a0014772.
Curtis, A. (2018). Individual, institutional and international: Three aspects of intercultural com-
    munication. In A. Curtis & R. Sussex (Eds.), *Intercultural communication in Asia: Education,
    language and values.* Cham: Springer.
Diller, A. (1980). Cross-cultural pain semantics. *Pain, 9*, 9–26.
Dworkin, R. H., Turk, D. C., Revicki, D. A., Harding, G., Coyne, K. S., Peirce-Sandner, S., Bhagwat,
    D., Everton, D., Burke, L. B., Cowan, P., Farrar, J. T., Hertz, S., Max, M. B., Rappaport, B. A.,
    & Melzack, R. (2009). Development and initial validation of an expanded and revised version

of the Short-Form McGill Pain Questionnaire (SF-MPQ-2). *Pain, 144*(1–2), 35–42. https://doi. org/10.1016/j.pain.2009.02.007.

Evans, S., & Bush, D. (2016). *Endometriosis and pelvic pain* (3rd ed.). Adelaide: Dr Susan F. Evans P/L.

Fabrega, H. J. (1976). Culture, language and the shaping of illness. *Journal of Psychosomatic Research, 20*, 323–337.

Fabrega, H. J., & Tyma, S. (1976). Language and cultural influences in the description of pain. *The British Journal of Medical Psychology, 49*(4), 349–371.

Fan, R. (2011). The Confucian bioethics of surrogate decision making: Its communitarian roots. *Theoretical Medicine and Bioethics, 32*(5), 301–313. https://doi.org/10.1007/s11017-011-9191-z.

Fernandez, E., & Boyle, G. L. (2001). Affective and evaluative descriptors of pain in the McGill Pain Questionnaire: Reduction and reorganization. *The Journal of Pain, 2*, 318–325.

Fernandez, E., & Towery, S. (1996). A parsimonious set of verbal descriptors of pain sensation derived from the McGill Pain Questionnaire. *Pain, 66*, 31–37.

Giles, H. (2016). *Communication accommodation theory: Negotiating personal relationships and social identities across contexts*. Cambridge: Cambridge University Press.

Goddard, C., & Ye, Z. (2014). Exploring "happiness" and "pain" across languages and cultures. *International Journal of Language and Culture, 1*(2), 131–148. https://doi.org/https://doi. org/10.1075/ijolc.1.2.01god.

Hadjistavropoulos, T., Craig, K. D., Duck, S., & Cano, A. (2011). A biopsychosocial formulation of pain communication. *Psychological Bulletin, 137*(6), 910–939. https://doi.org/https://doi. org/10.1037/a0023876.

Halliday, M. A. K. (1998). On the grammar of pain. *Functions of Language, 5*(1), 1–32.

Hasegawa, M. (2001). The McGill Pain Questionnaire, Japanese version, reconsidered: Confirming the theoretical structure. *Pain Research and Management, 6*, 173–180.

House, J. (2018). English as a global lingua franca: A threat to other languages, intercultural communication and translation? In A. Curtis & R. Sussex (Eds.), *Intercultural communication in Asia: Education, language and values*. Cham: Springer.

Institute of Medicine. (2011). *Relieving pain in America: A blueprint for transforming prevention, care, education, and research*. Retrieved on July 6, 2017, from https://www.ncbi.nlm.nih.gov/pubmed/22553896/

Iwasaki, N., Vinson, D. P., & Vigliocco, G. (2007). How does it hurt, kiri-kiri or siku-siku? Japanese mimetic words of pain perceived by Japanese speakers and English speakers. In M. Minami (Ed.), *Applying theory and research to learning Japanese as a foreign language* (pp. 2–19). Newcastle: Cambridge Scholars Publishing.

Kecskes, I. (2018). How does intercultural communication differ from intercultural communication? In A. Curtis & R. Sussex (Eds.), *Intercultural communication in Asia: Education, language and values*. Cham: Springer.

Kecskes, I., & Zhang, F. (2009). Activating, seeking and creating common ground: A socio-cognitive approach. *Pragmatics & Cognition, 17*(2), 331–355.

Ketovuori, H., & Pontinen, P. J. (1981). A pain vocabulary in Finnish – The Finnish Pain Questionnaire. *Pain, 11*, 247–253.

Kim, H. S., Schwartz-Barcott, D., Holter, I. M., & Lorensen, M. (1995). Developing a translation of the McGill Pain Questionnaire for cross-cultural comparison: An example from Norway. *Journal of Advanced Nursing, 21*(3), 421–426. https://doi.org/10.1111/j.1365-2648.1995. tb02722.xm.

Kim, M.-S., Klingle, R. S., Sharkey, W. F., Park, H. S., Smith, D. H., & Cai, D. (2000). A test of a cultural model of patients' motivation for verbal communication in patient-doctor interactions. *Communication Monographs, 67*(3), 262–283. https://doi.org/. https://doi. org/10.1080/03637750009376510.

Kövecses, Z. (2000). *Metaphor and emotion: Language, culture, and body in human feeling*. Cambridge: Cambridge University Press.

Kövecses, Z. (2008). The conceptual structure of happiness and pain. In C. Lascaratou, A. Despotopoulou, & E. Ifantidou (Eds.), *Reconstructing pain and joy: Linguistic, literary, and cultural perspectives* (pp. 17–33). Newcastle: Cambridge Scholars Publishing.

Kwok, W., & Bhuvanakrishna, T. (2014). The relationship between ethnicity and the pain experience of cancer patients: A systematic review. *Indian Journal of Palliative Care, 20*(3), 194–200. https://doi.org/10.4103/0973-1075.138391.

Lascaratou, C. (2007). *The language of pain*. Amsterdam/Philadelphia: John Benjamins.

Lascaratou, C. (2008). The function of language in the experience of pain. In C. Lascaratou, A. Despotopoulou, & E. Ifantidou (Eds.), *Reconstructing pain and joy: Linguistic, literary, and cultural perspectives* (pp. 37–57). Newcastle: Cambridge Scholars Publishing.

Lascaratou, C., & Marmaridou, S. (2005). Metaphor in Greek pain-constructions: Cognitive and functional perspectives. In S. Marmaridou, K. Nikiforidou, & A. Antonopoulou (Eds.), *Reviewing linguistic thought: Converging trends for the 21st century* (pp. 235–254). Berlin: Mouton de Gruyter.

Lian, A., & Sussex, R. (2018). Toward a critical epistemology for learning languages and cultures in 21st century Asia. In A. Curtis & R. Sussex (Eds.), *Intercultural communication in Asia: Education, language and values*. Cham: Springer.

Lim, T. S., & Bowers, J. W. (1991). Face-work: Solidarity, approbation, and tact. *Human Communication Research, 17*(3), 415–450.

Lwin, M. O., & Salmon, C. T. (2015). A retrospective overview of health communication studies in Asia from 2000 to 2013. *Asian Journal of Communication, 25*(1), 1–13.

Main, C. J. (2015). Pain assessment in context: A state of the science review of the McGill Pain Questionnaire 40 years on. *Pain*. https://doi.org/10.1097/j.pain.0000000000000457.

Mäntyselkä, P., Kumpusalo, E., Ahonen, R., Kumpusalo, A., Kauhanen, J., Viinamäki, H., Halonen, P., & Takala, J. (2001). Pain as a reason to visit the doctor: A study in Finnish primary health care. *Pain, 89*(2–3), 175–180.

Melzack, R. (1975). The McGill Pain Questionnaire: Major properties and scoring methods. *Pain, 1*, 277–299.

Melzack, R. (1987). The short-form McGill Pain Questionnaire. *Pain, 30*, 191–197.

Melzack, R., & Torgerson, W. S. (1971). On the language of pain. *Anaesthesiology, 34*(1), 50–59.

Menezes Costa, L., da Maher, C. G., McAuley, J. H., & Costa, L. O. P. (2009). Systematic review of cross-cultural adaptations of McGill Pain Questionnaire reveals a paucity of clinimetric testing. *Journal of Clinical Epidemiology, 62*(9), 934–943. https://doi.org/10.1016/j.jclinepi.2009.03.019.

Merskey, H., & Bogduk, N. (Eds.). (1994). *Classification of chronic pain, IASP task force on taxonomy* (2nd ed.). Seattle: IASP Press.

Mystakidou, K. (2002). Greek McGill Pain Questionnaire: Validation and utility in cancer patients. *Journal of Pain and Symptom Management, 24*, 379–387.

National Pain Strategy (Australia). (2011). Retrieved on July 7, 2017, from http://www.painaustralia.org.au/improving-policy/national-pain-strategy

Nayak, S. (2000). Culture and gender effects in pain beliefs and the prediction of pain tolerance. *Cross-Cultural Research, 34*, 135–151.

Nguyen, H. H. T. (2014). *The language of pain in Vietnamese*. St Lucia, Australia: University of Queensland PhD Dissertation.

Parker, M. A., Sneddon, A. E., & Arbon, P. (2010). The menstrual disorder of teenagers (MDOT) study: Determining typical menstrual patterns and menstrual disturbance in a large population-based study of Australian teenagers. *British Journal of Obstetrics and Gynaecology, 117*(2), 185–192.

Patients Beyond Borders. (n.d.). Accessed on 29 January 2017 from http://www.patientsbeyond-borders.com/medical-tourism-statistics-facts.

Pauwels, A. (1990). Health professionals' perceptions of communication difficulties in cross-cultural contexts. *ARAL, S7*, 93–111.

Perquin, C. W., Hazebroek-Kampschreur, A. A. J. M., Hunfeld, J. A. M., Bohnen, A. M., van Suijlekom-Smit, L. W. A., Passchier, J., & van der Wouden, J. C. (2000). Pain in children and adolescents: A common experience. *Pain, 87*(1), 51–58. https://doi.org/10.1016/S0304-3959(00)00269-4.

Pham, T. H. N. (2018). Confucian values as challenges for communication in intercultural workplace contexts: Evidence from Vietnamese –Anglo-cultural interactions. In A. Curtis & R. Sussex (Eds.), *Intercultural communication in Asia: Education, language and values*. Cham: Springer.

Rey, R. (1998). *The history of pain* (J. A. Cadden, & S. W. Cadden, Trans.). Cambridge, MA/London: Harvard University Press.

Rowbotham, S., Wardy, A. J., Lloyd, D. M., Wearden, A., & Holler, J. (2014). Increased pain intensity is associated with greater verbal communication difficulty and increased production of speech and co-speech gestures. *PLoS One, 9*(10), e110779. https://doi.org/10.1371/journal.pone.0110779.

Sakai, E. Y., & Carpenter, B. D. (2011). Linguistic features of power dynamics in triadic dementia diagnostic conversations. *Patient Education and Counseling, 85*(2), 295–298. https://doi.org/10.1016/j.pec.2010.09.020.

Sargent, C. (1984). Between death and shame: Dimensions of pain in Bariba culture. *Social Science & Medicine, 19*(12), 1299–1304. https://doi.org/10.1016/0277-9536(84)90016-9.

Sauver, J. L. S., Warner, D. O., Yawn, B. P., Jacobson, D. J., McGree, M. E., Pankratz, J. J., Rocca, W. A. (2013). Why patients visit their doctors: Assessing the most prevalent conditions in a defined American population. *Mayo Clinic Proceedings, 88*(1), 56–67. https://doi.org/https://doi.org/10.1016/j.mayocp.2012.08.020.

Scarry, E. (1985). *The body in pain: The making and unmaking of the world*. New York: Oxford University Press.

Stephens, R. (2009). Swearing as a response to pain. *Neuroreport, 20*, 1056–1060.

Strong, J., Mathews, T., Sussex, R., New, F., Hoey, S., & Mitchell, G. (2009). Pain language and gender differences when describing a past pain event. *Pain, 145*, 85–96.

Sullivan, M. D., & Derbyshire, S. W. (2015). Is there a purely biological core to pain experience? *Pain, 156*(11), 2119–2120.

Sussex, R. (2009). The language of pain in applied linguistics: Review article of Chryssoula Lascaratou's *The language of pain* (Amsterdam and Philadelphia: John Benjamins, 2007). *Australian Review of Applied Linguistics, 32*(1), 6.1–6.14. https://doi.org/10.2104/aral0906.

Sussex, R. (2012). Switching in international English. In A. Kirkpatrick & R. Sussex (Eds.), *English as an international language in Asia: Implications for language education* (pp. 175–190). Berlin/London: Springer-Verlag.

Sussex, R., & Kirkpatrick, A. (2012). A postscript and a prolegomenon. In A. Kirkpatrick & R. Sussex (Eds.), *English as an international language in Asia: Implications for language education* (pp. 223–231). Berlin/London: Springer-Verlag.

Todd, A. S., & Todd, S. F. (1993). *The social organization of doctor-patient communication* (2nd ed.). Greenwood: Ablex Publishing Corporation.

Towery, S., & Fernandez, E. (1996). Reclassification and rescaling of McGill Pain Questionnaire verbal descriptors of pain sensation: A replication. *The Clinical Journal of Pain, 12*(4), 270–276.

Wierzbicka, A. (1999). *Emotions across languages and cultures: Diversity and universals*. Cambridge: Cambridge University Press.

Wierzbicka, A. (2012). Is pain a human universal? A cross-linguistic and cross-cultural perspective on pain. Emotion Review, 4(3), 307–317. https://doi.org/10.1177/1754073912439761.

Wierzbicka, A. (2014). "Pain" and "suffering" in cross-linguistic perspective. *International Journal of Language and Culture, 1*(2), 149–173. https://doi.org/10.1075/ijolc.1.2.02wie.

Wiesenfeld-Hallin, Z. (2005). Sex differences in pain perception. *Gender Medicine, 2*, 137–145.

Wilkie, D. J., Savedra, M. C., Holzemer, W. D., Tesler, M. D., & Paul, S. M. (1990). Use of the McGill Pain Questionnaire to measure pain: A meta-analysis. *Nursing Research, 39*, 36–41.

Wittgenstein, L. (1953/1989). *Philosophical investigations*. Oxford: Basil Blackwell.

Wolff, J. L., & Roter, D. L. (2008). Hidden in plain sight: Medical visit companions as a resource for vulnerable older adults. *Archives of Internal Medicine, 168*(13), 1409–1415. https://doi.org/10.1001/archinte.168.13.1409.

Wolff, J. L., & Roter, D. L. (2011). Family presence in routine medical visits: A meta-analytical review. *Social Science & Medicine, 72*(6), 823–831. https://doi.org/10.1016/j.socscimed.2011.01.015.

Zborowski, M. (1969). *People in pain*. San Francisco: Jossey-Bass.

Functions of Humor in Intercultural Communication and Educational Environments

Kimie OSHIMA

Abstract Humor is important in its ability to help people to "think outside the box." It aids in the conceptualization of ideas that are outside of the framework of accepted norms. In this sense, it is a similar skill to having intercultural understanding and communication. It can also assist in the understanding and deconstructing of social and cultural expectations. It can function as a social lubricant, as well as be an antidote to inter-ethnic tensions, as seen in the successful use of ethnic jokes in a multi-ethnic society like Hawaii. It has also been shown that the type of environment created in the classroom by humor can motivate students, and by doing so contribute to building better teacher-student relationships. Humor promotes mental flexibility, which can help people to first understand, then adopt, new aspects of culture and communication, which can then be further developed through education.

1 Introduction

Having a sense of humor helps one to "think outside the box". It is helpful for imagining and understanding concepts outside the framework of one's own norms in terms of one's own cultural and social range. Among the several theories of humor that have been discussed, incongruity theory is one of the mainstream approaches:

> The notions of congruity and incongruity refer to the relationship between components of an object, event, idea, social expectation, and so forth. When the arrangement of the constituent elements of an event is incompatible with the normal or expected pattern, the event is perceived as incongruous (McGhee 1979, pp. 6–7).

This was more simply stated by Shultz (1976): "incongruity is usually defined as a conflict between what is expected and what actually occurs in the joke" (Schultz 1976, p. 12). This sense of incongruity can have beneficial outcomes in society, communication and learning. The present chapter investigates the role of humor in

K. OSHIMA (✉)
Foreign Language Department, Kanagawa University,
Yokohama, Kanagawa Prefecture, Japan
e-mail: k.oshima@english-rakugo.com

© Springer International Publishing AG, part of Springer Nature 2018
A. CURTIS, R. SUSSEX (eds.), *Intercultural Communication in Asia: Education, Language and Values*, Multilingual Education 24,
https://doi.org/10.1007/978-3-319-69995-0_10

communication and intercultural communication, both in their own right, and in the multicultural context of Hawaii, and in education. We devote special attention to Rakugo, a traditional Japanese humor genre, and how it can cross cultural boundaries when translated and adapted into English.

Having a sense of humor can help people to break through their own social and cultural expectations and understand themselves better. In this sense, it is a similar skill to intercultural understanding and communication. In order to understand a wide range of jokes or humorous episodes, one needs to have a certain amount of cultural and contextual knowledge. This fact is related to the notion that people with a well-developed sense of humor may be more skillful as intracultural and intercultural communicators (DiCioccio and Miczo 2014).

Humor can also function as an antidote for social friction, violence and aggression. This applies also to the function of ethnic humor in some multi-ethnic societies. To transform friction caused by differences in cultural behavior into laughter through the successful use of ethnic stereotypes is an effective way of mitigating the friction and tension among ethnic groups. As we shall see, Hawaii is a notably successful society where various ethnic groups coexist and yet maintain very positive ethnic relations (Lind 1967; Hormann 1972; Okamura 1995). Hawaii is well-known as a society where "everybody is a minority" (Yamanaka 1993, p. 65), because no single ethnic group is more than 20% of the population. Ethnic jokes work as a social lubricant within daily interethnic communication (Keller 1980; Hopkins 1991; Oshima 2000). The people of Hawaii are familiar with each other's ethnic features, and if not, they learn about each other through ethnic jokes.

Another aspect of humor is its functions in education. Studies such as Deneire (1995) and Morreall (1997) have shown that using jokes and creating a humorous environment in the classroom can help students to learn more efficiently and with a more positive attitude. Morreall (2008) states that:

> [...] humor can foster analytic, critical, and divergent thinking; catch and hold students' attention, increase retention of learned material, relieve stress, build rapport between teacher and students, build team spirit among classmates, smooth potentially rough interactions, promote risk taking, and get shy and slow students involved in activities (Morreall 2008, p. 465).

A number of studies on humor and education support this statement, as well as my own experience in teaching English language and intercultural communication using Rakugo scripts in my classroom. Rakugo is a traditional Japanese performing art with a history of approximately 400 years. I translate the scripts of stories into English and perform them around the world.[1] The translation process that involves translating humor and culture is challenging. And performance for non-Japanese audiences shows different aspects and values from Japanese audiences. Students learn some of the differences between Japanese and non-Japanese culture and

---

[1] I have been performing Rakugo in English since 1998, and have performed in more than 20 countries and regions, including the United States, Norway, Belgium, Germany, Australia, Israel, India, Pakistan, Brunei, Malaysia, Singapore, Thailand, and the Philippines.

Fig. 1 Bird or Rabbit?
(Morreall 1997, p. 105)

values, while at the same time developing their English language skills, through the humor in the English Rakugo scripts.

Humor can therefore help people to understand, adopt and adapt to different aspects of culture and communication.

2   Common Features of Humor and Intercultural Communication

As we have seen, humor is unexpected action or speech, which is different from one's norms. People from different cultures have different styles of communication – they may act and speak in unexpected ways that are different from each other. Spiegel (1972) characterizes this as: "humor arising from disjointed, ill-suited pairing of ideas of situations or presentations of ideas or situations that are divergent from habitual customs form the base of incongruity theories" (p. 7). It takes flexibility and creativity to be able to see what is not "normal", and to accept what one experiences with laughter. Humor is a communication skill. In order to create a joke and to understand a joke requires a certain amount of knowledge about language and cultural competence. Such skills and knowledge are also needed for effective intercultural communication.

Training programs and workshops to improve people's sense of humor can be conceived as similar to intercultural training. For example, Morreall (1997) asked trainees what they see in this figure (Fig. 1):

He explains that it takes mental flexibility to be comfortable with things that can be interpreted in more than one way. If we can see both the rabbit and the bird, we may have a higher tolerance for ambiguity, which is an important skill that is part of understanding humor. When we only see the bird, or only see the rabbit, we may have less mental flexibility than those who can see both, and may have a less developed sense of humor as well.

Some intercultural communication studies (Okabe 2002) have also used similar training methods, using famous artistic objects like such as "Rubens' vase" or the

Fig. 2 My wife and my
mother-in-law (Boring
1930, p 444: Reproduction
by William. E. Hill)

well-known illusion "My wife and my mother-in-law" (below), which shows that people have different perspectives, and understanding others means being able to see things from other people's perspectives. According to Okabe (2002), people see and recognize objects or concepts from their own personal and/or cultural perspectives. They may see one side of a thing, that part of the image which they recognize, and many times anything else becomes background noise. One such example is the illusion of "My wife and my mother-in-law". This shows that sometimes the "wife" is the focus image, in which case "my mother-in-law" becomes the background image, and vice versa. Often it is difficult to see both at the same time. Humor training can help people to realize how many concepts can be seen in a completely different light, depending on the cultural background of the viewer (Fig. 2).

There is now convincing evidence that having or developing a sense of humor can improve the development of intercultural communication skills (Davies 2015). When one has a sense of humor, one may be more able to understand and accept unexpected incidents or people's behavior that might otherwise seem strange or odd. A sense of humor may also help one to be more tolerant, understanding and accepting of other people's differences, to maintain good relationships with others, and to more easily adapt to different environments (e.g., Chapman 1983; Fine 1983; LeMasters 1975). These abilities are also important aspects of intercultural communicative competence (Oshima 2006b).

3   Ethnic Relations and Humor – The Case of Ethnic Jokes in Hawaii

Among the various types of jokes and humor, ethnic humor represents a distinct subset, as it requires participants to possess some prior understanding of ethnic characteristics or traits before the humor can be appreciated. Ethnic humor has strong connections with life style, physical and cultural characteristics, historical background, religious beliefs, and social and economic conditions, as well as the purported characteristics of the ethnic group concerned. In this sense, ethnic humor can be considered to be a highbrow rather than an insensitive type of humor.

Ethnic humor has a long and rich history in the traditional culture of Hawaii (Hopkins 1991). The enriching mixture of various cultures and peoples has provided the locals with a tolerant environment, which understands and accepts the nature of ethnic humor in multiethnic Hawaii (Hormann 1982). Ethnic humor has been developing strongly in Hawaii since the mid-nineteenth century, when a multiethnic and multicultural local society emerged as a result of worldwide immigration to Hawaii during the plantation era (1835–1900), when Hawaii started to encourage an influx of immigrants to serve as laborers in the sugar cane and pineapple plantations, especially from Asian countries. The complex mixture of ethnicities and cultures in contemporary Hawaiian society is directly related to this long history of immigrant labor (Lind 1967). Ethnic humor in Hawaii has been nurtured and maintained by indigenous Hawaiian and local communities as a positive contribution to the interactional well-being of the diverse ethnic groups living on the islands (Hopkins 1991).

As a result of this history and these conditions, people in Hawaii understand and respect each other's ethnic cultures. They believe that these ethnic cultures are part of a mature and developed multicultural society, so that local people are able to express stereotypes with pride and even joy. Okamura (1995) says, "It is widely believed by both academic researchers and laypersons that ethnic relations in Hawai'i are qualitatively 'better' than on the U.S. mainland and in other parts of the world (p. 246)". According to former Professor Fred Blake of the University of Hawaii, ethnic jokes serve as a healthy function in Hawaii because they can displace, diffuse and transform aggression (Keller 1980). Ethnic humor is an interethnic communication skill, which has developed as a device to lubricate daily communication and personal relationships among local people (Oshima 2000).

There was high expectation from many different groups, given the bi-racial background (a Kenyan father and white, Kansan mother) as well as his years spent living within the "Aloha Spirit" of Hawaii, that the then President of the United States, Barack Obama, would support and enhance ethnic relations with his governing style. According to the article "Hawaii as racial paradise? Bid for Obama Library invokes a complex past", Obama himself says,

> I do think that the multicultural nature of Hawaii helped teach me how to appreciate different cultures and navigate different cultures, out of necessity. [...] There just is a cultural bias

toward courtesy and trying to work through problems in a way that makes everybody feel like they're being listened to (Wu 2015).

Hawaii is unique in the United States in that healthy ethic humor is accepted by the majority of people. According to survey research among 604 local residents of Hawaii (Oshima 2000), 88% responded that not only are they are not offended by, but they are comfortable with telling and laughing at self-directed ethnic jokes – or jokes directed at their own ethnicity. As the sociologist Christie Davies stated in his book, *Ethnic humor around the world: A comparative analysis*:

> […] jokes provide insights into how societies work – they are not social thermostats regulating and shaping human behavior, but they are social thermometers that measure, record, and indicate what is going on (Davies 1990, p. 9).

In contrast, ethnic humor in the mainland states of the US or many other multiethnic regions is usually considered to show "discrimination" and "racial prejudice". Weaver (2014) says, "An alternative explanation for the existence of language and so are the result of intergroup relations imbued with historical power relations" (p. 215).

Frank DeLima and Mel Cabang are two of the leading ethnic-joke comedians in Hawaii. Although these comedians are consistently popular in Hawaii, their sense of humor is not easily understood in the mainland United States. Here is an example of an ethnic joke told by a high school student in Connecticut:

> Q: Two men jumped off from a tall building at the same time. One was Japanese, and the other was Chinese. Who hits the ground first?
> A: Who cares?
> (Oshima 2000, p. 45)

This joke is not an example of healthy ethnic humor. It promotes the notion of greater or lesser value placed on particular ethnicities. A healthy and positive ethnic joke creates laughter through recognition of ethnic characteristics and stereotypes in a respectable fashion, not to promote the notion of greater or lesser comparative worth of different races of people.

DeLima has a strong belief that his performances, which use ethnic humor to illuminate rather than denigrate, have positive social effects. In an interview with the author in 1995, he expressed the most important message he aims to deliver in his show:

> It is important to remember to respect each other and understand that all ethnic groups have something funny about them to each other. It is important to be able to laugh along with those people. That way, the differences can become a pleasant thing and funny instead of it's being something to defend and cause fighting. People are protective about their own ethnic groups and tend to forget that they are not perfect. There is no perfect race, no perfect culture, no perfect ethnic group. And that is why there are some things funny about them and we all should be able to laugh about it (interview with DeLima, Sep. 7, 1995).

One of DeLima's healthy ethnic jokes is presented below. Due to several instances in the history of Japanese rule over Korea, the older generations of the two countries tend not to get along as well as other ethnic groups. However, the tension is less prevalent among the younger generation in Hawaii, and certain jokes reflect this relationship:

Q: What do you get when a *Yobo* marries a *Buddah* head?[2]
A: Four angry parents.
(Hopkins 1991, p. 82)

With positive ethnic jokes it might be said that, although a script may be based on social observation, people seem to recognize that it is only a broad generalization, and that it is not representative of the particular race or personality traits of an individual.

There seems to be a particular tendency when telling ethnic jokes to talk about one's own ethnicity, and to laugh, which may be a reflection of the pride a person has in their own ethnicity. This confidence and pride are a direct result of the respect given and received within a cultural environment. This is the so-called "self-deprecating joke", which is the most basic and important part of beneficial ethnic humor. Ethnic jokes can also serve to highlight those qualities of a culture which are associated with specific ethnic characteristics, while at the same time exaggerating them. Many times these can be characteristics which are considered neutral to positive.

An example of such an ethnic joke would be:

Q: Why do the Japanese, the Chinese, and the Portuguese walk with small steps?
A: The Japanese wear tight dresses. The Chinese are tight. And Portuguese forget to cut the
    string holding the slippers together.
(Hopkins 1991, p. 40)

Avner Ziv proposes five functions of humor in *Personality and sense of humor*: the offensive function, the sexual function, the social function, the defensive function, and the intelligent function (Ziv 1984). Among these five functions, the social, defensive, and intelligent functions are all strongly related to the functions of ethnic humor. In its social function, common humor among people in a society can strengthen solidarity with a social group. Humor can lubricate communication and minimize conflict while sustaining human relations in a multiethnic society. With ethnic humor as a basis, society can recognize a person as one important component of a multiethnic society.

Self-deprecating jokes are generally considered to have a defensive function. A self-deprecating joke-teller is well aware that some of the characteristics of his/her ethnic background might seem funny to others, and instead uses these characteristics as a means of self-assertion. The joke-teller accepts the fact that their own ethnic group is at once virtuous and flawed – as are all ethnic groups. Defensively, one can take advantage of self-deprecating humor and avoid an offensive situation by laughing at one's own stereotypical flaws, as a pre-emptive strategy, before others point them out.

Special skill is required when a joke is told with ambiguous reference, in the form of a riddle, or with a reference to some shared knowledge. To fully understand and enjoy the specific reference of ethnic humor, one must possess this shared knowl-

---

[2] Humor sometimes creates its own new words in referring to a specific group. In Hawaii, nicknames for each ethnicity are those common words which are shared to make jokes more effective. *Yobo* is a nickname for Korean people, which comes from the Korean greeting, "*Yobo seyo*". *Yobo* literally means "sweet heart". *Buddah head* is a nickname for Japanese people, because many Japanese are Buddhists.

edge, and to a certain extent, the ability to solve problems. When people understand humor or jokes, it confirms their ability to grasp what is funny, and confirms their knowledge and intelligence in the solving of puzzles. Ethnic jokes certainly require an optimal amount of knowledge about various ethnicities and cultures, so that such jokes bring intellectual satisfaction to both joke-teller and the listener.

This function leads into the idea of using humorous stories and jokes in education. When certain jokes are studied, the learners acquire the social and cultural knowledge behind them. Thus, there are some potential benefits to using humor in an educational environment.

4 Humor in Education

A number of studies and research on humor in education have been carried out, and many have shown the benefits in using humor as a teaching tool to produce a positive pedagogical effect, to help create a more relaxed classroom atmosphere, and to increase student interest in and retention of material. For example, according to Garner (2006), some of the positive psychological effects of humor are to decrease stress, reduce anxiety, enhance self-esteem and improve camaraderie in the classroom, as well as increase student self-motivation. Each of these effects is beneficial in the learning process. Garner also points out the physiological effects of laughter, which improves respiration and circulation, lowers pulse rate, decreases blood pressure, oxygenates blood, and releases endorphins. These effects improve attention and lessen stresses that might adversely impact learning.

Studies such as Hill (1988) and Morreall (1997) have shown that using jokes and creating a humorous environment in the classroom can help students to learn more efficiently and with a more positive attitude. In Hill's (1988) view, "humor has a positive effect on the learning environment, to initiate, maintain, and enhance learner interest, and to facilitate retention" (pp. 20–24). Morreall (1997) also stated that: "The stage of our lives when we learn the fastest is precisely the stage when we take the most risks and are least afraid of mistakes – our first five years. [...] And humor can be a big help in setting a tone of acceptance of mistakes" (p. 140). In a humorous environment, students may be more receptive to new knowledge and different values, and as such may also be more accepting of the information presented by the instructor.

Some jokes involving historical events, ethnic issues, cultural values, social activities, and the politics of certain geographical areas can be effective materials to teach and learn about intercultural issues and values. Because effective humor delivers messages with an impact, the knowledge retained by the learner through jokes can become more stable and persist for longer periods of time. Moreover, jokes are naturally repeated by the learners. In my observations, which will be discussed in the following section, when students learn language, culture, or intercultural communication skills through humorous stories or jokes, students talk about what they have learned outside of the classroom. This can also help the learners to develop a better understanding and more stable knowledge of the subject matter they have acquired.

Some studies specifically indicate the advantages of using humor in language learning. Humor has been advocated as "a tool to make students sensitive to the structural and semantic differences between different languages" (Deneire 1995, p. 291). According to Deneire, jokes can direct learners' attention to phonology, morphology, lexicon, syntax and the cultural aspects of language:

Phonology
An American in a British hospital asks the nurse: "Did I come here to die?" The nurse
    answers: "No, it was yesterdie". (Nilsen 1989, p. 114)
Syntax + lexicon
Q: How do you make a horse fast?
A: Don't give him anything for a while. (Vega 1989, p. 60)

Bell (2014) found that some language teachers incorporate humor into the classroom in the belief that it facilitates learning by increasing students' interest and motivation:

Language play may be an important – perhaps even necessary - component of language acquisition, allowing learners to experiment with new voices and new ways of expressing themselves. [...] playing with and in a new language may work to draw learners' attention to form meaning relationships within the language being studied (Bell 2014, p. 672).

For the purposes of language acquisition, it can be effective to teach the structures and functions of the target language and culture through the use of humorous materials.

Although some jokes can have a positive effect on the learning process and enhance learner interest, Banas et al. (2011) point out that inappropriate humor in the classroom can be a distraction. For example, humor based on race, ethnicity, sex or political affiliation can have a negative effect, if it is felt by some learners to be offensive or aggressive. Wanzer et al. (2010), who developed the Instructional Humor Process Theory (IHPT),[3] also warn against the use of inappropriate instructional humor, which can negatively impact student motivation and learning, and erode student-teacher relationships as well. However, when humor is appropriately used by the teacher, it can increase students' cognitive and affective learning, and their willingness to engage in communication. Therefore, the materials must be carefully chosen and well planned to ensure that appropriate jokes, videos, or cartoons, for each age range are used (Garner 2006).

Another aspect of using humor in education that relates to the learning environment is student-teacher relationships. According to Van Giffen's (1990) study, there is a positive relationship between instructional humor and students' evaluations of teacher effectiveness, although students' perceptions were not necessarily associated with the teacher's warmth or friendliness. This means that using humor in class is more a matter of pedagogical skill rather than a feature of the personality of each instructor. Instructors should not be comedians in the classroom, which can distract

---

[3] IHPT proposes that the recognition of humor will increase students' attention and recall of class material if the humor is relevant, but students need to perceive and then resolve the incongruity in a humorous instructional message (Dunbar 2014).

students from learning. However, as Van Giffen's (1990) study showed, using humor as one of a repertoire of teaching skills can improve students' evaluations and help create a more positive attitude towards the teacher.

Murray (1983) conducted a study which showed that the use of humor was considered to be one of the five main teaching behaviors that distinguished "outstanding" from "average" and "poor" lecturers. Garner (2006) also found that that college students tended to strongly favor teachers who possess a sense of humor and rated these instructors with high evaluative scores. Therefore, humor in the classroom can serve as a bridge between educators and students and help to develop mutual understanding. Wanzer et al. (2010) also agree that appropriate humor can create a comfortable learning environment and improve relationships between students and teachers by reducing tension and anxiety.

According to these previous studies on humor in education, appropriate humorous material can help learners to retain their motivation and interest, reduce stress and anxiety, and improve the classroom environment and learning efficiency. Deneire (1995), who focused on learning language and culture using humor, found that understanding such classroom humor requires a high level of linguistic, sociolinguistic and discourse competence. Therefore, "the language learner will need to develop a certain level of cultural competence in the target language. Indeed, humor contains a lot of hidden cultural meaning and therefore functions as a social unifier within groups" (Deneire 1995, pp. 294–295).

Whether it is the study of language or culture, two closely related fields, my previous studies also support the finding that humorous materials keep students' attention, provide deeper insights into the culture of the language being studied, improve students' performance in speaking and listening tasks, and increase their willingness to study further (Oshima 2011). In next part of this chapter, I will present some materials that I have used to teach English language and inter-cultural aspects to Japanese students. These materials are based on Rakugo, a Japanese traditional performing art or comic story telling.

5 Translating Humor and Culture – Japanese Rakugo Comedy Scripts

Rakugo can be an effective tool to teach Japanese values, customs, history, communication style, manners, social norms, and family relations to students. Japanese students study what are the differences between their own cultures and others, as well as what extra cultural elements need further explanation during intercultural communication while speaking English. Rakugo, therefore, has been adopted as a means to learn intercultural communication and English language in Japanese English text books.[4]

---

[4] English textbooks authorized by Japanese Ministry of Education, Culture, Sports, Science, and Technology such as *New Crown* (Sanseido Publication), *New Horizon* (Tokyo Shoseki), *One World* (Kyoiku Shuppan) include Rakugo materials for students to learn Japanese culture and the English language.

Fig. 3 The author as a
Rakugo performer, seated
on a *zabuton* cushion in the
seiza position

I have been teaching intercultural communication and English through jokes and English translations of Rakugo scripts at universities in Tokyo since 2006. Since incorporating this material into my curriculum, I have noticed a marked improvement in my students' motivation to learn, their understanding of the materials, and the effectiveness of their learning.

Rakugo is one of the Japanese traditional performing arts and is best described as Japanese comic storytelling or "sit-down comedy" (as opposed to "stand-up comedy"). The performer tells a story as a single sketch, while kneeling on a thick cushion called a *zabuton* (Fig. 3).

The story consists of almost all dialogue and the performer acts out the different characters that appear in the story. The performer uses facial expressions, gestures and different tones of voice, changing the style and speed of speech to distinguish the characters, and all from a kneeling position.

The performer on the stage is equipped with two limited props, which are a folding fan (*sensu*) and a piece of cotton (*tenugui*). Those two items help the performer to express what happens in the story. For example, the fan can be used to represent chopsticks, a fishing pole, a writing brush, scissors, cigarettes, a sword, a pipe, and so on. The piece of cotton can be a book, a handkerchief, a wallet, a plate, a notebook, and so on. The audience is asked to use its imagination every time those items are used in the story.

The Rakugo tradition can be traced back as far as the 1600s, when Buddhist priests started telling funny stories about what was right and wrong about society, instead of giving serious lectures. In order to capture the people's attention, the priests created funny stories with punch lines illustrating the thoughts and theories of Buddhism. Many Rakugo stories are written by a well-known priest, Anrakuan Sakuden of Kyoto. In 1623 he published a storybook called *Sei-sui-sho* (*Wake up and laugh*) which contained over a thousand stories. Many classical Rakugo stories which are still popular and performed today are based on Sakuden's stories (Aiba 2009).

Until recently, Rakugo had not been introduced or performed internationally as much as the classical Japanese Kabuki or Noh musical dramas. This is because the attraction of Rakugo performance mostly relies on verbal elements rather than non-verbal, visual presentation. When the words and dialogues are not understood, Rakugo is not an engaging form of entertainment. The conversation between the characters, unexpected lines, puns, changes in tone of voice, pauses, and onomatopoeia are what is amusing about Rakugo. The visual attraction is much less important – as Rakugo is an art of the imagination. Simple stage setting and costume are established so that they do not prevent the audience from imagining the characters and scenes in the story. Good Rakugo makes the performer effectively disappear, and the story unfolds in front of the audience.

In order to introduce Rakugo to the rest of the world, I have translated many classical Rakugo stories, and I have been training to perform Rakugo since 1997. Throughout this time, translating Japanese humor and culture for a non-Japanese audience to understand the essence of Japanese values has always been a challenging process. The purpose of performing Rakugo in English in front of non-Japanese audiences is not only to introduce Japanese culture, but also to share the same sense of values and humor, and to laugh together to help establish better relationships. It takes creativity and flexibility, as well as elegance and narrative skills, to translate the culture in the scripts from Japanese to English.

For example, there is a story called "I hate manju" about a man who hates manju, a sweet dumpling and a Japanese delicacy. He is given a pile of manju by his friends because they want to see him struggle with the food. But the truth is, he loves manju and is happy to have a pile of them. When his friends ask him what he really hates, he answers, "Now I would really hate to have some hot green tea". It is easy to replace manju and tea with pizza and coke. Instead, however, I have some of the characters in this story talk about manju to give a hint how it goes well with hot green tea:

> "What? You hate manju? It has sweet soybean paste in it! It's delicious!"
> "I can't believe you don't like that soft warm steamed bun around the bean paste…!"
> "Yeah, I know, manju is everybody's favorite. They come in different flavors… some have really smooth bean paste, some have sweet potatoes, some have even chestnuts inside! You don't like any of them?"
> "You are crazy to hate manju!"

Through different scripts of Rakugo in English and Japanese, students learn what it takes to communicate an idea effectively across different cultures. The concept of ghosts, the social status of men and women, cultural customs, or reasons for making slurping sounds when eating or drinking, can be taken as understood in Japanese Rakugo, but they must be explicitly explained in English Rakugo scripts.

Styles of speech are also a reflection of culture and values. For example, indirect speech,[5] as a way to avoid conflicts and express politeness, is often seen in Rakugo scripts. Below is an example from "Catching a Bird":

> "So […], how have you been feeding yourself lately?"
> "Well, like this, I hold the rice bowl in my left hand and chopsticks in my right hand."
> "No, that's not what I mean. Where does the rice come from?"
> "From the rice cooker."
> "What about the rice in your rice cooker? Where does that come from?"
> "It comes from the rice chest."
> "What about the rice in your rice chest?"
> "It comes from the rice store."
> "What about the payment to the rice store? How do you pay him?"
> "I don't."

At the beginning of this conversation, the uncle asks his nephew, "How have you been feeding yourself lately?" For most Japanese, it is obvious that he means whether he is working and earning enough money to feed himself. But it would be rude to talk about money even between an uncle and a nephew, so the uncle asks the question about his nephew's money and (un)employment in a polite way, which is an indirect question.

According to Brown and Levinson (1978, 1987), one of the most important concepts of politeness is "face", so that politeness is about minimizing or avoiding face-threatening acts. Indirect questioning is a way to avoid losing one's face. In this case, the uncle tried to minimize the possibility of his nephew losing face in front of him. The nephew, on the other hand, is supposed to infer or sense the message from the uncle's inference and facial expression. However – and this is the humorous part of this conversation – the nephew appears to be unexpectedly foolish, in spite of his uncle's concern. As was stated earlier, the definition of humor is 'an unexpected act or speech.' The nephew's response is incongruous and humorous in a High Context[6] society such as Japan, where people usually understand indirect questions of politeness.

---

[5] Indirect speech, or indirect representation, is often expressed using euphemisms to deliver uncomfortable, taboo, or negative messages. It allows speakers to use milder words or non-verbal communication (Kume 2002). A question might be asked purely by indirect reference, leaving interpretation to the listener based on a shared knowledge of the context, whereas a direct question might be considered rude and harmful to the other person's feelings. Sometimes, when too vague, this communication style leads to misunderstanding.

[6] According to Hall (1976), Low Context refers to societies where people tend to have many connections but of shorter duration or for some specific reason. In these societies, cultural behavior and beliefs many need to be spelled out explicitly, so that those coming into the cultural environment, from outside, know how to behave appropriately. High Context refers to societies or groups where people have close connections over a long period of time. Many aspects of cultural behavior are not made explicit because most members know what to do and what to think from years of interaction with each other. People have clear boundaries, less verbal, and more internalized communication. Japan is considered to be a High Context society.

Conversation is an important element in Rakugo humor as well as in daily communication. The purpose of joking together is for people to share a common understanding and to relate to each other to establish, develop and maintain solidarity. Humor is not often effected by one person, but involves several people taking part by bouncing words back and forth. Therefore, in typical Japanese communication, jokes and humor do not usually function as "ice breakers" when people first meet each other. Instead, those present must be confident of sharing something in common, in order to enjoy communicative humor.

Often, many Japanese people are aware of the roles they are playing in humorous communication. Usually one among a group of people will undertake the role of the *boke* (ボケ the fool), and another will play the *tsukkomi* (ツッコミ the "sharp man"). The *boke*'s role is to make foolish or out-of-context statements and to engage in cognitive misunderstandings. *Boke* literally means vague, confused, addled, or befuddled. In contrast, *tsukkomi* means to thrust, to poke, or to be sharp or aggressive, so that role involves making statements to correct or to put down the *boke*. In such conversations, the *boke* is always followed by the *tsukkomi*, without whose responses the humorous conversation set cannot be completed. Such impulsive speech behavior, which is based on more spontaneous, witty, ironic comments, is referred to as "conversational humor" (Martin 2009; Takekuro 2005; Oshima 2013).

Although the roles of *boke* and *tsukkomi* are most commonly adopted in humorous conversational exchanges, there are others that individuals and their conversational groups may be aware of. There are special character roles in which one person might be canny or clever, another person stingy or mean, and so on. People will deliberately establish and exaggerate their own personalities or chosen characters in order to make the conversation funny. Such categories of roles or characters match the popular stereotypical characters found in Rakugo stories.

Rakugo contains many Japanese cultural elements that need to be introduced and explained to non-Japanese audiences, but on the other hand, the concepts or main ideas of Rakugo are often universal. Classical Rakugo stories that are still performed today have survived the last 400 years, in front of different audiences, from the 1600s. Japanese people of that time had different values and culture from the Japanese people of today. However, the same Rakugo stories still are making people laugh in the present day, which means that Rakugo stories contain a kernel of "universal humor" within Japanese society (Oshima 2006a). Many stories have been lost over time, but among over 2000 stories in the current repertoire, about 350–400 classical stories have survived.

The themes and central ideas of those surviving classical stories are: cunning, relations between men and women, death, power and authority, poverty, competition, and foolishness. These may be universal topics for jokes in many different counties, because they are based on general human instincts rather than on details belonging to specific cultural backgrounds (Ziv 1984). Rakugo humor works internationally when other modern Japanese comedy styles, based on present cultural and social concepts, have difficulties.

In my university course "Intercultural communication: Rakugo in English", students study English through Rakugo scripts, watching English Rakugo shows performed for non-Japanese audiences and performing short Rakugo stories and other jokes in English. The students also learn important concepts and skills related to and necessary for effective intercultural communication through translation work, as well as using gestures, facial expressions, and different tones of voice in performance. Through these kinds of activities, students learn what is specific to Japanese culture and what is universal.

In order to perform short Rakugo in the classroom, the students practise stories with other teachers and friends outside the classroom. This motivates students to practise English because when they tell funny stories, if they can tell them well, they are rewarded with positive responses, i.e., laughter. They also pay attention, listening carefully to other students' performances, or videos of Rakugo shows on world tours, because they want to understand the jokes and punch lines and laugh with others. Students learn what is or is not funny to non-Japanese audiences, and study the cultural and social reasons behind the humor.

The course teaching intercultural communication and English through English Rakugo scripts is effective because: (1) it increases students' attendance and participation; (2) humorous materials keep them motivated, concentrated, and maintain a positive atmosphere in classroom; and (3) it develops positive student-teacher relationships.

Many Japanese students face difficulties speaking in English, which is often because of poor language skills and limited abilities in intercultural communication and in humor. In High-Context societies like Japan, the information density, as well as the richness of context, are generally greater. Because of these reasons, less actually needs to be spoken to get the point across. What is more, given the isolation inherent in being an island nation, Japanese students have traditionally had fewer opportunities to explain or express themselves to the outside world. Through this course, however, students learn what it takes to understand other cultures in effective intercultural communication, and the English language skills needed for that purpose, from the perspective of humor.

6   Conclusion

Among the many fields of humor research such as health-care, communication, the workplace, psychology, sociology, linguistics, and philosophy, education is one of the latest to join the humor study movement. Traditionally, many teachers have suppressed instead of appreciating humor in the classroom. Playfulness and laughter were considered by some to be antithetical to the process of studying, and were viewed as distracting to learning (Bell 2014; Wanzer et al. 2010). Research in the field of humor, however, has persuaded some teachers to overcome this deep-rooted prejudice. Teachers and students have different values, perspectives, and cultures, and, as such, are constantly engaged in a form of intercultural communication, so that micro-level differences between even just two people can be seen as differences between cultures. In this way humor can contribute to building better teacher-student relationships, and can help students to learn more effectively.

Humor, as we have seen, can also help to build better relationships among people of different races, through the careful and the sensitive use of ethnic humor. More aggressive humor can be harmful when used to discriminate against a person or a group of people, and one must be aware of which types of ethnic jokes to tell, in which situations, and to whom, in order to have positive effects in interracial and intercultural communication. However, in some cases, ethnic jokes can be good material from which to gain insights into different cultures, races, histories, and help build positive relationships with other groups. When one is aware of the functions of humor and uses appropriate and harmless jokes in intercultural communication and in educational environments, humor can provide a very effective tool for communication.

As globalization and glocalization of the world have developed in recent decades, understanding each other through peaceful intercultural communication is an urgent matter among nations, races and individuals. Humor replaces aggression and helps to establish better relationships among people with different backgrounds. Humor can be considered to be a communication skill, and one that can be acquired through education. It may even be used as a "new" tool for global communication. Because most humor has a cultural background, many jokes may not be easily understood inter-culturally at once. However, jokes that center around universal humor can provide effective material to learn cultural differences and similarities.

Globalization could lead to the creation of global standards and universal values, and could possibly cause more conflict and boundaries as a backlash from entrenched cultures. Whereas localization respects diversities and differences to the extent that it could cause separation of different cultures and a lack in mutual communication. Bringing those two concepts together and promoting the idea of glocalization will take new skills of communication. Having a sense of humor can help one to imagine and understand new concepts outside of the framework of one's own norms. Such mental flexibility and creativity can also help people to understand, adopt and adapt new aspects of culture and communication, which can be developed through education.

References

Aiba, A. (2009). Owarai no rekishi (History of Japanese comedy). In *The Japan society for laughter and humor studies* (Ed.), Warai no seiki (Century of laughter), (pp.168–186). Osaka: Sogen-sha.

Banas, J., Dunbar, N., Rodriguez, D., & Liu, S. (2011). A view of humor in educational settings: Four decades of research. *Communication Education, 60*, 115–144.

Bell, N. (2014). Second language acquisition. In S. Attardo (Ed.), *Encyclopedia of humor studies* (Vol. 2, pp. 672–673). Los Angeles: SAGE Publications.

Boring, E. (1930). A new ambiguous figure. *American Journal of Psychology, 42*, 444–445.

Brown, P., & Levinson, S. (1978). Universals in language usage: Politeness phenomena. In E. N. Goody (Ed.), *Questions and politeness* (pp. 56–289). Cambridge: Cambridge University Press.

Brown, P., & Levinson, S. (1987). *Politeness: Some universals in language usage.* Cambridge: Cambridge University Press.

Chapman, A. (1983). Humor and laughter in social interaction and some implications for humor research. In P. McGhee & J. Goldstein (Eds.), *Handbook of humor research* (Vol. 1, pp. 135–157). New York: Springer-Verlag.

Davies, C. E. (1990). *Ethnic humor around the world: A comparative analysis.* Bloomington: Indiana University Press.

Davies, C. E. (2015). Humor in intercultural interaction as both content and process in the classroom. *International Journal of Humor Research, 28*(3), 375–395.

Deneire, M. (1995). Humor and foreign language teaching. *International Journal of Humor Research, 8*(3), 285–298.

DiCioccio, R., & Miczo, N. (2014). Intercultural humor. In S. Attardo (Ed.), *Encyclopedia of humor studies* (Vol. 1, pp. 387–388). Los Angeles: SAGE Publications.

Dunbar, N. (2014). Humor in education. In S. Attardo (Ed.), *Encyclopedia of humor studies* (Vol. 1, pp. 207–210). Los Angeles: SAGE Publications.

Fine, G. (1983). Sociological approaches to the study of humor. In P. McGhee & J. Goldstein (Eds.), *Handbook of humor research* (Vol. 1, pp. 159–181). New York: Springer-Verlag.

Garner, R. (2006). Humor in pedagogy: How ha-ha can lead to aha. *College Teaching, 57*(1), 177–180.

Hall, E. (1976). *Beyond culture.* Garden City: Anchor.

Hill, D. (1988). *Humor in the classroom: A handbook for teachers and other entertainers.* Springfield: Charles Thomas.

Hopkins, J. (Ed.). (1991). *Frank DeLima's joke book.* Honolulu: Bess Press.

Hormann, B. (1972). *Hawaii's mixing people – The blending of the races, marginality and identity in world perspective.* New York: Wiley and Sons, Inc..

Hormann, B. (1982). The mixing process. *Social Process in Hawai'i, 29*, 117–129.

Keller, M. (1980, Nov. 9). *Racial jokes seen easing aggressions.* Honolulu Star Bulletin, A3.

Kume, A. (2002). To mawashi ni soretonaku: Enkyoku hyogen (Talk around: Euphemism). In G. Furuta (Ed.), *Ibunka komyunikeshon ki-wado (Keywords in intercultural communication)* (pp. 106–107). Tokyo: Yuhikaku.

LeMasters, E. (1975). *Blue collar aristocrats: Life-styles at a working-class tavern.* Madison: University of Wisconsin Press.

Lind, A. (1967). *Hawaii's people.* Honolulu: University of Hawaii Press.

Martin, R. (2009). What's so funny? The scientific study of humor. In *Report on international symposium towards a general science of laughter and humor* (Vol. II, pp. 19–43). Suita: Kansai University.

McGhee, P. (1979). *Humor, its origin and development.* San Francisco: Freeman.

Morreall, J. (1997). *Humor works.* Amherst: HRD Press.

Morreall, J. (2008). Applications of humor: Health, the workplace, and education. In V. Raskin (Ed.), *The primer of humor research* (pp. 449–478). New York: Mouton de Gruyter.

Murray, H. (1983). Low-inference classroom teaching behaviors and student ratings of college teaching effectiveness. *Journal of Educational Psychology, 75*(1), 138–149.

Nilsen, D. (1989). Better than original: Humorous translations that succeed. *Meta, 34*(1), 112–124.

Okabe, R. (2002). Komyunikeshon to wa (What is communication). In G. Furuta (Ed.), *Ibunka komyunikeshon ki-wado (Keywords in intercultural communication)* (pp. 51–80). Tokyo: Yuhikaku.

Okamura, J. (1995). Why there are no Asian Americans in Hawai'i: The continuing significance of local identity. *Social Process in Hawai'i, 2*, 243–256.

Oshima, K. (2000). Ethnic jokes and social function in Hawai'i. *International Journal of Humor Research, 13*(1), 41–57.

Oshima, K. (2006a). Rakugo and humor in Japanese interpersonal communication. In J. M. Davis (Ed.), *Understanding humor in Japan* (pp. 99–109). Detroit: Wayne State University Press.

Oshima, K. (2006b). *Nihon no warai to sekai no humor (Laughter of Japan and humor of the world)*. Tokyo: Sekai Shiso Sha.

Oshima, K. (2011). Japanese cultural expressions seen in English Rakugo scripts. *Asian Englishes, 14*(1), 46–65.

Oshima, K. (2013). An examination for styles of Japanese humor: Japan's funniest story project 2010 to 2011. *Intercultural Communication Studies, 22*(2), 91–109.

Schultz, T. (1976). A cognitive-developmental analysis of humour. In J. Chapman & C. Foot (Eds.), *Humor and laughter: Theory, research, and applications* (pp. 11–36). London: John Wiley & Sons.

Spiegel, P. (1972). Early conceptions of humor: Varieties and issues. In J. Goldstein & P. McGhee (Eds.), *The psychology of humor: Theoretical perspectives and empirical issues* (pp. 4–39). New York: Academic Press.

Takekuro, M. (2005). Conversational jokes in Japanese and English. In J. M. Davis (Ed.), *Understanding humor in Japan* (pp. 85–98). Detroit: Wayne State University Press.

Van Giffen, K. (1990). Influence of professor gender and perceived use of humor on course evaluations. *International Journal of Humor Research, 3*, 65–73.

Vega, G. (1989). *Humor competence: The fifth component*. Purdue University, Unpublished M.A. thesis.

Wanzer, M. B., Frymier, A. B., & Irwin, J. (2010). An explanation of the relationship between humor and student learning: Instructional humor processing theory. *Communication Education, 59*, 1–18.

Weaver, S. (2014). Ethnic jokes. In S. Attardo (Ed.), *Encyclopedia of humor studies* (Vol. 1, pp. 214–215). Los Angeles: SAGE Publications.

Wu, E. (2015, Jan. 15). Hawaii as racial paradise? Bid for Obama Library invokes a complex past. Code switch: Frontiers of race, culture, and ethnicity. http://www.npr.org/blogs/codeswitch/2015/01/15/377197729/hawaii-as-racial-paradise-bid-for-obama-library-invokes-a-complex-past (Accessed on 27 July 2017)

Yamanaka, H. (1993). *Hawai (Hawaii)*. Tokyo: Chikuma Shobo.

Ziv, A. (1984). *Personality and sense of humor*. New York: Springer.

Part V
Identity

Emotional Branding on Social Media: A Cross-Cultural Discourse Analysis of Global Brands on Twitter and Weibo

Doreen D. WU and Chaoyuan LI

Abstract This chapter contributes to the ongoing debate of cultural influence and construction in the social media sphere by examining the discourse practices of sampled global brands in terms of emotional branding on Twitter and Weibo, the leading social networking sites in the US and China respectively. Findings suggest that there are more commonalities than differences in the thematic appeals used by the global brands across Twitter and Weibo. Instead of exhibiting a developmental divide, all three characteristic appeals of emotional branding (Pragmatist, Evangelist and Sensualist) co-exist across Twitter and Weibo. The brands also tend to use similar positive face strategies and relational rituals on both Twitter and Weibo. One notable difference consists in the tendency that corporate Weibo posts contain more emoticons, more intimate address forms, and more instances of small talk, which is a significant break-away from the established Chinese traditions of face and politeness in interpersonal interaction. Implications for corporate communication and higher education in the age of internationalization and digitalization are discussed.

1 Introduction

"Intercultural new media studies" is said to be the next frontier in intercultural communication (Wu and Li 2016). Part of the social reality today is the widespread adoption of myriad new communication technologies and platforms, which has led scholars to increasingly recognize that the study of culture should move beyond the

D. D. WU (✉)
CBS, The Hong Kong Polytechnic University,
Kowloon Hong Kong, Hong Kong SAR, People's Republic of China
e-mail: doreen.wu@polyu.edu.hk

C. LI
Department of Chinese and Bilingual Studies, The Hong Kong Polytechnic University,
Hong Kong, People's Republic of China
e-mail: chaoyuan.li@connect.polyu.edu.hk

© Springer International Publishing AG, part of Springer Nature 2018   225
A. CURTIS, R. SUSSEX (eds.), *Intercultural Communication in Asia:
Education, Language and Values*, Multilingual Education 24,
https://doi.org/10.1007/978-3-319-69995-0_11

fragmentary perspectives towards a more holistic view of culture that includes not only nation-state cultures, but organizational and technological cultures.

The present study attempts to contribute to the ongoing debate of cultural influence and construction in the social media sphere by examining the discourse practices of the global brands in their emotional branding with their followers on Twitter and Weibo, the two different social networking sites (SNSs) in the USA versus China. Specifically, the present study attempts to depart from the dichotomous perspective with pre-assigned cultural categories and to examine the actual instances of social media discourse, to better understand the nature of virtual language and culture and the ideology behind its construction, and to provide implications for the ever-changing world of higher education and internationalization.

2   Social Media and Intercultural Communication Studies

An increasing body of literature in the field of social media and intercultural communication studies has reinforced the belief that new communication technologies are anything but neutral instruments; rather, they are subject to cultural influences in various aspects related to particular communication circumstances and outcomes. Nonetheless, most previous studies in the field have been confined to a dichotomous perspective: the studies frequently draw on Hofstede's (1980, 2001) dimensions of nation-state cultures, or Hall's (1976) distinction of high- and low- context cultures, or Triandis' (1995) horizontal/vertical individualism/collectivism, and conclude with a simple account of dichotomous differences between the East and the West in the communication practices on social media.

For instance, comparing China and the US, Chu and Choi (2011) found that Chinese SNS users engaged in a greater level of information giving, information seeking, and pass-along behavior in SNSs than did their American counterparts. The results confirmed the respective cultural orientations of horizontal and vertical collectivism vs. individualism, pointing to the significant influence of national cultures on eWOM (electronic word-of-mouth) behavior. Further, Jackson and Wang (2013) surveyed the use of social networking sites (SNSs) by Chinese and American students, and found that collectivistic emphases on family and friends could be partly responsible for lesser use of SNSs by Chinese participants, while individualistic values of self, and having more but less close and enduring friendships, could explain US participants' greater use of SNSs. Similarly, Barker and Ota (2011) compared the use of Mixi and Facebook by Japanese and American females, and found that young American women preferred public expressions on Facebook, whereas Japanese young women were much more likely to communicate closeness via Mixi. In addition, Park et al. (2014) examined cross-cultural variations of the use of emoticons, and indicated that people from individualistic cultures tended to use horizontal and mouth-oriented emoticons such as:), in contrast to those in collectivistic cultures who preferred vertical and eye-oriented emoticons such as ^_^.

From the perspective of persuasive technology, Fogg and Iizawa (2008) analyzed how Facebook and Mixi were designed to influence users in relation to four activities: creating profile pages; inviting friends; responding to content by friends; and returning to the site often. Fogg and Iizawa concluded that Facebook's persuasive design is more assertive and mechanistic, whereas Mixi's design seems to be more subtle and indirect. The different styles in persuasive design were said to map to cultural differences between the two countries.

Cultural differences in corporate communications on social media have also been investigated and noted. For instance, Tsai and Men (2012) examined cultural differences in the use of communication appeals on corporate pages on China's Renren and America's Facebook. They found that value appeals in SNSs reflected dominant cultural values in different cultures: value appeals such as interdependence, popularity, high social status, luxury, emotions, and symbolic association were more common in collectivist, high-context societies such as in China, whereas individuality and hedonism were more frequently used in an individualistic society like the US.

Men and Tsai (2012) examined how companies use popular SNSs to facilitate dialogues with the public in China and the US, through a content analysis of 50 corporate pages with 500 corporate posts and 500 user posts from each. The study revealed that companies in both countries recognized the importance of SNSs in relationship development and employed the appropriate online strategies, but their specific tactics differed. Cultural differences among the types of corporate posts and public posts on SNSs indicated that culture played a significant role in shaping the dialogue between organizations and their public audiences in different countries.

Through a content analysis of microblogs of four smart-phone brands on Twitter[1] and Weibo[1], Ma (2013) found that consumers on both platforms were mostly used for sharing brand-central information and entertaining messages, but cultural values moderated specific types of content shared by consumers in significant ways. For example, US consumers showed significantly greater concern about unique product selling propositions and distinctive brand personalities, more eager for the special and the original, whereas Chinese consumers were more eager to know what was in vogue, and were more aware of status and prestige.

Although the study of websites seems to have been pushed into the background, as the medium is an "older" form of new media, a significant contribution of this line of research is that websites have incubated important conceptions of culture that are different from the traditional models offered by Hofstede (1980) or Hall (1976). Gallivan and Srite point out the importance of "articulating the cultural assumptions that are embedded into IT and explicitly evaluating whether these assumptions are congruent with potential adopters in other parts of the world"

---

[1] Twitter is the world's leading microblogging site, attracting around 320 million active users daily as of September 2015 (Twitter 2015). Weibo is a twitter-like service based in China and with Chinese-language interface, hosting more than 500 million users by the end of 2012 (*Global Times*, September 5, 2013), making itself the leading social networking service in China. Similar architecture of the two platforms has invited many studies using comparative data from them.

(2005, p. 296). They propose to move beyond the fragmentary perspectives to a more holistic view of culture that includes not only nation-state culture, but organizational and technological culture, which will lead to a more multi-layered conception of culture. Waters and Lo (2012), through a content analysis of Facebook profiles of 225 nonprofit organizations in the US, China, and Turkey, concluded that organizational uses of SNSs were only minimally affected by traditional cultural values, suggesting that global virtual cultures may be developing.

The present study thus attempts to contribute to the ongoing debate about cultural influence and construction in the social media sphere, by examining the discourse practices of the global brands in their processes of relational communication with their followers on Twitter and Weibo, the two different social networking sites (SNS) in the USA versus China.

3   Social Media and Emotional Branding by Corporations

The 2009 ENGAGEMENTdb Report measured the social media engagement and financial performance of the "world's most valuable brands" (e.g. Starbucks, Toyota, SAP, and Dell), revealing a direct and significant positive correlation between financial performance and the extent of social media engagement: the socially engaged brands were more financially successful. In 2014, Twitter narrowly surpassed Facebook to be the most frequently used new medium for corporate communication activities (Wright and Hinson 2014). Global brands and their multinational corporations have always been among the enthusiastic users of new communications technologies. Before the advent of social media, for global brands, it would have sufficed to have a corporate presence on their official websites. However, the age of social media requires these brands not only to be "present", but to actively engage with their key members of the public. For meaningful engagement and relationship-building between corporations and consumers to take place on social media, it requires the corporate branding discourse to move beyond transactional to emotional and relational to increase "site stickiness" and to "hook" followers tightly (Capozzi and Zipfel 2012, p. 339).

Since what is accentuated in the new protocols is relational and emotional communication, rather than transactional and informational communication between corporations and their customers (Blom et al. 2003; Wu and Feng 2015), emotional branding by corporations on social media becomes critical. Emotional branding can be defined as:

> [...] engaging the consumer on the level of senses and emotions; forging a deep, lasting, intimate emotional connection to the brand that transcends material satisfaction; [...] creating a holistic experience that delivers an emotional fulfillment so that the customer develops a special bond with and unique trust in the brand (Morrison and Crane 2007, p. 410).

Aiming at building consumers' attachment with a strong, specific, usage-relevant emotional response (e.g., bonding, companionship or love) to the brand (Roberts 2004; Rossiter and Bellman 2012), emotional branding directly appeals to the consumers' emotional state, needs and aspirations, and triggers an emotional response among consumers in their external corporate communication. Drawing on the case of the US, Gobe (2009, p. 128) identified three developmental phases of emotional branding: the Pragmatist Age (1940–1967), the Evangelist Age (1968–1989) and the Sensualist Age (1990–2009). Specifically, emotional branding in the Pragmatist Age emphasized products or service function, reliability and the pragmatic functions, as manifested by omnipresent advertising that dominated corporate communication at that time. The Evangelist Age represented philosophies of justice, equality and sensitivity to the environment, making people realize that they have power and could positively change the course of politics and the world. Finally, emotional branding discourse in the Sensualist Age is lifestyle-oriented and tends towards hedonism, glamour, fame and the individual expression, creating its own language, culture and symbols (Gobe 2009).

The unique merit of social media in humanizing or personifying corporations enables them to converse with the public using a conversational human voice. From a perception perspective, Kelleher and Miller (2006, p. 413) identified 11 defining aspects of the conversational human voice: it invites people to conversation; is open to dialogue; uses conversation-style communication; tries to communicate in a human voice; tries to be interesting in communication; provides links to competitors; uses a sense of humor in communication; attempts to make communication enjoyable; would admit a mistake; provides prompt feedback addressing criticism in a direct but uncritical manner; and treats me and others as being human.

Nonetheless, many studies of corporate/organizational communication on social media (e.g., Rybalko and Seltzer 2010; Seltzer and Mitrook 2007; Waters and Lo 2012) found that the dialogic potential of social media has not been fully utilized. Despite the plausibility of their conclusion, the studies often coded the content and technical features of social media pages, instead of examining the discourse characteristics of the actual messages. For instance, Rybalko and Seltzer (2010) recorded the presence of links to press releases or newsrooms, links to annual reports, links to Facebook, links to corporate websites, and whether questions are posed and user comments/questions are responded to on Twitter.

In view of the gaps, this chapter will present the results, findings and conclusions of a study designed to investigate the discourse realization of emotional branding, not only in terms of content of corporate updates but also the relational ritual and interactional strategies used to involve the brands' followers on social media. The emotional branding discourse by global brands on two dominant social networking site (SNS), Twitter, and its indigenous counterpart in China, Weibo, will be examined to further our understanding of cross-cultural corporate-public communication on social media.

4 Relational Ritual and Communication Across Cultures

In addition to the concerns and efforts by scholars of corporate communication in identifying the means of humanizing and personifying corporations in their relational communication with their stakeholders, scholars of interpersonal communication, particularly Interactional Sociolinguists, have long been concerned with describing and explaining how language is constructed for relational ritual and communication between people across cultures. The interdependence between people that constitutes a personal or social relationship derives in significant ways from their language use (Cappella 1988; Duck and Pittman 1993). The context of conversation, in which participants must coordinate their roles and contributions to the "joint project" of discourse moment by moment (Clark 1996), is a window through which this interdependence can be richly observed.

According to Interactional Sociolinguists, among the linguistic forms that are indexical of people's beliefs and evaluations regarding their relationships with others, one is the terms of address used in greeting each other. The choice of an address term is often governed by a number of factors, including the consideration of power and solidarity (see Brown and Gilman 1962). Gu (1990, p. 249) indicated that the choice of an address term in Chinese depends on the consideration of multiple variables: (1) kin or non-kin, (2) politically superior or inferior, (3) professionally prestigious or non-prestigious, (4) interpersonally familiar or unfamiliar, solidary or non-solidary, (5) male or female, (6) old or young, (7) on a formal or informal occasion, (8) family members or non-relatives, and (9) in public or at home. This wide array of variables suggests that the system of address forms in Chinese in contexts other than social media is highly complex and particularly indicative of power and social hierarchy.

Another type of linguistic form contributing to relational communication can be called small talk or phatic communication. The term *phatic* was first proposed by Malinowski (1923, p. 315) to refer to the role of talk in human sociality in that "each utterance is an act serving the direct aim of binding hearer to speaker by a tie of some social sentiment or other". Such communication is achieved "by the exchange of words, by the specific feelings which form convivial gregariousness, by the give and take of utterances which make up ordinary gossip" (Malinowski 1923, p. 315).

Cheepen and Monaghan (1990, p. 21) distinguished transactional and interactional language use, with the latter referring to phatic communication. Warren (2006, p. 101) further pointed out that conversations are often examples of both transactional and interactional language use, and that there could be primacy of interactional discourse over transactional, or the supremacy of so-called "idle chatter" or "small talk" over speech-in-action. Often the maintenance of the relationship is given prominence in a talk to the total exclusion of anything else. Warren (2006, p. 102) stated that "even the most routine of utterances should never be described as meaningless". Conversation is not talk for its own sake, but rather talk for the sake of building and maintaining social relationships.

Over the years, interactional sociolinguists have paid attention to comparing forms of phatic communication across cultures. For example, Chen (1993) compared Chinese and Americans in their responses to compliments in daily interaction, and found that while the Americans tended to accept compliments readily, the Chinese tended to show rejection or embarrassment over the compliments. The notion of positive politeness by Brown and Levinson (1978/1987) was then used to account for the behavior of the Americans, while the maxim of self-denigration in Chinese social interaction by Gu (1990) was used to account for the behavior of the Chinese.

Spencer-Oatey et al. (2000) undertook a similar study comparing the Chinese and the British in their varied ways of compliment responses, and came to a similar conclusion about the differences between the Chinese and the Westerners. Nonetheless, in 2010, Chen and Yang conducted a longitudinal study in compliment responses in Chinese, and found a tendency towards Westernization in Chinese compliment responses. The study revealed drastic changes in the way the Chinese in Xi'an city responded to compliments: in contrast to the overwhelming popularity of rejection in 1993 as found by Chen (1993), the 2010 Xi'an Chinese were found to largely accept compliments. The 2010 level of popularity of acceptance was so high that it was almost the same level as the English and German speakers. The study attributed this change to the influx of Western cultural influences that has occurred in the city of Xi'an since the early 1990s.

5 Methodology

5.1 Research Questions & Framework of Analysis

The present study, as noted above, aims to contribute to the ongoing debate of cross-cultural communication in the social media sphere by examining the discourse practices of emotional branding by global brands on two diverse social media platforms, Twitter versus Weibo. At least two dimensions have been identified as constituting the discourse realization of emotional branding: (1) thematic appeals, (2) interactional rituals and strategies. Specifically, two research questions will be addressed:

(1) What are the common and different thematic appeals used by global brands on Twitter versus on Weibo?
(2) What are the common and different interactional rituals and strategies adopted by global brands on Twitter versus on Weibo?

An integrated framework of analysis is built, incorporating a thematic analysis and an interactional analysis, to investigate the means of emotional branding by the leading brands in their English versus Chinese social media platforms. While the thematic analysis is employed to profile the brands' social media posts in terms of pragmatist, evangelist, and sensualist appeals, the interactional analysis investigates further the regular rituals and strategies of relational communication used, such as forms of greetings, phatic communication, and humor.

5.2   The Data

The data of the study consists of posts by nine of the World's Top 10 Best Brands (Forbes 2014), i.e., Apple, Google, Microsoft, IBM, Coca Cola, General Electric (GE), McDonald's, Intel, Samsung, and BMW, on Twitter[1] and Weibo[1] over a one-month period (1–30 Sept 2014). The dataset did not include posts by Apple, for the brand did not have official accounts on both platforms.

5.3   Thematic Analysis

Based on Gobe (2009), three possible themes of corporate posts on Twitter and Weibo have been identified: Pragmatist, Evangelist, and Sensualist. Pragmatist branding refers to the theme and content of the corporate posts centering on the pragmatic functions, reliability, endurance, convenience, and cost-effectiveness of the products or services provided by the brand. Evangelist branding content promotes virtues or positive values, such as peace, openness, justice, equality, humanitarianism, and sensitivity to the environment; while Sensualist branding content promotes themes of individual lifestyle and self-expression, hedonism, glamour and fame.

Unlike Gobe's (2009) view of the three themes as a temporal dimension that delineates different stages, we have found that the three themes co-exist in contemporary corporate communication. The global brands are actively involved in pragmatist emotional branding on Twitter and Weibo alike. For instance, a Microsoft tweet on September 16 reads:

Extract 1:
Microsoft @ Microsoft · Sept 16
Our new Universal Mobile Keyboard works on iOS, Android, and Windows Tablets. Check
  it out: msft.it/6013oB9
[Image omitted]

The tweet above explicitly promotes the compatibility of Microsoft's keyboard product. For today's increasingly mobile consumers who own and use a variety of mobile devices, compatibility is one of the most pragmatic functions, and is thus appealing to consumers. As an electronic products provider, Microsoft appeals to consumers' pursuit of compatibility and promotes its versatility. More traditional pragmatic emphasis such as product reliability is also promoted on Twitter, illustrated by an IBM tweet on September 13 that promotes the reliability of its cloud servers:

Extract 2:
IBM @ IBM · Sept 13
How @Intel and @softlayer are delivering trusted cloud platforms: ibm.co/X8TFot #IBM
  Cloud
[Image omitted]

The brands also promote their pragmatic values on Weibo. For example, McDonald's Weibo post in Extract 3 emphasizes the quality and cost-effectiveness of its new burger, the star product. The post is very much like a hard-sell advertisement that explicitly indicates the price of the product:

Extract 3: 继麦麦汉堡【10元天团】三足鼎力后,双层吉士成为最新"掌门堡"!它有才有料,还超值10元,还不快来膜拜?!

[图略]

9月27日 12:00 麦当劳的微博

Extract 3: Translation: Double-cheese Burger has become the new star burger! It's rich and delicious, and costs 10 yuan only! Why not hurry and have a try now?!

[Image omitted]

12:00 Sept 27 McDonald's Weibo

Technology brands like Google and Samsung also promote the convenience and versatility of their products on Weibo, illustrated by Extracts 4 and 5. In Extract 4, Google promotes its Google Glass as being convenient and easy to use, able to capture the full picture on various occasions. Extract 5 highlights the innovative features of Samsung's new smart phone: the S Pen and the multi-window display:

Extract 4: #Google 全球汇# Google glass能帮大家记住最美好和有趣的时刻。无论是一个人的自由、怡然,两个人的甜蜜还是三口之家的温馨,Google glass都能解放你的双手,帮童鞋们记录最完整的记忆。只需简单说出"ok glass",然后发出"take a picture"的英文口令,Google glass就会为您拍下最美的回忆啦~

[图略]

9月22日 11:33 谷歌的微博

Extract 4: Translation: Google glass can help you remember the best and fun moments. Whether it is freedom being alone, sweetness being with your love or warmth being with family, Google glass can always free your hands and record the fullest memory.

11:33 Sept 22 Google's Weibo

[Image omitted]

Extract 5: #星推荐#赞叹那水晶般的清晰画面,喜欢上触感升级再创奇迹的S Pen,着迷于更多便捷的随心多窗口,Samsung GALAXY Note 4,创新突破,让人轻易就会爱上的手机。

[图略]

9月29日 16:02 三星电子的微博

Extract 5: Translation: Marvel at the crystal clear picture, fall in love with the updated S Pen, be fascinated with the convenient multi-window display – Samsung GALAXY Note 4, the innovative phone you can readily fall in love with.

[Image omitted]

16:02 Sept 29 Samsung's Weibo

In addition to pragmatist branding, Evangelist branding content is also prevalent in the corporate posts on both Twitter and Weibo. The Evangelist theme is often related to corporate social responsibility (CSR). The publicity generated by CSR campaigns and presence on social media contributes to the positive image and reputation-building of the brands. A Google tweet in Extract 6 calls for universal access to and protection of the safety of the Internet. The pursuit of freedom, openness, and the safety of cyberspace is echoed by all users of the Internet, which at the same time presents Google as a caring Internet service provider with the same positive values:

Extract 6:
Google @ Google · Sept 10
The Internet belongs to everyone – and it's our job to protect it. Are you in?
[Image omitted]

IBM in Extract 7 shares a story of using its analytic tool in an Africa-aid project on Twitter, appealing to humanitarianism:

Extract 7:
IBM @ IBM · Sept 24
Here's how @IBMWatson is working in Africa through Project Lucy: [video URL link omitted]
[Image omitted]

CSR posts also occur frequently on Weibo, illustrated by Coca Cola (Extract 8) and GE (Extract 9). In Extract 8, Coca Cola promotes its sponsorship for a Chinese garden built in Washington D.C. and its contribution to China-US cultural exchanges:

Extract 8: 一座中国园林出现在异国的土地上,会是什么样子?美国华盛顿特区的国家植物园中,就坐落着一座中式花园。这座中国园林由一对中国设计师设计,展示着人与自然之间微妙的平衡,也是中美文化交流搭建的一座美丽桥梁。可口可乐也有幸参与其中并提供支持。
[图略]
9月29日 20:00 可口可乐的微博

Extract 8: Translation: What would it be like to have a Chinese garden on foreign soil? In the National Botanical Garden, there is a Chinese-style garden. The garden is a work by Chinese designers, demonstrating the human-nature balance, while also standing as a bridge for cultural exchanges between China and the US. Coca Cola is proud to be part of the project and have provided support for it.
[Image omitted]
20:00 Sept 29 Coca Cola's Weibo

General Electric broadcasts its health project for koalas in Australia, conducting reliable and humane checks for them to prevent infection and contagion. The action (as well as the post) appeals to people's love and care for the planet and for biodiversity:

Extract 9: #GE全球村#GE有爱又天才的科学家最近在为澳洲国宝考拉做超声检查,防治目前危机它们生存的传染病。为了及早诊断并减少传染,哥家科学家借鉴人体医学领域经验,将超声技术应用到病菌检测中,操作简单,效果精确,而且全程无痛,让这些人见人爱的小家伙看病时也能保持"萌萌哒"。
[图略]
9月1日 19:37 通用电气的微博

Extract 9: Translation: GE's loving and talented scientists are conducting ultrasonic imaging tests for koalas in Australia, to detect and prevent contagious diseases that threaten their lives. GE scientists have drawn on experience from medical care for humans to provide painless testing for the cute ones.
[Image omitted]
19:37 Sept 1 GE's Weibo

Furthermore, Sensualist branding is also common on both Twitter and Weibo platforms, illustrated by BMW's status-promoting tweet in Extract 10 and Samsung's Weibo post in Extract 11:

Extract 10:
BMW @ bmw · Sept 26
All eyes on me. All roads become red carpets wherever the BMWi8 goes.
[Image omitted]

Extract 10 personifies BMW's product as a super star walking the red carpet, attracting enormous attention, thus appealing to consumers' desire uniqueness, individuality, and being the focus of the crowd.

Extract 11: #星娱乐#喜欢他帅气的侧脸,喜欢他安静的性格……暗恋的小心思那么多,最终也只是幻化成手机中一张偷拍的照片……那一刻悸动的美好,经历过就不会忘,年轻真好。[emoticon: Smile]
[图略]
9月26日 09:01 三星的微博

Extract 11: Translation: Liked his handsome face, liked his quiet character [...] So many fond feelings of a secret admirer ended up as a picture taken secretly and saved in the phone [...] The beauty of the moment shall never be forgotten. So good to be young.
[Image omitted]
9:01 Sept 26 Samsung's Weibo

At first sight, Extract 11 does not seem to promote any product, but emphasizes the beauty of being young. By thematizing its content into a romantic experience shared by many young people, the Samsung post appeals to the feelings of a secret admirer and implicitly promotes its product – the smart phone as a camera.

6   Interactional Analysis

This interactional analysis of corporate tweets/posts aims to identify the solidarity-building strategies and verbal rituals, which function to address followers in a conversational human voice, in order to maximize their emotional attachments to the brands. We identified three verbal rituals and strategies as being employed to close the psychological and cognitive distance between the corporations and their followers on Twitter and Weibo: (1) intimate address forms, (2) phatic communication, and (3) humor and jokes.

6.1   Intimate Address Forms

Intimate address forms refer to the forms that are used interpersonally between people who are very familiar, close or in intimate relationships, and often take place in the private domain. These are different from regular daily interactions, in which the choice of an address form can be subject to a consideration of many variables such as kin versus non-kin, superior versus inferior, public versus private, etc. In contrast, the use of address forms on social media platforms tends to be simple, casual or intimate. Examples of address forms used by some of the global brands on Twitter are as follows:

Extract 12:
McDonald's @ McDonalds · Sept 24
Hey @lenadunham, we wanted to confirm your reservation. The corner booth is waiting for **you**!

Extract 13:
McDonald's @ McDonalds · Sept 28
My coffee is **your** coffee. Visit us 'till 9/29 for a small @McCafe coffee during breakfast.

Extract 14:
Samsung USA @ Samsungtweets · Sept 25
Bakers, start your ovens: it's pie season.

Extract 15:
Samsung USA @ Samsungtweets · Sept 28
Indulge **your** inner foodie with these must-have apps: ….

On the Chinese Weibo, the corporations use and create a range of intimate forms to address the followers and themselves. Some of these forms are general intimate address forms borrowed from those used frequently in daily interactions on Weibo, e.g., "童鞋(们)" ("classmates"), "小伙伴们" ("folks"), "(各位)亲(们)" ("dear"), "粉丝们" ("fans"), as well as first names (e.g., Jenny). Others are brand-specific address forms that are often initiated or suggested by brands and also adopted by followers. For example, self-appellation forms include "麦麦(家)" ("Maimai/Wheat", McDonald's), "哥" ("Brother", GE), "小可" ("Little Co", Coca Cola), etc. Brand followers are called "星迷" ("star fans", Samsung's followers), "英粉" ("Intel fans", Intel's followers), or "麦粒(们)" ("wheat grain", McDonald's followers). Such casual as well as brand-specific address terms play an important role in building emotional attachments between the brands and the followers.

6.2   Phatic Communication

As indicated earlier, phatic communication refers to small talk, including routine utterances which are seemingly purposeless but contribute significantly to relational communication by building "convivial gregariousness" and binding the addressee to the addresser using "a tie of some social sentiment or other" (Malinowski 1923, p. 315). We can observe that many tweets by the corporations are purely relational tweets with hashtags manifesting ritualized small talk. For instance, Coca Cola sends "good morning" tweets almost every day (Extract 11 as an example). If the "good morning" tweets said the two words "good morning" every day, it would become boring; therefore, Coca Cola resorts to sharing chicken-soup content (i.e. content containing warm, touching, or inspirational lines or life stories) in its morning tweets while marking these tweets with a hashtag "Coca Cola. Good morning". The hashtag not only serves to topicalize, and thus ritualize the phatic communication of "Good morning", but also makes explicit the purpose of its chicken-soup content and thus the tweet. This design grants dual functions of the tweet: the phatic "good morning" function and the thematic "chicken-soup":

Extract 16:   细雨从星星上落下,浸湿痛苦,称为我们的一部分。九月结束时,请唤醒
我。——Wake me up when September ends#可口可乐.晨安#
[图略]
9月30日 09:15可口可乐中国的微博

Extract 16: Translation: Here comes the rain again, falling from the stars, drenched in my
pain again, becoming who we are. Wake me up when September ends. – Wake me up
when September ends #Coca Cola Good morning#
[image omitted]
9:15 Sept 30 Coca Cola's Weibo

Below are more instances of phatic communication by the global brands on
Twitter and Weibo:

Google (Twitter): Happy Grandparents' Day!
McDonald's (Twitter): Commute conquered.
McDonald's(Twitter):There'sonlyonewaytoshakehandstoday.#ChocolateMilkShakeDay.
Samsung (Weibo): #星暖语#总是抱怨梦想的不可实现性,却从未怀疑自己是否足够努
力,真正强大的人,是在暮色之后,面对疲惫和困扰,依然咬住牙继续前进的人。坚
持一下,或许就能收获到意想不到的奇迹。晚安～ (Translation: People always com-
plain about how far away the dream is, but never doubt whether they are trying hard
enough. The true man is someone who still fights with clenched teeth when it goes dark.
Persevere and you may get a miracle. Good night~).
McDonald's (Weibo): 最爱你的人是我,我怎么舍得让你错过早餐!唤醒你的味蕾的除
了麦麦,还有永远都想和你好在一起的最佳"早餐小伙伴",把TA＠出来,从此每一
天的早餐都有滋有味!(Translation: I'm the one who loves you most and how do I have
the heart to see you go without breakfast! Your taste buds are not only woken up by
Maimai (McDonald's), but by the breakfast partner who wants to spend time with you
every day. Come @ him/her and have a sweet breakfast every morning!)
Microsoft   (Weibo):   秋季美剧即将回归,大家最期待的美剧是哪部?(Translation:
American TV series are coming back! Which one is your favorite?)

6.3   Humor and Jokes

Humor and jokes could be defined as anything "funny, amusing, or laughable"
(Attardo 1993). Humor and joke-telling have long been regarded by Interactional
Sociolinguists as an important means of accomplishing relational work and boost-
ing solidarity (Holmes and Schnurr 2005). Norrick (1989, p. 118) indicates that
"joke telling counts as positive politeness, [...] as an invitation to demonstrate
membership and solidarity". Below are some instances of humor and jokes posted
by the global brands on both Twitter and Weibo.:

Google (Twitter): Mr. Yeti? Can we call you Bigfoot? Or do you prefer
Sasquatch?#OkGoogle?#NationalComicBookDay.
McDonald's (Weibo): 麦麦今天给大家粗一个心理测试,题目:你会怎样度过这个美好的
周末呢?A 在家吃麦麦发呆,B去电影院吃麦麦欣赏大片,C带着麦麦去郊外野餐,D和
好伙伴们去公园享受麦麦野餐。测试答案如下:资深麦粒,鉴定完毕!! (Translation:
Maimai is giving you a fun test today, a multiple choice. Question: How will you spend
this great weekend? A. Daydream at home while eating McDonald's; B. Go to the cinema
while eating McDonald's; C. Bring McDonald's and go for a picnic in the suburbs;
D. Have a McDonald's picnic in the park with friends. Key: A veteran McDonald's fan!)

7 Conclusion

The present study has attempted to contribute to the emerging research on intercultural new media studies by examining the discursive practices of the global brands in their emotional branding on Twitter versus Weibo, the leading social networking sites (SNSs) in USA versus China respectively. Specifically, this study has attempted to depart from the dichotomous perspective with the pre-assigned cultural categories and to examine the actual instances of social media discourse, so as to better understand the nature of virtual language and culture and the ideology behind its construction, and to provide implications for the changing world of higher education and internationalization.

It is found that there are more commonalities than differences in the thematic appeals used by the global brands on Twitter versus Weibo. Instead of exhibiting a developmental divide, as indicated by Gobe (2009), all the three characteristic appeals of emotional branding, i.e., Pragmatist, Evangelist, and Sensualist appeals, exist across Twitter and Weibo. Hybridized appeals are also observed, notably pragmatist blended with Evangelist or with Sensualist branding, demonstrating the extent of multi-valued emotional branding. Furthermore, the global brands tend to use similar positive face strategies and daily rituals on both Twitter and Weibo. Nonetheless, the actual wording and topics in the English versus the Chinese versions can be different according to their different targeted stakeholders on Twitter versus Weibo. For example, compared with Twitter posts (tweets), Weibo posts, their Chinese counterparts, contain more emoticons, more intimate address forms, and more instances of small talk as well. What is worthy of notice is that the Chinese traditions of face and politeness in interaction (as postulated by many previous scholars, such as Gu 1990) are no longer applicable to describe or explain Chinese social interactions on social media such as Weibo.

This chapter thus concludes that given the ever increasing development of digitalization and the ever increasing usage of SNS/social media for human interactions, we need to reexamine our orthodox notions or theorizations of intercultural communication, redefine the existing notions or develop new notions for a better description and explanation of the emerging global virtual language and culture. Furthermore, in our future development of curriculum for higher education in a changing world of internationalization, we need to move beyond the learning of cultural practice as confined by nation-states but turn our attention to the emerging cultural practice with the growth of advanced communication and technological services. We also need to be acutely aware that internationalization is not equal to globalization or homogenization, i.e., inclusion of the local, context- and individual-sensitive learning dimension as well as the global, universal dimension is important in the curriculum of internationalization. Finally, as suggested in the prevalent use of solidarity-building strategies and daily verbal rituals by the global brands on the social media platforms, our curriculum development, the teaching learning process of higher education in this world of increasing market economy, democracy and liberalization, should include not only formal or elite language education but also the informal, non-elite language education.

Acknowledgement This work was supported by RGC Directly Allocated Research Grant, Hong Kong (#4-ZZFB).

References

Attardo, S. (1993). Violation of conversational maxims and cooperation: The case of jokes. *Journal of Pragmatics, 19*, 537–558.

Barker, V., & Ota, H. (2011). Mixi diary versus Facebook photos: Social networking site use among Japanese and Caucasian American females. *Journal of Intercultural Communication Research, 40*(1), 39–63.

Blom, J., Kankainen, A., Kankainen, T., & Tiitta, S. (2003). Location-aware multi-user messaging: Exploring the evolution of mobile text-based communication services. *Helsinki Institute for Information Technology Technical Report 2003-2*. Retrieved 11 November 2014, from www. hiit.fi/publications/pub_files/hiit2003-2.pdf

Brown, R., & Gilman, A. (1962). The pronouns of power and solidarity. *American Anthropologist, 4*(6), 24–69.

Brown, P., & Levinson, S. (1978/1987). *Politeness: Some universals in language usage.* Cambridge: Cambridge University Press.

Capozzi, L., & Zipfel, L. B. (2012). The conversation age: The opportunity for public relations. *Corporate Communications: An International Journal, 17*(3), 336–349.

Cappella, J. N. (1988). Personal relationships, social relationships, and patterns of interaction. In S. Duck (Ed.), *Handbook of personal relationships* (pp. 325–342). New York: Wiley.

Cheepen, C., & Monaghan, J. (1990). *Spoken English: A practical guide.* London: Pinter.

Chen, R. (1993). Responding to compliments: A contrastive study of politeness strategies between American English and Chinese speakers. *Journal of Pragmatics, 20*(1), 49–75.

Chen, R., & Yang, D. (2010). Responding to compliments in Chinese: Has it changed? *Journal of Pragmatics, 42*, 1951–1963.

Chu, S., & Choi, S. M. (2011). Electronic word-of-mouth in social networking sites: A cross-cultural study of the United States and China. *Journal of Global Marketing, 24*, 263–281.

Clark, H. H. (1996). *Using language.* Cambridge: Cambridge University Press.

Duck, S., & Pittman, G. (1993). Social and personal relationships. In M. L. Knapp & J. A. Daly (Eds.), *The Sage handbook of interpersonal communication* (pp. 676–695). Thousand Oaks: Sage.

Fogg, B. J., & Iizawa, D. (2008). Online persuasion in Facebook and Mixi: A cross-cultural comparison. In H. Oinas-Kukkonen, P. H. M. Harjumaa, K. Segertahl, & P. Ohrstrom (Eds.), *Persuasive technology: Third international conference, PERSUASIVE 2008 proceedings* (pp. 35–46). Berlin: Springer.

Forbes. (2014). *The world's most powerful brands.* Retrieved 12 October 2014 from: http://www. forbes.com/powerful-brands/

Gallivan, M., & Srite, M. (2005). Information technology and culture: Identifying fragmentary and holistic perspectives of culture. *Information and Organization, 15*, 295–338.

Global Times. (2013). *Sina Weibo users now need employment documents to get verified ID, September 5.* Retrieved 27 October 2015 from: http://www.globaltimes.cn/content/808980. shtml

Gobe, M. (2009). *Emotional branding: The new paradigm for connecting brands to people* (Revised ed.). New York: Allworth Press.

Gu, Y. (1990). Politeness phenomena in modern Chinese. *Journal of Pragmatics, 14*, 237–257.

Hall, E. T. (1976). *Beyond culture.* New York: Doubleday.

Hofstede, G. (1980). *Culture's consequences: International differences in work-related values.* Beverly Hills: Sage.

Hofstede, G. (2001). *Culture's consequences: Comparing values, behaviors, institutions, and organizations across nations*. Beverly Hills: Sage.

Holmes, J., & Schnurr, S. (2005). Politeness, humor and gender in the workplace: Negotiating norms and identifying contestations. *Journal of Politeness Research, 1*(1), 121–149.

Jackson, L. A., & Wang, J. (2013). Cultural differences in social networking site use: A comparative study of China and the United States. *Computers in Human Behavior, 29*, 910–921.

Kelleher, T., & Miller, B. (2006). Organizational blogs and the human voice: Relational strategies and relational outcomes. *Journal of Computer-Mediated Communication, 11*, 395–414.

Ma, L. (2013). Electronic word-of-mouth on microblogs: A cross-cultural content analysis of Twitter and Weibo. *Intercultural Communication Studies, 22*(3), 18–42.

Malinowski, B. (1923). The problem of meaning in primitive languages. In C. K. Ogden & I. A. Richards (Eds.), *The meaning of meaning* (pp. 296–336). London: Kegan Paul, Trench, Trubner.

Men, L. J., & Tsai, W. S. (2012). How companies cultivate relationships with publics on social network sites: Evidence from China and the United States. *Public Relations Review, 38*, 723–730.

Morrison, S., & Crane, F. G. (2007). Building the service brand by creating and managing an emotional brand experience. *Journal of Brand Management, 14*(5), 410–421.

Norrick, N. R. (1989). Intertextuality in humor. *Humor, 2*(2), 117–139.

Park, J., Baek, Y. M., & Cha, M. (2014). Cross-cultural comparison of nonverbal cues in emoticons on Twitter: Evidence from big data analysis. *Journal of Communication, 64*, 333–354.

Roberts, K. (2004). *Lovemarks: The future beyond brands*. New York: Powerhouse Books.

Rossiter, J., & Bellman, S. (2012). Emotional branding pays off: How brands meet share of requirements through bonding, companionship and love. *Journal of Advertising Research, 52*(3), 291–296.

Rybalko, S., & Seltzer, T. (2010). Dialogic communication in 140 characters or less: How Fortune 500 companies engage stakeholders using Twitter. *Public Relations Review, 36*, 336–341.

Seltzer, T., & Mitrook, M. A. (2007). The dialogic potential of weblogs in relationship building. *Public Relations Review, 33*, 227–229.

Spencer-Oatey, H., Ng, P., & Li, D. (2000). Responding to compliments: British and Chinese evaluative judgments. In H. Spencer-Oatey (Ed.), *Culturally speaking: Managing rapport through talk across cultures* (pp. 98–116). London: Continuum.

Triandis, H. C. (1995). *Individualism and collectivism*. Boulder: Westview Press.

Tsai, W., & Men, L. R. (2012). Cultural values reflected in corporate pages on popular social network sites in China and the United States. *Journal of Research in Interactive Marketing, 6*(1), 42–58.

Twitter. (2015). *About Twitter*. Retrieved 27 October 2015 from: https://about.twitter.com/zh-hans/company

Warren, M. (2006). *Features of naturalness in conversation*. Amsterdam/Philadelphia: John Benjamins Publishing Company.

Waters, R. D., & Lo, K. D. (2012). Exploring the impact of culture in the social media sphere: A content analysis of nonprofit organizations' use of Facebook. *Journal of Intercultural Communication Research, 41*(3), 297–319.

Wright, D. K., & Hinson, M. D. (2014). An updated examination of social and emerging media use in public relations practice: A longitudinal analysis between 2006 and 2014. *Public Relations Journal, 8*(2), 1–36.

Wu, D. D., & Feng, W. (2015). Pragmatist, evangelist, or sensualist? Emotional branding on Sina Weibo. In P. P. K. Ng & C. S. B. Ngai (Eds.), *Role of language and corporate communication in Greater China* (pp. 225–239). Berlin: Springer.

Wu, D. D., & Li, C. (2016). Sociolinguistic approaches for intercultural new media studies. *Intercultural Communication Studies, 45*(2), 14–31.

China's Fluctuating English Education Policy Discourses and Continuing Ambivalences in Identity Construction

Yihong GAO

Abstract Foreign language education policies constitute an important aspect of China's reconstruction of its linguistic and cultural identities in an increasingly globalized world. China's English language education policies in the past three decades have undergone fluctuations, which can be roughly categorized into the following stages: (1) the *opening up* of English education from the late 1970s to the mid-1990s, and related to this, the euphoria for learning English. (2) The *speeding up* of English education from the mid-1990s to the first decade of the new millennium, and related to this, the anxiety regarding "too much time and too little effect." (3) The *slowing down* or *losing direction* as shown in a recent debate over a proposed English education policy reform from 2013 to 2014. Related to this is the fear that English education will have a negative effect on Chinese language proficiency and cultural identity. These changes have been reflected in and constructed by policy related discourses, including those of the national policy makers, education institutions and experts, and ordinary learners and netizens. The above policy and attitudinal fluctuations over 30 years can be contextualized and interpreted as being emblematic of issues in China's history over the last 150 years. An ambivalent psychological complex towards self and "the West" is revealed, situated in China's semi-colonial and semi-feudal history, beginning with the Opium Wars in 1840, when China faced foreign invasions and was forced to open its markets and partially give up sovereignty. It was in that context that the ambivalence was developed, i.e., the strong desire for the English language through which new technologies can be learned to strengthen the nation, and the fear that this foreign language will threaten Chinese identity. A brief historical analysis shows that the status of English in China has been fluctuating for the past 150 years. Such ambivalences and fluctuations have become a "*habitus*" (Bourdieu, P. *Language and symbolic power.* (J. B. Thompson Ed.; G. Raymond & M. Adamson Trans.). Cambridge: CUP, 1991), i.e., durable "structuring structures" of the collective mind. English has become a screen with two sides: on one side is projected the Chinese dream of becoming strong; and on

Y. GAO (✉)
Institute of Linguistics and Applied Linguistics, School of Foreign Languages, Peking University, Beijing, People's Republic of China
e-mail: gaoyh@pku.edu.cn

© Springer International Publishing AG, part of Springer Nature 2018   241
A. CURTIS, R. SUSSEX (eds.), *Intercultural Communication in Asia:*
Education, Language and Values, Multilingual Education 24,
https://doi.org/10.1007/978-3-319-69995-0_12

the other side is projected the nightmare of losing national identity. This self-perpetuating ambivalence helps to explain the fluctuations of China's English language education policies. In the context of increased globalization, when English is becoming a de-territorialized resource, the habitual defense mechanism is no longer effective, and it may well hinder national and individual development. The durable yet not eternal *habitus* can be transformed, and alternative strategies are to be conceived. Instead of a screen, English can be taken as a mirror, from which we can perceive our complex needs, desires, and emotions. With a clear self-perception, we can probably be free from compulsory policy and mood swings, feel more confident about our native cultural identity, and be ready to take on the identity of a "dialogical communicator" (Gao, Lang Intercult Commun 14(1):1–17, 2014) in intercultural communication.

1   Introduction

To meet an increasingly globalized world, China's English education policies face some emerging and continuing challenges. As an integral part of China's reconstruction of its linguistic and cultural identities, English education policies involve interaction between different forces, including the "hard" increases like those of the economy and internationalization, and "soft" language ideologies. A crucial challenge comes from the incompatibility of two beliefs about language and cultural identity: (1) English is the key to individual success and national prosperity; (2) English is an invading force that will hamper the maintenance of the Chinese language and cultural/national identity.

The struggle between these two competing ideologies can be seen from the changes of China's English education policies over the past three decades, and related to this, the very evident emotions that loom large in society. These changes can be roughly divided into three phases: (1) the *opening up* of English education from the late 1970s to the mid-1990s, characterized by the *euphoria* for learning English; (2) the *speeding up* of English education from the mid-1990s to the first decade of the new millennium, marked by an *anxiety* regarding "too much time and too little effect" in achieving the expected results; (3) the *slowing down* or *losing direction*, as shown in a recent debate between 2013 and 2014 over a proposed English education policy reform. Related to this is the *fear* that English education will hamper Chinese language proficiency and cultural identity.

Previous studies on foreign language policies have already categorized the key stages of historical development, and identified some general themes. Shen (2012) and O'Regan (2014) provided overviews of the development of foreign language education policies in contemporary east Asia, especially Japan, Korea and China. The changes of foreign language education policies are mostly associated with the nations' political history, international relations, and economic development. Typically, governments realized the need for English education when their countries faced Western military, political and economic threats in the nineteenth century, and the need was accelerated in the process of globalization. Descriptions of China's foreign language education history have been provided by a number of scholars (e.g., Adamson 2002; Cai 2006; Gao 2009; Hu 2003; Lam 2002; Wen and Hu 2007; Yang 2000; Zhao and Campbell 1995). The stages of development have been categorized, with common findings. There have been some critical reflections (e.g., Hu 2003) on existing problems, such as rapid changes of policy following political situations and over-concentration on English, accompanied by neglect of other foreign languages. In recent years, the proposed English entrance examination reform, signaling a slowing down in English language education, also attracted focused critical discussion, evaluation, and policy suggestions (e.g., Cheng 2014). However, there were a few studies from a social psychological perspective which dealt with not only the historical backgrounds but also the internalized *habitus* (Bourdieu 1991), or "structuring structures" for repeated behaviors (Gao 2009).

This chapter will examine the above three stages of China's English education policy and related emotions in the past three decades from a social psychological perspective. This effort is meant in a sense as critical self-reflection, as I am a member in the community of Chinese educators of English, who is involved in the discussed process of history. In this chapter I will focus more on the third stage, as this is still ongoing and has been less studied. While providing my descriptive account of the three stages, I will cite sample discourses at three levels – the government (policy documents or policy makers' words), educational institutions (state-run universities and private enterprises; educational experts; mass media), and individuals (ordinary learners and teachers; netizens). I will then contextualize and reinterpret the policy and attitudinal fluctuation of the most recent 30 years in terms of the history of China over the last 150 years. An ambivalent psychological complex towards self and "the West" is revealed, situated in China's semi-colonial and semi-feudal history, beginning with the Opium Wars in the mid nineteenth century. This ambivalence involves the desire for the English language through which new technologies can be learned to strengthen the nation against foreign invasion, and the fear that this foreign language will threaten to undermine Chinese identity.

Such ambivalent attitudes, ideologies and related fluctuations have become what the French sociologist Bourdieu (1977, 1991) calls a "*habitus*", i.e., durable structuring structures of the mind that generate policy-making practices and discourses which are not necessarily rational. According to Bourdieu, *habitus* is historically acquired and embodied in the individual. "Each individual system of dispositions may be seen as a structural variant of all the other group or class *habitus[es]*" (1977, p. 86). *Habitus* is durable, but not eternal (Bourdieu and Wacquant 1992). It is far from being simply a "mechanical reproduction of the initial conditions" (Bourdieu 1977, p. 95). Such a nature provides opportunities for change.

In light of Bourdieu's concept of *habitus*, combined with general insights from psychoanalysis regarding the impact of early traumatic experience on later life (Mitchell and Black 1995), I will propose that English to the Chinese has been a screen onto which ambivalent feelings carried from traumatic historical experiences have been projected and replayed. In the new context of globalization, such an old defense mechanism of self-perpetuation is no longer effective. It is suggested that English can be taken as a mirror, from which we can reflect on our multiple needs, desires and identities. With a clear self-perception, we can be relatively free from extreme ambivalences, and search for more creative solutions to the challenges of globalization. A few suggestions will be made for future lines of policy.

2   Stages of China's Foreign Language Education Policy, and Related Emotions

2.1   Opening Up *with Euphoria*

After a long period of isolation from the rest of the world, the opening up of China's foreign (English) education, together with its economic reform, began in the late 1970s. This opening was associated with the mastery of an instrument for economic growth and wealth, and related to this, the identity of a strong nation.

On January 18, 1978, China's Ministry of Education (MOE) issued the Protocol for 10-Year Full-Time Teaching in Elementary and Secondary Schools. It was stipulated that for schools meeting the necessary conditions, foreign (English) language classes should begin from Grade 3 in elementary school, and the total teaching hours over 8 years should amount to 1,080. On February 17, the State Council endorsed the MOE document which resumed the key university position of two foreign language institutes, in Beijing and Shanghai respectively. On March 4th, MOE made public its decision to send about 300 students and visiting scholars abroad that year.

A National Symposium on Foreign Language Education was held by the MOE from August 29 to September 10, 1978. This symposium was regarded as an event of "bringing order out of chaos". Liao Chengzhi, Vice Chairman of the NPC (National People's Congress) Standing Committee, presented a speech entitled "Speeding up the education of foreign language talents". The "uselessness of foreign languages" was criticized. The symposium called for "greater, faster, better and cheaper ways for the education of all-rounded foreign language talents. [...] Not being able to learn a foreign language well is not only a professional failure, but also a political failure" (Higher Education Research Institute, Sichuan Institute of Foreign Languages 1993, p.135).

It is interesting and important to note that "greater, faster, better, and cheaper" was a slogan which originated in China's Great Leap Forward from 1958 to 1961, an economic and social campaign aimed at unrealistic rapidity of industrialization. The campaign led to a great imbalance of the national economy; it produced exaggeratedly high figures of production, and at the same time was at least partially responsible for high numbers of deaths from starvation. While the failure of the

Fig. 1 English Corner, Fudan University, Shanghai, 1984 (Source of photo: *Southern Weekend* (南方周末): http://ndnews.oeeee.com/html/201310/31/443348.html. Accessed on March 19, 2014.)

campaign has been recognized, the unrealistic desire for rapid growth and its discourse representation has been sustained, and were reproduced in, the *opening up* stage of FL education in China.

Euphoria, excitement, and passion permeated university campuses and society in general. "English Corner", a special time-place for communication in English only, quickly flourished on university campuses in the 1980s (Fig. 1). As seen in this photo, the corner goers were not particularly young in age, their clothes were old-styled and reminiscent of the previous era, but the eagerness and enthusiasm on their faces were intense and new. Despite specific content talked about, that English as used in this "corner" became a symbol for the new opening.

In the 1980s and 1990s, English in formal school education increased by leaps and bounds, in the formulation of teaching guidelines, the recovery and expansion of English major programs, and English education research projects (Higher Education Research Institute, Sichuan Institute of Foreign Languages 1993). Meanwhile, private enterprises of English education began to emerge, adding to the "heat" of English learning. A representative case is Li Yang's "Crazy English".

Li Yang set up his "Li Yang International English Promotion Studio" in 1994. His "Crazy English" quickly swept China with its loudly shouted English sentences. At the beginning of a documentary "Crazy English" (produced and directed by Zhang Yuan 1999)[1]. Li walked in the snow with a group and shouted loudly: "Crazy world! Crazy study! Crazy English! Crazy Everything! Crazy every day! I love this crazy game! Crazy! Crazy! Crazy!". Figure 2 is an impressive advertising picture widely

---

[1] Access to the documentary film: http://v.ku6.com/show/CXaHTsDMX3A7QioU.html?nr=1.

Fig. 2 "Carry forward the national spirit; Stimulate patriotic passion" ("Crazy English" in the Forbidden City, Beijing, 1998) (Source of photo: "Li Yang's Crazy English", accessed on March 19, 2014. The same photo of lower resolution without attached caption or with other captions can be found at multiple websites on January 1, 2016, e.g., Beidu Baike: http://baike.baidu.com/subview/5440/6535113.htm)

seen in China, portraying Li Yang shouting English in the Forbidden City, i.e., the center of China's traditional culture, supposedly "carrying forward the national spirit and stimulating patriotic passion", as the Chinese caption says. While the relation between the English shouting and Chinese patriotism is curiously unclear, the passion transmitted is immediately evident and very striking.

Alongside patriotism, economic success was a practical motivation that private institutions focused on so as to attract learners, as seen in the words of another advertisement:

> "Ignite your English potential immediately! Change your life like a magic!"
> "Who else wants to transform from a victim of deaf and dumb English to a respected English expert, even an international bilingual elite long dreamed for?"
> "The only trainer in China who can help trainees to conquer English in half a year, and turn English competence into a sizable amount of cash […] money […] and wealth in one year!"

Individual learners were indeed motivated and jointly contributed to the craze for English. In a qualitative study on trainees of Crazy English carried out at the turn of the millennium (Shen and Gao 2004, pp. 198–199), individual learners expressed their ideas which were highly congruent with the institution: Crazy English "was a positive word", it "refers to the pursuit of a goal with extremely high commitment"; "only in this way can one succeed." Those who are "crazy" are "persistent" or "fanatical", which in turn means "rationally dedicated to one's goals".

As shown above, the English euphoria was pervasive and consistent at different levels of discourse in the *opening up* period – the "greater, faster, better, and cheaper" of the government, the "craziness" of educational institutions, and the fanaticism of individual learners. In this opening up of the nation to the world,

English was taken as a symbol as well as an instrument for individual success and national prosperity.

2.2 Speeding Up with Anxiety

The *speeding up* of English education from the mid-1990s to the first decade of the new millennium was a natural development of the *opening up*, and in the same direction. The prototypical emotion related, however, was negative rather than positive. The growth in the economy called for faster development of English education, which apparently lagged behind and generated feelings of anxiety and frustration.

"Too much time, too little effect" At a symposium on FL education reform held on June 28, 1996, Vice Premier Li Lanqing stated: "There is a common problem of spending much time and achieving only limited results. This problem requires urgent inspection and solution". He also compared China with other nations:

> Due to inappropriate teaching methods, the general FL proficiency of Chinese intellectuals has fallen behind not only developed countries such as Germany, but also many developing countries such as India, Pakistan, Bangladesh, Indonesia, Thailand, Singapore, Malaysia and the Philippines. This has not only become an obstacle and weakness in our learning of advanced science and technology, opening up to and having collaborative exchanges with the external world, but also made us suffer losses. (Li 1996, p.4)

Cen Jianjun, the MOE official in charge of foreign language education, echoed this evaluation:

> The disparity between China's FL education and development of economy, science and technology is becoming increasingly great each year. [...] The speed of reform is seriously hampered by the overly low FL proficiency of our university students. (Cen 1998, p.13)

Vice Premier Li's negative evaluation was quickly shortened into a phrase "too much time; too little effect" (feishi dixiao) and became a topic for heated discussion in the mass media as well as academia. Support for this negative assessment was prevailing. In a paper published in *China Youth Daily* (March 10, 1999), a government official newspaper, University English professor Jing Shenghua portrayed English education in China as "a kettle of lukewarm water that will never boil". A more commonly known concept was "dumb English", meaning not being able to speak after learning English for many years. Dai Weidong (2001), president of the Shanghai Foreign Studies University, stated that a major problem of China's English education is "too much time and too little effect". There were also different voices, though rather weak. For instance, Hu Zhuanglin (2002), a senior professor from Peking University, stressed that Chinese students learn English as a foreign rather than second language, implying the fallacy of the belief that China was "falling behind" ESL (English as a second language) countries such as India.

It is evident that the assessment and anxiety of "too much time; too little effect" at least partially resulted from the "greater, faster, better, and cheaper" expectation.

The disparity was between the gradual development in reality and the expected great leap forward.

Exam-oriented Anxiety One area where the anxiety was clearly manifested was in the national standard tests of English, particularly the "College English Test" (CET), with its two levels, Band 4 (CET-4) and Band 6 (CET-6), both targeted at university students other than those majoring in English. The development of CET-4 and CET-6 was organized by the MOE in late 1986, and the tests were formally implemented in 1987. For university students majoring in English, there is a separate national standard test called "Test for English Majors" (TEM), with its two levels Band 4 (TEM-4) and Band 8 (TEM-8). The formal implementation of TEM started from 1991. In terms of proficiency level, CET-4 is intermediate, CET-6 and TEM-4 are upper intermediate, and TEM-8 is advanced. It is claimed that these tests were "to push forward the implementation of English teaching guidelines, to objectively and accurately assess university students' English competence, and to improve the level of English education in China".[2] The impact of these tests, especially CET, which involved students of various majors, was enormous. For a long period of time, CET-4 results were tied to student graduation, university ranking, and English teacher evaluation. Only at the beginning of the new millennium, in 2005, did the MOE decide to lessen the importance of this test and stop issuing certificates showing satisfactory CET performance. Since then universities have gradually disconnected CET-4 results from student graduation, although the test has remained influential.

The anxiety the tests generated among students was intense. The following are citations of student journals and interviews from a longitudinal study (Gao et al. 2013):

> A gray April just passed, and an agonizing June is coming. From last December to this June, there were English tests one after another. I am really worried. CET-4 made my hair turn gray and turned me into a Santa Clause. TEM-4 gave me such a hard blow that I totally became an April fool. Now everyone is busy preparing for CET-6, the most important exam at university, similar to the university entrance examination. To pass these tests, I have spent a lot of time. (Xiao Tan, English Journal 11)

> My (CET-4) score was one point lower than the passing line. […] I was really upset about it. You know, as I failed CET-4, I didn't get the scholarship. Though I was elected as an excellent class leader, this title was not conferred by the university. And then, when they were recruiting volunteers for the Olympic Games, they wouldn't allow me to take the (recruiting) test. Oh, my god! (Xu Jiayi, Interview 5, translated from Chinese).

Although there were different voices among English educators, the anxiety of "too much time and too little effect" was dominant, and was largely consistent across social levels. The "too much and too little" anxiety and frustration, as can be

---

[2] Baidu Encyclopaedia (百度百科): http://baike.baidu.com/link?url=DV6uqpqmwshVhaILjd3OhM 1UKmBE5r8TgU5nXhlMa-K0_LI5BgpVYfJzwJbZD50OQFM24rtfQuJYVSVEkoFugKhttp:// baike.baidu.com/link?url=DV6uqpqmwshVhaILjd3OhM1UKmBE5r8TgU5nXhlMa-K0_ LI5BgpVYfJzwJbZD50OQFM24rtfQuJYVSVEkoFugK . Accessed on January 1, 2015. "College English Band 4" (大学英语四级考试).

seen in its development, was generated against the expectation of "greater, faster, better, and cheaper".

2.3 The Slowing Down or Losing Direction with Fear

While the "too much but too little" anxiety was still burning, a different kind of emotion was simmering, i.e., the fear (and sometimes anger) that English education would harm the maintenance of the Chinese language and Chinese national identity. Such emotions were easily ignited by international and domestic events. In reaction to NATO's bombing of the Chinese embassy in Yugoslavia in May, 1999, Peking University students put up a slogan "Say no to TOEFL and GRE; say yes to the fight against US imperialism!" (bu kao Tuo bu kao G, yixinyiyi da meidi!). More than a decade later, when the 6th edition of the *Modern Chinese Dictionary* (2012) included some 200 "letter words", mostly acronyms or mixed acronyms such as "DNA", "NBA" and "T恤"(T-shirt). Over a hundred scholars wrote a joint report, accusing the compilers and publisher of destroying the purity of the Chinese language, thus violating China's Law of National Language and Writing System. This event generated a heated social debate. When a policy reform in English college entrance examination was discussed during 2013 and 2014, the fear was highlighted all the more.

Proposed Policy Change Regarding English Exams In November 2013, the 3rd Plenary Session of the 18th CPC (the Communist Party of China) Central Committee called for further education reforms regarding entrance examinations. Following this call, local governments discussed similar plans for senior high school and college entrance examination reform, language exams being at its core. The rationale of the reform was to "let English return to its due (instrumental) position", and to "highlight the importance of the Chinese mother tongue in education". Specific measures included a gradual score increase for Chinese, a decrease in the score for English, and eventually moving the responsibility of running English exams from state-run institutions (schools and MOE delegated organizations) to "social institutions" (private enterprises). In December 2013, the government of Beijing Municipality released a potential plan to be implemented from 2016. According to this plan, for senior high school entrance exams, the total score for Chinese will be raised from 120 to 150; that for English will be reduced from 120 to 100. For university entrance exams, the total score for Chinese will be raised from 150 to 180; that for English will be reduced from 150 to 100. Similar policy changes were discussed in other big cities and provinces. The reform was to temper "the overheated English learning in China", and to "emphasize the assessment of mastery of excellent Chinese cultural traditions".[3] On May 9, 2014, the announcement that

---

[3]Yesky (天极网): http://news.yesky.com/hot/119/35496119.shtml. Accessed on March 19, 2014. "Vigorous reforms of Senior High and College Entrance Exams in Beijing: English Scores Will Decrease and Chinese Scores Will Increase from 2016" (北京中高考大改革 2016年起降低英语分提高语文分).

"English will be removed from the university entrance exam from 2016" at the national level became explosive news for the public.[4]

However, this reform plan was not eventually adopted for implementation. On September 3, 2014, four months after the media announcements in May, "The State Council's Views on the Implementation of Deepened Enrollment Exam Reform" was formally released. It stipulated that "the subjects of Chinese, mathematics, and foreign language in university entrance exams will remain unchanged; so will their scores. [...] Two exam opportunities will be provided for the foreign language".[5] So the proposed reform was aborted for the moment. The status of English in the university entrance exams fluctuated, from being taken "out of" the package altogether, to an increase from one exam opportunity to "two opportunities" each year. The temperature of English education did not cool down; the focus of policy discourse shifted, from "letting English return to its due (instrumental) position" and "highlighting the importance of the Chinese mother tongue in education", to battling against "one test to determine the whole life, which make students overburdened".

A new round of the reform effort came about in March 2017, when NPC representative Li Guangyu made a proposal at the annual NPC meeting, i.e., removing English from university entrance exams, and changing the status of English in elementary and secondary schools from required course to elective course. The reason he provided, based on his investigation, was that English learning took too much time and was a big burden for Chinese school children. This proposal triggered a new round of the old debate.[6]

Media Presentation The proposed reform of removing English from entrance exams was presented in the mass media, with interesting metaphors. One of them was a "tug of war" between Chinese and English (Fig. 3); another was "filling competing water tanks" (Fig. 4, with water in the English tank reduced, and that in the Chinese tank added). Still another one was fervently "cooling down the English fever" (Fig. 5, with the cloud and rain representing the reform plan, and the fire representing various English training classes). Commonly implied is the ideology that English and Chinese education are in conflict and involved in a win-or-lose game.

Discourses of Educational Institutions A retrospective look at the debate of the reform from the end of 2013 to the first half of 2014 shows different voices from

---

[4]Sina Guangduang (新浪广东): http://gd.sina.com.cn/qy/news/2014-05-10/07461150.html. Accessed on November 1, 2014. "English out of College Entrance Exam from 2016 Is a Rumor" (2016年英语正式退出新高考纯属网络传言).

[5]Library of Law (法律图书馆网): http://www.law-lib.com/law/law_view.asp?id=461340. Accessed on November 1, 2014. "The State Council's Views on the Implementation of Deepened Enrollment Exam Reform" (国务院关于深化考试招生制度改革的实施意见).

[6]China Youth Online (中青在线): http://news.cyol.com/content/2017-03/08/content_15721094.htm. Accessed on May 29, 2017. "A One-Sided Opinion of Removing English from University Entrance Exam? Observation of NPC and CPPCC meetings" (一边倒支持高考取消英语?两会青观察).

Fig. 3 Tug of War between Chinese & English (Source of photo: Jinghua (精华在线): http://www.jinghua.com/exam/newsinfo_21571.html. Accessed on March 19, 2014.)

Fig. 4 Filling Competing Water Tanks (Source of photo: Tencent Education (腾讯教育): http://edu.qq.com/a/20131023/006389.htm . Accessed on March 19, 2014.)

educational institutions, educators, and netizens. The interaction of oppositional voices might have influenced the decision making of the government.

The New Oriental School, a representative private enterprise in English teaching, expressed a favorable attitude regarding reducing the scores of English in entrance exams. Yu Minhong, head of the New Oriental School, expressed his opinion before attending the annual meeting of the Chinese People's Political Consultative Conference (CPPCC) on March 3, 2014. He believed that as long as English held a certain proportion in the university entrance exam, even if reduced to a mere 20 points, "students would work very hard for those 20 points."[7] Yet Yu was against Li Guangyu's proposal

---

[7]Yinchuan News (银川新闻网): http://www.ycen.com.cn/jypd/jyzx/201403/t20140305_37344.html. Accessed on March 19, 2014. "Yu Minhong: Support for English Score Reduction in Entrance Exam; No Influence on Training Market" (俞敏洪：支持高考英语降分 不影响培训市场).

Fig. 5 Fervently Cooling Down the English Fever (Source of photo: Xinhua (新华网): http://news.xinhuanet.com/comments/2013-10/24/c_117853417.htm . Accessed on March 19, 2014.)

of removing English altogether, as stated during his attendance of the CPPCC in March 2017. Yu regarded Li's proposal as "too hasty" and "even reckless," as "the world now is not isolated, and it is beneficial for children to learn English."[8]

It remains interesting to observe whether commercial benefits might be part of the debate drive. While reducing the score of English in the officially implemented college entrance examination, the proposed reform (2013–2014) would make "social institutions" such as the New Oriental School responsible for standard English tests. The redistribution of testing authority would bring great economic benefit to these "social" (private) institutions.

University English educators expressed mostly negative opinions. They typically stressed the importance of English education in terms of "foreign language strategies of the nation." Cai Jigang, head of Steering Committee for College English Teaching in Shanghai, published a newspaper article in the *Wenhui Daily* on December 12, 2013, stating that the standard of English education should be raised rather than lowered from the perspective of "national strategies" in "national and international contexts." Cheng Xiaotang (2014), dean of School of Foreign Languages, Beijing Normal University, published a journal article to argue against "letting English return to its due instrumental position." On June 14, 2014, the first "Symposium on Foreign Language Entrance Exam Reform" was jointly organized by the editorial department of *Foreign Languages*, an academic journal run by Shanghai Foreign Studies University, and the School of Foreign Languages, Beijing Normal University. Participants (e.g., Chen Lin, Hu Zhuanglin and Cheng Musheng) were mostly university English educators with a high reputation. Based on the symposium consensus, the 15 participants wrote a letter to Vice Premier Liu Yandong

---

[8]China Youth Online (中青在线): http://news.cyol.com/content/2017-03/08/content_15721094.htm.

on July 20, 2014, arguing for the importance of "foreign language strategies of the nation." They made several suggestions to the government, such as organizing a hearing concerning the necessity and feasibility of the proposed reform, and its possible impact.

Debate Among Netizens   The general public also paid great attention to the reform. For the 2013 public appraisal of "Top 10 Language Events" on sina.com, the English entrance exam reform ranked number one.[9] Heated debates appeared on various Internet forums. A study on 1,023 comments posted by 804 netizens on website of Tencent News from May 18 to June 6, 2014 showed that 75.4% of the comments were negative and 24.6% were positive about English learning (Luo 2015).

The following are some opposing arguments for and against the discussed reform:

> For: When English is dashing forward, the Chinese language and culture is falling behind.
> Against: The Chinese language and culture has nothing to do with English. Are you prepared to trip others just because YOU are faltering?
> For: Shouldn't there be a priority order when it comes to transmission of the national language and learning of a foreign language?
> Against: Why should the issue between L1 and L2 be a zero-sum game? When a "national" prefix is added to the language, it surely suggests a lack of confidence.
> For: Chinese children will be misled to be subservient to foreigners, and lack national awareness. Good students all hope to go abroad or even emigrate. What's the value of consuming Chinese resources for the development of foreign countries? What's the point of using one's own money to raise others' kids?
> Against: Your kids went to play at your neighbor's home, and you think the problem is your kids have legs. If their legs are broken, they will then stay home. How ridiculous and short-sighted![10]

In fact, similar debates among netizens had been going on a decade before. On the forum "Guantian Tea House," for example, a netizen said "Only slaves need to learn their masters' language!". Those who supported English proposed "Learning the enemies' strengths so as to conquer them", and "We should learn English with clenched teeth!" (Gao 2009). Before the reform plan was released there had been already a loud outcry in the public for cooling down English education: "English exam has become a huge cancerous tumor"; "bombard the exam system of college English"; "the Chinese nation is experiencing a new round of 'the Opium War' brought about by the invasion of English" (Zhu and Yang 2004, pp. 11–12).

The fear and anger concerning the loss of native language and cultural identity were deeply entrenched in discourses at various levels. From the debate concerning the most recent reform plan, one can perceive English education in China vacillat-

---

[9] Sina Investigation (新浪调查): http://survey.news.sina.com.cn/result/87778.html. Accessed on November 1, 2014. "Top 10 Language Issues of Public Sentiment, 2013" (2013年语言文字舆情十大热点事件评选).

[10] Chinese Quora(知乎): http://www.zhihu.com/question/22224453. Accessed on November 1, 2014. "Why Should There Be Changes in College Entrance Exam of English, Regarding Its Form and Weight?" (为什么要改革英语高考考试形式，并调整其在招生录取中的权重?)

ing between different directions. One can also hear more diverse voices, and the dynamism of interaction among them.

3   Sociohistorical Context: 30 years in 150 years

3.1   English Education in China's Modern History

As shown above, the trajectory of China's English language education in the past three decades can be roughly categorized as opening up and euphoria, from the late 1970s to the mid-1990s, speeding up and related anxiety from the mid-1990s to the first decade of the new millennium, and the slowing down or losing direction and related fear in recent years. The fluctuations of these 30 years can be better understood when situated in the larger context of China's 150-year modern history. This modern history started with the two Opium Wars (1840–1842; 1856–1860) in the mid-nineteenth century, when China, a previously self-enclosed and self-centered "Central Kingdom," was first hit by the imposition of the power of Great Britain and its allies, and was forced to cede territory, open treaty ports, and pay indemnities. Thus China underwent a transformation from a feudal society to a semi-feudal and semi-colonial society. It was faced with the "strengths of the ships and cannons" of the West, so that the Chinese government realized the importance of learning from the West. A "Self-Strengthening Movement" (Yangwu Yundong) was launched from the 1860s and 1890s, aiming at learning from the West, focusing on science and technology, building up China's industries and military force, and the navy in particular. It is important that the literal name for "Self-strengthening Movement" is "Westernization Movement", showing the instrumental rationale and tension in this lesson. While ship building and other military related industries were promoted, students were sent abroad to study. Tongwenguan (School of Combined Learning), the first institution for training translators, was established by the government in 1862, targeting at introducing Western works to the Chinese. The guiding principles of the Self-Strengthening Movement were conceptualized in two sentences: "learning the enemies' strengths in order to conquer them",[11] and "Chinese learning for *ti* (essence); Western learning for *yong* (utility)."[12] Whereas the former positions the movement in relation to the foreign powers, the latter connects it to China's own cultural traditions and attempts to provide order between conflicting cultural traditions. That is, Chinese learning has priority over Western learning. The Self-Strengthening Movement ended in failure, marked by the Chinese navy's complete destruction in the first Sino-Japanese War (1894–1895). The failure can be partially attributed to the superficiality of learning from the West at the technological level, without substantial reforms at the government/institutional level (Gao 2009).

---

[11] "师夷长技以制夷",from *Graphic Records of Overseas Countries* (《海国图志》)edited by Wei Yuan(魏源). The editing of the serial book started in 1842, and reached 50 volumes in 1852.
[12] "中学为体, 西学为用", from "Encouraging Learning"(《劝学篇》) by Zhang Zhidong (1898).

To recapitulate, modern Chinese foreign language education, marked by the establishment of Tongwenguan, was situated in a sociohistorical context of national crisis. While setting up the objective and priority order, the "learn and conquer" and *"ti-yong"* principles highlighted the conflicting tension between the battling or competing "Self" and the "West". The same tension can be seen in the naming of "Yangwu Yundong" ("Westernization Movement" in the sense of "Self-Strengthening Movement"). China's loss in the first Sino-Japanese War and the failure of the Self-Strengthening Movement added to its national shame, and painfully deepened the sense of national identity. Despite the failure of the Self-Strengthening Movement, the *ti-yong* order has been maintained as a central principle over several generations. The specific themes varied with the sociohistorical background and international relations in different periods, as did English education policies and their implementations. A brief summary of the situations during these 150 years is presented in Table 1.

The above summary shows that the fluctuation of China's English language education policies and emotions is deeply rooted in China's modern history, since its contact with the West in the Opium Wars. To a great extent, the *opening up, speeding up*, and *slowing down* or *losing direction* in the recent 30 years are but a repetition of what had been going on since the mid-nineteenth century. A common pattern can be discerned.

3.2   English as a Screen for Projection

English is a screen. On each of its sides is projected a different inner perception, and language ideology. On one side are projected the angel, heaven, the Chinese dream to be strong, successful, and prosperous. Related to this is the ideology of English as a key to strong nation building. On the other side are projected the devil, hell, and the nightmare of being invaded and oppressed. Associated with this is the ideology of English as a killer of the national language and national identity. The screen itself is not altogether empty and transparent. It is color tinted, and it may enact dreams or nightmares. Yet in the development of history, English education has already become an abstract symbol, or to be more exact, a signifier with two signifieds: the dream of a strong nation, and the nightmare of national identity loss. The two ideological discourses have alternated to be in the dominant position during different historical periods. Confrontations and alternations of the discourses may also be found within the same period. The ambivalent psychological complex has been reproduced through discourses of the government, educational institutions and individual learners. The policy fluctuation and attitudinal ambivalence have become a *habitus* (Bourdieu 1991) or "structuring structures" in Chinese culture. The Opium Wars over a century ago were a historical reality. The contemporary "new Opium War" against the "spiritual Opium" of English is a discursive construction, with its own psychological reality. The psychological complex rooted in a historical trauma has continuously enacted reproduction of the imagined enemy. Self-repeating the

Table 1 The historical status of English language in China

Period	Time	Historical background	Status of english	*Ti-Yong* relation	Characteristics of english education
Late Qing Dynasty	1861–1911	The two Opium Wars (1940s–1960s) brought great challenges and humiliation to China's ability of protecting itself against Western invasions	English as a vehicle for gaining access to Western science and technology; "Learning the enemies' strengths in order to defeat them"	"Chinese learning for *ti* (essence); Western learning for *yong* (utility)." Technological utility only.	On the curriculum of institutions set up to facilitate transfer of scientific knowledge; after 1903, included on the curricula of secondary and tertiary institutions
The New Cultural Movement	1911-1923	The New Cultural Movement (1917–1923) launched criticism of the Confucian tradition and introduced various "isms" from abroad; Linguistic reform from classical Chinese to modern Chinese	English as a vehicle for exploring Western philosophy and other ideas	Western *ti* (schools of ideas/"isms") entered the scene of China's sociocultural transformation.	On the curricula of secondary and tertiary institutions
The Republican Era	1924–1949	China aligned more with the West against Japan. The ruling party Guomindang sought support from the US, and followed the model of US education system for some time.	English as a vehicle for diplomatic, military and intellectual interaction with the West	Primarily *yong* (military, diplomatic, political utilities)	On the curricula of secondary and tertiary institutions

(continued)

Table 1 (continued)

Period	Time	Historical background	Status of english	Ti-Yong relation	Characteristics of english education
PRC Before the Cultural Revolution	1949–1960	In the early, 1950s China was closely aligned with the Soviet Union against the West, but the Sino-Soviet relationship broke in the late 1950s.	The status of English declined while that of Russian was boosted. The trend was reversed in late 1950s.	Status of *yong* fluctuated. English fell out of favor for political reasons; later considered valuable for modernization.	On the curricula of very few secondary and tertiary institutions in 1950s. Promoted on the curricula of secondary and tertiary institutions in early 1960s.
PRC During the Cultural Revolution	1966–1976	A radical political movement to re-establish class struggle. Education in general suffered greatly.	English was associated with imperialism and capitalism; Western learning was repudiated.	If any *yong* at all, as an instrument of political propaganda.	Removed from the curricula of secondary and tertiary institutions; later restored, though rather sporadically
PRC Reform Era	1978 onwards	Economic reform and development; transformation from planned economy to market economy; China entered the WTO.	English seen as an essential instrument for modernization.	Great value of *yong*; as an instrument for economic development	Strongly promoted on the curricular of secondary and tertiary institutions.

Gao in Lo Bianco, Orton and Gao (2009, pp. 61–62)

traumatic experience serves to maintain the sensitive and not strong enough national identity.

The psychological complex should be understood in this sociohistorical context, with its rationale. It is unrealistic to expect the pendulum swing discussed above to disappear in a short time. However, a historically situated understanding does not mean there are no alternatives to the pendulum swing. In the contemporary context of globalization, the old *habitus* may not be the most effective strategy for national identity building. New ways forward need to be explored.

4   From a Screen of Projection to a Mirror of Reflection

From a social constructivist perspective, social phenomena are discursively negoti-ated and constructed, without denying the existence of sociohistorical facts (Fairclough 2006). Bourdieu (1990, p. 123), who labeled his own theoretical stance "constructivist structuralism" or "structuralist constructivism", integrated a social constructivist perspective that allowed for changes. When discussing its character-istics, Bourdieu has said that *habitus* is durable, but not eternal (Bourdieu and Wacquant 1992). In other words, *habitus* is subject to gradual moderation and reconstruction. In light of such a perspective, the pendulum swing does not have to go on forever. Globalization has brought about not only challenges but also oppor-tunities for breaking the cycle. In this new context, English is being de-territorialized; it has been taken as a wide range of legitimate varieties of "World Englishes" (Kachru 1992) tied up with local cultures, or a lingua franca with communicative functions but largely without "native speakers" (Seidlhofer 2011). In many parts of the world, English education has given up standards centered on "native speakers," and has been adjusted to objectives such as communicative "capability" rather than native-speaker-centered communicative "competence" (Widdowson 2013).

If we believe that English can be de-territorialized, it no longer poses an unavoid-able imperialist threat to national identities. Consequently, the habitual psychologi-cal defense mechanism and resulting policy pendulum swing do not have to be the only choice. Instead of a screen for projection, English may be taken as a mirror of reflection, from which we can perceive and examine various ambivalent needs, desires, and feelings. When our own ambivalences are clearly seen, we can take a more creative stance to education in national and global languages, to the mainte-nance of native cultural identity, and to the development of a global identity. A "productive orientation" (Fromm 1948) can be taken to transcend oppositions, with the two sides positively reinforcing each other, in a "1+1>2" manner to create some-thing which is more than the sum of its parts (Gao 2001). The identity of "dialogical communicator" will then be developed (Gao 2014). Distinguished from the "faithful imitator" whose L2 use and cultural conduct are strictly modeled on the native speaker, the "legitimate speaker" who claims equal rights with native speakers in their distinct L2 use, the "playful creator" who constructs unconventional hybrid language use for their self-expression, the Bakhtinian "dialogical communicator" converses – speaks and listens – on the basis of respect and reflection, in interpersonal communication. In intra-subject communication, i.e., dialogues between different consciousness or "voices", the "dialogical communicator" has a reflective sensitiv-ity, ready to discern, expand, deepen and reorganize various kinds of consciousness within him- or herself.

Such productive and dialogical efforts can be made at practical levels. For exam-ple, instead of letting English be dropped from examinations to make room for Chinese, we may think of how to enhance the English expression of Chinese cul-ture. In English teaching materials and teaching at various levels, it is desirable and feasible to guide students in describing certain aspects of their local culture, e.g., family food, scenic spots, historical figures, and regional cultural specialties. Practicum can be designed to relate to the local context, for example by having the students role-play as international tourist guides in local museums, or presenting exhibits on the internet for students in other parts of the world. While English competitions in recitation, speech, and debate have flourished in China for many years, other contests such as English translation of Chinese classics can also be held. Some interesting attempts have already been made. In the new college English textbook compiled by Wen Qiufang and associates, for instance, law students were invited to mount a defense from a cultural perspective for the victim in an intercultural conflict, triggered by the use of traditional Chinese "Gua Sha" treatment.[13]

In this chapter, I have roughly divided English education policies in the past three decades into three stages, each with its prominent emotion: the *opening up* with euphoria, the *speeding up* with anxiety, and *slowing down* or *losing direction* with fear. To better understand this fluctuation, I have further situated these policies in China's modern history, during the past 150 years. It is pointed out that to a great extent, the fluctuation of the last 30 years is but a repetition of what has been happening for 150 years. My view is that while similar concerns and dilemmas exist in other nations with a history of foreign invasions, China is quite distinct in its context-shaped social psychology. With its historical experience of traumatization through foreign invasions, it is not easy to develop fully open attitudes towards the "invasion" of foreign languages. On the other hand, as China has never been fully colonized and used the colonizers' language as the official language, it is not easy to develop an attitude and identity to "own" (a local variety of) the English language. China's ambivalence towards English is very deep.

Globalization has provided new opportunities for breaking the cycle. Instead of taking English education as a screen of projection, we should take it as a mirror of critical self-reflection, from which we can perceive clearly our own conflicting needs, desires, feelings and identities. The screen projection is largely unconscious and passive, whereas the mirror reflection involves conscious acts of active agents. With a clear perception of ourselves and of our environment, we can then be less "crazy", and gradually move beyond the compulsive pendulum swing and oppositional thinking. Then our national and global identities will be constructed in peace, and in a mutually enhancing manner.

Acknowledgement This chapter is based on an earlier paper in Chinese, "A Mirror for Reflection vs. a Screen for Projection" (投射之 "屏幕" 与反观之 "镜子"), *Foreign Language Learning Theory and Practice* (《外语教学理论与实践》) 149:1-7. Efforts are made to update the data and further the discussion. The author would like to thank Professor Roland Sussex and Professor Andy Curtis for their helpful comments, suggestions and editing work during the revision of this paper.

---

[13] *Gua Sha* is a treatment in traditional Chinese medicine, which commonly leaves red spots of inner bleeding on skin. The movie *The Gua Sha Treatment* is about Sino-US cultural differences, and intercultural (mis)communication. When the Chinese grandpa performed Gua Sha on his grandson in the US context, the family was sued because of "child abuse". A chain of intercultural conflicts followed, but were eventually resolved.

References

Adamson, B. (2002). Barbarian as a foreign language: English in China's schools. *World Englishes, 21*(2), 231–243.

Bourdieu, P. (1977). *Outline of a theory of practice*. Cambridge: Cambridge University Press.

Bourdieu, P. (1990). *In other words* (M. Adamson Trans.). Stanford: Stanford University Press.

Bourdieu, P. (1991). *Language and symbolic power*. (J. B. Thompson Ed.; G. Raymond & M. Adamson Trans.). Cambridge: Cambridge University Press.

Bourdieu, P., & Wacquant, L. (1992). *An invitation to reflexive sociology*. Chicago: University of Chicago Press.

Cai, J. G. (蔡基刚). (2006). *College English teaching: Review, reflection and research* (《大学英语教学:回顾、反思和研究》). Shanghai: Fudan University Press.

Cen, J.J. (岑建君). (1998). College English teaching reform should look to the future(大学英语教学改革应着眼于未来). *Foreign Language World* (《外语界》), *4*, 12–17.

Cheng, X. T. (程晓堂). (2014). Thoughts on current adjustment of English language education policies (关于当前英语教育政策调整的思考). *Curriculum, Teaching Material and Method* (《课程·教材·教法》), *5*, 58–64.

Dai, W. D. (戴炜栋). (2001). The phenomenon of "too much time and too little effect" in foreign language teaching (外语教学的"费时低效"现象). *Foreign Languages and Their Teaching* (《外语与外语教学》), *7*, 10–14.

Fairclough, N. (2006). *Language and globalization*. London: Routledge.

Fromm, E. (1948). *Man for himself*. London: Routledge & Kegan Paul.

Gao, Y. H. (2001). *Foreign language learning: "1+1>2"*. Beijing: Peking University Press.

Gao, Y. H. (2009). Sociocultural contexts and English in China: Retaining and reforming the cultural *habitus*. In J. Lo Bianco, J. Orton, & Y. H. Gao (Eds.), *China and English: Globalization and the dilemmas of identity* (pp. 56–78). Bristol: Multilingual Matters.

Gao, Y. H. (2014). Faithful imitator, legitimate speaker, playful creator and dialogical communicator: Shift in English learners' identity prototypes. *Language and Intercultural Communication, 14*(1), 1–17.

Gao, Y. H. & Project Group (高一虹等). (2013). *College students' English learning motivation and self-identity development – A four-year longitudinal study* (《大学生英语学习动机与自我认同发展—四年五校跟踪研究》). Beijing: Higher Education Press.

Higher Education Research Institute, Sichuan Institute of Foreign Languages (Ed.). (1993). (四川外国语学院高等教育研究所编), 1993, *Annals of foreign language education in China* (《中国外语教育要事录》). Revised and approved by Department of Higher Education, Ministry of Education (国家教委高等教育司审订). Beijing: Foreign Language Teaching and Research Press.

Hu, W. Z. (2003). A matter of balance – Reflections on China's language policy in education. In W. Z. Hu (Ed.), *ELT in China 2001* (pp. 107–127). Beijing: Foreign Language Teaching and Research Press.

Hu, Z. L. (胡壮麟). (2002). The issue of "too little effect" regarding English teaching in China (中国英语教学中的"低效"问题). *Foreign Language Teaching Abroad* (《国外外语教学》), *4*, 3–7.

Kachru, B. (1992). *The other tongue: English across cultures* (2nd ed.). Urbana: University of Illinois Press.

Lam, A. (2002). English in education in China: Policy changes and learners' experiences. *World Englishes, 21*(2), 245–256.

Li, L. Q. (李岚清). (1996). Improve methods and quality of foreign language teaching (改进外语教学方法,提高外语教学水平). *Teaching and Teaching Material* (《教学与教材研究》), *6*, 4–5.

Luo, Z. P. (罗正鹏). (2015). Chinese netizens' language attitudes towards English in the context of college entrance examination reform (高考英语改革背景下中国网民的英语语言态度). *Journal of Tianjin Foreign Studies University* (《天津外国语大学学报》), *6*, 57–63.

Mitchell, S. A., & Black, M. J. (1995). *Freud and beyond: A history of modern psychoanalytical thought*. New York: Basic Books.

O'Regan, J. (2014). *English as a global language and the situation of East Asia. Talk at the school of foreign languages*, Beijing Normal University. June 4, 2014.

Seidlhofer, B. (2011). *Understanding English as a Lingua Franca*. Oxford: Oxford University Press.

Shen, L. X. & Gao, Y. H. (沈莉霞、高一虹). (2004). What "Crazy English" means to Chinese students (疯狂英语对于学习者的意义). In Y. H. Gao and Project Group (高一虹等), *The social psychology of English learning by Chinese college students* (《中国大学生英语学习社会心理》), Chapter 9 (pp. 190–201). Beijing: Foreign Language Teaching and Research Press.

Shen, Q. (沈骑). (2012). *Development of foreign language education policies in contemporary East Asia* (《当代东亚外语教育政策发展研究》). Beijing: Peking University Press.

Wen, Q. F., & Hu, W. Z. (2007). History and policy of English education in mainland China. In Y. H. Choi & B. Spolsky (Eds.), *English education in Asia: History and policies* (pp. 1–32). Seoul: AsiaTEFL.

Widdowson, H. (2013). *Competence and capability: Rethinking the subject English*. The 11th Asia TEFL Conference, Manila October 2013.

Yang, Y. (2000). *History of English education in China*. ERIC, ED441347.

Zhao, Y., & Campbell, K. P. (1995). English in China. *World Englishes, 14*(3), 377–390.

Zhu, L.Z. & Yang, A.X. (朱鲁子、杨艾祥). (2004). *English learning: Possessed by the devil* (《走火入魔的英语》). Changsha: Hunan People's Press.

Part VI
Conclusion

Conclusion

Roland SUSSEX and Andy CURTIS

Abstract The rapidly increasing profile of English in communication in Asia has given rise to some concerns about the integrity both of Asian languages and about the frameworks which have been applied to the study of intercultural communication in Asia. However, as the chapters in this volume have shown, research on interpersonal intercultural communication is beginning to yield an enhanced understanding of Asian values, content and strategies. In particular, research on intercultural communication within Asia is beginning to reflect new perspectives on Asian contexts in terms of empirical studies, theories and methodologies, and more nuanced conceptual frameworks. Seeing active intercultural communicating as being the result of emergent values and negotiated strategies and solutions points the way to an understanding of intercultural communication in Asia which more prominently reflects Asian values, with important implications for education and the new ways in which intercultural communication is being conceptualized today.

Asia is not only loosely defined; it is also a rapidly moving target. It comprises a set of disparate societies undergoing rapid and radical change in different ways and at different paces in different locations, with globalizing and glocalizing tendencies often in considerable tension. But Asia nonetheless has some coherence, as we saw in the Introduction to this volume (and see Kim 2010), in terms of geography and historical ideologies, and more recently in terms of geo-politics and economics, as the three large states (China, India, Japan) are joined by the nations of the Association of South-East Asian Nations (ASEAN). Asia is the site of wide-ranging social, economic and cultural changes as traditional and national boundaries are blurred in a

R. SUSSEX (✉)
School of Languages and Cultures, and Institute for Teaching and Learning Innovation,
The University of Queensland, St Lucia, QLD, Australia
e-mail: sussex@uq.edu.au

A. CURTIS
Graduate School of Education, Anaheim University, Anaheim, CA, USA
e-mail: andycurtiswork@gmail.com

© Springer International Publishing AG, part of Springer Nature 2018
A. CURTIS, R. SUSSEX (eds.), *Intercultural Communication in Asia:
Education, Language and Values*, Multilingual Education 24,
https://doi.org/10.1007/978-3-319-69995-0_13

variety of ways (Lian and Sussex 2018), which centrally involve intercultural communication.

The Third Macao International Forum, held in December 2014, began in this Asian context with three questions – the challenges of intercultural communication for:

- the boundaries that still intersect society in spite of – of because of – globalization;
- ideological issues and values;
- educational policy makers and deliverers.

The chapters in this collection have addressed these questions and the links between them in focused studies which have confirmed the relevance and importance of these three meta-questions to an understanding of intercultural communication in Asia.

We can identify a number of emerging directions for Asia in intercultural communication (Chen 2006). These arise directly from the intersection of the current literature with the input of the present volume.

English is the dominant trans-national language force in Asia. Cheng, echoing Crystal (2009), puts it like this:

> English became a powerful language as a result of political and military power initially, of science and technology power in the sixteenth to seventeenth century, of economic power in the nineteenth century and of cultural power in the twentieth century. Therefore, in order to understand the power of English, we need to understand the people who are using the English language today, especially those outside the 'English-dominant' countries such as United States of America, Canada, England and Australia (Cheng 2012, p. 327).

English is also, and as a consequence, the pre-eminent transplanted component of intercultural communication in Asia. Consistent with its role in globalization, it has also dominated the cross-cultural communication literature: comparisons of cultures have overwhelmingly involved English with another language, where English is usually American English. The "other" language tended to be Spanish in earlier research into intercultural communication, but Asian languages are now increasingly prominent (Kim 2010, p. 168).

The burgeoning presence of English in public, commercial, educational and cultural life in Asia has given rise to substantial misgivings about the possibly noxious effect of English on homeland languages. But as House (2018) has showed, English as a lingua franca (and see Canagarajah 2007) is not necessarily accompanied by negative or subtractive effects on the languages and countries where it is used as a lingua franca. On the contrary, the interaction of English and local languages can be creative and rich, and need pose no necessary threat to homeland languages, which will continue to be used as languages of identification. This scenario has been played out in language-in-education policy discussions in China (Gao 2018), where earlier overheated enthusiasm for English has been tempered by concerns for the integrity of Chinese language and culture. This policy debate is far from finished, but there is an emerging direction of both/and rather than either/or, where English is finding a more collaborative, rather than competitive-confrontational, profile in language-in-education policy in China.

It is not only in China that the ubiquitous presence of the **forms** of the English language have prompted concerns about national identity: might English overlay, or disadvantage, or even drive out not only homeland languages, but also homeland cultural institutions and practices? This concern, understandably, persists. But as Wu and Li (2018) demonstrate, online social media like Weibo show only selective influences from exogenous sources like English. Their approach is also part of a rise of a more Asian perspective on intercultural communication (Ito 1992). First, the typical "Asian" stereotypes like collectivism and indirect talking (Sussex and Curtis 2018; Kim 2010) are being modified by a perspective which is more nuanced and discriminating, as Asian cultures emerge as pluralistic and more clearly differentiated. Hitherto the literature on intercultural communication has tended to view Asian cultural communicative behaviours from the point of view of Western values, including typically Western-developed theories of politeness (Brown and Levinson 1987), power and individualism (Hofstede 1980, 1991).

Critiques of this perspective are starting to present an Asian view: studies of politeness as not just a matter of individualism/collectivism and face (Gu 1990; Mao 1994; Lim 1994); and studies of humour (Oshima 2018; Miczo and Welter 2006). This research problematizes the key vectors of intercultural communication in different ways. A corollary is a change from a centripetal to a combined centripetal-centrifugal profile of Asian research into intercultural communication. Until the last decade, and in some instances more recently, research into intercultural communication in Asia has been predominantly centripetal, involving the importation of Western theories, methodologies and techniques. This profile is starting to be balanced by a more centrifugal component, as Asian work – not only on Asian data – establishes itself in the international journals, conferences and publishing houses (Kim 2001). We can look forward to more in-depth Asian analyses of Western, and especially American, cultural practices.

A key to these intercultural communicating contexts is interpersonal negotiation. For example, Pham (2018) highlights the importance of how interlocutors evaluate the fit between language and culture. Although both speakers in her data – the male Anglophone employer and the female Vietnamese employee – obviously share a functionally effective level of English language, the difficulties arise with the less obvious cultural values.

Let us explore this in more detail. The Vietnamese employee speaks English as a second language (L2), and works in a cultural framework with elements of English as a second culture (let us call it "C2") combined with her native Vietnamese first culture ("C1"). The Anglo employer has L1 English, and on the evidence operates within C1 English (whether he has assimilated much of Vietnamese culture is not evident from the data presented here). The crucial domain is the coexistence of English C2 with Vietnamese C1 in the Vietnamese employee's interpersonal interactions in English, and how these are perceived (if at all) and interpreted by the Anglo employer.

It is this potential dissonance between language (L) and culture (C) which plays a key role in intercultural mis-communication. With languages and cultures it is important to know whether an interlocutor is using a first language (L1) and what that language is. It is equally important, though often covert (and only marginally taught (Snow 2018)), to know whether the interlocutor is using a first culture (C1) and what that culture is.

In **intra**cultural communication (Kecskes 2018) both speakers share a first language $(L1_x)$. In such a situation, as Kecskes argues, common ground is assumed: the culture components are taken as given and congruent $(C1_x)$. And the language performance of an interlocutor gives rich cues about their level of competence. A conversation between a speaker with $L1_x$ and another with $L2_x$ (say English as a Second Language in this case) can be functionally and informationally successful.

To return to Pham's example: how much of the culture of the target language (English) is the non-native speaker using or understanding? How much do they **think** they understand and activate? To what extent does the Anglo employer realize this? In Pham's data, the problems arise specifically with the expectations of cultural fit which arise from the non-native speaker's competence level in English.

This is where the negotiation of culture-neutral spaces becomes relevant. Curtis (2018) has considered the Internet as a "culture-neutral" space, in the sense of a space in which there is no particular culture that can be identified or specified using the usual parameters. House (2018) addresses aspects of English as a lingua franca and its "culture-neutrality". What does this mean in terms of speakers bringing cultural values to an intercultural interaction? If not, what elements, and from which cultures, are brought into the interaction, and how do the speakers become aware of them and negotiate them, probably on an ongoing basis, as the interaction progresses? Does the notion of "cultura franca" (Sussex and Curtis 2018) stand scrutiny, paired with lingua franca? This is an area which calls for empirical investigation.

In this intersection between L and C we also find an immediate link with the intra–/inter-cultural framework presented by Kecskes (2018). In his analysis, the greater the competence in a language, the closer the interaction is to intra-cultural communication. As the speakers move away from language competence, the common ground on which they communicate becomes increasingly emergent and a matter of negotiation; less a matter of societal assumptions and more a matter of individual intervention and interaction as the speakers build functional bases for communication, starting from the point of view of their individual ethnicities. In these kinds of interactions, language usage itself relies less on conventional patterns and more on creative contribution to suit the needs of the interaction. The context of communication in intercultural communication cannot rest on shared assumptions, in the way that it tends to do in intracultural communication. We see, in the words of Kecskes (2018), "a more conscious approach to what is said, and how it is said". In intercultural communication in Asia, whether involving English as a lingua franca and/or a cultura franca (Sussex and Curtis 2018), the fundamentally **constructed emergent** nature – "artifact" in Curtis's terms (2018) – of communication is in need of close empirical investigation. One way of addressing Kecskes's concept of a gradient between intracultural and intercultural communication is in the interplay between L and C.

Parallel to these trends, empirical, descriptive and analytical coverage of key domains in Asia will continue their current rapid growth (e.g. on politeness: Gu

1990; Lim 1994; Mao 1994). A key factor here is the Internet and digital cultures. As Lian and Sussex (2018) argue, the Internet makes the task of interpreting inter-cultural messages – or at least of determining the cultural content of messages – much more the responsibility of the individual. Unlike traditional teacher-centred learning, with its structured curriculum and pedagogy, Internet-oriented learning requires the engagement of the learner directly in evaluating language and cultural meaning. As a result, we need to extend the role of the Internet and social media from one of facilitating technologies to include the role of conceptual shapers of intercultural communication. The Internet and digital technologies have become an epistemology, a way of thinking about reality, in a way which brings to mind the Sapir-Whorf Hypothesis and the relation of language to cognition (Sung 2015). And in turn technology involves social contexts and online social capital, a topic to which the *Asian Journal of Communication* devoted a special issue in 2011 (Issue 5; and see Park et al. 2014). We need to move the Internet and social media from the role of facilitating technologies to the role of conceptual shapers of intercultural communication. This includes mobile technologies (Qiu 2010).

The literature is already seeing the appearance of Asian studies of advertising (Cheong et al. 2010), media (Iwabuchi 2010), and public health communication (Lwin and Salmon 2015). There are also studies of communicating behaviour in email and social media (Wu and Li 2018); inter-Asian comparisons of values (Sar and Rodriguez 2014); and media coverage, both inter-Asian (Zhang 2012) and contrast-ing China and the USA (Zhang et al. 2013). The Internet and digital cultures, pre-cisely because of their ability to bring languages and cultures into contact with low costs in access and physical mobility, have not only accelerated intercultural contacts in Asia, but have also changed the nature of those contacts. Japanese emojis, to take a single but emblematic example, have materially altered the content and style of com-munications on email and via SMS and social media, across languages and cultures, to the point where the "tears of joy" emoji was crowned by the Oxford Dictionary the "Word of the Year" for 2015 (Oxford Dictionaries 2015). Japanese advances in car-toon animation have also established a meme of their own (Cooper-Chen 2012).

The demands of intercultural communicative competence are also shifting the emphases of practitioners of both intercultural communication and educators. Intercultural communication is finding a much-delayed place in language curricula, especially but not only in English. Snow (2018) advocates introducing into lan-guage curricula components of intercultural communication, specifically to address ethnocentrism, stereotyping and in-group bias. This shift belongs with the re-balancing of language curricula in the direction of "communicacy" (Sussex and Kirkpatrick 2012), or the capacity to be an expert communicator. Under communi-cacy we find an openness to variation and non-standard language, including switch-ing; an ability for repair and recovery from failed communications; and negotiation and accommodation. Here communicators will mutually shift towards the other's cultural space, perhaps involving something like a shared "third place" (Lo Bianco et al. 1999) as a negotiated "common ground" (Kecskes 2018). We can expect that acts of intercultural communication will be more like rolling asymmetric negotia-tion, in Pennycook's sense (2012), in an emergent communicative collaboration.

As English continues to grow as the lingua franca of Asia, and as endocultural and Anglo-exocultural practices rise, there will be a continuing need for the role of education in preparing Asian speakers for communication across language and cultural boundaries. At the present time (Snow 2018), while instruction in the English language is being sustained (albeit with some challenges from within the curriculum – see Gao 2018), the nature of cultural communication and cultural awareness remains relatively less studied. The initial focus for such educational reform, in Snow's analysis (2018), rests in training non-English speakers to be alert to, and to implement, Anglo-cultural values in their interactions with Anglos, especially with reference to ethnocentrism, stereotypes and in-group values.

But in communications between Asians there is also the question of non-Anglo values when English is used, and when it is not. Such communication points of nexus can play out in multi-cultural street-scapes and street semiotics (Radwańska-Williams 2018). With potentially more dire medical consequences, they can impact on conversations relating to questions of pain and its expression, especially between patients and health care professionals (Sussex 2018).

And behind these factors, at a more generic level, are emotional intelligence and social intelligence (Wawra 2009), or competence in empathy and interaction. We might postulate an intercultural communication intelligence, close to intercultural competence, which was the subject of a special issue (48, 2015) of the *International Journal of Intercultural Relations*. A slightly different approach to this question, and one which is more generic, is "cultural intelligence" (Presbitero 2016), which both activates the cultura franca concept (Sussex and Curtis 2018) as a set of common cultural practices, and manages modifications to and departures from the cultura franca in individual intercultural interactions.

Underpinning this notion of cultura franca are the networks of values which inform and underpin intercultural communication in Asia. One common manifestation is the Anglo < > indigenous-homeland juxtaposition as described by Pham (2018), especially when English is used as the language of communication. Such situations typically involve L1 English combined with C1 (first culture) English, as used by native Anglophone speakers when interacting with homeland speakers of Asian languages in English as a second language (L2) and second culture (C2). But increasingly, as Asians communicate with each other in English across language and culture borders, L2 and C2 English will become more common. In such a situation, as Lian and Sussex (2018) note, "foreigners" (i.e. people who do not speak the language of the country of communication) are increasingly expected to speak English: as when a Thai person, say, communicates in English in Korea with a Japanese person. Whether they will use Anglo cultural values, or cultural values congruent with their own L1, is something which has so far received less attention. As Oshima has shown (2018), it is possible to perform Japanese values of culture, drama and humour in English, while at the same time preserving the ethos of Japanese, together with the dress, conventions and format of *rakugo*. Furthermore, in L2 English interactions between speakers of different Asian languages, for example Vietnamese and Chinese, it is not difficult to observe modes of culture implementation which unmistakably rest on "CHC" (Confucian Heritage Culture) (Watkins and Biggs 1996) principles and traditions. The speakers achieve comfortable and effective communication, even though in practice they are coding C1 (Confucian) messages in L2 English. Here English is not evidently intruding negatively on communication (House 2018).

The multi-disciplinary nature of intercultural communication will certainly continue to grow. But it will do so with a new and emphatic Asian flavour, stemming not only from Asia as a source of data for studying intercultural communication, but also as a new source of interpretation, analysis and theory based on principles which are not built uniquely on the Western paradigms which have dominated intercultural communication thus far.

These tendencies also require renewed consideration of the role of English as L and C in Asia in the wake of the United States' recent distancing of itself from Asia, for instance in the cancelling of the Trans Pacific Partnership (TPP) trade agreement in January, 2017. There is no indication that English as L will **not** continue to be the dominant lingua franca in Asia, though Chinese will certainly make inroads into this position, especially in direct interactions with Chinese institutions and enterprises. This position of English as lingua franca looks solid – though not necessarily beyond challenge or modification. What is less clear is the C role of Anglo values, especially if the USA adopts a confrontational posture vis-a-vis its relations with Asia. Certain aspects of the new American administration, not least the tenor of US President Trump's modes of public speech, tweets and public comments, reflect an American posture which sounds less collaborative and consultative than before, in economic or geo-political terms. Though these are early days in the Trump administration, we may anticipate a period of substantial and prolonged uncertainty. In this scenario both L1 and L2 speakers, and C1 and C2 culture activators, may find a need to negotiate, and in some instances re-negotiate, the bases of their communication.

We can now summarize four key outcomes of the present volume, as it looks ahead to future studies of intercultural communication in Asia:

1. There is a need for extensive and deep empirical studies of intercultural communication in the broad sense, and of acts of intercultural communication, in Asia, and comparing Asian to non-Asian languages and cultures (Morris 2014).
2. These studies need to be seen not just through the lens of Western intellectual models and methodologies, but also from the viewpoint of Asian language and culture values and practices seen in Asian terms.
3. In the interaction between L and C in intercultural communications in Asia, we need to bear in mind the gradient between intra- and inter-cultural communication, as presented by Kecskes (2018). To what extent can this gradient be segmented and analyzed into clusters of factors and features, or are the factors and features part of a continuum which is both variable and potentially in motion during the course of every intercultural interaction?
4. Acts of intercultural communication need to be seen as emergent, the result of negotiation through interaction. They are artifacts, constantly being both constructed and interpreted. And they are not just interpersonal. Learners using the Internet (Lian and Sussex 2018) need to exercise critical cultural judgement if they are to understand the cross-cultural significance of the material which they find, and to relate it to their existing networks of knowledge.

These four points of focus have been given additional emphasis by developments in the use of public language over 2016 and into 2017. The Oxford Dictionaries chose "post-truth" as their Word Of The Year for 2016, reflecting the violations of truth and openness which had occurred in Britain during the discussions leading to the Brexit vote in 2016, as well as to the events and tenor of the 2016 American Presidential election. These problems have been intensified by the ubiquity of the Internet and social media, and their role in influencing public opinion. The invention of the term "agnotology" in early 2017 to refer to the production of ignorance, and the study of how it influences people, is another indication of the ways in which the integrity of talk, both in general and especially in public discourse, has been altered. There has been little commentary on the role of post-truth or agnotology in intercultural communication. But given the increased unknowns in **inter**cultural communication, the potential for misinformation and misunderstanding must be even higher than in **intra**cultural communication. We need to become much more alert, informed and critical consumers of the messages we receive, and the cultural and other values in which they are embedded; and less judgemental if we encounter speech or values – like Chinese *guanxi* and *mianzi*, for instance (Sussex and Curtis 2018) – which do not accord at once with our own.

This is not just a call to arms on behalf of a scholarly discipline. To recapitulate a quotation from Kim which we used in the Introduction, and which now appears less hyperbolic than we suggested earlier,

> Intercultural communication is arguably the most serious of all the problems confronting humankind, and is the single most vital domain in social science (2010, p. 177).

References

Brown, P., & Levinson, S. (1987). *Politeness: Some universals in language usage*. Cambridge: Cambridge University Press.

Canagarajah, S. (2007). Lingua Franca English, multilingual communities, and language acquisition. *Modern Language Journal, 91*, 932–939.

Chen, G.-M. (2006). Asian communication studies: What and where to now. *Review of Communication, 6*(4), 295–311.

Cheng, L. (2012). The power of English and the power of Asia: English as lingua franca and in bilingual and multilingual education. *Journal of Multilingual and Multicultural Development, 33*(4), 327–330.

Cheong, Y., Kim, K., & Zheng, L. (2010). Advertising appeals as a reflection of culture: A cross-cultural analysis of food advertising appeals in China and the US. *Asian Journal of Communication, 20*(1), 1–16.

Cooper-Chen, A. (2012). Cartoon planet: The cross-cultural acceptance of Japanese animation. *Asian Journal of Communication, 22*(1), 44–57.

Crystal, D. (2009). *The future of language*. London: Routledge.

Curtis, A. (2018). Individual, institutional and international: Three aspects of intercultural communication. In A. Curtis & R. Sussex (Eds.), *Intercultural communication in Asia: Education, language and values*. Cham: Springer.

Gao, Y. H. (2018). China's reconstruction of linguistic identities: Emerging and perpetuating challenges in intercultural communication. In A. Curtis & R. Sussex (Eds.), *Intercultural communication in Asia: Education, language and values*. Cham: Springer.

Gu, Y. (1990). Politeness phenomena in modern Chinese. *Journal of Pragmatics, 14*, 237–257.

Hofstede, G. (1980). *Culture's consequences: International differences in work-related values.* Beverly Hills: Sage.

Hofstede, G. (1991). *Cultures and organizations: Software of the mind.* London: McGraw Hill.

House, J. (2018). English as a global lingua franca: A threat to other languages, intercultural communication and translation? In A. Curtis & R. Sussex (Eds.), *Intercultural communication in Asia: Education, language and values.* Cham: Springer.

Ito, Y. (1992). Theories on intercultural communication styles from a Japanese perspective: A sociological approach. In J. Blumler, J. McLeod, & K. Rosengren (Eds.), *Comparatively speaking: Communication and culture across space and time* (pp. 238–268). Thousand Oaks, CA: Sage.

Iwabuchi, K. (2010). Globalization, East Asian media cultures and their publics. *Asian Journal of Communication, 20*(2), 197–212.

Kecskes, I. (2018). How does intercultural communication differ from intracultural communication? In A. Curtis & R. Sussex (Eds.), *Intercultural communication in Asia: Education, language and values.* Cham: Springer.

Kim, Y. Y. (2001). *Becoming intercultural: An integrative theory of communication and cross-cultural adaptation.* Thousand Oaks, CA: Sage.

Kim, M.-S. (2010). Intercultural communication in Asia: Current state and future prospects. *Asian Journal of Communication, 20*(2), 166–180.

Lian, A., & Sussex, R. (2018). Toward a critical epistemology for learning languages and cultures in 21st century Asia. In A. Curtis & R. Sussex (Eds.), *Intercultural communication in Asia: Education, language and values.* Cham: Springer.

Lim, T.-S. (1994). Facework and interpersonal relationships. In S. Ting-Toomey (Ed.), *The challenge of facework: Cross-cultural and interpersonal issues* (pp. 209–229). Albany, NY: State University of New York Press.

Lo Bianco, J., Liddicoat, A. J., & Crozet, C. (Eds.). (1999). *Striving for the third place: Intercultural competence through language education.* Deakin: Australian National Languages and Literacy Institute.

Lwin, M. O., & Salmon, C. T. (2015). A retrospective overview of health communication studies in Asia from 2000 to 2013. *Asian Journal of Communication, 25*(1), 1–13.

Mao, L. M. R. (1994). Beyond politeness theory: 'Face' revisited and renewed. *Journal of Pragmatics, 21*, 451–486.

Miczo, N., & Welter, R. E. (2006). Aggressive and affiliative humor: Relationships to aspects of intercultural communication. *Journal of Intercultural Communication Research, 35*(1), 61–77.

Morris, P. K. (2014). Comparing portrayals of beauty in outdoor advertisements across six cultures: Bulgaria, Hong Kong, Japan, Poland, South Korea, and Turkey. *Asian Journal of Communication, 24*(3), 242–261.

Oshima, K. (2018). Functions of humor in intercultural communication: Disarm, tolerance, and solidarity. In A. Curtis & R. Sussex (Eds.), *Intercultural communication in Asia: Education, language and values.* Cham: Springer.

Oxford Dictionaries. (2015). https://blog.oup.com/2015/11/oxford-dictionaries-word-of-the-year-2015-emoji-face-tears-joy/. Accessed 2 Jul 2017.

Park, N., Song, H., & Lee, K. M. (2014). Social networking sites and other media use, acculturation stress, and psychological well-being among East Asian college students in the United States. *Computers in Human Behavior, 36*, 138–146.

Pennycook, A. (2012). Lingua francas as language ideologies. In A. Kirkpatrick & R. Sussex (Eds.), *English as an international language in Asia: Implications for language education* (pp. 137–154). Berlin and London: Springer-Verlag.

Pham, T. H. N. (2018). Confucian values as challenges for communication in intercultural workplace contexts: Evidence from Vietnamese – Anglo-cultural interactions. In A. Curtis & R. Sussex (Eds.), *Intercultural communication in Asia: Education, language and values.* Cham: Springer.

Presbitero, A. (2016). Cultural intelligence (CQ) in virtual, cross-cultural interactions: Generalizability of measure and links to personality dimensions and task performance. *International Journal of Intercultural Relations, 50*, 29–38.

Qiu, J. L. (2010). Mobile communication research in Asia: Changing technological and intellectual geopolitics? *Asian Journal of Communication, 20*(2), 213–229.

Radwańska-Williams, J. (2018). The linguistic landscape of Macao. In A. Curtis & R. Sussex (Eds.), *Intercultural communication in Asia: Education, language and values*. Cham: Springer.

Sar, S., & Rodriguez, L. (2014). The effectiveness of appeals used in Cambodian and Vietnamese magazine ads. *Asian Journal of Communication, 24*(6), 529–548.

Snow, D. (2018). Intercultural communication in English courses in Asia: What should we teach? In A. Curtis & R. Sussex (Eds.), *Intercultural communication in Asia: Education, language and values*. Cham: Springer.

Sung, C. C. M. (2015). Sapir-Whorf hypothesis. In J. M. Bennett (Ed.), *The SAGE encyclopedia of intercultural competence* (Vol. 2, pp. 741–742). Thousand Oaks: Sage. http://dx.doi.org. ezproxy.library.uq.edu.au/10.4135/9781483346267.n245.

Sussex, R. (2018). Pain as an issue of intercultural communication. In A. Curtis & R. Sussex (Eds.), *Intercultural communication in Asia: Education, language and values*. Cham: Springer.

Sussex, R., & Curtis, A. (2018). Introduction. In A. Curtis & R. Sussex (Eds.), *Intercultural communication in Asia: Education, language and values*. Cham: Springer.

Sussex, R., & Kirkpatrick, A. (2012). A postscript and a prolegomenon. In A. Kirkpatrick & R. Sussex (Eds.), *English as an international language in Asia: Implications for language education* (pp. 223–231). Berlin/London: Springer.

Watkins, D. A., & Biggs, J. B. (Eds.). (1996). *The Chinese learner: Cultural, psychological, and contextual influences*. ERIC Document ED405401. https://eric.ed.gov/?id=ED405410

Wawra, D. (2009). Social intelligence. *European Journal of English Studies, 13*(2), 163–177.

Wu, D. D., & Li, C. L. (2018). Emotional branding on social media: A cross-cultural discourse analysis of global brands on Twitter and Weibo. In A. Curtis & R. Sussex (Eds.), *Intercultural communication in Asia: Education, language and values*. Cham: Springer.

Zhang, W. (2012). The effects of political news use, political discussion and authoritarian orientation on political participation: Evidences from Singapore and Taiwan. *Asian Journal of Communication, 22*(5), 474–492.

Zhang, D., Shoemaker, P. J., & Wang, X. (2013). Reality and newsworthiness: Press coverage of international terrorism by China and the United States. *Asian Journal of Communication, 23*(5), 449–471.

Contributors

Andy CURTIS received both his M.A. in applied linguistics and English language teaching and his Ph.D. in international education from the University of York in England. From 2007 to 2011, he was the director of the English Language Teaching Unit at the Chinese University of Hong Kong and a professor in the Faculty of Education there. Prior to 2007, he was the executive director of the School of English at Queen's University in Ontario, Canada, and a professor at the School for International Training in Vermont, USA.

Andy is currently working with the Graduate School of Education at Anaheim University, which is based in California, USA. From 2015 to 2016, he served as the 50th president of the TESOL International Association – the largest international language teaching association in the world, with more than 50,000 core and affiliate members in more than 150 countries. In 2016, he received one of the association's 50-at-50 Awards, when he was voted one of the Fifty Most Influential Figures in the Field, over the last 50 years.

Andy has published more than 100 articles, book chapters, and books, including the second edition of *Learning About Language Assessment: Dilemmas, Decisions, and Directions* (2015, National Geographic/Cengage Learning), coauthored with Kathi Bailey. He is also the editor of a new nine-book TESOL Press series, *ELT In Context*, published between 2015 and 2017, and the editor of a new five-book series, *Applied Linguistics for the Language Classroom*, published in 2017 by Palgrave Macmillan, which includes his book, *Language Teaching Methods and Methodologies: The Centrality of Context*.

Over the last 25 years, Andy has been invited to present to around 25,000 teachers in 50 countries, in Europe, Asia, Africa, and the Middle East, as well as in North, South, and Central America. He is based in Ontario, Canada, from where he works as a consultant for teaching and learning organizations worldwide.

© Springer International Publishing AG, part of Springer Nature 2018
A. CURTIS, R. SUSSEX (eds.), *Intercultural Communication in Asia: Education, Language and Values*, Multilingual Education 24,
https://doi.org/10.1007/978-3-319-69995-0

Yihong GAO   obtained her M.A. degree in linguistics from Durham University (UK) in 1983, Ed.M. in TESOL from Boston University (USA) in 1988, and Ph.D. in linguistics from Peking University in 1992. Currently, she is professor of linguistics and director of the Research Institute of Linguistics and Applied Linguistics, School of Foreign Languages, Peking University. She is also vice president of the China English Language Education Association and served as the president of the Association of Chinese Sociolinguistics. Her major research interest lies in the social psychology and sociocultural contexts of foreign language learning and teaching. Her publications include *Culture and Foreign Language Teaching* (1997, second author, collaboration with HU Wenzhong), *Understanding and Transcending Linguistic and Cultural Differences* (2000), *Foreign Language Leaning: "1+1>2"* (2001), *The Social Psychology of English Learning by Chinese College Students: Motivation and Learners' Self-Identities* (2004, first author), and *College Students' English Learning Motivation and Self-Identity Development: A Four-Year Longitudinal Study* (2013, first author).

Juliane HOUSE   received her first degree in English and Spanish translation and international law from Heidelberg University; her B.Ed., M.A., and Ph.D. in applied linguistics from the University of Toronto, Canada; and honorary doctorates from the University of Jyväskylä, Finland, and the University Jaume I, Castellon, Spain. She is emeritus professor of applied linguistics at the University of Hamburg, Germany, and a founding member of the German Science Foundation's *Research Centre on Multilingualism*, where she was principal investigator of several projects on multilingual communication and translation. She also directed a project on multilingualism and multiculturalism in German universities.

She is past president of the International Association for Translation and Intercultural Studies (IATIS) and now directs a Ph.D. program in applied linguistics at Hellenic American University in Athens, Greece. Her research interests include contrastive pragmatics, discourse analysis, politeness theory, English as a lingua franca, intercultural communication, and translation. She has published widely in all these areas. Her latest books include *Translation: A Multidisciplinary Approach* (Palgrave Macmillan), *Translation Quality Assessment: Past and Present* (Routledge), *Translation as Communication Across Languages and Cultures* (Routledge), and *Translation: The Basics* (Routledge).

Istvan KECSKES   is professor of linguistics and education at the State University of New York, Albany, USA, where he teaches graduate courses in pragmatics, second language acquisition, and bilingualism and directs the English as a second language Ph.D. and M.A. programs. Professor Kecskes is the president of the American Pragmatics Association (AMPRA).

Some of his books and papers have been quite influential in the fields of pragmatics and bilingualism. *Foreign Language and Mother Tongue* published by Erlbaum in 2000 was the first book that described the effect of the second language on the first language. His paper on dueling contexts published in the *Journal of Pragmatics* in 2008 is one of the most quoted papers according to the journal's website. His latest books are *Intercultural Pragmatics* published by Oxford University Press in 2013, an edited volume titled *Research in Chinese as a Second Language* published by De Gruyter in 2013, and another volume edited with Jesus Romero-Trillo *Research Trends in Intercultural Pragmatics* published by De Gruyter also in 2013.

Dr. Kecskes is the founding editor of the linguistics journal *Intercultural Pragmatics* and the Mouton Series in Pragmatics published by Mouton de Gruyter (Berlin/New York), as well as the new bilingual (Chinese-English) journal *CASLAR (Chinese as a Second Language Research)* published by Mouton and the *Journal of Language Aggression and Conflict* published by John Benjamins (Amsterdam/Philadelphia) (co-founder Pilar Garces Blitvich). He sits on the editorial board of the *Journal of Pragmatics* (Elsevier), *Pragmatics and Society* (Benjamins), *International Journal of Multilingualism* (Taylor & Francis), *Lodz Papers in Pragmatics* (De Gruyter), *International Journal of Language and Culture* (Benjamins), and the *Journal of Foreign Languages (Waiguoyu)* published in China. Dr. Kecskes is also on the editorial board of four book series: Pragmatics, Philosophy & Psychology (Springer), Series in Pragmatics (Cambridge Scholarly Publishing), Pragmatic Interfaces (Equinox), and Studies in General Linguistics (Hungarian Academy of Sciences).

Dr. Kecskes received a senior fellowship from the Rockefeller Foundation in the Rockefeller Research Center in Bellagio, Italy, in 2004; a senior fellowship from the Mitteleuropa Foundation, Bolzano, Italy, in 2005; an honorary professorship from Zhejiang University, Hangzhou, in 2009; a Yunshan chair professorship from Guangdong University of Foreign Studies, Guangzhou, China, in 2011; and a distinguished visiting professorship at Monash University, Melbourne, Australia, in 2013.

He is the recipient of the Chancellor's Excellence in Research Award of the State University of New York, the codirector of the Barcelona Summer School on Bilingualism and Multilingualism, the chairman of CASLAR (Chinese as a Second Language) movement, and also the director of the biannual conference on intercultural pragmatics.

LI Chaoyuan is a Ph.D. student in the Department of Bilingual and Chinese Studies, the Hong Kong Polytechnic University. Her research interests include sociolinguistics and intercultural communication.

Andrew LIAN is professor of foreign language studies, School of Foreign Languages, Suranaree University of Technology, Nakhon Ratchasima, Thailand. He is also professor of postgraduate studies in English language education at Ho Chi Minh City Open University, HCMC, Vietnam, and professor emeritus of languages and second language education at the University of Canberra, Canberra, ACT, Australia. He is the current president of AsiaCALL, the Asia Association of Computer-Assisted Language-Learning, a research and professional association focusing on the uses of technology to enhance second/foreign language-learning in Asian contexts.

Andrew Lian specializes in issues of knowledge and meaning-construction as well as postmodern approaches to learning and teaching (languages). He is one of the three "pioneers" of the modern era of technology-enhanced language-learning in Australia (with Roly Sussex and Jack Burston), beginning his work in the area in the early 1980s. Prior to coming to Thailand, he held five (full) professorial appointments and department headships in Australia (Bond University, James Cook University, University of Canberra) and the USA (Rice University, Western Illinois University).

He is on the advisory or editorial boards of eight international peer-reviewed journals. His current research interests include the development of rhizomatic, technology-supported, self-regulating language-learning environments (including personal learning environments), especially the uses of multimedia databases and the conceptualization and construction of awareness-raising tools for language learners. Now that he has officially "retired" from full-time work, he is able to work full time.

Kimie OSHIMA, Ph.D. is currently a professor at Kanagawa University in Yokohama since April of 2014. Previously, she was teaching at Bunkyo Gakuin University in Tokyo from 2003 to March of 2014. She has been teaching sociolinguistics, intercultural communications, humor studies, and English skills. Her research topics are English as international language, English for Japanese speakers, humor in communication and business, and English rakugo (Japanese sit-down comedy). Her recent publications are *English Rakugo in the Classroom* (2013) (Sansei-do publications: Tokyo), "Common features of Japanese English and Hawaiian Creole: Case study of Japanese business persons" (2012) (Bunkyo Gakuin University Press, No.11, 97–114), "Japanese cultural expressions seen in English rakugo scripts" (2011) (Asian Englishes Vol.14-1, 46–64).

Thi Hong Nhung PHAM did her B.A. in English language teaching from Hue University of Education in 1997 and then obtained her M.A. and Ph.D. both in applied linguistics with the University of Queensland, Australia, and a diploma in language teaching management with Cambridge ESOL in 2011. She is a lecturer at Hue University of Foreign Studies (formerly Hue University, College of Foreign Languages), in Hue City, Vietnam, where she has taught intercultural communication, pragmatics, and second language acquisition to TESOL students. She is deputy rector of the university, in charge of graduate studies and research since 2009, and director of Hue Culture and Language Centre since 2010.

Pham is head of the *MOET* (English textbook) quality control committee and is also senior consultant of the Vietnamese National Foreign Language Project 2008–2020. Pham's recent publications include 2 books titled *Communicating with Vietnamese in Intercultural Contexts: Insights into Vietnamese Values* (2011, published by Vietnamese Educational Publishing House) and *Pragmatics for Language Teachers: Developing Pragmatic Competence for EFL Learners* (2013, Hue University Press). Her recent articles are "Strategies employed by the Vietnamese to respond to compliments and the influence of compliment receivers' perception of the compliment on their responses" (*International Journal of Linguistics,* 6(2), 2014), "Linguistic and cultural constraints in Vietnamese general practitioners' act of initiating clinical information-seeking process in first encounters with outpatients" *(Theory and Practice in Language Studies,* 4(6), 2014), "How do the Vietnamese lose face? Understanding the concept of face through self-reported, face loss incidents" (*International Journal of Language and Linguistics,* 2(4)-in press, 2014), "Vietnamese orientation towards interdependent self: Evidence from the act of self-introduction," and "Assessing EFL learners' pragmatic competence through their ability to identify pragmatic violations" (respectively, in *Vietnamese Journal of Linguistics,* 2 (248), 4(271), 2013). Pham's current research interests include clinical pragmatics and intercultural communication.

Joanna RADWAŃSKA-WILLIAMS was born in Warsaw, Poland, and spent a part of her childhood in London, England. She received her B.A. with a double major in English and linguistics (awarded with highest honors, 1981) and her Ph.D. in linguistics (1989) from the University of North Carolina at Chapel Hill. Her dissertation was published as *A Paradigm Lost: The Linguistic Theory of Mikołaj Kruszewski* (Amsterdam: John Benjamins, 1993). Her research interests include the history of linguistics, language teaching methodology, poetics, semiotics, and inter-disciplinary applications of linguistics, and she has authored or coauthored over 40 journal articles and book chapters in these fields. She is a coauthor of the *Polish Language Learning Framework* (New York: Polish Institute of Arts and Sciences of America, 2002). Her publications include the book chapters "The Native Speaker as a Metaphorical Construct" in *Metaphors for Learning: Cross-Cultural Perspectives* (edited by Erich A. Berendt; Amsterdam: John Benjamins, 2008) and "Chomsky's Paradigm: What It Includes and What It Excludes" in *Chomskyan (R)evolutions* (edited by Douglas A. Kibbee; Amsterdam: John Benjamins, 2010). She is currently the general editor of *Intercultural Communication Studies*, the official journal of the International Association for Intercultural Communication Studies.

Joanna has taught Slavic linguistics at the State University of New York at Stony Brook (1989–1994) and the University of Illinois at Chicago (1994–1995) and English linguistics at Nanjing University (1996–1999) and the Chinese University of Hong Kong (1999–2003). In 2003, she joined Macao Polytechnic Institute, where she has served as a professor of English in the School of Business, the School of Languages and Translation, and the MPI-Bell Centre of English.

Joanna is a poet, and her poetry has been anthologized in several collections, including *Lingua Franca: An Anthology of Poetry by Linguists* (edited by Donna Jo Napoli and Emily Norwood Rando; Lake Bluff, Illinois: Jupiter Press, 1989), *Montage of Life* (Owings Mills, Maryland: The National Library of Poetry, 1998), and *I Roll the Dice: Contemporary Macao Poetry* (edited by Christopher Kit Kelen and Agnes Vong; Macao: Association of Stories in Macao, 2008).

Don SNOW has a B.A. in history from the College of Wooster, an M.A. in English (TESOL) from Michigan State University, and a Ph.D. in East Asian language and culture from Indiana University. He has taught courses in language, culture, and linguistics for over two decades in universities such as Nanjing University, Zhongshan University, and the Chinese University of Hong Kong and has also played administrative roles with institutions such as the College of Wooster, the Amity Foundation, and Shantou University. He is currently professor and director of the Language and Culture Center at Duke Kunshan University.

Don has published journal articles on topics ranging from self-directed language learning to diglossia to written forms of Chinese vernaculars. His books include *More Than a Native Speaker: An Introduction for Volunteers Teaching English Abroad* (TESOL Publications, revised edition 2006), *Encounters with Westerners: Improving Skills in English and Intercultural Communication* (Shanghai Foreign Language Education Press, 2004/2014), *From Language Learner to Language Teacher* (TESOL Publications, 2007), and *Cantonese as Written Language: The Growth of a Written Chinese Vernacular* (Hong Kong University Press, 2004).

In such free time as his work allows, Don enjoys listening to and making music, hiking, drinking tea, and sitting down with a good book. He also stays in shape as a language learner by studying different varieties of Chinese and is currently attempting to learn a little Suzhounese and Shanghainese.

Roland (Roly) SUSSEX was professor of applied language studies at the University of Queensland, where he had taught and researched since 1989. Before that, he taught linguistics and Russian at the University of Reading (UK) and Monash University in Melbourne and was the foundation professor of Russian at the University of Melbourne from 1977 to 1989. He is currently research professor in the Institute for Teaching and Learning Innovation and the School of Languages and Cultures, at the University of Queensland.

He was chair of the Library Board of Queensland from 2009 to 2014 and deputy chair from 2014 to 2017. He was president of the Alliance Française of Brisbane from 2010 to 2017. His current research is located in the triangle between language, culture and society, and technology. He is cochief investigator in the PainLang Research Group at the University of Queensland, which is investigating communication and language in the diagnosis, treatment, and management of pain (http:// www.uq.edu.au/painlang/).

His recent major publications include *The Slavic Languages* with Paul Cubberley (Cambridge University Press, 2006) and *English as an International Language in Asia: Implications for Language Education* by Andy Kirkpatrick and Roland Sussex (Eds) (Berlin and London: Springer-Verlag, 2012). Roly writes a weekly column on language for the Brisbane *Courier Mail* and has been broadcasting every week to *Queensland* on ABC radio since 1997 and for the last decade to South Australia. He was awarded the Medal of the Order of Australia in 2012 and was appointed a Chevalier des Palmes Académiques by the French Government in 2017.

Doreen D. WU (Ph.D. from the University of Florida, USA) is an associate professor in the Department of Chinese and Bilingual Studies, The Hong Kong Polytechnic University. She also serves as the program leader for doctor of applied language sciences (DALS), Faculty of Humanities, The Hong Kong Polytechnic University.

Doreen's recent research interests include glocalization and corporate communications, multilingualism and multiculturalism in media communication of cultural China, and transcultural branding. Among her works are editor of the *Discourses of Cultural China in the Globalizing Age* (2008, The Hong Kong University Press); coeditor of "Media discourse in Greater China," special issue for *Journal of Asian-Pacific Communication*, 2009, Vol. 19(2); and coeditor of "Media discourses & cultural globalisation: A Chinese perspective," special issue for *Critical Arts,* 2011, Vol. 25(1).

Doreen serves on the editorial boards for a number of important international and local journals devoted to multilingual and multicultural studies, e.g., *Critical Arts* (Routledge), *East Asian Pragmatics* (Equinox), *Journal of Multicultural Discourses* (Routledge), *Contemporary Linguistics* (Chinese Academy of Social Sciences, PRC), and *Modern Foreign Languages* (Zhejiang University, PRC). She is also an advisory board member for both the International Association for Intercultural Communication Studies (IAICS) and the China Association for Intercultural Communication (CAFIC).

Printed by Printforce, the Netherlands